Gary Rhodes 365/

Gary Rhodes

365/ One year. One book. One simple recipe for every day.

Gary Rhodes

Photographs by Lottie Davies

MICHAEL JOSEPH
an imprint of
PENGUIN BOOKS

MICHAEL JOSEPH

Published by the Penguin Group
Penguin Books Ltd, 80 Strand, London WC2R 0RL, England
Penguin Group (USA) Inc., 375 Hudson Street, New York, New York 10014, USA
Penguin Group (Canada), 90 Eglinton Avenue East, Suite 700, Toronto, Ontario, Canada M4P 2Y3
(a division of Pearson Penguin Canada Inc.)
Penguin Ireland, 25 St Stephen's Green, Dublin 2, Ireland (a division of Penguin Books Ltd)
Penguin Group (Australia), 250 Camberwell Road,
Camberwell, Victoria 3124, Australia (a division of Pearson Australia Group Pty Ltd)
Penguin Books India Pvt Ltd, 11 Community Centre,
Panchsheel Park, New Delhi – 110 017, India
Penguin Group (NZ), 67 Apollo Drive, Rosedale, North Shore 0632, New Zealand
(a division of Pearson New Zealand Ltd)
Penguin Books (South Africa) (Pty) Ltd, 24 Sturdee Avenue,
Rosebank, Johannesburg 2196, South Africa

Penguin Books Ltd, Registered Offices: 80 Strand, London WC2R 0RL, England

www.penguin.com

First published 2008

1

Text copyright © Gary Rhodes, 2008

Photographs copyright © Lottie Davies

The moral right of the author has been asserted

Printed in Germany by Mohn Media
Colour reproduction by Altaimage Ltd

A CIP catalogue record for this book is available from the British Library

ISBN: 978–0–718–15315–1

Contents/

Introduction 8

Cook's notes 10

Starting the day 22
Breakfast; Brunch

Midweek lunch 68

Afternoon tea 94
High tea and treats; Teatime for children

Simple midweek suppers 148
For one; For two; For four

Weekend eating 226
Saturday lunch; Saturday night entertaining;
Sunday lunch; Light weekend suppers

Special occasions 410
Valentine's; Easter; Christmas

Potatoes and vegetables 448

Sauces 462

Index 468

This book is for somebody who has provided me with a decade of dedication. She always has a smile and keeps everyone happy while managing a huge collection of different requirements every day, knowing instinctively how to mix and turn them into something quite smooth; everything falling into place.

So a very special thank-you to my personal assistant, Lissanne Kenyon, for her commitment 365 days of the year.

Thanks, Lissanne

x

introduction

How lovely it would be to find the time to eat freshly prepared food every day of the year. This may have been the way in days of old, but as we know, times move on and with that, habits change.

The kind of food we eat changes too and we are lucky to have been introduced to so many different cuisines from across the world, due mainly, I suspect, to the ease of travel. There's Indian, Chinese, Japanese, Italian and Spanish and the list goes on. Many of these are readily available for home delivery and fresh and frozen dishes wait to be picked up from every supermarket shelf.

So in today's world of ease and convenience, why this book?

Well, on a quite rare sunny summer's day in 2007, friends were due round for one of those late alfresco lunches. Thinking about the company and the flavours I wanted to share, I decided that it was going to be all about freshness and simplicity. For me, this was to be a bowl of tomato and basil risotto, crisp summer salad leaves with a light vinaigrette, followed by a platter of British, French and Italian cheeses. The risotto was simply one pan on the stove, the arborio rice loosened with hot water straight from the kettle, a stock cube sprinkled over to enhance and lift the rice. Bread, biscuits, fresh fruit and good wine were all that were needed to accompany our meal.

As we all, just under a dozen in total, tucked in beneath those welcome rays of sunshine, conversation, as it so often does, turned to food. Many of our friends made much the same statement: 'If only I knew how to prepare such simple, beautiful and tasty food, I would be cooking every single day of the year'!'

So here it is, *365*.

This is a book that can be followed as freely as you wish. As you'll see, the recipes are divided into chapters relevant not to a particular day of the year, but to the time of day or an occasion in the week. Please, however, don't allow these categories to become set in stone. I'm purely offering guidance as to when the recipes might suit, but all are very willing to be juggled around.

You'll also notice that to simplify the cooking of many dishes I've used what I call convenience foods, such as chopped tomatoes, tins of cannellini or haricot beans and frozen peas, mingling them amongst the fresh produce. Do remember also that good ingredients, cooked simply, need little help to explain themselves and it's worth every effort to see what's seasonal and available when choosing recipes to cook. With these common aims, you'll see that the new recipes blend very nicely with those I've chosen to include from *Keeping it Simple* and *Time to Eat*.

And if this still sounds a bit daunting, then may I suggest creating a new habit by cooking fresh food at least one day a week? Soon this new cooking habit will become an obsession and you'll find yourself reaching for your pan more often, the new habit having become an old one and this being one good old habit that dies hard.

I do hope you enjoy reading and choosing from amongst these pages. The greatest social meeting place in the world is at the dinner table. It's the spot that draws family and friends together to enjoy what? Good company with good food. This book offers 365 recipes to do exactly that and to remind us that it is good food that makes people happy, whatever the effort, time or expense that goes into preparing it.

To sum up, I'll leave you with a handful of words that I more than believe in.

'Enough is as good as a feast' John Heywood (1497–1580)

Cook's notes/

General
Nuts and spices
Fish and seafood
Eggs
Fruit and vegetables

I've provided here a few pages of straightforward cooking skills to learn from or just to quickly refer back to when needed. Where these techniques appear in the recipes, I've cross-referenced you to here, but if you've already mastered a skill, you can of course carry straight on.

General

butter

Like most chefs, I generally use unsalted butter when I'm cooking to give me total control over the seasoning. However, this is not essential with savoury foods, so use whatever you have.

eggs

All the eggs I use are large free range.

oven temperatures

I have given these in Celsius, Fahrenheit and a gas mark for all the recipes, but if you want to use your fan oven, check your manufacturer's recommendations before referring to my conversion table below to set the right temperature:

140°C	275°F	fan oven 120°C	gas 1
150°C	300°F	fan oven 130°C	gas 2
170°C	325°F	fan oven 140°C	gas 3
180°C	350°F	fan oven 160°C	gas 4
190°C	375°F	fan oven 170°C	gas 5
200°C	400°F	fan oven 180°C	gas 6
220°C	425°F	fan oven 200°C	gas 7
230°C	450°F	fan oven 210°C	gas 8
240°C	475°F	fan oven 220°C	gas 9

spoon measurements

All spoon measurements are level unless otherwise specified.

salt and pepper

I use both coarse sea salt and table salt in my cooking. I also prefer the taste and texture of white pepper to black, but use whatever you prefer. If possible, grind white peppercorns in a peppermill unless ground white pepper is specified.

stocks

Home-made stock is lovely, but it's certainly not quick and simple to make, and these days there are lots of instant varieties on offer. Try one of the tubs of liquid stocks available in the chilled cabinets or a tin of consommé, which provides the richest of flavours. Beef is the easiest to get hold of and it suits most meat and chicken dishes, while game consommé is the one to use for game dishes and duck.

- If you're making your stock using cubes, look for the rectangular ones with a paste-like texture, rather than the crumbly cubes, and add just half a cube to the recommended water quantity for a fresher, less artificial flavour. For a clear finish, boil the water in a saucepan, whisk in the cube and simmer for 1 to 2 minutes to clarify.

Nuts and spices

Buy in small quantities and store in an airtight tin to keep them as fresh as possible.

toast pine nuts or sesame seeds

- Fry the nuts or seeds in a dry wok or frying pan until toasted and golden brown, then remove from the pan to prevent further cooking.

toast spices

- Fry the spices in a dry pan until toasted and golden brown, then remove from the pan to prevent further cooking.

Fish and seafood

Most fish you buy these days have already been cleaned, scaled and often filleted. If in doubt, your fishmonger is a good source of advice and will usually happily prepare or fillet a fish for you.

scaling fish

- Over newspaper or under running water, grip the tail and, using the back of a knife, work against the surface of the fish, pushing towards the head. Don't apply too much pressure as this could pierce the skin. Once cleaned, rinse and pat dry.

pinboning fish

- Many round fish have a line of fine bones within the fillet. It's good to check that these have been removed by running your hand from head to tail along the fillet, then using a pair of tweezers to remove any that you might find.

filleting and trimming herrings

- Remove the head of the herring to expose the backbone and provide guidance for your knife to follow. With the back of the fish facing towards you, cut as close as possible above the bone. Once the flesh is loosened, place a hand flat on top of the fillet and, with sweeping movements, cut through and as close to the bone as possible until the fillet is removed.

- The small pin bones left in the fillet can be removed with tweezers, before turning the fish and repeating the same process. Trim the tail using kitchen scissors.

gutting and cleaning sardines

- Push the scales off and away. Cut from the anal fin vent towards the head, exposing the entrails. These can now be pulled free by hand, cutting away any left behind. Remove also the thin blood line running with the central bone before rinsing until clean.

filleting flat fish

- Lay the fish dark skin side up, noting the central lateral line running from top to tail. Cut as close as possible around either side of the head, then cut down to the backbone following the lateral line. Insert the knife at the head end and begin to cut, keeping the knife as flat as possible, in short, sweeping movements against the bones, towards the tail. Lift the fillet as it loosens and finish off by cutting around the edge of the fins to remove. Turn the fish round to remove the other fillet. To remove the last two, turn the fish over and repeat the same process.

filleting round fish

- Place the fish with its back towards you. Cut and release the fillet around the head as close as possible, then cut horizontally into the fish, following the backbone to the tail. Continue these cuts and movements, keeping the blade close to the bones. Once the fillet begins to be released, it can be lifted revealing the direction to be taken. Upon reaching the rib bones, simply continue filleting as close to them as possible. Fine rib bones can be cut through and the bones removed with tweezers or pliers once the fillet is taken out. Turn the fish over and repeat the same process.

peeling and deveining prawns

- To peel prawns, twist the heads off and peel away the shell, leaving the fan tails intact.
- To devein, cut down the back of the prawns using a sharp knife and remove the thin digestive tract.

butterfly prawns

- Simply cut slightly deeper while deveining to open up the backs, cutting virtually halfway through the meat to create a natural butterfly shape.

cleaning mussels

- Wash the mussels under cold running water, scraping away any barnacles and pulling out the beards that protrude from between the closed shells. If any mussels are found slightly open, a short, sharp tap should make them close, letting you know they are still alive. Any that don't close should be discarded.

preparing cooked lobster

- Hold the lobster's body in one hand and firmly grasp the tail in the other, twist and pull the tail away. Lay the tail flat. Using a large knife, split the tail in half lengthways before removing the meat from the shell. Grasp the claws near the lobster body and, with a firm twist, remove. Crack the claws with the back of a heavy knife and remove the meat and nuggets, leaving the claws whole.

preparing cooked crab

- Once cooked, remove the claws and legs from the crab, break them open with a nutcracker or with a sharp tap from the back of a knife and remove the meat. Detach the body from the back shell and, once turned, pull away the bony pointed flap. Insert a knife between the shell and body and twist firmly to release the meat. Any grey-looking gills should be discarded along with the stomach sac, which can be detached by applying pressure to the small piece of shell situated just behind the eyes. Pour away any excess water from the shell. The brown meat can now be spooned out and pushed through a sieve. Quarter the central body and remove all the white meat with a pick or skewer, add to the white claw meat and check through with your fingertips to remove any splinters of shell.

Eggs

A cooked egg is not only a delicious, simple meal on its own, but a way of adding more weight to a salad or a plate of cold cuts.

scrambling eggs

- Beat the eggs to combine the yolks with the whites. Melt a large knob of butter in a saucepan or frying pan and, once bubbling but before it browns, pour in the eggs, seasoning them with salt and pepper. Turn and stir the eggs fairly vigorously with a wooden spoon, covering every corner of the pan.

- For the simplest eggs, cook them with just the knob of butter and season with salt and pepper. If you prefer a really soft, moist texture, you can add milk, cream or water, but it's best to add no more than a tablespoon per egg because too much liquid can leave a puddle of eggy cream.

- Once the eggs start to set and get lumpy, but still have a soft consistency, remove the pan from the stove. The secret of scrambled eggs is to always take them off the heat slightly underdone. They will continue to cook in the pan or even on the plate.

poaching eggs

The eggs need to be as fresh as possible, otherwise the egg whites tend to spread on contact with the water. If you don't think your eggs are really fresh, add a drop of vinegar to the water to help set the whites.

- Crack the eggs into cups and whisk a deep saucepan of vigorously simmering water in a circular motion. Always poach in deep water. The deep water makes the whites collect around the yolks and the eggs become quite bulbous as they travel to the bottom of the pan. Pour each egg into the middle of the spinning water to pull and set the white around the yolk, and poach for 3 to 4 minutes until the white has set but the yolk still has a runny, warm consistency. Lift the eggs out with a slotted spoon and drain on kitchen paper.

- Eggs can be poached in advance and refreshed in iced water. Reheat in simmering water for 1½ to 2 minutes.

frying eggs

- Heat a knob of butter in a small, non-stick frying pan over a medium to low heat until the butter begins to bubble but not burn. Crack in the eggs and fry for 30 seconds until the white begins to set, then begin to baste the yolk with the butter. Once cooked, lift out the eggs and pour the butter over.

boiling eggs

- Carefully lower room-temperature eggs into a saucepan of water that is boiling, but not too rapidly, and place on the pan's bottom to prevent cracking. If you want to boil a lot of eggs, make sure you have a large saucepan, otherwise the temperature of the water will be reduced, making timings harder.

These cooking times treat the eggs like a sirloin steak, with timings for rare, medium and well done. The timings are for room-temperature eggs (add 30 seconds for cold), timed from the point they hit the water:

	medium	large
very soft	3½ minutes	4 minutes
soft	4½ minutes	5 minutes
medium	5½ minutes	6 minutes
hard (but with a moist centre)	7 minutes	8 minutes
well done	9 minutes	10 minutes

Once done, run quickly under water to stop the cooking.

Fruit and vegetables

When garden-fresh, fruit and vegetables need little preparation. Rinse your produce in cold water or wipe clean if delicate and drain well or pat dry.

soaking dried mushrooms

- Soak for 20 to 30 minutes in warm water. Once softened, scoop the mushrooms from the water, squeezing any excess juices back into the bowl, and keep the mushroom-flavoured water to one side. Drain the water through a fine sieve to remove any impurities, leaving you with an instant mushroom stock.

peeling tomatoes

- To remove the skins from tomatoes for a smooth finish to your sauce or soup you will need to blanch them. Remove the eye with the point of a sharp knife and cut a cross in the opposite end. Plunge the tomatoes into boiling water for 10 to 15 seconds before plunging into iced water. Once cold, the skin peels away easily and the tomatoes can be halved and deseeded before cutting into cubes or strips.

peeling peppers

- Preheat the grill. Put the peppers under the grill and allow them to reach a deep, almost burnt, colour before turning and repeating until completely coloured. The peppers can now be peeled while still warm or placed in a plastic bag and left to cool before peeling.

segmenting oranges or grapefruit

- Top and tail the fruit. The rind and pith can now be removed by cutting in a sawing motion down the sides. To release the segments, cut between each membrane, saving all the juice.

Starting the day/

Is there any better way to wake up your day than with a special breakfast? Of course, in today's busy world we don't always have time for the full monty, but for those who do like to kick-start their morning with flavour, I have included a few quick ideas for smoked haddock with eggs and an honest, straight-up bacon butty (brown sauce optional). And for those who are looking for a quick but still healthy breakfast, there are sunshine-enticing breakfast smoothies.

However, I have saved the best for the weekend. There's our great English breakfast of course, with all the trimmings, but also a vegetarian version that any meat eater would be happy to enjoy. And if you do have a little more time, then nothing sets up a relaxed weekend quite like brunch. A wonderful excuse to invite friends over for food that's as unfussy to cook as it is enjoyable to eat, you'll find that the Cumberland sausage and red onion tart is exactly the sort of thing you should make. If your friends are expecting scrambled eggs on toast, then bringing this out of the oven will certainly surprise them.

Starting the day/

Breakfast

Bacon and onion potatoes

Omelette

Smoked haddock-topped eggs with melting Lancashire cheese

Grilled kipper and granary fried bread

Bacon butty

Vegetarian full English

Full English breakfast

Sausage sandwich with sweet and sour tomatoes and onions

Scrambled egg mushroom muffins

Chocolate and nut pancakes with maple syrup

Grilled gingerbread slice with crushed banana and yoghurt

Strawberry and orange smoothie

Thick banana and coconut smoothie

bacon and onion potatoes

These potatoes are lovely with just about any dish but I particularly like to have them with a fried or poached egg for breakfast. This is also a great way to use up leftover boiled potatoes.

Cook the potatoes in their skins in boiling salted water for 20 to 25 minutes until tender. Drain and chop into bite-sized chunks.

In a hot frying pan, fry the bacon and potatoes in a tablespoon or 2 of olive oil for a few minutes before stirring in the onion. Cook until golden brown.

Season with salt and pepper.

serves four

4–5 large potatoes or 1kg (2¼lb) new potatoes
6–8 rashers of streaky or back bacon, roughly chopped
olive oil
3 onions, sliced
salt and pepper

omelette

French-style omelettes are best cooked until just set, leaving a soft centre and not allowing the outside to colour and become leathery. For breakfast, fillings such as cheese, onion, ham or tomatoes can be added to the omelette.

Break the eggs into a bowl and whisk together with a fork. Meanwhile warm a 15cm (6 inch) non-stick omelette pan over a medium heat, add the butter and swirl around the pan to cover the base and the sides.

Season the eggs with salt and pepper. Once the butter begins to foam, add the egg mixture and move the pan back and forth, stirring the eggs until a soft scrambled consistency is reached. Spread the base of the pan with the egg and leave until just set.

Hold the pan at an angle, slide the omelette towards the edge and fold it in, then fold the other side over to create a cigar shape. Turn the omelette out on to a plate and serve.

serves one

3 eggs
15g (½oz) butter
salt and pepper

smoked haddock-topped eggs with melting lancashire cheese

A simple open omelette with thinly sliced smoked haddock warmed through with melting Lancashire cheese (Cheddar, Gruyère or mozzarella would also melt beautifully). Using six eggs, the omelette can be divided into two or four.

serves two–four

175g (6oz) smoked
haddock fillet, skinned
a knob of butter
6 eggs, beaten
salt and pepper
75–100g (3–4oz)
  Lancashire cheese, grated

Slice the smoked haddock as thinly as you would smoked salmon. Preheat the grill.

Melt the butter in a 17–20cm (7–8 inch) frying pan over a medium heat and swirl around to cover the base and sides. Season the eggs with salt and pepper and once the butter begins to foam, add the eggs, moving the pan back and forth and stirring until a soft, scrambled consistency is reached before removing from the heat.

Cover the eggs with the smoked haddock and top with the cheese. Put beneath the grill, melting the cheese until it begins to lightly bubble. The omelette is now ready to cut and serve.

more
- Chopped chives can be added to the beaten eggs for a cheese and onion taste.

grilled kipper and granary fried bread

Brown bread and butter is the classic accompaniment for kippers. Here I've used a thick slice of granary loaf fried in lots of butter to give a crisp contrast to the melting kipper.

Preheat the grill. Lightly grease a baking tray and place the kipper, flesh-side up, on top. Dot about 15g (½oz) butter over the kipper and grill for 4 to 5 minutes until the butter begins to sizzle.

Meanwhile, melt the remaining butter in a pan and once bubbling, fry the granary bread for 2 to 3 minutes on each side until crispy and golden brown.

Pull away the central bone from the kipper and serve with the fried bread and, if using, the lemon wedge, drizzling any butter from the baking tray over the fillet.

serves one

1 kipper, head and tail
 removed
40g (1½oz) butter
1 thick slice of granary
 bread
wedge of lemon (optional)

more
- Try a breakfast or brunch kipper with warm, buttery wilted spinach.

bacon butty

The picture speaks for itself. This is one of my favourites and a recipe that will always live on. Adding mayonnaise or mustard-flavoured crème fraîche and rocket leaves on a slice of beef tomato to the roll gives a more 'continental' breakfast or brunch.

serves one

4–5 rashers of streaky
  bacon, halved
1 roll or bap
softened butter, for
  spreading
tomato ketchup or brown
  sauce (optional)

Heat a large frying pan and, once hot, lay the rashers in the pan and fry over a fierce heat to prevent any juices boiling the bacon. Cook the bacon until golden brown and crispy, the rashers frying in their own fat.

Meanwhile, preheat the grill. Split the roll or bap in two, liberally butter each side and toast the cut sides to a golden brown.

Stack the bacon rashers in the roll with a dollop of ketchup or brown sauce, if using.

vegetarian full english

The basic three components – tomatoes, mushrooms and a poached egg
– are listed together, while the sweetcorn pancakes and sweet potatoes and
onions are separate recipes. This gives you the choice of cooking as many
or as few as you wish. Everything serves four.

sweet potatoes and onions

2 large sweet potatoes,
  roughly chopped
1 large onion, sliced
2 tablespoons olive oil
salt and pepper

Preheat the oven to 200°C/400°F/gas 6. Mix together the sweet
potato and onion and put into a small roasting tray. Drizzle with
the olive oil, season with salt and pepper and bake for 25 to 30
minutes until tender.

eggs, tomatoes and mushrooms

4 tomatoes, halved
8–12 button or open cup
  mushrooms
olive oil, for drizzling
a large knob of butter, plus
  extra for spreading
sea salt and pepper
2 thick slices of bread
4 poached eggs
  (see page 18)

Preheat the grill. Bring a large saucepan of water to a rapid
simmer, ready for poaching the eggs.

Put the tomatoes and mushrooms on a baking tray, drizzle the
tomatoes with olive oil and divide the butter among the mushrooms,
seasoning with salt and pepper. Grill for 8 to 9 minutes until tender.
Meanwhile, butter the bread and toast until golden brown.

Poach the eggs.

Halve the toasts, top with the poached eggs and serve with the
tomatoes and mushrooms.

sweetcorn pancakes

100g (4oz) self-raising flour
1 egg
80–100ml (3–3½fl oz) milk
salt and pepper
1 small tin of sweetcorn,
  drained
olive or vegetable oil

Whisk together the flour, egg and enough milk to loosen.
Season with salt and pepper. Stir in the sweetcorn.

Heat a little oil in a large non-stick frying pan. Drop 2 tablespoons
of batter per pancake into the pan, adding as many as the pan
has room for.

Cook over a low to medium heat for 2 to 3 minutes, then turn and
fry for a further few minutes until golden brown. Keep the
pancakes warm while frying the remainder. The recipe will make
about eight to twelve pancakes.

full english breakfast

I've kept most of the elements of this large breakfast plate separate, leaving you with the choice. Each recipe serves four.

sauté potatoes

450g (1lb) potatoes
3–4 tablespoons olive or
  vegetable oil
a knob of butter
salt and pepper

Cook the potatoes in their skins in boiling salted water for 25 to 30 minutes until cooked through. Drain and leave to cool before peeling. Cut the potatoes into 5mm (¼ inch) slices.

Heat the oil in a large frying pan and fry the potatoes, including any crumbly broken pieces, over a medium heat until golden brown. Turn the potatoes and fry until crispy. Add the knob of butter and season with salt and pepper.

sausages

8 sausages
olive or vegetable oil

Pan-fry the sausages in a drizzle of oil over a medium heat for 10 to 15 minutes until completely golden brown.

black pudding

4 slices of large black
  pudding or 8–12 slices
  from small puddings
a large knob of softened
  butter

Preheat the grill. Lay the black pudding slices on a grill tray, brush each with the butter and grill for a few minutes on each side until crispy on the outside and soft in the centre.

bacon

8 rashers of back bacon or
  8–12 rashers of streaky
  bacon

Preheat the grill. Grill the bacon for 5 to 6 minutes, leaving it for an extra few minutes if preferred crispy.

fried egg, tomatoes and mushrooms

4 tomatoes, halved
8 flat mushrooms
olive oil
a large knob of softened
  butter
salt and pepper
15g (½oz) butter
4 eggs

Preheat the grill. Put the tomatoes and mushrooms on a baking tray, drizzle the tomatoes with olive oil and brush the softened butter over the mushrooms. Season with salt and pepper and grill for 8 to 9 minutes.

Fry the eggs (see page 19)

sausage sandwich with sweet and sour tomatoes and onions

Fry the sausages in a dash of olive oil over a medium heat until well coloured all round and firm to the touch.

Meanwhile, in a separate pan, fry the onion in a drop of olive oil until softened with burnt tinges. Add the cherry tomatoes and cook until they start to break down. Season with salt and pepper.

Whisk together the ketchup, vinegar and honey with the 2 tablespoons of olive oil, adding the mustard if using. Season and stir into the onions.

Slice each of the sausages into three strips. Arrange on half the bread slices, spoon the tomatoes and onions on top and close with the other slices of bread.

serves four

450g (1lb) sausages
2 tablespoons olive oil, plus
   extra for frying
2 onions, sliced
12–15 cherry tomatoes,
   halved
salt and pepper
1 teaspoon tomato ketchup
1 teaspoon white wine
   vinegar
½ teaspoon honey
½ teaspoon Dijon mustard
   (optional)
8 slices of bread

more

- You could spread mayonnaise on the bread.
- Sauté some sliced mushrooms with the onions.

scrambled egg mushroom muffins

serves two–four

2 muffins, halved
15g (½oz) butter, plus extra
  for spreading and
  scrambling
100g (4oz) mushrooms,
  sliced or quartered
6 eggs
salt and pepper
1 heaped teaspoon
  chopped chives
Parmesan cheese, for
  grating

Preheat the grill. Brush each muffin half with butter and toast under the grill until golden.

Melt the butter in a frying pan and, once foaming, add the mushrooms and fry over a medium to hot heat for 1 or 2 minutes until softened. Spoon on top of the muffins.

Meanwhile, beat the eggs to combine the yolks with the whites. Melt a large knob of butter in a saucepan or frying pan and, once bubbling but before it browns, pour in the eggs, seasoning them with salt and pepper. Turn and stir the eggs fairly vigorously with a wooden spoon, covering every corner of the pan.

Top the muffins with the scrambled eggs, sprinkle over the chives and grate Parmesan cheese on top of each one.

chocolate and nut pancakes with maple syrup

makes 25–30 pancakes

175g (6oz) self-raising flour
50g (2oz) cocoa powder
25g (1oz) butter
200ml (7fl oz) milk
2 eggs, beaten
100g (4oz) caster sugar
salt
75g (3oz) pecan nuts,
  chopped
vegetable oil, for frying
maple syrup, to serve

Sift together the flour and cocoa powder. Melt the butter and whisk in the milk, eggs, sugar and a pinch of salt. Pour into the flour and whisk vigorously before stirring in the pecan nuts.

Gently heat a frying pan with a trickle of oil. Spoon in the batter to make five to six pancakes and cook for a few minutes until small bubbles appear on the surface and the pancakes are ready to be turned. Fry for a further 1 to 2 minutes, remove from the pan and wrap in a warm tea towel while cooking the remaining pancakes.

Serve with maple syrup.

grilled gingerbread slice with crushed banana and yoghurt

serves four

4 slices (approximately
1.5cm/⅝ inch thick) of
  gingerbread cake
softened butter, for
  spreading (optional)
2 large or 4 small bananas
a squeeze of lime
1 small pot of natural
  yoghurt

Preheat the grill. Spread the gingerbread slices with butter, if using.

Put the slices on a baking tray, butter-side up, and toast under the grill to a golden brown.

Meanwhile, peel the bananas, add to a bowl and crush with a fork as smooth or as coarse as you wish. Add a squeeze of lime for a citrus bite and to prevent the banana from discolouring.

Arrange the hot gingerbread on plates or in bowls, scoop a dollop of banana on top of each one and offer the yoghurt separately.

strawberry and orange smoothie

serves one–two

100g (4oz) strawberries,
 roughly chopped
100ml (3½fl oz) orange
 juice
1 tablespoon natural
 yoghurt

Put all the ingredients into a blender and blend until smooth.

Serve over ice or in a cooled glass.

thick banana and coconut smoothie

serves one–two

1 banana, peeled
150ml (3½fl oz) coconut
 milk
a generous squeeze of lime
4–5 ice cubes

Place all the ingredients in a blender and blitz until smooth.

Pour into a glass to serve.

more

- For more of a 'piña colada' flavour, add 100ml (3½fl oz) pineapple juice.

Starting the day/

Brunch

Pea pancakes and grilled bacon

Cumberland sausage and red onion tart

Bacon and egg risotto

Charcuterie board with celeriac coleslaw

Warm chorizo and goat's cheese salad with raspberry vinaigrette

Black pudding and bacon with honey apples and yoghurt rocket

Black pudding with blue cheese, celery and apple salad

Warm gammon and pineapple with English leaves

Cured ham with a carpaccio sauce

Sautéed kidneys and chipolatas with mushrooms and garlic toasts

Glazed horseradish tuna with spring onion potatoes

Golden oatmeal herrings

Smoked salmon and poached egg muffins

Warm salmon on brown bread

Smoked haddock, poached egg and sorrel hollandaise

Crab salad with crispy poached egg

Crushed champ kippers with wilted watercress

Grilled mackerel with Calvados apples

Red wine and mushroom poached eggs on toast

Bacon and egg salad

Home-made salad cream with new potatoes, eggs and red onions

Red Leicester mushrooms

Leeks and red onions with a warm poached egg

Oyster mushroom and spinach pancakes

pea pancakes and grilled bacon

Place the peas, egg, egg yolk, flour and cream or milk in a food processor and blitz to a slightly chunky or smooth consistency. Season with salt and pepper. Heat a frying pan, add the butter and cook until a sizzling nutty brown before stirring into the mix.

Wipe the frying pan clean and add a trickle of oil. Drop 2 to 3 tablespoons of the mix into the pan for each pancake (a lightly greased stainless steel ring can be used for a perfect round shape). Cook three to four pancakes at a time over a medium heat for 2 to 3 minutes, then turn and cook for a further 1 to 2 minutes. Remove the pancakes and keep warm while frying the remainder of the mix (it should make about twelve pancakes).

Meanwhile, preheat the grill. Lay the bacon on a grill tray and grill for 5 to 6 minutes, leaving for an extra few minutes if preferred crispy.

The pancakes and bacon can now be stacked, with about three pancakes and six half rashers of bacon for each portion.

more

- Maple syrup is very tasty with the bacon, a little drizzled over the rashers.

serves four

225g (8oz) frozen petits
  pois, defrosted
1 egg
1 egg yolk
3 tablespoons plain flour
3 tablespoons double
  cream or milk
salt and pepper
50g (2oz) butter
vegetable oil, for frying
8-12 rashers of streaky
  bacon, halved

cumberland sausage and red onion tart

A large 'Catherine wheel' Cumberland sausage is featured in this recipe. It's a good idea to become friendly with your local butcher, who I'm sure will be more than happy to make one of these for you.

serves six–eight

3 knobs of butter, plus extra for greasing
3 large red onions, sliced
2 tablespoons red wine vinegar
1 heaped tablespoon redcurrant jelly
salt and pepper
1 sheet of ready-rolled puff pastry
1.35kg (3lb) Cumberland sausage, about 23–25cm (9–10 inches) in diameter

Melt a knob of butter in a frying pan and, once foaming, add the red onion and cook over a medium heat until softened. Pour in the red wine vinegar and stir over a fierce heat until it has totally evaporated. Spoon in the redcurrant jelly, reduce the temperature and cook until the onions are sticky. Season with salt and pepper and leave to cool.

Preheat the oven to 220°C/425°F/gas 7.

Cut out a 25cm (10 inch) disc from the pastry. Butter a baking tray, place the pastry on top and prick all over with a fork. Spread the onion over the pastry to cover, top with the sausage and pierce the end with one or two cocktail sticks to help maintain the wheel shape. Brush with a knob of melted butter. Bake for 20 to 25 minutes until the pastry is crisp and the sausage is golden brown.

For some extra colour, brush with the last knob of butter and finish under a preheated grill.

more

- If only basic Cumberland sausages are available, the pastry can be cut into individual rectangles and the onions and two sausages put on top of each one before baking.

bacon and egg risotto

serves four

olive oil
75g (3oz) butter
1 onion, finely chopped
6–8 rashers of streaky or
  back bacon, cut into strips
  or cubes
350g (12oz) risotto rice
1–1.2 litres (1¾–2 pints)
  chicken stock
  (see page 13)
50g (2oz) Parmesan
  cheese, grated (optional)
salt and pepper
4 poached eggs
  (see page 18)

Heat the olive oil and half the butter in a large shallow pan or deep frying pan. Add the onion and bacon and lightly fry for 6 to 8 minutes.

Over a gentle heat, add the rice and stir for a minute, allowing the rice to be coated with the butter without colouring. Heat the stock in a small saucepan. Add a ladleful or two of the gently simmering stock, stirring gently.

Once the stock has been absorbed, add a further ladleful, stirring and adding more as it continues to be absorbed. Continue this process for 15 to 20 minutes, at which point the rice should be tender and creamy, but still maintaining the slightest of bites.

Meanwhile, bring a large saucepan of water to a rapid simmer, ready for poaching the eggs. Add the remaining butter and Parmesan cheese to the risotto, if using, and season. The risotto can now be left to rest with a lid on while the eggs are poached.

Spoon the risotto into bowls, top each with an egg and drizzle with olive oil.

charcuterie board with celeriac coleslaw

Charcuterie literally means cooked meat and covers a whole range of salamis, hams and terrines, with Parma, Bayonne, Serrano and Ibérico hams (Italian, French and Spanish) probably the best known.

Cut away the tough skin of the celeriac and slice on a mandolin into fine sticks. Core the apples and pears and cut into sticks on the mandolin, leaving the skin on.

Mix together the fruit, celeriac, celery, onion, if using, and walnuts. Stir in the lemon juice and season with salt and pepper.

Mix the mayonnaise with the mustard, adding all the mayonnaise for a looser dressing. Spoon the sauce through the salad and check for seasoning.

Arrange the charcuterie on a board or platter with the coleslaw.

serves six–eight

1 small or ½ large celeriac
2 apples
2 pears
4 sticks of celery, peeled and thinly sliced
1 small red onion, very thinly sliced (optional)
100g (4oz) walnuts, chopped
juice of 1 lemon
salt and pepper
200–300g (7–10oz) mayonnaise
1 teaspoon Dijon or wholegrain mustard
mixed charcuterie, about 200–300g (7–10oz) per person

more

- For an extra nutty taste or as an alternative to the walnuts, add a tablespoon or two of toasted sesame seeds.

warm chorizo and goat's cheese salad with raspberry vinaigrette

serves four

for the raspberry vinaigrette

4 tablespoons olive oil, plus extra for cooking
2 tablespoons raspberry vinegar
a pinch of caster sugar
½ teaspoon Dijon mustard (optional)
salt and pepper

100–200g (4–7oz) mixed or single variety salad leaves
2–3 spring onions, thinly sliced
225g (8oz) goat's cheese, broken into chunks
300g (10oz) chorizo sausage, peeled and cut into 1cm (½ inch) thick slices

Whisk together the olive oil, vinegar and sugar, adding the mustard if using. Season with salt and pepper.

Mix together the salad leaves and spring onion and gently toss with the goat's cheese.

Heat a large frying pan with a drizzle of olive oil. Fry the chorizo, turning, for 3 to 4 minutes. Spoon the sausage into the salad, whisk any fat released into the vinaigrette and drizzle over the leaves.

more

- A little natural yoghurt can be sprinkled over the salad for a creamier finish.
- A few fresh raspberries can be added to enhance the flavour of the vinaigrette.

black pudding and bacon with honey apples and yoghurt rocket

Heat a large frying pan. Add the rashers to the dry pan and as the bacon fat melts, the rashers will become crispy. Once the fat has been released, add the black pudding and fry for a few minutes on each side.

Meanwhile, peel the apples, divide each one into eight wedges and remove the core before halving each wedge into chunks. Melt the butter in a separate pan. Once foaming, fry the apple over a medium to high heat until golden. Stir in the honey and cook until it begins to caramelize.

Whisk the lime juice, if using, into the yoghurt, season with salt and pepper and fold in the rocket leaves.

Arrange the black pudding, bacon and honey apples on warm plates, finishing with the yoghurt rocket.

serves two

4–6 rashers of streaky bacon
6 thick (1.5–2cm/⅝–¾ inch) slices of black pudding
2 apples
a large knob of butter
1 tablespoon honey
a squeeze of lime juice (optional)
1–2 tablespoons natural yoghurt
salt and pepper
2 handfuls of rocket

black pudding with blue cheese, celery and apple salad

serves four

2 baby black puddings,
   halved, or 8 thick slices of
   a large black pudding
1 large knob of butter
100ml (3½fl oz) single
   cream or crème fraîche
50g (2oz) blue cheese,
   finely crumbled
juice of ½ lime
pepper
2 handfuls of curly endive
2 handfuls of rocket leaves
4 spring onions, sliced
2 sticks of celery, peeled
   and sliced
2 apples, sliced or cut into
   chunks

Preheat the grill. Butter the black pudding, place on a baking tray and grill for 5 to 6 minutes until almost crispy on top.

Meanwhile, in a pan warm together the cream or crème fraîche and blue cheese. Once smooth, remove from the heat, add the lime juice and season with a twist of pepper.

Mix together the salad leaves, spring onion, celery and apple and dress with the warm blue cheese cream to coat.

Put the black pudding on plates and arrange the salad over and around.

warm gammon and pineapple with english leaves

serves four

for the salad
1 small cos
1 small round lettuce
1 little gem
1 small bunch of watercress

1 small ripe pineapple,
   peeled, cored and cut into
   1cm (½ inch) cubes
2 tablespoons light soft
   brown sugar
sea salt and pepper
100ml (3½fl oz) pineapple
   juice
150ml (5fl oz) sour cream
a squeeze of lime or splash
   of balsamic vinegar
   (optional)
1 tablespoon sunflower or
   groundnut oil
2 x 175–225g (6–8oz)
   gammon steaks (smoked
   or unsmoked), cut into
   1cm (½ inch) cubes
a knob of butter

Tear the salad leaves into a salad spinner or colander, rinse lightly and leave to drain.

Heat a large non-stick frying pan. Add the pineapple, sprinkle with the sugar and fry quickly over a high heat, allowing the sugar to lightly caramelize. Season with sea salt and a generous twist of black pepper.

Pour the juice over the pineapple and bring to a simmer. As the fruit cooks, the syrup will begin to thicken. After a few minutes, drain the pineapple in a sieve over a bowl and keep the fruit to one side. Whisk the sour cream into the syrup in the bowl, seasoning if needed. For a slightly sharper taste, add the lime or balsamic.

Reheat the frying pan and add the oil. Quickly pan-fry the diced gammon for a few minutes until tender and golden. Season with salt and pepper and finish with the butter.

Divide the salad leaves between four plates, topping each with the pineapple and gammon before drizzling liberally with the pineapple-flavoured sour cream.

cured ham with a carpaccio sauce

Any cured ham would be wonderful with this carpaccio sauce (usually served with the Italian classic of thinly sliced raw beef). A few salad leaves, such as rocket, and perhaps some Parmesan shavings and crusty bread create an easy brunch, lunch or supper.

Arrange the ham to cover the plates.

Whisk together the mayonnaise, Worcestershire sauce, lemon juice and milk or water, seasoning with salt and pepper. The sauce can be drizzled in a rustic fashion over the ham or offered separately along with the olive oil.

serves four

225–350g (8–12oz) thinly sliced cured ham, such as Parma, Bayonne, Serrano, jambon d'Ardennes or Ibérico
150g (5oz) mayonnaise
2 teaspoons Worcestershire sauce
2 teaspoons lemon juice
2 tablespoons milk or water
salt and pepper
olive oil

sautéed kidneys and chipolatas with mushrooms and garlic toasts

serves four

1 onion, sliced
100g (4oz) small button
  mushrooms
olive oil
4 tomatoes, deseeded and
  roughly chopped
200ml (7fl oz) chicken or
  beef stock (see page 13)
salt and pepper
6 lambs' kidneys, trimmed
  and halved
12 chipolata sausages
1 tablespoon chopped
  parsley

for the garlic toasts

2 cloves of garlic, finely
  crushed
4 tablespoons olive oil
12 slices of French bread

In a large shallow pan, fry the onion and mushrooms in olive oil until golden brown, then add the tomato and cook until softened. Pour in the stock, bring to a simmer for 5 to 6 minutes and season with salt and pepper.

Meanwhile, warm a splash or two of olive oil in another frying pan and, once smoking, sauté the kidneys and chipolatas for 3 to 4 minutes until well coloured. Season with salt and pepper, then add to the sauce and simmer gently for 1 to 2 minutes before adding the parsley.

Preheat the grill. Mix together the garlic and olive oil, brush it liberally on the bread slices and place them on a baking tray. Toast under the grill until golden brown on both sides and serve with the kidneys and chipolatas.

more

- English mustard and white wine vinegar will add a touch of heat and sharpness to the dish.

glazed horseradish tuna with spring onion potatoes

This horseradish glaze is quite fiery, but the quantity of horseradish cream can be reduced, or increased. Marinated in lemon oil, the hot new potatoes are delicious with this dish, but can be simply rolled in butter instead.

serves four

675g (1½lb) new potatoes
150ml (5fl oz) olive oil
3 teaspoons lemon juice
salt and pepper
2 slices of crustless bread,
  soaked in water
1 teaspoon white wine
  vinegar
2 egg yolks
2 tablespoons horseradish
  cream
1 tablespoon chopped
  chives
4 x 150g (5oz) tuna steaks
1 bunch of spring onions,
  thinly sliced

Cook the potatoes in boiling salted water for 20 minutes or until cooked through. Drain and halve into a bowl. Whisk together 4 tablespoons of the olive oil and the lemon juice, seasoning with salt and pepper. Pour the dressing over the potatoes and mix together well. Cover with clingfilm and keep warm to one side.

Squeeze any excess water from the soaked bread and place it in a small bowl or blender with the vinegar and egg yolks. Using an electric hand whisk or the blender, blitz until smooth, slowly pouring in all but a tablespoon of the remaining olive oil, a little at a time, as you would when making mayonnaise. Once mixed in, fold in the horseradish cream and chives and season with salt and pepper.

Preheat the grill and dry the tuna steaks on kitchen paper. Warm an ovenproof frying pan with the remaining olive oil. Once hot, fry the tuna steaks for 1 to 2 minutes on each side before spooning the horseradish cream over generously. Pop the tuna under the grill, glazing to a golden brown.

Stir the spring onions into the potatoes and serve with the tuna.

more
- A few salad leaves or sprigs of watercress are the perfect accompaniment to help mop up the horseradish glaze.

golden oatmeal herrings

Preheat the grill. Lightly grease a baking tray with a knob of the butter, season with salt and pepper and lay the herring fillets on top.

Mix together the oatmeal, breadcrumbs and sultanas and season. Brush each of the fillets on the skin side with the beaten egg before topping with the oatmeal crumbs. Melt the remaining butter and trickle over the fillets.

Grill the herrings for just a few minutes (4 to 5 minutes maximum) until golden brown. Put the herrings on plates, add a little squeeze of lemon from one of the quarters to any remaining butter on the tray and trickle it around each fillet. Serve with the lemon quarters.

serves two–four

50g (2oz) butter
salt and pepper
4 large herring fillets,
   soaked and trimmed
   (see page 14)
40g (1½ oz) pinhead
   oatmeal
40g (1½ oz) fresh white
   breadcrumbs
40g (1½ oz) golden
   sultanas, chopped
1 egg, beaten
1 lemon, quartered

more

- A splash of whisky mixed into the cooked butter adds a Scottish touch, from where the dish was born.
- The fillets can also be pan-fried in butter.

smoked salmon and poached egg muffins

serves four

4 poached eggs
  (see page 18)
2 muffins, halved
softened butter, for
  spreading
1 pack of sliced smoked
  salmon (approximately
  200–225g/7–8oz)
120ml (4fl oz) crème
  fraîche
½–1 teaspoon Dijon
  mustard
1 lemon, quartered
salt and pepper

Bring a large saucepan of water to a rapid simmer and poach the eggs.

Meanwhile, preheat the grill, lightly butter the muffins and toast to a golden brown. Top each muffin with smoked salmon and a warm poached egg.

Mix together the crème fraîche, mustard and a few drops of lemon juice from one of the quarters. Season with salt and pepper and spoon the sauce over the eggs, serving the lemon quarters on the side.

more

- Why not try some chopped chives or chervil mixed with the crème fraîche or sprinkled on top with a trickle of olive oil.

warm salmon on brown bread

The salmon takes less than 10 minutes to cook and during that time, the rest of the sandwich is prepared. A thick slice of smoked salmon would also work very well, with the sandwich then taking just a few minutes to make.

Heat a non-stick frying pan with the butter or oil. Once sizzling, season the salmon with salt and pepper and lightly fry, skinned-side down, for 3 to 5 minutes. Turn the fillets and remove the pan from the stove. The residual heat in the pan will continue to cook the fish for a further minute or so. Meanwhile, stir together the cucumber, lime juice and the sugar, if using, and season with salt and pepper.

Spread the bread liberally with the mayonnaise before adding the cucumber. Place the salmon on the cucumber to complete the open sandwich.

more
- Chopped dill can be added to the cucumber.

serves two

a large knob of butter or 1 tablespoon olive oil
2 x 100–175g (4–6oz) slices of salmon fillet, skinned and pinboned (see page 14)
salt and pepper
½ small cucumber, peeled or not, sliced
a squeeze of lime juice
a pinch of sugar (optional)
2 thick slices of brown or granary bread
mayonnaise, for spreading

smoked haddock, poached egg and sorrel hollandaise

It's important that this quick hollandaise sauce is made first and kept warm while poaching the smoked haddock and eggs.

serves four

1 x quick hollandaise sauce
  (see page 464)
300ml (10fl oz) milk
4 x 100–175g (4–6oz)
  smoked haddock fillets
4 poached eggs
  (see page 18)
a knob of butter
100g (4oz) rocket
1 bunch of watercress, main
  stalks removed
salt and pepper
10–12 sorrel leaves,
  chopped

Make the hollandaise. Bring a large saucepan of water to a rapid simmer, ready for poaching the eggs. Bring the milk and the same amount of water to boil in a pan large enough to hold the haddock.

Put the haddock in the milk and gently simmer for 3 to 4 minutes until just firm to the touch. Meanwhile, poach the eggs.

Heat the butter in a frying pan or wok. Once bubbling, add the rocket and the washed and well-drained watercress, seasoning with salt and pepper. The leaves will take just a moment to wilt and can then be divided among four plates.

Using a fish slice, carefully lift the haddock, peeling away the skin if left on and arrange on the plates with the eggs. Stir the sorrel into the hollandaise and spoon over the top.

crab salad with crispy poached egg

serves four

225g (8oz) new potatoes
4 poached eggs
  (see page 18)
salt and pepper
1 egg, beaten with 1
  tablespoon milk
75g (3oz) dried white
  breadcrumbs
3 plum tomatoes, peeled,
  deseeded and cut into
  cubes (see page 20)
4 tablespoons olive oil
2 tablespoons lemon juice
2–3 tablespoons crab or
  lobster bisque (optional)
75ml (3fl oz) crème fraîche
175g (6oz) white crabmeat
a handful or two of mixed
  salad leaves
vegetable oil

Cook the new potatoes in boiling salted water for 20 minutes until tender. Bring a large saucepan of water to a rapid simmer and poach the eggs.

Plunge the eggs into iced water. Pat dry with kitchen paper, season with salt and pepper and dip into the beaten egg followed by the crumbs. Refrigerate until needed.

Whisk the tomato cubes together with the olive oil, lemon juice and tomatoes, allowing them to gently break. Season with salt and pepper.

Whisk the bisque, if using, into the crème fraîche and season with salt and pepper. Drain the potatoes, slice and season with salt and pepper, stirring in enough of the bisque crème fraîche to bind. Divide among four plates, spooning any extra sauce around. Top with the crabmeat and a few mixed leaves and drizzle with the tomato dressing.

Heat enough oil in a wok or small saucepan to cover the crumbed eggs. Drop the eggs in carefully and fry over a medium heat until golden. Drain on kitchen paper and arrange the eggs on top of the salads.

crushed champ kippers with wilted watercress

Cook the potatoes in boiling salted water for 20 to 25 minutes before draining and crushing coarsely with a potato masher or fork.

Melt 25g (1oz) of the butter in a saucepan and, once bubbling, throw in the spring onions, stirring for 30 to 60 seconds until they begin to soften. Add the onions to the crushed potatoes and season with salt and a generous twist of pepper.

Meanwhile, preheat the grill. Grease a baking tray and place the kippers on top, skin-side down. Top with two or three knobs of butter and grill for 4 to 5 minutes. Once cooked, pull away the central bone and discard, separating the chunky flakes with two forks.

Melt the remaining butter and, once foaming, drop the washed and well-drained watercress sprigs into the butter. Season with salt and pepper. As soon as the leaves wilt, spoon on to plates with a pile of champ topped with the flakes of kipper. Mix any butter left on the tray with the lemon juice and drizzle over the top.

serves four

450g (1lb) floury potatoes, peeled and quartered
50–75g (2–3oz) butter, plus 2 or 3 extra knobs
1 bunch of spring onions, finely shredded
sea salt and pepper
2 kippers, heads and tails removed
2 bunches of watercress, main stalks removed
a few drops of lemon juice

more
- Top the kippers with a dollop of crème fraîche or natural yoghurt.

grilled mackerel with calvados apples

If you don't have Calvados, try a generous splash of cider or whisky.

serves four

4 x 225–300g (8–10oz) whole mackerel fillets, gutted and cleaned
melted butter, for brushing
sea salt and pepper
40g (1½ oz) butter
3 apples, peeled, cored and cut into 1–2cm (½– ¾ inch) chunks
1–2 measures (25–50ml/1– 2fl oz) of Calvados
100ml (3½fl oz) apple juice

Preheat the grill. Using a sharp knife, score the mackerel three to four times on each side. Grease a baking tray and sprinkle with salt and pepper. Lay the fish on top, brush with butter and season. Cook beneath the grill for 4 to 5 minutes until crispy on both sides.

Meanwhile, melt a knob of the butter in a large frying pan and, once foaming, add the apple and fry over a high heat until it starts to colour. Carefully pour over the Calvados and allow it to ignite and bubble until almost evaporated. Add the apple juice and simmer until just half is left. Shaking the pan, add the remaining butter and serve with the crispy mackerel.

red wine and mushroom poached eggs on toast

serves two

300ml (10fl oz) red wine
1 heaped teaspoon caster sugar
50g (2oz) butter, plus extra for spreading
1–2 handfuls of mushrooms (whatever you have), sliced
salt and pepper
2 thick slices of crusty bread
4 poached eggs (see page 18)

Simmer the red wine with the sugar in a small saucepan until just a quarter is left.

Meanwhile, heat a frying pan with a small knob of the butter and, once sizzling, add the mushrooms and fry over a high heat until well coloured. Season with salt and pepper. Whisk the remaining butter into the wine sauce before pouring over the mushrooms. Keep warm.

Preheat the grill and bring a large saucepan of water to a rapid simmer, ready for poaching the eggs. While poaching the eggs, toast the bread on one side under the grill, then butter the other side and return to the grill, toasting that side until golden.

Arrange the eggs on the toasts, spooning the red wine mushrooms over the top.

bacon and egg salad

Streaky bacon works well in this salad, but here I've chosen a cured ham, which crisps up very nicely. The dressing for the salad is flavoured with a blue cheese such as Roquefort, Gorgonzola, Dolcelatte or Stilton, but can be substituted with a soft goat's cheese if preferred.

Crumble the blue cheese in a food processor and blend with the crème fraîche and a twist of pepper.

Warm a little oil in a frying pan and, once hot, fry the slices of ham for a minute until crispy. Mix the salad leaves with the dressing, scatter them over the plates and top with the crispy ham.

Add the butter to the frying pan and, once foaming, crack the eggs into the pan and fry and baste with the butter until the white is set and the yolk is soft.

Place the eggs on top of the salad to serve, drizzling any butter over the top.

serves two

50g (2oz) blue cheese
6 tablespoons low-fat crème fraîche
pepper
vegetable oil
2–4 slices of Bayonne, Parma or Serrano ham
100g (4oz) mixed salad leaves
a large knob of butter
2 large eggs

home-made salad cream with new potatoes, eggs and red onions

serves four

450g (1lb) new potatoes
4 eggs
1 red onion, finely chopped
coarse sea salt and pepper
olive oil

for the salad cream

1 tablespoon plain flour
4 teaspoons caster sugar
2 teaspoons English
 mustard powder
salt
2 eggs
100ml (3½fl oz) white wine
 vinegar
150ml (5fl oz) double cream
a squeeze of lemon juice

Cook the new potatoes in boiling salted water until just overcooked. Boil the four eggs for 7 to 8 minutes.

For the salad cream, mix together the flour, sugar, mustard and a pinch of salt. Beat in the 2 eggs and white wine vinegar. Place the bowl over a pan of simmering water and stir for 5 to 6 minutes until warmed and thickened. Remove the bowl from the heat and leave to cool. Once cold, stir in the cream and lemon juice. This makes 200–300ml (7–10fl oz) salad cream, which will keep refrigerated for 1 to 2 weeks.

Break the warm overcooked potatoes into a bowl. Peel the boiled eggs, cut into large pieces and add to the potatoes with the red onion. Season with salt and pepper, drizzle with olive oil and serve with the salad cream.

more

- A few chopped chive stalks could be sprinkled over the top.

red leicester mushrooms

serves six

6 large flat mushrooms,
   stalks trimmed
salt and pepper
50g (2oz) butter, plus extra
   for greasing
3 red onions, sliced
100g (4oz) Red Leicester
   cheese, grated
50g (2oz) Gruyère or
   Emmental cheese, grated
100ml (3½fl oz) double
   cream

Lightly butter a baking tray. Place the mushrooms on the tray, stalk-side up. Season with salt and pepper. Using half the butter, put small knobs on each of the mushrooms.

Melt the remaining butter in a large deep frying pan and, once sizzling, add the onion and fry over a medium to hot heat for 8 to 10 minutes until softened and lightly coloured. Season with salt and pepper.

Meanwhile, preheat the grill and cook the mushrooms for 6 to 8 minutes until tender. Spoon the onion on top of the mushrooms.

Mix the two cheeses in a bowl and stir in the cream. Top each of the oniony mushrooms with the cheese mixture and return under the grill until the cheese has melted to a golden brown.

leeks and red onions with a warm poached egg

serves four

2 knobs of butter
3 large red onions, chopped
grated zest of ½ orange
1 teaspoon red wine
   vinegar
1 tablespoon blackcurrant
   cordial or crème de cassis
salt and pepper
4 poached eggs (see
   page 18)
1–2 large leeks, shredded
1 x red wine mustard
   dressing (see page 466)

Melt a knob of butter in a pan and, once foaming, add the red onion and orange zest and soften without colouring. Pour in the red wine vinegar and simmer until it evaporates, then add the blackcurrant cordial or cassis and cook for a further 5 to 6 minutes. Season with salt and a twist of black pepper.

Meanwhile, bring a large saucepan of water to a rapid simmer and poach the eggs.

Melt the remaining butter in a frying pan, add the leek with a few tablespoons of water, cover and steam for 2 to 3 minutes. Stir the leeks and season with salt and pepper.

Place the red onion on to plates, top with the leeks and warm poached eggs and drizzle the red wine mustard dressing liberally over the eggs.

oyster mushroom and spinach pancakes

Sift the flour and salt into a bowl. Whisk the egg and the milk into the flour until smooth, adding the parsley if using. Warm a 17–20cm (7–8 inch) frying pan (preferably non-stick) over a medium heat and lightly oil. Pour in just enough batter to coat the base of the pan. Cook for a minute until golden brown, turn the pancake and cook for a further minute. Keep warm while cooking the remainder of the pancakes (the mixture should make about eight).

Melt the butter in a large shallow pan and, once sizzling, fry the mushrooms to quickly colour and soften. Season with salt and pepper and remove from the pan. Return the pan to the heat, add the washed and well-drained spinach and soften over a fierce heat, allowing any water to evaporate. Season with salt and pepper. Add the mushrooms to the spinach along with the crème fraîche and Parmesan, if using.

Spoon the filling on to one half of each pancake, fold over the other halves and serve.

serves four

for the pancakes
100g (4oz) plain flour
a pinch of salt
1 egg
300ml (10fl oz) milk
1 tablespoon chopped
 parsley (optional)
vegetable oil

a knob of butter
100g (4oz) oyster
 mushrooms, torn into
 strips
salt and pepper
350g (12oz) spinach leaves
2–3 tablespoons crème
 fraîche
2 tablespoons grated
 Parmesan cheese
 (optional)

Midweek lunch/

The midweek lunch must be the most neglected of meals. While the French and Spanish look forward to a tasty, freshly prepared lunch after a morning's hard work, we British treat ourselves to a plastic-wrapped sandwich and packet of crisps. We may not be able to change our whole lifestyle (siesta, anyone?) but we are all entitled to good, enjoyable food as part of our everyday life.

The new British midweek lunch I'm thinking of should arrive from stove to table within half an hour, like the grilled buffalo mozzarella with garlic, lemon and courgettes, ready in less than ten minutes. It might be made from ingredients you want to use up from your fridge – a couple of leftover courgettes for a soup with tomato and red onion bruschetta or an odd piece of cheese for melting over hot asparagus spears and ham. It may be something simple to eat on your own, like fiery mushrooms on toast, or enjoyed in company, like charred squid with passion fruit, pineapple and sesame leaves, but it should never compromise on flavour.

I don't like to eat heavily at midday and I think the best midweek lunch is carbohydrate-light but packed with goodness and energy for the afternoon ahead. With that in mind, I've chosen lots of fish. Quick to cook, light and healthy, it's a perfect midweek lunch.

Midweek lunch/

Courgette soup with tomato and red onion bruschetta

Butternut squash soup

Cherry tomato soup

Broken feta cheese salad with apples and pears

Three bean salad

Red and white chicory salad with a rhubarb vinaigrette

Fennel, asparagus, grapefruit and apple

Hot potato salad with melting raclette

Avocado and courgette salad with lime

Grilled buffalo mozzarella with garlic, lemon and courgettes

Gorgonzola, Parma ham and rocket pasta

Pasta with chicken, sage and onion butter

Fiery mushrooms on toast

Asparagus and ham glazed with Cheddar and Parmesan

Fried bacon pieces with spinach and prawns

Salmon with a salted tomato and herb salad

Salmon cutlets with minted leeks and peas and a sweet lemon dressing

Grilled tuna with a niçoise salsa

Sweet sesame mackerel with banana chutney

Potted mackerel

Steak Diane

Charred squid with passion fruit, pineapple and sesame leaves

Roast chicken with goat's cheese and fresh herb butter

courgette soup with tomato and red onion bruschetta

Boil some water in a kettle. Put the chopped courgettes into a saucepan and pour 600ml (1 pint) boiling water on top. Bring to the boil and cook for 6 to 7 minutes until tender. Season with salt and pepper and liquidize in a blender until smooth.

Meanwhile, rub the cut side of the garlic halves over both sides of the toasted bread. Mix together the tomato, onion and basil with a drop or two of olive oil.

Season with sea salt and pepper and arrange the topping on the toasts.

Offer the toasts alongside the soup or place in the bowls and pour the soup around them.

serves four

450g (1lb) courgettes,
  roughly chopped
salt and pepper

for the bruschettas
1 clove of garlic, peeled and
  halved
4 thick slices of French
  bread or ciabatta, toasted
2 plum tomatoes, deseeded
  and cut into thin strips
1 small red onion, thinly
  sliced
4 basil leaves, shredded
olive oil
sea salt and pepper

more
- One vegetable stock cube can be crumbled over the courgettes before adding the boiling water, if preferred.
- A buffalo mozzarella can be divided into four and lightly melted on top of each toast before spooning on the tomato.

butternut squash soup

serves four

2 tablespoons olive oil
1 large onion, sliced
1 clove of garlic, crushed
675g (1½lb) butternut
  squash, peeled, deseeded
  and cut into cubes
¼ teaspoon ground ginger
600ml (1 pint) vegetable
  stock (see page 13)
100ml (3½fl oz) orange
  juice
salt and pepper
6 tablespoons single cream,
  crème fraîche or natural
  yoghurt

Warm the olive oil in a large saucepan and add the onion and garlic. Cook over a low heat until soft but without colour. Add the butternut and ginger and gently cook for 5 minutes. Add the vegetable stock and the orange juice and simmer for 20 to 30 minutes until the butternut is tender.

Purée the soup in a blender or food processor until smooth and season with salt and pepper. Return the soup to a clean pan, ready to warm through when needed.

To serve, stir the cream into the hot soup or drizzle in swirls on top. Serve with crusty bread.

cherry tomato soup

serves four–six

olive oil
2 red onions, sliced
2 cloves of garlic, crushed
2 tablespoons red wine
  vinegar
500g (1lb 2oz) cherry
  tomatoes, halved
300ml (10fl oz) passata
450ml (16fl oz) vegetable
  stock (see page 13)
sea salt and pepper
torn basil leaves, to serve
  (optional)

Heat some olive oil in a large, deep frying pan. Add the onion and garlic and fry over a medium heat until softened and lightly coloured. Spoon in the vinegar and allow it to boil until very little of the liquid is left.

Add the cherry tomatoes and continue to fry for 10 minutes.

Pour in the passata and stock, bring to a simmer and gently cook for a further 10 minutes.

Finish with a sprinkling of sea salt, twist of pepper and the basil, if using.

broken feta cheese salad with apples and pears

Mix together the salad and chicory leaves in a bowl. Core and slice the apple and pear and add to the salad with the chopped walnuts and feta.

Whisk together the vinegar, sugar and oils, seasoning with salt and a twist of pepper. Spoon the dressing over the salad, gently mixing it all together before dividing among the plates.

serves two–three

1 bag of mixed salad leaves
1 chicory head, trimmed
  and divided into leaves
1 apple
1 pear
a handful of roughly
  chopped walnuts
225g (8oz) feta cheese,
  broken into pieces
2 tablespoons cider vinegar
pinch of caster sugar
2 tablespoons walnut oil
2 tablespoons groundnut
  oil
sea salt and pepper

more

- Add a squeeze of lemon or lime juice to the dressing.
- A few sprigs of chervil, parsley or chive stalks can be added to the salad.

three bean salad

French beans, runner beans and cannellini beans are the three featured in this recipe. The cannellini beans (Italian haricot beans) also help flavour the dressing.

serves four

175g (6oz) fine French beans
175g (6oz) runner beans
400g (14oz) tin of cannellini beans, drained
100ml (3½fl oz) low-fat crème fraîche
½ teaspoon Dijon mustard
1 teaspoon sherry vinegar
salt and pepper
2 tablespoons pine nuts
225g (8oz) mixed salad leaves
2 large shallots, sliced into rings
olive oil

Trim only the tops from the French beans. Top and tail the runner beans, removing the side strings. At an angle, slice the runner beans into thin strips.

Put 50g (2oz) of the cannellini beans, the crème fraîche, mustard and vinegar into a blender or food processor and blend to a smooth dressing with a coating consistency. Season with salt and pepper.

Preheat the grill. Spread the pine nuts on a baking tray and toast until golden.

Plunge the runner and French beans into a large saucepan of boiling salted water. Cook for a few minutes until tender, but with a slight bite. Drain and leave to cool until just warm.

Put the salad leaves and shallot rings into a large bowl, add the remaining cannellini beans and the warm beans and season with salt and pepper. Divide the salad among the plates, spoon over the dressing and sprinkle with the pine nuts. Drizzle with the olive oil before serving.

more

- Many other flavours can be added to the salad, with peppers and tomatoes working particularly well with the dressing.
- Serve with slices of toasted ciabatta or French bread spread with garlic butter.

red and white chicory salad with a rhubarb vinaigrette

This is quite a lively salad with the bitter chicory and sharp rhubarb slightly calmed by the vinaigrette. It's best to use the sweet forced rhubarb in season between January and April, but if only the green main crop is available, replace the teaspoon with a tablespoon of sugar.

Boil the orange juice, sugar and ginger until just a third of the liquid is left. Add the rhubarb, return to the boil and remove from the heat. Whisk in the vinegar and olive oil and season with salt and pepper.

Scatter the chicory leaves and spring onions over four plates or bowls and drizzle with the rhubarb vinaigrette just before serving.

serves four

juice of 2 oranges
1 teaspoon caster sugar
a pinch of ground ginger
1 stick of forced rhubarb,
  cut into small cubes
1 tablespoon red wine
  vinegar
3 tablespoons olive oil
salt and pepper
4 red chicory heads, leaves
  separated
4 white chicory heads,
  leaves separated
2 spring onions, thinly sliced

fennel, asparagus, grapefruit and apple

This salad works well with soft, creamy goat's cheese. If you fancy cooking, breadcrumbed and deep-fried goat's cheese is even better. Whichever you fancy, simply sit it on top and enjoy the whole salad.

serves four–six

2 medium or 4 baby fennel
  bulbs
8–10 asparagus spears
1 grapefruit, segmented
  (see page 20)
1 red apple
1 green apple
1 small or ½ medium
  melon, skinned, deseeded
  and chopped
15–20 crispy crostini
  (optional)
1 x cream vinaigrette
  (see page 466)
1 bag of mixed salad leaves

Remove the outside layer from the fennel and discard, shredding the bulb finely, preferably on a mandolin. Cut the woody base from each asparagus and slice the spears thinly lengthways, again on a mandolin if possible.

Halve the grapefruit segments. Quarter each apple and remove the core, cutting each piece into thin slices.

Mix all the vegetables and fruits together in a bowl with the crostini, if using, drizzling with the creamy vinaigrette. Top with the salad leaves, finishing with another drop or two of dressing.

more

• A trickle of walnut or olive oil can be drizzeled over the salad

hot potato salad
with melting raclette

Raclette is famous for its melting abilities and sweet, nutty flavour, particularly on potatoes. This salad can be served with ham, salami, salad or pickles, but works equally well on its own for lunch or topped with a poached egg.

serves four

650g (1½lb) new potatoes
6 spring onions, thinly sliced
sea salt and pepper
juice of 1 lemon
4 tablespoons olive oil
350g (12oz) raclette
  cheese, rind removed and
  thinly sliced

Cook the potatoes in boiling salted water for 20 minutes or until tender. Drain, cut in half and scatter into an ovenproof dish. Sprinkle the spring onions on top and season with salt and a twist of pepper.

Preheat the grill. Mix the lemon juice with the olive oil and spoon over the potatoes. Arrange the raclette slices overlapping on top and place under the grill until the cheese has melted.

more

- A few spoonfuls of crème fraîche can be added to the potatoes before topping with the cheese.
- If serving with a poached egg, a crisp green salad is a good accompaniment.

avocado and courgette salad with lime

Trim the ends of the courgettes and, with a Y-shaped potato peeler, slice lengthways into long, thin strips.

Whisk together the lime juice, olive oil and sugar, seasoning with salt and a twist of pepper before stirring in the mint.

Add the avocado and courgette to the dressing and gently fold in the rocket.

serves two–four

4 small or 2 medium
  courgettes
2 tablespoons lime juice
2 tablespoons olive oil
½ teaspoon caster sugar
sea salt and pepper
1 heaped teaspoon
  chopped mint
1 avocado, peeled and cut
  into 8 wedges
a large handful of rocket
  leaves

more

Here's a few extras to consider for this salad:

- toasted pine nuts
- lime segments
- crispy iceberg leaves

grilled buffalo mozzarella with garlic, lemon and courgettes

The garlic and lemon purée provides a pungent sharpness for the mozzarella. Any purée not used will keep refrigerated for a few days. Here the mozzarella is quickly grilled, but it can also be served as it is, at room temperature.

serves two–four

6 large cloves of garlic, peeled
milk, to cover
½ lemon, cut into small cubes
2 courgettes, thinly sliced
¼ teaspoon salt
flour, for dusting
2 buffalo mozzarellas, halved
a knob of softened butter, for brushing
sea salt and pepper
2 tablespoons hazelnut or walnut oil

Put the garlic in a small saucepan with enough milk to cover and bring to a simmer. Cook gently for 15 to 20 minutes until the garlic is tender, then drain the milk. Purée the cloves in a small food processor. Add the lemon to the garlic and blend, leaving it slightly coarse.

Meanwhile, mix the courgette slices with the ¼ teaspoon of salt and leave to stand in a colander for 15 to 20 minutes. This releases excess water from the courgettes, leaving them tender.

Preheat the grill. Lightly flour the cut side of the mozzarella and brush with the softened butter. Place on a baking tray, buttered side up and put below the heated grill, as close to the heat as possible. Cook for a minute or two, allowing the butter and flour to colour. Season with sea salt and pepper.

Spoon the courgette on to plates, season with pepper and drizzle with the hazelnut or walnut oil. Top with the warm mozzarella and a small dollop of the garlic and lemon purée.

gorgonzola, parma ham and rocket pasta

serves two

50g (2oz) butter
150ml (5fl oz) single
  cream
175g (6oz) Gorgonzola
  cheese, crumbled
50g (2oz) grated mozzarella
200–250g (7–9oz) dried
  pasta
1 large handful of rocket
  leaves
pepper
4 slices of Parma ham, torn
  into pieces
4 tablespoons walnut oil,
  optional

Warm the butter and single cream together in a pan, add the Gorgonzola and mozzarella and gently melt over a low heat.

While making the sauce, cook the pasta until tender. Drain and add to the finished sauce with the rocket. Season with a twist of pepper and divide the pasta into bowls. Arrange the Parma ham on top.

Drizzle with the walnut oil just before serving, if using.

pasta with chicken, sage and onion butter

serves four

olive oil
2 large chicken breasts,
  skinless and sliced into
  thin strips
salt and pepper
2 large red onions, sliced
1 clove of garlic, crushed
100g (4oz) butter
1 small bunch of sage,
  leaves torn into pieces
400–500g (14–18oz) dried
  pasta

Heat a large deep frying pan with some olive oil. Season the chicken strips with salt and pepper, add to the hot oil and fry over a high heat, turning once or twice.

Add the onion and garlic to the pan with a large knob of the butter and continue to fry for 5 to 6 minutes.

Add the remaining butter and sage, seasoning with salt and pepper.

While making the sauce, cook the pasta until tender. Drain and add to the finished sauce.

fiery mushrooms on toast

This is delicious to eat as a quick lunch and almost becomes a full meal when accompanied by a tossed green salad.

Preheat the grill. Mix together the garlic, chilli and red onion, if using, stirring in half the olive oil to loosen.

Place the mushrooms flat-side down on a greased baking tray. Spoon the garlic chilli mix over each one, seasoning with a sprinkling of sea salt. Grill not too close to the heat for 10 to 12 minutes until tender.

Meanwhile, toast the bread on both sides and keep warm. Spoon the mushrooms on to the bread and sprinkle with the parsley.

Mix together the remaining oil, vinegar and any cooking juices and drizzle over generously.

serves four

2 cloves of garlic, chopped
2 fresh red chillies, thinly sliced
½ small red onion or 1 shallot, very thinly sliced (optional)
4 tablespoons olive oil
butter, for greasing
8 large Portobello mushrooms
sea salt
4 thick slices of French bread
a handful of curly parsley, roughly chopped
1 tablespoon red wine vinegar

asparagus and ham glazed with cheddar and parmesan

serves four

2 bunches of asparagus
   (8–10 spears per person)
salt and pepper
a large knob of butter
4 slices of ham
100g (4oz) Cheddar
   cheese, grated
100g (4oz) Parmesan
   cheese, grated

Preheat the grill.

Snap the woody end from each asparagus spear. Place the spears in a deep saucepan, boil a kettle and pour the water over them, adding a pinch of salt. Reheat until boiling and cook for 2 to 3 minutes until just tender. Drain, adding the butter and seasoning with salt and pepper.

Put half the spears in an earthenware dish and top with 2 slices of ham, leaving the asparagus tops exposed.

Mix the two cheeses together and scatter half over the ham. Place under the grill until just beginning to melt. Top with the remaining spears, ham and cheese and return under the grill until melted with a light golden finish.

fried bacon pieces with spinach and prawns

serves two–four

225g (8oz) pancetta cubes
a knob of butter
225g (8oz) peeled prawns
225g (8oz) washed and
   ready-to-eat baby spinach
salt and pepper
1 lemon, quartered
   (optional)
100–150ml (3½–5fl oz) sour
   cream (optional)

Fry the pancetta in a hot pan for a few minutes until golden brown. Pour away the majority of the pancetta fat and add the butter. Once foaming, add the prawns.

After a minute or two, stir in the spinach, seasoning with salt and pepper. When the leaves begin to wilt, the dish is ready to divide between the plates. Offer the lemon quarters and sour cream separately, if using.

salmon with a salted tomato and herb salad

This recipe makes a light lunch for four, but adding a green salad and warm new potatoes would make it more substantial. The selection of herbs also doesn't have to be as wide as I've chosen.

Halve the tomatoes horizontally, seasoning the cut sides with a generous sprinkling of sea salt and a twist of pepper.

Whisk together the olive oil, lime juice and herbs, seasoning with salt and pepper.

Pat the salmon dry on kitchen paper. Trickle a little oil into a non-stick frying pan over a medium heat. Add the butter and, once bubbling, cook the fish gently for 3 to 4 minutes before turning the fillets and removing the pan from the heat. The residual heat in the pan will continue to cook the fish for a further minute or so.

While the salmon is resting, divide the tomatoes among the plates, spooning over the herb dressing. Place the salmon beside the tomatoes to serve.

serves four

16–20 cherry tomatoes
sea salt and pepper
4 tablespoons extra-virgin olive oil, plus a trickle for cooking
1 tablespoon lime juice
1 tablespoon chopped mixed herbs (tarragon, chervil, basil, chives, coriander)
4 x 100g (4oz) salmon fillets, skinned and pinboned (see page 14)
15g (½oz) butter

salmon cutlets with minted leeks and peas and a sweet lemon dressing

Any leftover dressing can be kept in an airtight container in the refrigerator for several weeks. In fact, if you add the lemon grass, the longer the dressing is left to infuse, the better the flavour becomes. Drizzle over fish, chicken or salads.

serves two for lunch

for the sweet lemon dressing
50g (2oz) caster sugar
juice of 2 lemons
1 strip of lemon zest
1 stick of lemon grass, finely shredded (optional)
150ml (5fl oz) olive oil
salt and pepper

1 large leek, finely shredded
150ml (5fl oz) double cream
50g (2oz) frozen petits pois, defrosted
salt and pepper
1 sprig of mint, leaves chopped
350–450g (12–16oz) salmon fillet, skinned and pinboned (see page 14)
25g (1oz) butter

For the dressing, boil the sugar, lemon juice, zest and lemon grass, if using, with 50ml (2fl oz) water and simmer for several minutes. Remove from the heat and leave to infuse for 30 to 60 minutes before straining (see above). Whisk together with the olive oil and season with salt and pepper, then pour into a screw-top jar ready for shaking when needed.

Cook the leek in boiling salted water for 2 to 3 minutes. Boil the cream in a pan to a spoon-coating consistency, add the peas and leeks and season with salt and pepper before stirring in the mint.

Meanwhile, cut slices through the salmon fillet to create eight cutlet-shaped portions. Melt the butter in a large non-stick frying pan and, once foaming, add the cutlets. Cook quickly over a medium to hot heat for just a minute, then turn over and fry for a further 30 seconds. Serve with the creamy leeks and peas and a good drizzle of the sweet lemon dressing.

grilled tuna with a niçoise salsa

A ridged grill pan is ideal for cooking the tuna here, those bitter, burnt lines adding earthiness to the dish. However it isn't essential; a frying pan will do.

Cook the potatoes in boiling salted water for 20 minutes or until cooked through. When they have cooled down, peel them. Cook the beans in boiling salted water until tender, but still with a bite. Drain, running them under cold water to stop the cooking.

Cut the beans, potatoes, spring onions, tomatoes, pepper, anchovy fillets and olives into small pieces.

Put the eggs into a pan of boiling water and boil them for 8 minutes before running under cold water – this will cook the eggs through but leave a slight gooeyness to the texture. The eggs can now be shelled and chopped. Mix the eggs with the garlic, herbs and olive oil and season with salt and a twist of pepper. In a large bowl, spoon this dressing over the vegetables, mixing them all together.

Preheat the grill pan until hot. Brush the tuna steaks with olive oil, season with salt and a twist of pepper and lay on the pan. Grill for 1 to 2 minutes on each side before serving with a spoonful or two of Niçoise salsa.

serves four

4 large new potatoes
50g (2oz) fine French beans
2 spring onions
3 plum tomatoes, deseeded
1 small yellow pepper
4 anchovy fillets
8 pitted black olives
2 eggs
½ clove of garlic, crushed
½ tablespoon chopped chives
½ tablespoon chopped chervil
3 tablespoons olive oil, plus extra for brushing
salt and pepper
4 x 150g (5oz) tuna steaks

more

- Mix or drizzle a little low-fat crème fraîche over the salsa for a creamier flavour.

sweet sesame mackerel with banana chutney

serves four

for the banana chutney
1 tablespoon olive oil
1 small onion, chopped
1 teaspoon light soft brown
  sugar
2 bananas (best underripe),
  cut into chunks
1 tablespoon white wine
  vinegar
½ teaspoon allspice
salt and pepper
1 teaspoon chopped fresh
  coriander (optional)

4 mackerel fillets, skinned
  and pinboned
  (see page 14)
1 egg yolk
2 tablespoons sesame
  seeds, toasted
  (see page 13)
1 tablespoon light soft
  brown sugar

To prepare the chutney, warm the olive oil in a pan with the onion and cook, without colouring, for several minutes until softened. Add the sugar and bananas, increase the heat and allow them to slightly colour and begin to soften. Add the vinegar and allspice, season with salt and pepper and cook for 2 to 3 minutes before removing from the heat. Stir in the coriander, if using, before serving.

Preheat the oven to 200°C/400°F/gas 6.

Brush the skinned side of the mackerel fillets with the egg yolk. Mix together the sesame seeds and sugar and sprinkle liberally on top of the fillets to cover. Lay on a buttered baking tray and bake for 5 to 7 minutes until just firm to the touch, before serving with a spoonful of banana chutney.

more

- Quickly blitzing the sesame seeds and sugar in a coffee grinder would give a more rustic texture.
- A ripe avocado and a squeeze of lime could be added to the chutney.

potted mackerel

Serve with crusty bread and drizzled salad leaves – it needs no more.

serves four–six

2 large fresh mackerel
  fillets, skinned and
  pinboned (see page 14)
3 smoked mackerel fillets,
  skinned
3 tablespoons Greek-style
  natural yoghurt
1 heaped teaspoon
  horseradish cream
salt and pepper
¼ teaspoon paprika
juice of 1 lime
75g (3oz) softened butter

Place the fresh mackerel fillets in a small roasting tray and pour over boiling water to cover. Place over a medium heat and return the water to a simmer, then remove from the stove and leave to cool. Pat the fillets dry on kitchen paper before flaking into pieces.

Break the smoked mackerel into pieces, removing any pin bones. Put the smoked and flaked fresh fish in a food processor, add all the remaining ingredients except the butter and blitz until smooth. Stir in 50g (2oz) of the butter, then spoon the mixture into four to six ramekins or one kiln jar.

Melt the remaining butter and spoon a little over each ramekin, barely enough to cover. Refrigerate to set. Serve immediately or, if kept refrigerated, the potted mackerel will last for 2 to 3 days.

steak diane

A French classic, this is a quickly fried steak with a peppered cream sauce, sharpened with mustard.

serves four

4 x 75g (3oz) fillet or sirloin
  steaks
salt and pepper
a knob of butter
1 shallot, finely chopped
350g (12oz) button
  mushrooms, sliced
1 tablespoon red wine
  vinegar
100–150ml (3½–5fl oz)
  double cream
1 teaspoon Dijon or
  wholegrain mustard

Season the steaks with salt and a twist of black pepper. Melt the butter in a large frying pan and, once foaming, add the steaks and fry for 2 minutes on each side. Remove from the pan and keep warm.

Add the shallots and mushrooms to the pan and fry for 3 to 4 minutes until softened and with a little colour. Season with two to three twists of pepper. Add the red wine vinegar and boil until almost dry. Stir in the cream and mustard and season with a pinch of salt. The sauce is ready to spoon over the steaks.

charred squid with passion fruit, pineapple and sesame leaves

The vinaigrette recipe will make more than is needed for this dish, but it can be kept refrigerated in a screw-top jar for several weeks. It is a lovely dressing for any salad.

serves two–four

for the passion fruit and pineapple vinaigrette
50ml (2fl oz) passion fruit juice
100ml (3½fl oz) pineapple juice
a pinch of cayenne pepper
a pinch of saffron (optional)
50ml (2fl oz) sesame oil
100ml (3½fl oz) groundnut oil
salt

350g (12oz) cleaned squid
vegetable oil
salt and pepper
a handful of washed and ready-to-eat baby spinach
1 tablespoon sesame seeds, toasted (see page 13)

Whisk together all the ingredients for the vinaigrette. Season with a pinch of salt and pour into a screw-top jar or bottle, ready to shake before using.

Split the squid in half, if large, and cut into two to three pieces. Lightly oil each piece, season and place on a very hot grill pan or hot frying pan. Cook for 1 to 2 minutes on each side until the edges are charred.

Meanwhile, dress the spinach with the vinaigrette, arrange on four plates and sprinkle with the toasted sesame seeds. Scatter the squid on top, liberally drizzling with the vinaigrette before serving.

roast chicken with goat's cheese and fresh herb butter

Once carved, the chicken is best served in a sandwich with good crusty bread and crisp sprigs of watercress.

Preheat the oven to 200°C/400°F/gas 6.

Using your fingers, from the neck end of the chicken loosen the chicken skin from the breast.

Beat together the soft butter, goat's cheese and herbs. Season with salt and pepper. Divide the mix between the breasts, pushing it under the skin and patting it into an even layer.

Brush the chicken with butter and season with salt and pepper. Place in a roasting tray and cook for about 1 hour. To check the bird is cooked, pierce between the thigh and breast with a skewer and check that the juices run clear. Leave to rest for 15 minutes before carving.

serves two–four

1.6–1.8kg (3½–4lb) chicken
50g (2oz) softened butter, plus extra for brushing
50g (2oz) goat's cheese
1 tablespoon chopped chives
1 tablespoon chopped parsley
1 tablespoon chopped tarragon
coarse sea salt and pepper

more

• Extra additions to the goat's cheese butter could be grated lemon zest or chopped shallots.

Afternoon tea/

Afternoon tea is one of our proudest traditions, and the delight of baking –
the simple beating and whisking as well as the eating – offers time in the day
to pause and enjoy simple pleasures. Opening a packet of biscuits just doesn't
fill your house with the smell of a freshly baked black cherry sponge or warm
buttermilk scones with clotted cream and strawberry jam. A cake is always the
perfect excuse for inviting over friends and this chapter is real indulgence, with
a whole array of sweet things to choose from and some savoury offerings as well.

There are recipes for children's teatime here too. The nursery tea of crumpets
and milk puddings may be a thing of the past, but children still need comforting,
tasty food when they get home from school and want feeding quickly. Even if
you don't have anyone in your house worrying about homework or wearing
school uniform, you might still find real macaroni cheese, crunchy fish strips
with an avocado dip and Wensleydale patties entice your family in for tea.

Afternoon tea/

High tea and treats

Smoked salmon, trout and mackerel open sandwiches

Prawn and cucumber sandwiches with chive cream and a tomato dressing

Blackberry and almond tart

Orange flan, strawberries and orange curd cream

Hazelnut cake with frangelico cream

Raspberry clafoutis

Chocolate and caramel shortbread

Buttermilk mini scones

Banana, pecan and honey cakes with espresso butter cream

White chocolate cheesecake

Black cherry Victoria sponge cake

Lemon meringue tartlets

Honeycomb caramel slice

smoked salmon, trout and mackerel open sandwiches

These are particularly good with chunky, crusty granary or wholemeal breads.

For the smoked salmon sandwiches, divide each grapefruit segment into three or four chunks and mix with the avocado and olive oil. Spoon on to the bread and season with a generous twist of pepper, a pinch of sea salt and top with cress or rocket, if using. Arrange the slices of salmon on top.

For the smoked trout sandwiches, bind the little gem leaves with the dressing. Spoon on to the bread and arrange the pieces of smoked trout on top.

For the smoked mackerel sandwiches, stir together the apple, spring onion, sugar and vinegar. Stir in the torn pieces of smoked mackerel, adding enough cream to bind. Season with salt and pepper and spoon on to the bread.

serves four–six

for the smoked salmon
1 grapefruit, segmented
  (see page 20)
1 large avocado, peeled and
  chopped
a few drops of olive oil
bread
sea salt and pepper
sprigs of baby watercress,
  mustard cress or rocket
  (optional)
225g (8oz) sliced smoked
  salmon

for the smoked trout
1 little gem, leaves separated
½ x cream vinaigrette
  (see page 466)
bread
2 smoked trout fillets, each cut
  into 4 neat pieces

for the smoked mackerel
1 apple, quartered and chopped
1 spring onion, peeled and thinly
  sliced
¼ teaspoon caster sugar
2 teaspoons cider vinegar
225g (8oz) smoked mackerel
  fillet, broken into bite-sized
  pieces
2–3 tablespoons sour cream
salt and pepper
bread

prawn and cucumber sandwiches with chive cream and a tomato dressing

These ingredients combine as you eat to create an alternative cocktail sauce flavour, the tomato mingling with the crème fraîche to give a much lighter finish than the original. I prefer to serve on white bread, especially on baguettes or rolls.

serves four

for the tomato dressing
1 tablespoon tomato ketchup
1 tablespoon white wine vinegar
1 teaspoon Dijon mustard
4 tablespoons olive oil
salt and pepper

100ml (3½fl oz) crème fraîche
1 tablespoon chopped chives
a squeeze of lemon juice
bread rolls or baguettes
½ small cucumber, peeled and thinly sliced
300g (10oz) peeled Atlantic prawns, left whole or halved

To make the tomato dressing, simply whisk all the ingredients together and season with salt and pepper.

Stir together the crème fraîche, chives and lemon juice, seasoning with a pinch of salt and a twist of pepper. Spread on the halved baguettes or rolls and top with slices of cucumber.

Season the prawns with sea salt and pepper and spoon on top of the cucumber before drizzling with the tomato dressing.

blackberry and almond tart

serves six

275–350g (10–12oz) ready-
  made shortcrust or puff
  pastry
3 tablespoons blackberry or
  blackcurrant jam
2 eggs
100g (4oz) caster sugar
100g (4oz) softened butter
100g (4oz) ground almonds
175g (6oz) blackberries

Preheat the oven to 170°C/325°F/gas 3.

Roll out the pastry on a lightly floured surface into a circle large enough to line a 23cm/9 inch non-stick tart tin (preferably loose-bottomed). Lift the pastry on to the rolling pin and place in the tart tin, easing the pastry into the bottom and corners of the tin and trimming off any excess overhanging pastry.

Prick the base well with a fork. Spoon and spread the jam over the base, then refrigerate for 20 minutes.

In a food processor, blend together the eggs, sugar, butter and almonds until totally combined. Spread the almond mix into the tart case and place the blackberries on top.

Bake the tart for 40–45 minutes until golden brown and firm to the touch.

more

- Eat warm or cold with pouring cream.
- The tart can be dusted with icing sugar before serving.

orange flan, strawberries and orange curd cream

serves eight

butter, for greasing
3 eggs
100g (4oz) caster sugar
finely grated zest of 1
  orange
75g (3oz) plain flour
75g (3oz) ground almonds
½ teaspoon baking
  powder
100g (4oz) melted butter
8 tablespoons double or
  whipping cream
8 tablespoons orange curd
250g (9oz) orange
  marmalade
1–2 punnets of strawberries

Preheat the oven to 190°C/375°F/gas 5. Generously butter a 20–25cm (8–10 inch) fluted tart tin or flan dish.

In an electric mixer or by hand, whisk together the eggs, sugar and orange zest until pale, thick and creamy. Sift the flour and mix together with the ground almonds and baking powder, then fold into the creamy mix.

Slowly pour in the melted butter and stir in with a spoon. Pour the mixture into the buttered tin and bake for 12–15 minutes until risen, golden and spongy to the touch.

Whisk the cream and orange curd in a bowl until soft peaks form.

In a small saucepan, simmer together the marmalade and 100ml (3½fl oz) water until the marmalade is completely melted. The sauce can be strained or left chunky.

Cut a wedge of the warm or cold flan and drizzle over the warm sauce. Serve with a large spoonful of the orange curd cream and fresh strawberries.

hazelnut cake with frangelico cream

Preheat the oven to 180°C/350°F/gas 4.

Line an 18cm (7 inch) loose-bottomed cake tin with buttered greaseproof paper.

Grind the hazelnuts finely in a food processor. Put the digestive biscuits into a plastic bag and crush with a rolling pin. Using an electric mixer, beat together the butter and sugar until creamy.

Sift the flour into a bowl and mix together with the hazelnuts and digestives. Slowly add the dry mix to the creamy butter, followed by one egg at a time, stirring until smooth.

Spoon the mix into the tin, smoothing the top. Bake for 25 to 30 minutes until the cake is just beginning to come away from the sides of the tin and is golden and firm in the middle. Leave to cool before removing from the tin. The cake can be served cold or each slice lightly warmed in the microwave.

To make the Frangelico cream, pour the cream into a bowl with the icing sugar and Frangelico. Whip to a light soft peak stage and dollop on top of the cake slices. Warm chocolate sauce drizzled over the top of the cake would be delicious.

serves four–six

for the hazelnut cake
150g (5oz) skinned
  hazelnuts
25g (1oz) digestive biscuits
175g (6oz) butter
100g (4oz) caster sugar
25g (1oz) self-raising flour
3 eggs

for the Frangelico cream
150ml (5fl oz) double cream
1 heaped tablespoon icing
  sugar
3 tablespoons Frangelico
  liqueur

more
- The warm chocolate sauce featured on page 467 is delicious drizzled over this cake.

raspberry clafoutis

This recipe is more or less fruit baked in a sweet Yorkshire pudding batter. The batter can be flavoured with lemon or orange zest or a flavoured liqueur. Blackberries also work really well in place of raspberries.

serves four

2 large eggs
75g (3oz) caster sugar, plus
  extra for dusting
40g (1½oz) plain flour
100ml (3½fl oz) double
  cream or crème fraîche
100ml (3½fl oz) milk
butter, for greasing
225g (8oz) raspberries

Preheat the oven to 180°C/350°F/gas 4.

Whisk together the eggs and sugar. Sift over the flour and whisk well before stirring in the cream or crème fraîche and milk. Leave to rest for 10 minutes.

Lightly butter one large or four individual baking dishes and sprinkle with sugar to coat. Scatter the raspberries in the dish and gently pour over the batter.

Bake for 20 to 25 minutes until the batter is just firm to the touch. If it is too soft in the centre, bake for a further 5 minutes. Allow the clafoutis to cool slightly before serving, perhaps with some pouring cream over the top.

chocolate and caramel shortbread

serves six–eight

300g (10oz) plain flour, plus
  extra for rolling
225g (8oz) softened butter
100g (4oz) icing sugar
1 egg yolk
225g (8oz) plain chocolate,
  broken into pieces
200g (7oz) Nestlé Carnation
  caramel cream
  (condensed milk caramel)

Preheat the oven to 180°C/350°F/gas 4.

Sift the flour into a large bowl and beat with the butter. Stir in the icing sugar and egg yolk. Shape into a ball and roll out on a lightly floured surface into a 20cm (8 inch) disc.

Place the shortbread disc inside a 20cm (8 inch) loose-bottomed flan tin and prick all over with a fork. Bake for 20 to 25 minutes. Leave to cool slightly before removing from the tin.

Melt the chocolate in a small bowl over warm water (or microwave for 10 to 15 seconds). Stir in the caramel cream, adding more if preferred. Spread the chocolate caramel over the shortbread and leave to cool before serving.

buttermilk mini scones

Having made many scones over many years, I've found this recipe produces the best of the lot. The buttermilk gives a rich finish and they are very moist too. The dough can be made up to 24 hours in advance. Simply wrap in clingfilm and refrigerate until needed.

makes about 15 mini scones

225g (8oz) plain flour
15g (½ oz) baking powder
25g (1oz) caster sugar
50g (2oz) butter, cut into
  cubes
150ml (5fl oz) buttermilk
1 egg, beaten

Preheat the oven to 220°C/425°F/gas 7. Sift the flour and baking powder into a bowl. Add the sugar and rub in the butter until it resembles fine breadcrumbs. Stir in the buttermilk, a little at a time, to form a smooth dough.

Wrap in clingfilm and rest in the refrigerator for an hour or two. Unwrap the mixture and roll out on a lightly floured surface until 1–1.5cm (½–⅝ inch) thick. The scones can now be cut using a 3cm (1¼ inch) pastry cutter, not twisting the cutter as this tends to create an uneven rising. Brush each scone lightly with the beaten egg.

Place the scones on a greaseproof-paper-topped baking tray and bake for 8 to 10 minutes until golden. Remove and allow to cool slightly.

Serve the scones while still warm (they can be left to completely cool and microwaved quickly to rewarm), preferably with our British classics of strawberry jam and clotted cream.

more
- One the scones are cut, any pastry trimmings can be re-rolled and a few more scones cut.

banana, pecan and honey cakes with espresso butter cream

These little cakes are individual versions of a banana loaf. For the butter cream, there is no need to have a coffee machine. A good-quality instant coffee, made very strong, is fine.

makes 12

for the banana, pecan and honey cakes
225g (8oz) self-raising flour, sifted
100g (4oz) butter, plus extra for greasing
4 ripe bananas, mashed
50g (2oz) dark soft brown sugar
4 tablespoons honey
50g (2oz) pecan nuts, chopped
4 eggs

for the espresso butter cream
100g (4oz) butter
100g (4oz) icing sugar
50–75ml (2–3fl oz) cold espresso coffee

Preheat the oven to 180°C/350°F/gas 4.

Grease a non-stick individual Yorkshire pudding or muffin tray.

Put all the cake ingredients into a food processor and blitz until well combined.

Spoon the mixture into the moulds, filling until just a few millimetres from the top. Bake for 25 to 30 minutes. Remove the tray from the oven and leave to rest for 5 to 10 minutes before turning out the cakes.

Meanwhile, beat together the butter and icing sugar until light and creamy before folding in the espresso coffee. The butter cream is now ready to be scooped and spread on every bite of cake.

white chocolate cheesecake

For the biscuit base, crush the biscuits in a food processor until they form crumbs. Melt the butter and chocolate together and stir into the crumbs. Press the crumb mix into the base of a 20–25cm (8–10 inch) loose-bottomed cake tin and refrigerate to set.

For the cheesecake, whip the cream until soft peaks form and set aside. Beat together the crème fraîche, cream cheese and brown sugar until smooth. Place the white chocolate in a bowl and melt over a pan of simmering water. Once melted, stir in the crème fraîche mixture and then fold in the lightly whipped cream.

Spoon the cheesecake mixture on top of the biscuit base and smooth down. Refrigerate for 2 to 3 hours to set. When you're ready to serve, loosen around the cheesecake with a warm knife before lifting from the tin (if you have a blowtorch, quickly blasting around the outside of the tin will help to release the cheesecake with ease).

For the topping, put all the ingredients into a bowl and sit it over a pan of gently simmering water to melt, stirring until combined. The topping can now be spread to cover the cheesecake or simply piped into wild lines, offering any extra topping on the side.

serves six–eight

for the biscuit base
225g (8oz) chocolate HobNob biscuits
50g (2oz) butter
50g (2oz) dark chocolate

for the cheesecake
150ml (5fl oz) whipping cream
200ml (7fl oz) crème fraîche, at room temperature
200g (7oz) full-fat soft cream cheese, at room temperature
50g (2oz) light soft brown sugar
300g (10oz) white chocolate, chopped

for the chocolate topping
100g (4oz) dark chocolate, chopped
1 teaspoon liquid glucose
50ml (2fl oz) double or whipping cream
15g (½oz) butter

black cherry victoria sponge cake

serves eight

175g (6oz) self-raising flour
1 level teaspoon baking
  powder
175g (6oz) butter, at room
  temperature, plus extra
  for greasing
175g (6oz) caster sugar
grated zest of 1 orange or 1
  lemon
a few drops of vanilla
  essence
3 eggs, at room
  temperature
milk, to loosen
icing sugar, for dusting

for the filling
150ml (5fl oz) double cream
200g (7oz) black cherry jam

Preheat the oven to 170°C/325°F/gas 3. Lightly grease two 20cm (8 inch) in diameter and 2.5cm (1 inch) deep cake tins with a little butter and line the bottoms with greaseproof paper.

Sift the flour and baking powder into a bowl. Put the butter, caster sugar, zest and vanilla essence in another bowl and, using an electric hand whisk, beat together for 1 to 2 minutes until light and creamy. Add the eggs one at a time and beat until totally combined. Fold in the flour. The mixture should drop off a spoon easily, but if it is too thick, loosen with a little milk.

Divide the mixture between the two tins, smoothing the tops. Bake in the centre of the oven for 20 to 25 minutes. To check the sponges are cooked, press your finger gently on top and the imprint should spring back. If it doesn't, bake for a further 5 minutes.

Remove the cakes from the oven and leave to rest for a few minutes, then run a knife around the edges, turning the cakes out on to a wire rack. Remove the greaseproof paper and leave to cool completely.

Whip the double cream to a soft peak and fold in the cherry jam. Spread the cherry cream over one of the sponges and sit the other sponge on top, then dust with icing sugar.

more

- A splash of Amaretto liqueur stirred into the cherry cream enriches the flavour of the cherries.

lemon meringue tartlets

These tartlets are filled with ready-made crunchy meringues bound in a lemon curd cream.

makes eight

butter, for greasing
flour, for dusting
225g (8oz) ready-made
  sweet shortcrust pastry
175g (6oz) lemon curd
200ml (7fl oz) double cream
50g (2oz) ready-made
  meringues

Butter and flour eight small tartlet cases, about 7.5–9cm (3–3½ inches) in diameter. Roll the pastry out very thinly on a lightly floured surface and divide into eight, lining each tartlet case, leaving any excess hanging over the side. Refrigerate for 20 minutes before trimming for a neat finish.

Preheat the oven to 200°C/400°F/gas 6. Line each case with greaseproof paper, fill with baking beans or rice and bake for 20 minutes. Remove the paper and beans and continue to bake for a further 5 minutes. Leave to cool, then remove the pastries from the tins.

In a large bowl, whisk together the lemon curd and double cream to a soft peak. Coarsely crumble the meringues and stir into the cream. Spoon the filling into the tartlets and they are ready to eat.

more

- Strawberries can be mixed in or offered alongside.

honeycomb caramel slice

serves six

1 sheet of ready-rolled puff
   pastry
icing sugar, for dusting
200g (7oz) Nestlé Carnation
   caramel cream
   (condensed milk caramel)
200ml (7fl oz) double cream
2 Crunchie bars, coarsely
   crushed
cocoa powder (optional)

Preheat the oven to 220°C/425°F/gas 7.

Cut the pastry to a 20–23cm (8–9 inch) width (any extra can be frozen). Line a baking tray with greaseproof paper, dusting it liberally with icing sugar. Top with the puff pastry, also dusting it liberally with icing sugar. Bake for 25 to 30 minutes until risen and golden brown. Once cooked, cut the pastry into two long rectangles.

In a large bowl, whisk together the caramel and cream to a soft peak and fold in the crushed Crunchie bar. Spoon the cream on to one of the pastries and top with the other pastry slice. Dust liberally with icing sugar and then add a light dusting of cocoa powder, if using, to give a cappuccino-style finish.

more

- Chopped bananas or toasted almonds can be added to the cream or sprinkled on the pastry before topping with the cream.

Afternoon tea/

Teatime for children
(or adults who like to eat early!)

Sage and onion porkies

Tomato soup, spaghetti and meatballs

Pancakes

Cheddar cheese and onion Scotch pancakes

Baked potatoes with sour cream, chives and bacon

Pasta with tomato, mozzarella and basil

Ham, cheese and onion spaghetti

Bacon, potato and cheese frittata

Macaroni cheese

Ratatouille omelette

Crunchy fish strips with an avocado dip

Fish cake fingers

Wensleydale patties

Lamb cutlets with creamy mint peas

Sticky lemon chicken

Crispy Parmesan chicken with basil tomatoes

Bolognese

Sticky sausage and onions

Barbecued spare ribs

Chicken and bacon sticks

Pork and peas risotto

Chicken skewers with peanut sauce

Apple mascarpone salad with warm sausage chunks

Raspberry mascarpone oat pud

Chocolate brownie gypsy pudding

White chocolate cream with mango sauce

Strawberry Eton mess with raspberry sauce

sage and onion porkies

These little burgers are simply pork sausages, a packet of sage and onion stuffing and one egg. Leftover mash or new potatoes sautéed in butter with fresh vegetables or frozen peas help create a full meal. Alternatively, place in a roll or between two slices of bread.

Remove the skin from the sausages. Place the meat in a bowl and stir in the stuffing and egg, seasoning with salt and pepper.

Divide the mixture into eight and shape as burgers.

Heat 2 tablespoons of the oil in a large frying pan and pan-fry the porkies over a medium heat for 5 to 6 minutes on each side until cooked through.

serves four

450g (1lb) pork sausages
85g (3½oz) packet of dried
  sage and onion stuffing
1 egg
salt and pepper
sunflower or vegetable oil

more

- A coarsely grated apple can be added to the mix.
- This recipe also creates easy meatballs. Simply roll the mixture into small balls and pan-fry before piercing with cocktail sticks. Smooth apple sauce or a flavoured mayonnaise are tasty dips to accompany.

tomato soup, spaghetti and meatballs

This recipe belongs to my wife Jennie and it's become a household favourite. The soup can be left chunky, but we prefer it blitzed and smooth.

serves four

2 tablespoons olive oil
2 onions, sliced
¼ teaspoon chilli powder
1 red pepper, roughly chopped
600g (1lb 5oz) tomatoes, quartered
400g (14oz) tin of chopped tomatoes
1–1.2 litres (1¾–2 pints) chicken stock (see page 13)
450g (1lb) minced beef or sausages
salt and pepper
1 egg, if using mince
¼ packet spaghetti, snapped into 5cm (2 inch) pieces

Warm a saucepan with the olive oil. Add the onion and cook over a medium heat until softened. Add the chilli powder and cook for a further couple of minutes before stirring in the pepper and fresh tomatoes. Once they begin to soften, add the tinned tomatoes and half the stock and simmer for 20 to 25 minutes.

Meanwhile, warm the remaining stock in a large saucepan until simmering. Skin the sausages or season the mince and stir in the egg. Shape into Malteser-sized balls and drop into the stock for 10 minutes to poach until succulently tender.

Cook the pasta until tender and meanwhile ladle the soup into a blender and whizz until smooth (or leave it rustic and chunky). Stir the pasta and meatballs as they are ready into the soup, loosening with any of the meatball cooking liquor if preferred. Check for seasoning and serve.

more

- This soup is delicious with lots of crusty bread for dunking.

pancakes

Accompany these pancakes with lemon juice and sugar, golden syrup or honey, strawberry jam or, during our summer months, red berries.

makes 15–20 pancakes

225g (8oz) plain flour
a pinch of salt
2 eggs
600ml (1 pint) milk
50g (2oz) unsalted butter, melted
vegetable oil

Sift the flour and salt into a bowl, whisking in the eggs and milk until smooth, before stirring in the melted butter.

Warm a 17–20cm (7–8 inch) frying pan, preferably non-stick, over a medium heat and lightly oil. Add a small ladleful of batter, tilting and rotating the pan to spread the mix and cover the base. Cook for a minute until golden brown. Turn the pancake over and cook for a further 45 to 60 seconds.

The pancake is ready to serve or can be stacked between squares of greaseproof paper while you cook the remainder.

cheddar cheese and onion scotch pancakes

serves six

225g (8oz) self-raising flour
½ teaspoon salt
½ teaspoon mustard powder (optional)
2 eggs
150ml (5fl oz) milk
100g (4oz) Cheddar or Cheshire cheese, grated
1 large onion, grated
pepper
vegetable oil

Sift the flour, salt and mustard powder, if using, together into a large bowl. Add the eggs and milk and whisk to make a smooth batter. Stir in the cheese, onion and a twist of pepper.

Heat a large frying pan and brush with oil. Using a tablespoon, drop the batter into the pan in batches of five to six pancakes. Cook over a medium heat for 2 to 3 minutes before turning over and continuing to cook for a further 2 minutes. Place the pancakes inside a clean folded tea towel while frying the remainder of the batter.

baked potatoes with sour cream, chives and bacon

To guarantee a crisp-skinned and fluffy-textured baked potato, a floury rather than starchy variety of potato is the best choice. Should you prefer the skins to be softer, wrap the potatoes in foil.

serves four

4 baking potatoes
sea salt and pepper
100g (4oz) cubes of
  pancetta or bacon
4 tablespoons sour cream
1 tablespoon chopped
  chives

Preheat the oven to 220°C/425°F/gas 7. Prick the potatoes to release the steam created during baking. Scatter a little sea salt on a baking tray to prevent the skins from burning, place the potatoes on the salt and bake in the middle of the oven for 1 to 1½ hours.

Fry the bacon in a dry frying pan until coloured, then reduce the heat and continue to cook until crispy and crunchy. Dry the bacon pieces on kitchen paper.

To serve, cut a cross in the top of each potato. Using a clean cloth, squeeze from the base so the four quarters open. Top with a spoonful of sour cream, a scattering of chives and the crispy bacon.

pasta with tomato, mozzarella and basil

In a large bowl, mix the tomato, mozzarella, red onion, basil and olive oil together.

While making the sauce, cook the pasta until tender. Drain and add to the finished sauce. Season with sea salt and a twist of pepper.

serves four

8 tomatoes, quartered, deseeded and cut into chunky cubes
225g (8oz) mozzarella, cut into small cubes or grated
1 red onion, thinly sliced
1 small bunch of basil, torn
6 tablespoons olive oil
400–500g (14–18oz) dried pasta
sea salt and pepper

ham, cheese and onion spaghetti

Cook the spaghetti until tender. Meanwhile, melt half the butter in a large frying pan and gently cook the onion until softened.

Add a few tablespoons of water along with the ham and, once warm, stir in the rest of the butter to create a sauce.

Drain the pasta, add to the sauce and season with salt and pepper. Stir in half the cheese and drizzle liberally with olive oil, offering the remaining cheese to sprinkle over the top.

serves four

400g (14oz) spaghetti or any other pasta
50g (2oz) butter
1 onion, grated (or thinly sliced spring onions)
6–8 slices of ham, torn or chopped
salt and pepper
100g (4oz) Parmesan or Cheddar cheese, grated
olive oil

bacon, potato and cheese frittata

A frittata is an Italian flat omelette, called a tortilla in Spain, which is completely cooked through, unlike the soft-centred French omelette.

serves four

2 medium–large potatoes, quartered
225g (8oz) cubes of bacon, pancetta or ham
25g (1oz) butter
6 spring onions, finely chopped
6 eggs
100g (4oz) Cheddar or Gruyère cheese, grated
salt and pepper

Cook the potatoes in boiling salted water for 20 to 25 minutes or until cooked through. Drain and leave to cool slightly before peeling and cutting into cubes.

Heat a non-stick frying pan, preferably 20cm (8 inches) in diameter. Fry the bacon or pancetta, if using, until golden, then drain off any excess fat. Add the butter, diced potatoes and half the spring onions, cooking for a few minutes over a low heat.

Beat the eggs, adding half the cheese. Season with the salt and pepper. Pour the eggs over the bacon and potatoes. Stir gently in the pan for a few minutes, allowing the frittata to cook over a very low heat until it begins to set, leaving just a moist surface. Preheat the grill.

Sprinkle the remaining spring onions and cheese on top and warm under the grill until the top has set and the cheese melted. Cut the frittata into wedges to serve.

macaroni cheese

serves two

200g (7oz) macaroni
150ml (5fl oz) single cream
100ml (3½fl oz) crème
  fraîche
100–150g (4–5oz) cheese,
  such as Cheddar or
  Gouda, grated
a splash of milk
salt and pepper

Preheat the oven to 220°C/425°F/gas 7.

Cook the macaroni until tender, then drain.

Warm together the cream, crème fraîche and 100g (4oz) of the cheese over a gentle heat until melted, not allowing the sauce to boil. Loosen with milk until a sauce consistency and season with salt and pepper. Mix the sauce with the macaroni.

Transfer the macaroni to an earthenware dish, sprinkle the remaining cheese over the top and colour under a preheated grill.

ratatouille omelette

serves four

50ml (2fl oz) olive oil, plus
  extra for drizzling
25g (1oz) butter
2 red peppers, cut into
  strips
1 green pepper, cut into
  strips
1 yellow pepper, cut into
  strips
1 small aubergine or half a
  large, cut into cubes
1 large courgette, halved
  and cut into thick pieces
1 clove of garlic, crushed
4 spring onions, sliced
salt and pepper
10 beaten eggs
75g (3oz) Pecorino or
  Parmesan cheese, grated

Heat the olive oil and butter in a large deep frying pan. Add the peppers, aubergine, courgette and garlic and stir over a high heat until they begin to colour. Reduce the heat slightly and continue to cook for a further 10 to 12 minutes until all are tender. Add the spring onions and season with salt and pepper.

Over a low heat, pour the beaten eggs into the ratatouille and stir gently for 1 to 2 minutes, allowing the omelette to set and brown on the base.

Preheat the grill. Sprinkle the cheese over the omelette and melt under the grill. Drizzle with olive oil and serve in wedges, hot, warm or cold.

more

- There are many other cheeses that can be used in place of the Pecorino or Parmesan. For a calmer finish try Cheddar, gouda or emmental.

crunchy fish strips with an avocado dip

Put the avocado into a food processor with the lime juice and mayonnaise. Season with a pinch of salt and blitz until smooth. Refrigerate the dip until ready to serve.

Cut the lemon sole into strips about the length and width of your little finger and season with salt and pepper. Lightly dust a handful at a time in flour, then coat in the egg and breadcrumbs. Continue with the remainder, keeping the strips separate to prevent them from becoming soggy.

Heat the oil in a large pan or deep-fat fryer to 180–190°C (350–375°F) and fry a handful of strips for 1–2 minutes until crispy golden brown. Using a slotted spoon, lift them from the oil on to a kitchen-paper-lined plate or tray. Once the oil is back to the correct temperature, continue to fry the remainder.

Stack a plate or bowl with the crunchy fish strips and serve with the avocado and lime dip.

serves four

1 ripe avocado, roughly
  chopped
juice of 1 lime
100g (4 oz) mayonnaise
salt and pepper
550g (1¼lb) lemon sole
  fillets, skinned and
  pinboned (see page 14)
flour, for dusting
2 beaten eggs
100g (4oz) fresh white
  breadcrumbs
oil, for deep-frying

more

- Plaice, dab or flounder can be used instead of the lemon sole.
- For a lemon bite, add the finely grated zest of a lemon to the breadcrumbs.
- Also lovely with lemon mayonnaise in place of the avocado dip.

fish cake fingers

Pollack, a cousin of the cod, is a fish not given the respect it deserves. It is very economical and has texture and flavour its cousin would be proud of. These are best made several hours in advance or even the day before to nicely firm up before frying.

serves four

sea salt and pepper
butter, for greasing
4 medium jacket potatoes
350g (12oz) pollack, coley
  or haddock fillets, skinned
  and pinboned
  (see page 14)
juice of 1 lemon
1 tablespoon mayonnaise
1 heaped tablespoon
  chopped flat-leaf parsley
  (optional)
flour, for dusting
2 eggs, beaten
150g (5oz) dried
  breadcrumbs
vegetable oil

Preheat the oven to 200°C/400°F/gas 6. Scatter a little sea salt on a baking tray, prick the potatoes with a fork and place on top. Bake for 1 to 1¼ hours, then scoop out and crush the flesh in a bowl.

Meanwhile, lightly butter a baking dish, sprinkle it with salt and pepper and place the pollack on top. Season the fish, squeeze over most of the lemon juice and add about 150ml (5fl oz) water. Cover and bake for 8 to 10 minutes, then leave to cool. Flake the pollack and mix with the potato, mayonnaise, a squeeze of lemon juice and the parsley, if using. Season with salt and pepper.

Divide the mixture into 12 to 16 pieces and roll them into cylinders or shape in rectangles. Dust each finger with flour, then egg and finally the breadcrumbs to coat. Refrigerate for several hours to firm before frying.

Heat a frying pan with enough oil just to cover the base. Fry the fish cake fingers for 3 to 4 minutes on each side until crispy golden brown. Blot on kitchen paper before serving with a choice of ketchup, mayonnaise, lemon wedges or a few salad leaves with Caesar dressing (see page 464).

wensleydale patties

serves two–three

100g (4oz) Wensleydale
  cheese, grated
150g (5oz) fresh white
  breadcrumbs
2 spring onions, finely
  shredded
a pinch of English mustard
  powder
2 egg yolks
salt and pepper
1 heaped tablespoon
  chopped parsley (optional)
1 egg, beaten
2 tablespoons olive oil

Preheat the oven to 180°C/350°F/gas 4.

Mix the cheese with 75g (3oz) of the breadcrumbs, the spring
onions, mustard powder and egg yolks and season with salt and
pepper.

Divide the mixture into six and shape into flat, round patties.

Mix together the remaining breadcrumbs and the parsley, if using.
Dip the patties in the beaten egg and then coat with the crumbs.

Heat the oil in a frying pan and fry the patties over a medium heat
until golden brown, finishing them in the oven for 4 to 5 minutes to
cook through.

more

• Lancashire or Cheshire cheese could replace the Wensleydale.

lamb cutlets with creamy mint peas

serves four

12 lamb cutlets
25–50g (1–2oz) softened
  butter
salt and pepper
450g (1lb) fresh or frozen
  peas (podded weight if
  fresh)
100ml (3½fl oz) double
  cream
2 teaspoons chopped mint

Preheat the grill. Place the lamb cutlets on a grill tray with a rack,
brush with half the butter and season with the salt and pepper.
Cook under the grill for about 5 minutes on each side, brushing
with the remaining butter once turned. Meanwhile, plunge the
peas into a pan of boiling salted water and cook until tender.
Drain well.

Warm the cream in a saucepan. Add the peas and mint and bring
to the boil to thicken the cream. Season with salt and pepper
before serving with the lamb cutlets.

sticky lemon chicken

The cooking time in this recipe may seem a bit long for chicken pieces, but this is intentional, the succulent meat just falling off the bone.

serves four

4 large chicken legs, halved
salt and pepper
olive oil
1 tablespoon golden syrup
finely grated zest and juice
 of 1 large lemon

Preheat the oven to 200°C/400°F/gas 6.

Season the chicken legs with salt and pepper. Heat an ovenproof braising pan or roasting tray on top of the stove with some olive oil and lay in the chicken, skin-side down. Fry for a few minutes until golden, turning each piece, before roasting in the oven for 35 to 40 minutes.

Meanwhile, mix together the golden syrup, lemon zest and juice. Spoon it over the chicken for the last 5 minutes of cooking until the pieces are sticky and ready to eat.

crispy parmesan chicken with basil tomatoes

serves four

4 chicken breasts, skinless
salt and pepper
flour, for dusting
75g (3oz) fresh white
 breadcrumbs
50g (2oz) finely grated
 Parmesan cheese
2 beaten eggs
olive oil
a large knob of butter
6 tomatoes, halved
1–2 cloves of garlic, thinly
 sliced
sea salt
a handful of basil leaves
4 wedges of lemon

Lightly bat the chicken breasts between sheets of clingfilm until about 5mm–1cm (¼–½ inch) thick. Season with salt and pepper, then dust in flour to coat, tapping away any excess. Mix together the breadcrumbs and Parmesan. Dip the escalopes in the egg, followed by the Parmesan breadcrumbs.

Heat some olive oil with the butter in a large frying pan. Once sizzling, add the escalopes and cook for 3–4 minutes on each side until crispy and golden.

Meanwhile, preheat the grill and put the tomato halves on a baking tray, topping each with a slice of garlic. Season with a good twist of pepper and a sprinkling of sea salt. Drizzle with olive oil and grill until soft and juicy.

Tear the basil leaves and scatter them over the tomatoes with a drizzle of olive oil. Serve with the escalopes and a wedge of lemon.

bolognese

A classic from northern Italy, this recipe sticks close to the original, needing a few hours of slow simmering for the beef to soften and the flavours to blend.

serves four

100g (4oz) cubes of
  pancetta
25g (1oz) butter
1 large onion, finely
  chopped
1 large carrot, finely
  chopped
2 sticks of celery, finely
  chopped
500g (1lb 2oz) lean minced
  beef
salt and pepper
300ml (10fl oz) milk
300ml (10fl oz) red wine
400g (14oz) tin of chopped
  tomatoes
400ml (14fl oz) tin of beef
  consommé

Heat a large saucepan over a medium heat. Add the pancetta and fry for a few minutes until golden brown, then remove from the pan and keep to one side.

Add the butter along with the chopped vegetables and cook over a low heat for 10 to 15 minutes. Season the beef with salt and pepper and add to the vegetables, increasing the heat and cooking the beef until brown. Pour in the milk and cook until well absorbed before adding the red wine. Bring to the boil and simmer until just half the liquid is left.

Add the pancetta, tomatoes and half the consommé and return to a simmer. Cover with a lid and cook over a low heat for 2 hours, stirring occasionally. Add the remaining consommé if needed and check the seasoning before serving.

sticky sausage and onions

serves four

vegetable oil
450g (1lb) sausages
1 large onion, sliced
a knob of butter
salt and pepper
4 thick slices of bread, such
  as ciabatta or bloomer
olive oil, for drizzling
4 tablespoons clear honey
2 tablespoons wholegrain
  mustard (optional)

Warm 2 tablespoons of the vegetable oil in a frying pan, add the sausages and fry for 10 to 15 minutes over a medium heat until golden.

Meanwhile, in a separate pan, fry the onion in a drizzle of vegetable oil and the butter until soft and a rich golden brown. Season with salt and pepper.

Drizzle the bread slices with a little olive oil before toasting, frying or grilling to a golden brown.

Mop away excess fat from the sausage frying pan with some kitchen paper, add the honey and mustard, if using, and roll the sausages in the pan, allowing each to become well coated.

Arrange the sausages on the toasted bread and spoon the onions on top.

more

- Little burnt tinges around the toast create a bitter-sweet taste with the sticky honey sausages.

barbecued spare ribs

For maximum flavour, these should be planned 24 hours in advance.

serves five–six

1.5kg (3¼lb) short-cut pork
 spare ribs
6 tablespoons tomato
 ketchup
2 tablespoons red wine
 vinegar
2 tablespoons soy sauce
2 tablespoons
 Worcestershire sauce
3 tablespoons honey
1 teaspoon Dijon mustard
2 cloves of garlic, crushed
1 nugget of fresh ginger,
 finely grated (optional)

Cut the pork into individual ribs.

Bring a large pan of water to the boil before adding the ribs and simmering rapidly for 50 to 60 minutes until tender. Once cooked, remove and leave to cool.

Whisk together the remaining ingredients, including the ginger if using. Add the ribs to the marinade, cover and refrigerate for a minimum of 6 hours and preferably 12 to 24 hours.

Preheat the oven to 200°C/400°F/gas 6. Put a wire rack over a large roasting tray, arrange the ribs on the rack and roast for 30 to 40 minutes. During the last 10 to 15 minutes of cooking, baste the ribs with any remaining marinade until they are deeply rich and sticky.

chicken and bacon sticks

serves four

4 chicken breasts
6 rashers of streaky bacon,
 cut in half
salt and pepper
3 knobs of butter
olive oil
1 tablespoon capers
 (optional)
a squeeze of lemon juice

Soak four bamboo skewers in cold water for 20 to 30 minutes.

Place each of the chicken breasts between two sheets of clingfilm and gently pound with a small saucepan until approximately 1cm (½ inch) thick. Cut each breast lengthways into three strips.

Lay a half rasher of bacon on each strip of chicken and roll into mini Catherine wheels, threading three wheels on to each skewer.

Preheat the grill. Lightly grease a baking tray with olive oil and sprinkle it with salt and pepper. Place the skewers on the tray. Using a knob of butter brush each of the skewers before drizzling with olive oil.

Cook the chicken under the grill for 5 to 6 minutes on each side until golden brown.

Melt the remaining 2 knobs of butter in a small pan and, once foaming, add the capers, if using, lemon juice and a pinch of salt and pepper. Spoon over the skewers and serve.

pork and peas risotto

This simple risotto is a great way of using up leftover slow-roasted hand, shoulder or belly of pork; cuts which, when reheated, maintain a soft, buttery succulence.

serves four–six

1 litre (1¾ pints) chicken
  stock (see page 13)
75g (3oz) butter
2 onions, finely chopped
350g (12oz) risotto rice
  (carnaroli or arborio)
225–350g (8–12oz) cooked
  pork, roughly chopped
100g (4oz) frozen petits
  pois, defrosted
salt and pepper

Heat the stock in a saucepan until gently simmering.

Melt half the butter in a large pan. Add the onion and cook gently, without colouring, for 7 to 8 minutes until softened.

Stir in the rice and cook for a further 1 to 2 minutes. Pour in a ladleful of stock and cook over a medium heat, stirring continuously. Once the stock has almost evaporated, add a couple more ladlefuls and continue this process for 17 to 20 minutes. The risotto is ready once the rice is tender, but with a slight bite.

Put the pork into a bowl, add a couple of tablespoons of water, cover with clingfilm and microwave until hot. Add the peas and pork to the risotto and stir in the remaining butter. Season with salt and pepper before serving.

chicken skewers with peanut sauce

A satay usually demands the meat to be marinated, but here the chicken is left plain with an optional marinade, for a richer flavour, listed below. These chicken skewers go really well with buttered and herby new potatoes, which also enjoy being dipped in the peanut sauce.

serves 4

4 chicken breasts, skinless
salt and pepper
vegetable oil

for the peanut sauce
225g (8oz) crunchy or
  smooth peanut butter
100–150ml (3½–5fl oz)
  coconut milk
2 tablespoons soy sauce
3 teaspoons mild sweet
  chilli sauce
juice of 1 lime

Soak twenty bamboo skewers in cold water for 20 minutes.

Cut each chicken breast into four or five strips, pierce one piece of chicken on to each skewer and season with salt and pepper. Heat a little vegetable oil in a frying pan and fry the chicken until completely golden brown and firm to the touch.

Meanwhile, warm together in a saucepan the peanut butter and 100ml (3½fl oz) of the coconut milk, then add the remaining ingredients. The sauce should be a thick coating consistency. If it's too thick, add the remaining coconut milk and top up with water if needed.

The chicken skewers and peanut sauce are now ready to serve.

more

- For the marinade, mix together 4 tablespoons soy sauce, 4 tablespoons teriyaki sauce, 1 teaspoon finely chopped fresh ginger, 1 crushed clove of garlic and 50ml (2fl oz) pineapple juice. Steep the chicken in the marinade for a minimum of 1 to 2 hours.

apple mascarpone salad with warm sausage chunks

Everybody loves sausages, but this recipe also offers children a refreshingly crisp apple salad.

serves four–six

2–3 tablespoons vegetable oil
450g (1lb) plain or flavoured pork sausages
200ml (7fl oz) apple juice
50ml (2fl oz) crème fraîche
50g (2oz) mascarpone
1 teaspoon cider vinegar or lime juice
salt and pepper
1 red apple, cored and sliced
1 green apple, cored and sliced
1 bag of mixed salad leaves

Heat a large frying pan with the oil and fry the sausages for 8 to 10 minutes until completely cooked and golden brown.

Meanwhile, boil the apple juice until just 50ml (2fl oz) of the liquid is left. Whisk the juice together with the crème fraîche, mascarpone and cider vinegar or lime juice and season with salt and pepper.

Mix the apple with the salad leaves and enough dressing to coat. Slice the sausages and arrange on plates with the salad or simply mix the whole lot together.

raspberry mascarpone oat pud

This is simply a great way of using up cold leftover porridge (obviously without salt) and turning it into a delicious pudding.

serves four

200g (7oz) cold porridge
2–3 tablespoons golden syrup
250g (9oz) mascarpone cheese
100ml (3½fl oz) crème fraîche
1–2 punnets of raspberries
maple syrup (optional)

Beat the cold porridge in a bowl to soften and add the golden syrup and mascarpone followed by the crème fraîche.

Lightly crush half of the raspberries with a fork and add to the mixture, leaving a slightly rippled effect.

Divide the remaining raspberries among bowls or glasses, saving a few to decorate, before spooning the mascarpone porridge on top. This tastes at its best chilled with a drizzle of maple syrup.

chocolate brownie gypsy pudding

This is like a toffee mousse with chocolate brownies in it - very sweet but very moreish. You'll want to go back for seconds.

serves four–six

175g (6oz) chocolate brownies, cut into 1cm (½ inch) pieces
410g (14oz) tin of evaporated milk
225g (8oz) dark muscovado sugar

Preheat the oven to 200°C/400°F/gas 6.

Scatter the chocolate brownie pieces into a 25cm (9–10 inch) x 1.5cm deep flan dish.

Using an electric mixer whip the evaporated milk and muscovado sugar together on the highest setting until it slightly thickens, the sugar dissolves and there are no granular bits left. Put the brownies into a dish and pour the mixture over. Put in the oven for 10 minutes and eat at room temperature.

white chocolate cream with mango sauce

In a small saucepan, bring 100ml (3½fl oz) of the cream to the boil. Add the chocolate, stirring until completely melted. Pour the chocolate cream into a bowl and leave to cool.

Meanwhile, whiz the chopped mango and caster sugar in a blender until smooth. Strain through a sieve.

Whip the remaining cream to soft peaks, folding in the cooled chocolate to complete the mousse. If too loose, continue to whisk to a soft peak.

Serve a dollop of the white chocolate cream drizzled with the mango sauce.

serves four–six

for the white chocolate cream
300ml (10fl oz) double cream
225g (8oz) white chocolate, finely chopped

for the mango sauce
1 large mango, skinned and roughly diced
1 tablespoon caster sugar

more

- Puff pastry palmiers, available in most large stores, are perfect for dipping in the mousse.
- Strawberries and raspberries go very well with this chocolate cream.

strawberry eton mess with raspberry sauce

To make the raspberry sauce, blitz the berries and icing sugar to a purée in a blender. Push through a sieve and add a drop of water if too thick.

Break the meringues into chunky pieces. Roughly chop two thirds of the strawberries, halving the remainder. Whip the double cream to a soft peak and fold in the chopped strawberries, broken meringues and half of the raspberry sauce to create a ripple effect.

Divide the 'mess' among the bowls and finish with the remaining strawberries and a drizzle of raspberry sauce.

serves four–six

225g (8oz) raspberries
50g (2oz) icing sugar
4 individual meringues
450g (1lb) strawberries, hulled
600ml (1 pint) double cream

Simple midweek suppers/

Cooking supper in the middle of the week has at times been a rare pleasure for a chef like me, so I think I enjoy even more the challenge of preparing a comforting meal over which I can relax, catch up with my wife and sons and talk over the day. Midweek suppers are unpredictable and while I may find time to make an anchovy gremolata butter to accompany crispy slices of liver, on other evenings I have barely the energy to cook pasta for a pesto linguine with extra Parmesan and balsamic tomatoes. I've thus made all these recipes quick to prepare, with some, like the creamed mushrooms with fresh herbs, needing so little of your time.

I've also split the chapters into cooking for one, for two and for four. I find that I cook quite differently for one than for two or more and while I love tucking into a steak sandwich with bittersweet onions on my own in front of the telly, I like to share my pan-fried brill with red wine cockles with a hungry table. And who likes to look around their kitchen at lots of mess? My best midweek suppers are served from the saucepan or pot they were cooked in, with the minimum of after-dinner washing-up.

Simple midweek suppers/

Cooking for one

Pesto linguine with balsamic tomatoes

Grilled Portobello mushroom steaks, chips and tomatoes

Dover sole with hot lemon butter

Red mullet with fennel and olives

Tuna steak with red wine mushrooms

Grilled plaice with chives and capers

Surf 'n' turf

Steak sandwich with bittersweet fried onions

Courgette and bean sprout stir-fry

T-bone steak with melting Roquefort cherry tomatoes

Bowl of broccoli with a Gorgonzola swirl

Quick seared duck à l'orange

Lemon and parsley crusted lambs' kidneys

pesto linguine with balsamic tomatoes

Cook the pasta in boiling salted water until tender with a slight bite.

Meanwhile, season the tomatoes with salt and a twist of pepper and drizzle them quite liberally with the olive oil and balsamic vinegar.

Drain the pasta, spoon into a large bowl and stir in the butter and pesto. The Parmesan can now be grated or shaved using a vegetable peeler and scattered over the top. Serve the tomatoes alongside the pesto linguine

serves one

100g (4oz) dried linguine or
  spaghetti
8–10 cherry tomatoes,
  halved
salt and pepper
olive oil
balsamic vinegar
a knob of butter
2 tablespoons basil pesto
Parmesan cheese, for
  grating or shaving

more

- A teaspoon of chopped shallots or chives can be added to the tomatoes, or a few fresh basil leaves to complement the pesto.

grilled portobello mushroom steaks, chips and tomatoes

serves one

1–2 large baking potatoes
2 tablespoons olive oil, plus
  extra for drizzling
sea salt and pepper
a handful of cherry
  tomatoes, halved
2 large Portobello
  mushrooms, stalks
  removed

Preheat the oven to 220°C/425°F/gas 7.

Leaving the skin on, cut the potatoes into thick chips and dry on kitchen paper. On a large baking tray, mix the potatoes with a tablespoon of olive oil and bake for 25 minutes, then turn and bake for a further 20 to 25 minutes until crispy golden brown. Season with a pinch of salt.

Season the tomatoes with salt and pepper. About 5 to 10 minutes before the chips are ready, pop the tomatoes, cut-side up, on to the baking tray with the chips.

Heat a grill pan. Brush the mushrooms with the remaining tablespoon of olive oil and grill, flat-side up, for just a few minutes before turning. Grill for a further few minutes, only allowing the mushrooms to begin to soften to maintain all their tasty juices and firm texture. Season with salt and pepper.

The mushroom 'steaks' and chips are ready to serve with the cherry tomatoes drizzled with olive oil.

dover sole with hot lemon butter

I'm using fillets here, but the Dover sole can also be cooked whole and the frying time increased by a few minutes. Either way, cooking fish doesn't get any easier than this.

Pat the sole fillets dry on kitchen paper before lightly dusting in flour.

Heat a spoonful or two of olive oil in a large non-stick frying pan. Once the oil is hot, fry the fillets over a medium to high heat, without shaking the pan, for 3 to 4 minutes until they are a rich golden brown.

Season the fillets with salt and pepper before adding the butter to the pan and squeezing a wedge of lemon juice over them. Turn the fillets, then remove the frying pan from the heat.

After a minute of sitting in the hot pan, the fish are ready to serve. Spoon over the lemon butter and serve with the remaining lemon wedge.

serves one

450–550g (1–1¼lb) Dover
  sole, filleted, skinned and
  pinboned (see page 14)
flour, for dusting
olive oil
salt and pepper
15g (½oz) butter
2 wedges of lemon

more

- Although Dover sole is listed, lemon sole or plaice makes a very good second choice.
- Extra flavours can be added to the lemon butter, sizzling it again just before spooning over the fish. Try a couple of teaspoons of capers or some herbs, such as tarragon, chives or parsley.

red mullet with fennel and olives

serves one

1 small fennel bulb
1 plum tomato
6–8 green olives, halved
4 tablespoons olive oil
sea salt and pepper
a squeeze of lemon
1 x 350–400g (12–14oz)
  red mullet, scaled, filleted
  and pinboned
  (see page 14)
flour, for dusting
a large knob of butter

Remove the fennel top, saving any fronds. Shred the fennel very finely, preferably on a mandolin, and place in a bowl. With the point of a knife, remove the eye from the tomato and place in the bowl with the fennel. Cover with boiling water from the kettle and, after 10 to 12 seconds, refresh the tomato and fennel under cold water before draining.

Peel, halve and deseed the tomato before cutting into cubes and mixing with the fennel and green olives. Add the olive oil, season and squeeze over the lemon.

Lightly dust the skin side of the mullet fillets with flour and season with salt and pepper. Melt the butter in a frying pan and, once foaming, add the fillets, skin-side down, and fry for 3 to 4 minutes until golden brown. Turn the fillets and fry for a further 1 to 2 minutes.

Add any saved fronds to the fennel salad and serve with the red mullet.

more

• Fresh dill or tarragon could supplement the fennel fronds.

tuna steak with red wine mushrooms

serves one

olive oil, for cooking
175g (6oz) tuna steak
salt and pepper
2 knobs of butter
1 shallot, sliced in rings
75–100g (3–4oz) wild,
  chestnut or button
  mushrooms, sliced
1 glass of red wine
1 teaspoon sugar

Heat a frying pan with a few drops of olive oil, season the tuna with salt and pepper and sear the fillet for a couple of minutes on each side until tender and pink. Remove the fish from the pan and keep warm.

Add a knob of butter to the pan and, once sizzling, sauté the shallot rings and mushrooms quickly before adding the wine and sugar. Boil until a syrupy consistency is reached, stir in the remaining butter and season with salt and pepper.

The red wine mushrooms are now ready to spoon on top of the tuna.

grilled plaice with chives and capers

serves one

25g (1oz) butter, plus extra
  for greasing and brushing
sea salt and pepper
450–675g (1–1½lb) plaice,
  trimmed
1 heaped teaspoon
  chopped chives
1 teaspoon capers,
  chopped if large
½ lemon

Preheat the grill. Grease a baking tray with butter and sprinkle with salt and pepper. Lay the plaice, white skin-side up, on the tray, brush with a little butter and season with sea salt only.

Put the fish beneath the grill and cook for 8 to 10 minutes until golden brown.

Meanwhile, stir together the 25g (1oz) butter with the chives and capers, add a squeeze of lemon juice and season with salt and pepper. Scoop a dollop or two of the butter over the plaice.

surf 'n' turf

serves one

3–4 raw tiger prawns,
  peeled
2 tablespoons mayonnaise
1 heaped teaspoon tomato
  ketchup
a splash of brandy
  (optional)
salt and pepper
1 small clove of garlic,
  crushed
1 teaspoon chopped chives
1–2 squeezes of lemon
  juice
25g (1oz) softened butter,
  plus an extra knob
olive oil
175g (6oz) sirloin or
  fillet steak
a handful of lettuce leaves

Soak a bamboo skewer in cold water for 15 minutes. Dry on kitchen paper and pierce the prawns on to the skewer.

To make the cocktail sauce, mix together the mayonnaise and ketchup, adding the brandy if using. If too thick, loosen with a splash or two of water. Season with salt and pepper.

Stir the garlic, chives and a squeeze of lemon juice into the softened butter and season.

Heat the olive oil in a frying pan and once smoking, season the steak and fry for a few minutes on each side for a pink finish. Remove from the pan and leave to rest. Add the knob of butter with the prawn skewer to the hot pan, season and cook for a further minute or two on each side, finishing with a squeeze of lemon juice.

Arrange the lettuce leaves on a plate, topping with the cocktail sauce and the prawn kebab. Sit the steak next to the salad and spoon a large dollop of garlic and chive butter on top.

steak sandwich with bittersweet fried onions

serves one

2 tablespoons olive oil
1 onion, sliced
100–175g (4–6oz) sirloin
  steak
salt and pepper
a knob of butter
1 teaspoon honey
1 heaped tablespoon
  mayonnaise
1 teaspoon wholegrain
  mustard
1 baguette, split in half
a few salad leaves
  (optional)

Heat the olive oil in a large frying pan. Fry the onion over a high heat for 5 to 6 minutes until rich golden brown with a burnt tinge before pushing to one side and making space for the steak.

Season the steak with salt and pepper. Put the butter in the pan and once sizzling, fry the steak for a few minutes on each side for a tender pink finish. Remove, then stir the honey into the onion for a sweet bitter taste.

Mix together the mayonnaise and mustard and spread it on the bread. Place the salad leaves, if using, on one half of the bread, spooning the onions on to the other half. The steak can now be sliced before laying on top of the onions. The sandwich is now ready to close and enjoy.

courgette and bean sprout stir-fry

serves one

oil, for cooking
a knob of butter
225g (8oz) courgettes, cut
  into cubes
50g (2oz) bean sprouts
1 bunch of spring onions,
  shredded
salt and pepper
a pinch of sugar
1 tablespoon sesame oil
2–3 tablespoons oyster or
  worcestershire sauce
  (optional)

Heat a wok or frying pan and add the oil. Once hot, add the butter and the courgettes and cook for 2 minutes, then add the bean sprouts and spring onions.

Continue to cook for 1 to 2 minutes, then season with salt and pepper and the sugar. To finish, drizzle over and stir in the sesame oil and oyster or worcestershire sauce, if using.

t-bone steak with melting roquefort cherry tomatoes

serves one

450–600g (1lb–1lb 5oz)
 T-bone steak
salt and pepper
2 tablespoons olive oil
1 tablespoon finely chopped
 shallots
100g (4oz) cherry tomatoes,
 halved
50g (2oz) Roquefort
 cheese, crumbled into
 small pieces

Preheat a frying pan and the grill.

Season the steak with salt and pepper, drizzling over half a tablespoon of olive oil, and fry for 3 to 4 minutes on each side until medium rare to medium.

Meanwhile, in a small frying pan, cook the shallots in the remaining olive oil for a few minutes. Add the tomatoes and continue to fry over a high heat until they soften. Season with salt and pepper. Top the steak with the tomatoes and Roquefort and place the pan under the preheated grill until the cheese melts before serving with any juices drizzled over the top.

bowl of broccoli with a gorgonzola swirl

This recipe can be multiplied for many, but stands as one of the simplest quick meals for one, full of natural flavour.

serves one

a knob of butter
½ small onion, finely
 chopped
175g (6oz) broccoli, roughly
 chopped and the stalk finely
 chopped
salt and pepper
25–50g (1–2oz) Gorgonzola
 cheese, softened
50ml (2fl oz) half-fat crème
 fraîche
slices of toasted crusty bread

Melt the butter in a small saucepan. Once bubbling, add the onion and cook over a low heat for 5 to 6 minutes until softened. Pour in 300ml (10fl oz) water and bring to the boil before adding a pinch of salt and the broccoli. Cook for a further 5 to 6 minutes until the broccoli is tender and ready to blend until smooth (a handheld blender will do the job quite comfortably). If slightly too thick, add a splash or two of water to loosen. Season with salt and pepper.

Meanwhile, cream together your preferred quantity of Gorgonzola with the crème fraîche, leaving it as coarse or smooth as you wish.

The soup is ready to serve, finishing with a swirl of Gorgonzola cream and lots of hot toast for dunking.

quick seared duck
à l'orange

serves one

1 carrot, peeled and cut into
  matchsticks
100ml (3½fl oz) orange
  juice
½ teaspoon honey
50g (2oz) mangetout or
  French beans
1 teaspoon sesame seeds,
  toasted
a large knob of butter
salt and pepper
olive oil
1 duck breast, skinned and
  sliced into thin strips
a handful of rocket or
  watercress sprigs
1 orange, segmented
  (see page 20)

Put the carrot, orange juice and honey into a saucepan and
simmer for 5 to 6 minutes until the carrot is tender and half the
juice is remaining.

Cook the mangetout or beans in boiling salted water until tender,
drain and add to the carrot. Stir in the sesame seeds and butter
and season with salt and pepper.

Heat a frying pan or wok with a splash of olive oil. Once smoking,
quickly fry the duck strips for about 30 seconds. Season and add
to a plate with the carrot, mangetout and orange segments before
topping with the salad leaves and drizzling with any remaining
dressing.

lemon and parsley crusted lambs' kidneys

A garlicky slow-roasted beef tomato is included to complete the meal.

Preheat the oven to 180°C/350°F/gas 4. Put the tomato halves on a lightly oiled baking tray, cut-side up. Top each with 2 slices of garlic, season and trickle with olive oil. Bake for 20 to 25 minutes.

Meanwhile, cut through the kidneys without separating them completely. Heat a frying pan with a few drops of olive oil, add the kidneys, cut-side down, and fry for 1 to 2 minutes on each side. Season with salt and pepper and brush the kidneys with Dijon mustard.

Preheat the grill. Mix together the breadcrumbs, parsley and lemon zest and spoon over the kidneys. Trickle with olive oil and grill until golden brown and crispy.

Put the kidneys and tomato halves on a plate, add the butter and lemon juice to the tomato juices and spoon over the kidneys.

serves one

1 beef tomato, halved
1 clove of garlic, sliced
 into 4
sea salt and pepper
olive oil
2 large lambs' kidneys,
 skinned
Dijon mustard, for spreading
50g (2oz) fresh white
 breadcrumbs
1 tablespoon chopped flat-
 leaf parsley
grated zest and juice of ½
 lemon
a knob of butter

Simple midweek suppers/

Cooking for two

British sausage soup

Open spinach and ricotta ravioli with pine nuts and parmesan

Aubergine, red onion and mozzarella bake

Creamed mushrooms with fresh herbs

Moules marinières

Scallop salad

Tiger prawns and tomatoes with basil and garlic mayonnaise

Quick curried prawns

Fish and chips for two

John Dory with sautéed honey sesame courgettes

Crab and spinach omelette with lobster cream

Quick-fry monkfish and curry dip with banana, cucumber and apple

Salmon skewers with pistachio lime yoghurt

Fresh tuna with mango, apple, orange and curry vinaigrette

Stir-fried chicken with tomatoes, basil and crispy Parmesan

Chicken and chorizo sausage stew

Lemon and chilli sesame pork with mangetout

Black pepper lamb steak with pomegranates

Spiced lamb with mango, apple and cucumber salad

Bittersweet beef fillet leaves

Seared beef with Provençal tomatoes and mustard watercress

Crisp liver slices with anchovy gremolata butter

Venison sausages with red wine onions and blackcurrants

british sausage soup

This soup carries a bit of French and Italian influence, but the main feature is definitely British.

Melt the butter in a large saucepan, add the onion, carrot, celery and garlic and cook for 5 to 6 minutes. Stir in the haricot beans, top with the stock and bring to a simmer.

Meanwhile, fry the sausages in the olive oil until completely golden brown. Add the sausages to the soup and simmer gently for 20 minutes.

Remove the sausages from the pan and cut into thick pieces before returning them to the soup. Season with salt and pepper before sprinkling the herbs on top.

serves two

25g (1oz) butter
1 onion, chopped
1 large carrot, chopped
2 sticks of celery, chopped
1 clove of garlic, crushed
400g (14oz) tin of white
   haricot beans, drained and
   rinsed
600ml (1 pint) chicken stock
   (see page 13)
450g (1lb) British pork
   sausages
2 tablespoons olive oil
salt and pepper
1 tablespoon mixed
   chopped chives and
   parsley

more
- Chopped tomatoes add a sweet 'Italian' touch.
- The beans can be replaced with 1 or 2 chopped potatoes.

open spinach and ricotta ravioli with pine nuts and parmesan

serves two

2 sheets of dried lasagne
sea salt and pepper
25g (1oz) butter
3 spring onions, chopped
225g (8oz) spinach
freshly grated nutmeg
100g (4oz) ricotta cheese
1 tablespoon olive oil
2 tablespoons pine nuts
6–8 sage leaves, torn
a squeeze of lemon
fresh Parmesan shavings,
  to serve

Cook the pasta in boiling salted water until tender, drain and halve each sheet to give you four squares.

Meanwhile, melt half the butter in a large shallow pan and fry the spring onion for a minute or two. Add the washed and well-drained spinach and stir over a high heat until the leaves have wilted. Season with salt, pepper and a pinch of grated nutmeg. Remove from the heat and break the ricotta among the leaves.

Lay a pasta sheet in each of two bowls, spoon on the spinach and ricotta and top with the remaining pasta.

Quickly heat another pan with the olive oil and remaining butter. Add the pine nuts and, once golden brown, sprinkle in the sage leaves with a squeeze of lemon. Drizzle over the ravioli with shavings of Parmesan.

more

- For a 'meatier' flavour, add a handful of wild mushrooms to the spinach.

aubergine, red onion and mozzarella bake

A bowl of rocket and watercress, drizzled with olive oil and a few dots of balsamic vinegar will help make this a complete meal for two.

serves two

3 tablespoons olive oil
2 medium aubergines, cut into 2.5cm (1 inch) cubes
2 red onions, halved and sliced
salt and pepper
100ml (3½fl oz) crème fraîche
2 tablespoons mayonnaise
2 tablespoons dried breadcrumbs
4 tablespoons grated mozzarella

Preheat the oven to 200°C/400°F/gas 6. Heat the olive oil in a large frying pan. Once smoking, scoop the aubergine and onion into the pan and fry for a few minutes over a high heat until slightly golden. Season with salt and pepper.

Mix together the crème fraîche and mayonnaise before stirring into the aubergine and shaking it into a 600ml (1 pint) baking dish.

Combine the breadcrumbs and mozzarella, sprinkle over the aubergines and bake for 10 to 15 minutes until piping hot and golden. If slightly undercoloured, simply finish beneath a preheated grill.

creamed mushrooms with fresh herbs

These are particularly delicious with poultry and fish dishes or spooned over a bowl of pasta or a jacket potato.

serves two

350g (12oz) button or
  chestnut mushrooms,
  thickly sliced
100ml (3½fl oz) double or
  whipping cream
a squeeze of lemon juice
salt and pepper
milk, to loosen
1 tablespoon chopped
  mixed herbs (chives,
  parsley and tarragon)

Place the mushrooms in a frying pan with the cream and lemon juice, seasoning with salt and pepper.

Cook over a low heat, allowing the mushrooms to soften as the cream warms. If the cream becomes too thick, loosen with a splash or two of milk. Simmer very gently until completely tender before stirring in the herbs.

moules marinières

serves two

1kg (2¼lb) mussels
50g (2oz) unsalted butter
1 small onion, finely
  chopped
1 glass of white wine
1 tablespoon chopped
  parsley
a squeeze of lemon

Clean the mussels by washing them under cold running water, scraping away any barnacles and pulling out the beards that protrude from between the closed shells. If any mussels are found slightly open, a short, sharp tap should make them close, letting you know they are still alive. Any that don't close should be discarded.

Put the mussels, a third of the butter, the onion and white wine into a large saucepan (it's important that the saucepan is only half full of mussels for even cooking).

Cover with a lid and cook over a high heat for 6 to 8 minutes, shaking the pan and stirring the mussels from time to time until they have all opened.

Spoon the mussels into bowls, discarding any that have not opened. To finish, whisk the remaining butter, parsley and a squeeze of lemon into the cooking juices and spoon them over the steaming mussels.

scallop salad

serves two

1 thick slice of crusty bread,
  cut into cubes
olive oil
sea salt and pepper
2 large shallots, cut into
  rings
a pinch of sugar
8 black olives, pitted and
  halved
6 marinated anchovies
a large handful of mixed
  salad leaves
a knob of butter
5 scallops, halved
½ lemon
1–2 tablespoons crème
  fraîche (optional)

Fry the bread croutons in olive oil until crispy and golden brown. Season with salt and keep to one side.

Reheat the pan with a drop more olive oil and fry the shallots over a fierce heat for just a minute or two until well coloured. Add the sugar and season, then spoon into a large bowl.

Toss the croutons, olives, anchovies and salad leaves with the shallots and divide between two plates.

Heat the frying pan, add the butter and, once foaming, quickly sear the scallop slices for no more than a minute, then turn and fry for a further 30 to 60 seconds. Season and scatter amongst the salads, drizzling each one with olive oil and a generous squeeze of lemon juice. The crème fraîche can then be trickled over the salad if desired.

tiger prawns and tomatoes with basil and garlic mayonnaise

This recipe would also make a great starter for four if you're entertaining friends.

Spoon the mayonnaise, herbs and garlic into a small food processor and whiz to mix together, finishing with the lemon juice and a twist of pepper.

Stir just enough extra-virgin olive oil into the tomato to loosen and add the balsamic vinegar. Season with salt and pepper.

Heat a frying pan with the knob of butter. Once sizzling, cook the prawns for 1 to 2 minutes on each side until they turn pink. Season with salt and pepper.

Spoon the tomato dressing over the prawns and serve with the basil and garlic mayonnaise in a small bowl ready for dipping.

serves two

100g (4oz) mayonnaise
2 tablespoons chopped basil
1 tablespoon chopped flat-leaf parsley
2 cloves of garlic, chopped
a squeeze of lemon juice
sea salt and pepper
extra-virgin olive oil, to loosen
2 plum tomatoes, peeled and diced (see page 18)
a dash of balsamic vinegar
a knob of butter
12 large raw tiger prawns, peeled and deveined (see page 16)

quick curried prawns

This dish can be eaten as a main course with plain rice, or served just warm with torn or shredded iceberg leaves for an alternative prawn cocktail.

serves two

12 large raw tiger prawns,
  peeled and deveined,
  saving all the
  heads and shells
  (see page 16)
vegetable oil
a large knob of butter
salt and pepper

for the sauce
a knob of butter
2 tablespoons brandy
1 teaspoon curry powder
150ml (5fl oz) chicken stock
  (see page 13)
200ml (7fl oz) double cream
salt and pepper
a squeeze of lime

To make the sauce, melt the butter and gently fry the prawn heads and shells for 5 to 6 minutes.

Pour in the brandy and cook until the liquid is almost dry before adding the curry powder, stock and cream. Simmer rapidly until just two thirds of the liquid is left and it has reached a sauce consistency. Strain through a fine sieve, squeezing out any juice from the shells. Season with salt and pepper and finish with a squeeze of lime.

Heat a frying pan with a drop or two of the vegetable oil. Add the butter and, once it begins to sizzle, fry the prawns for just a couple of minutes before turning and frying for a further 2 minutes until pink. Season with salt and pepper and stir in the curry sauce.

more

- A teaspoon or two of mango chutney can be added to the sauce with the stock and cream for a sweeter curry taste.

fish and chips for two

Preheat the oven to 190°C/375°F/gas 5. In a wok or deep frying pan, heat 6–7cm (2½–3 inches) of oil over a low heat until just warm.

Dry the potato sticks on kitchen paper and gently drop into the oil, simmering for 5 to 7 minutes until they have become tender without colouring. Increase the heat to 170–180°C (325–350°F) and fry to a crisp golden brown. Using a slotted spoon, lift on to a baking tray topped with kitchen paper and keep warm in the oven.

For the batter, whisk together the flour, a pinch of salt and the beer (this can be liquidized for a really smooth mixture). Season the fish with salt and pepper and totally immerse in the batter, holding above the bowl for a few seconds to allow any excess batter to drop back in.

Carefully lower the fillets into the oil and fry for 4 to 5 minutes until golden brown and crisp. Drain on kitchen paper and serve with the home-made chips and lemon wedges.

serves two

vegetable oil
3 large potatoes, cut into 5–10mm (¼–½ inch) thick sticks
100g (4oz) self-raising flour
salt and pepper
150ml (5fl oz) beer or stout
2 x 150–175g (5–6oz) haddock fillets, pinboned (see page 14)
2 lemon wedges

more

- The chips can be quickly dipped back into the hot oil once the fish has been fried to guarantee a crisp finish.

john dory with sautéed honey sesame courgettes

The shape of the John Dory fillets means they can naturally be split into 'fish fingers' before cooking, as you can see in the photo.

serves two

2 tablespoons sour cream
1 teaspoon clear honey
salt and pepper
olive oil
15g (½oz) butter, plus a
  knob for frying
225g (8oz) courgettes,
  sliced
2 teaspoons sesame seeds,
  toasted (see page 13)
2 x 175g (6oz) John Dory
  fillets, skinned and
  pinboned (see page 14)
flour, for dusting

Mix together the sour cream and honey, seasoning with salt and pepper. Heat some olive oil and the butter in a large saucepan and add the courgettes. Season with salt and pepper and fry for 5 to 6 minutes until golden brown and tender. Stir in the sesame seeds.

While cooking the courgettes, dry the John Dory on kitchen paper and season with salt and pepper before lightly flouring.

Heat some more olive oil and the knob of butter in a non-stick frying pan. Fry the fish for 4 to 5 minutes until golden brown before turning and removing from the heat. The residual heat in the pan will continue the cooking.

Spoon the honey sour cream over the courgettes before dividing between your plates. Place the John Dory on top of, or beside, the courgettes and serve drizzled with the juices from the pan.

more

- This dish can also be made with turbot, cod, monkfish, sea bass or tuna.
- Fresh chopped herbs, shallot rings and halved cherry tomatoes all work very well mixed in with the courgettes.

crab and spinach omelette with lobster cream

serves two

6 eggs
150ml (5fl oz) tinned lobster
  bisque
1–2 tablespoons half-fat
  crème fraîche
a squeeze of lemon
salt and pepper
2 knobs of butter
100g (4oz) white crabmeat
2 handfuls of washed and
  ready-to-eat baby spinach
  leaves

Using three eggs per person, crack into two separate bowls and whisk with a fork.

Heat the lobster bisque, adding the crème fraîche and a squeeze of lemon. Season with salt and pepper.

Over a medium heat, warm a 15–18cm (6–7 inch) non-stick omelette pan. Add a knob of butter and, once foaming, stir in half the crabmeat and spinach leaves, seasoning with salt and pepper. As the leaves begin to wilt, pour in a bowl of the beaten egg, stirring until a soft scrambled consistency is reached. Cover the base of the pan with the egg and cook for a further 30 to 60 seconds until just beginning to set.

Hold the pan at an angle, slide the omelette towards the edge and fold it in, folding the other side over to create a cigar shape. Turn the omelette out on to a plate and keep warm while the remaining omelette is made. Finish both with a spoonful or two of the warm lobster cream.

quick-fry monkfish and curry dip with banana, cucumber and apple

Cut the cucumber and apple into matchsticks. Peel and slice the banana and toss together with the cucumber and apple, stirring in the cumin seeds and chopped coriander leaves. Season with salt and pepper, drizzle over half the lime juice and a little walnut or groundnut oil to barely coat and finish the salad.

Season the monkfish fingers and lightly dust with flour. Heat the vegetable oil in a frying pan or wok and, once smoking, scatter in the fingers, frying over a high heat for a few minutes until a rich golden brown. Add the butter and, once foaming, squeeze over the remaining lime juice.

Serve the monkfish fingers with the salad and curry mayonnaise.

serves two

¼ cucumber
1 apple
1 banana
½ teaspoon cumin seeds, toasted (see page 13)
a few sprigs of fresh coriander, leaves roughly chopped
salt and pepper
juice of 1 lime
walnut or groundnut oil
300–350g (10–12oz) monkfish fillet cut into fingers
flour, for dusting
2 tablespoons vegetable oil
a knob of butter
1 x curry mayonnaise (see page 465)

more
- Chicken breast fingers will work just as well with the salad and dip.

salmon skewers with pistachio lime yoghurt

serves two

for the pistachio lime yoghurt
25g (1oz) peeled pistachios
75ml (3fl oz) natural yoghurt
a squeeze of lime
salt and pepper

350g (12oz) salmon fillet,
  pinboned (see page 14)
  and cut into 8 square
  chunks
1 tablespoon olive oil, plus
  extra for drizzling
a large knob of butter
1 courgette, cut into
  matchsticks
1 green apple, cut into
  matchsticks
4 breakfast radishes, cut
  into matchsticks
sea salt and pepper
a squeeze of lime

Soak two bamboo skewers in cold water for 20 minutes.

Blend together the pistachios and yoghurt, ideally in a coffee grinder or mini food processor, until slight chunky-smooth. Add a squeeze of lime and season with salt and pepper.

Pierce four pieces of salmon on to each skewer, leaving a slight gap between the chunks. Heat a large frying pan with the oil and butter and, once foaming, fry the skewers for just 2 to 3 minutes before turning and cooking for a further 1 to 2 minutes.

Meanwhile, mix together the courgette, apple and radish matchsticks, season and drizzle with olive oil and a squeeze of lime. Scatter on to two plates, put the salmon skewers on top and serve with a spoonful or two of the pistachio yoghurt.

fresh tuna with mango, apple, orange and curry vinaigrette

serves two

for the curry vinaigrette
2 tablespoons lemon juice
1 small clove of garlic, crushed
1 level teaspoon Dijon mustard
1 level teaspoon Madras curry powder
½ teaspoon grated fresh ginger
50ml (2fl oz) vegetable oil
50ml (2fl oz) olive oil

1 orange, segmented (see page 20)
1 green apple, sliced
1 shallot, sliced into rings
a handful of mixed salad leaves
1 small mango, peeled and sliced
a knob of butter
2 x 150–175g (5–6oz) tuna steaks
sea salt and pepper

To make the vinaigrette, put the lemon juice, garlic, mustard, curry powder and ginger in to a blender and blitz, adding the oils slowly to emulsify. Strain through a sieve into an airtight jar.

Mix the orange segments with the apple slices, shallot rings and salad leaves and liberally drizzle over some of the curry vinaigrette. Arrange the mango slices between two plates and place the dressed salad on top.

Melt the butter in a hot frying pan and, once bubbling, season the tuna steaks and fry for 2 minutes before turning over and cooking for a further minute, leaving a moist, pink centre. The fish is now ready to serve on top of the salad.

more
- Any leftover dressing can be kept refrigerated for up to 2 weeks and used to accompany almost any salad.

stir-fried chicken with tomatoes, basil and crispy parmesan

Preheat the oven to 180°C/350°F/gas 4.

Mix together the tomatoes, garlic and 2 tablespoons of the olive oil in a roasting tray and season with salt, pepper and a pinch of sugar.

Bake for 20 to 25 minutes until the tomatoes have softened and released their juices, creating a dressing with the olive oil.

Meanwhile, divide the Parmesan into two circles on a non-stick baking tray and place in the oven for 10 to 12 minutes until melted. Remove and leave to cool and set into two crispy wafers.

During the last 10 minutes of baking the tomatoes, season the chicken with salt and pepper. Heat a wok or large frying pan with the remaining olive oil. Once hot, fry the chicken, allowing the pieces to become a rich golden brown before adding the butter and onion and cooking for 6 to 7 minutes until tender. Finish with a squeeze of lemon.

Divide the chicken among the plates, spooning over the soft tomatoes. Sprinkle with the basil and top with the Parmesan wafers.

serves two

175g (6oz) punnet of cherry
  tomatoes, halved
1 clove of garlic, chopped
3 tablespoons olive oil
sea salt and pepper
a pinch of sugar
50g (2oz) Parmesan
  cheese, grated
2 chicken breasts, skinned,
  each cut into 5 or 6 pieces
a knob of butter
1 small onion, thinly sliced
a squeeze of lemon
a handful of small basil
  leaves

chicken and chorizo sausage stew

serves two

2 tablespoons olive oil
175g (6oz) small chorizo
    sausages, sliced into 1cm
    (½ inch) thick pieces
1 large onion, sliced
400g (14 oz) tin of cannellini
    beans, drained and rinsed
400g (14 oz) tin of chopped
    tomatoes
2 plum tomatoes, quartered
    and deseeded
2 chicken breasts, skinless
salt and pepper
a pinch of sugar

Heat a deep frying pan or saucepan with a tablespoon of the olive oil. Quickly fry the chorizo until coloured and its oils have been released.

Reduce the heat slightly, stir in the onion and cook for a few minutes until it begins to soften. Add the cannellini beans and tinned tomatoes, topping up with half a tin of water to loosen. Halve the tomato quarters and stir them into the stew, simmering gently for 10 to 15 minutes.

Meanwhile, cut the chicken into bite-sized pieces and season with salt and pepper. Heat a separate frying pan with the remaining olive oil. Fry the chicken for 6 to 7 minutes until golden brown and firm to the touch. Spoon the chicken into the stew and season with salt, pepper and the sugar before serving.

more

- 100–150ml (3½–5fl oz) of passata can be added for a looser, richer sauce.

lemon and chilli sesame pork with mangetout

serves two

100g (4oz) mangetout
olive oil
2 shallots, peeled and
  sliced
2 medium red chillies,
  halved, deseeded and
  very thinly sliced
zest and juice of 1 lemon
350g (12oz) pork fillet or
  loin, sliced into thin strips
sea salt and pepper
2 teaspoons sesame seeds,
  toasted (see page 13)
a knob of butter

Snap away the tops of the mangetout, plunge into rapidly boiling salted water for 1 minute, drain and keep to one side.

Heat a wok or frying pan with a splash of olive oil and fry the shallots, chilli and lemon zest over a medium heat for a few minutes until the shallots are just beginning to soften.

Season the pork with salt and pepper. Increase the heat in the pan, add the pork and fry for just a few minutes until the pork is golden brown. Stir in the mangetout, sesame seeds, butter and lemon juice (using just half if it's a particularly juicy fruit) to finish the dish.

more

- A dollop of natural yoghurt, crème fraîche or sour cream can be added or offered separately for a creamier dish.
- A trickle or two of sesame oil can also be drizzled on top to enrich the flavour of the toasted seeds.

black pepper lamb steak with pomegranates

A handful or two of rocket leaves loosely bound with a dollop of crème fraîche is all you really need to help this meal along.

Halve the pomegranates, scooping out the seeds from one half while juicing the remainder on a lemon squeezer.

Heat the olive oil in a large frying pan and season the lamb steaks with the black pepper and sea salt. Add a knob of butter to the pan and fry the steaks for 4 to 5 minutes on each side, cooking to a medium pink. Remove the steaks and leave to rest for a few minutes.

Pour away any fat from the pan, add a few tablespoons of water and the pomegranate juice and bubble fiercely until syrupy. Stir in the remaining butter before straining through a fine sieve and adding the pomegranate seeds.

Add any released lamb juices to the pomegranate syrup before drizzling around the lamb to serve.

serves two

2 pomegranates
1 tablespoon olive oil
2 x 225–300g (8–10oz) lamb steaks
1 heaped teaspoon black peppercorns, coarsely crushed
sea salt
2 knobs of butter

more
- A few dots of grenadine syrup can be added to the pomegranate sauce to give a sweeter contrast to the black pepper.

spiced lamb with mango, apple and cucumber salad

serves two

2 x 200g (7oz) leg of
  lamb steaks
salt and pepper
150ml (5fl oz) natural
  yoghurt
juice of 1 lime
1 teaspoon medium curry
  powder
1 small clove of garlic,
  finely chopped
1 heaped tablespoon
  chopped mint
2 tablespoons vegetable oil
1 mango, peeled and cut
  into cubes
1 apple, cored and cut into
  cubes
¼ cucumber, peeled and
  cut into cubes
1–2 handfuls of salad or
  baby spinach leaves

Cut away the bone from each lamb steak and, using a meat tenderizer, bat the steaks into large escalopes between 5 and 10mm (¼–½ inch) thick. Season with salt and pepper.

Whisk together 2 tablespoons of the yoghurt, the juice of ½ lime, the curry powder and garlic. Dip and coat the escalopes in the mix, leaving to infuse while the salad is prepared. To make the dressing, whisk the remaining yoghurt, lime juice and mint together, seasoning with salt and pepper.

Heat the oil in a large frying pan or grill pan. Once hot, cook the lamb for 3 to 5 minutes on each side, maintaining a pink centre. Remove from the heat and allow to rest.

Meanwhile, arrange the fruit, cucumber and salad leaves or spinach on the plates, drizzle over the dressing and serve with the spiced lamb.

bittersweet beef fillet leaves

serves two

1 tablespoon vegetable oil
2 x 100g (4oz) beef fillet
  steaks
salt and pepper
1 teaspoon honey
2 teaspoons red wine
  vinegar
2 tablespoons olive or
  walnut oil
2 handfuls of mixed
  green salad leaves

Heat a frying pan with the vegetable oil. Once smoking, season the beef fillets with salt and pepper. Fry the two steaks in the pan over a high heat for a few minutes, allowing them to colour until almost burnt before turning and repeating. A few minutes on each side will give a medium-rare finish. The burnt tinges provide the bitter flavour. Remove and set aside to rest.

Slightly reduce the heat and add the honey. Once bubbling, remove the pan from the heat and stir in the vinegar and oil. Season with salt and pepper.

The beef fillet can now be sliced and served with the salad leaves, drizzled with the honey dressing.

more

- Crispy crostini toasts (available ready-made) and chunks of blue cheese or Brie make tasty additions.

seared beef with provençal tomatoes and mustard watercress

serves two

3 plum tomatoes
2 small cloves of garlic,
  each cut into 3 pieces
1 teaspoon dried Provençal
  herbs
sea salt and pepper
4–5 tablespoons olive oil
2 x 100g (4oz) beef fillet
  steaks
2 tablespoons sour cream
1 heaped teaspoon English,
  Dijon or wholegrain
  mustard
1 bunch of watercress

Preheat the oven to 200°C/400°F/gas 6. Halve the tomatoes, put in a small roasting tray, cut-side up, and top each with a slice of garlic. Sprinkle with the Provençal herbs, season with salt and pepper and drizzle with 4 tablespoons of the olive oil. Roast for 20 to 25 minutes until completely cooked and softened.

Heat a frying pan with the remaining olive oil. Season the steaks with salt and a generous twist of pepper and sear for 2 to 3 minutes on each side for a pink finish.

Stir together the sour cream and mustard and mix gently with the watercress leaves to coat. Season with salt and pepper. Divide the watercress, steaks and tomatoes between your plates and drizzle with any tomato juices left in the roasting tray.

more
- The steaks can be split into two thinner slices each and seared for literally a minute on each side.

crisp liver slices with anchovy gremolata butter

Gremolata is an Italian mixture of lemon zest, garlic and parsley, here bound in butter with chopped anchovy.

Beat together the butter, anchovy fillets, lemon zest, garlic and parsley and season with a twist of pepper.

Mix together the breadcrumbs and Parmesan and season with salt and pepper. Lightly dust the liver slices with flour and dip them into the egg before coating with the Parmesan crumbs.

Heat the olive oil with the knob of butter in a large frying pan. Once sizzling, fry the crumbed liver for 2 to 3 minutes on each side until golden and crispy.

To serve, top each slice of liver with a dollop of the softened butter.

serves two

for the butter
60g (2½oz) softened butter, plus an extra knob for frying
2–3 anchovy fillets, chopped
finely grated zest of ½ lemon
1 small clove of garlic, crushed
1 heaped teaspoon chopped parsley
pepper

25g (1oz) fresh white breadcrumbs
25g (1oz) Parmesan cheese, finely grated
salt and pepper
2 x 150–175g (5–6oz) calves' or lambs' liver slices, 1–2cm (½–¾ inch) thick
flour, for dusting
1 egg, beaten
2 tablespoons olive oil

venison sausages with red wine onions and blackcurrants

All you need with this is a dollop of mash.

serves two

3 tablespoons vegetable oil
400g (14oz) venison
  sausages (about 6
  sausages)
3 red onions, sliced
1 tablespoon demerara
  sugar
2 tablespoons red wine
  vinegar
1 tablespoon crème de
  cassis (blackcurrant
  liqueur) (optional)
1 glass of red wine
200ml (7fl oz) beef stock
  (see page 13)
75g (3oz) blackcurrants
  (fresh or frozen)

Preheat the oven to 180°C/350°F/gas 4. Warm 2 tablespoons of the oil in a braising pan and, once hot, fry the sausages quickly to colour. Remove from the pan, add the remaining oil and sauté the onion until golden brown.

Stir in the demerara sugar and red wine vinegar and simmer until almost dry and becoming sticky. Pour in the cassis, if using, along with the red wine and beef stock.

Throw the sausages back in, bring to a simmer and cook in the oven for 20 to 25 minutes, adding the blackcurrants for the last 10 minutes of cooking.

Simple midweek suppers/

Cooking for four

Coconut rice and peas with butternut squash

Watercress, leek and potato soup

Prawns, pancetta, pasta

Pasta carbonara

Pasta with spinach and melting brie

Linguine and pesto frittata with asparagus, spinach, peas

Parmesan risotto

Macaroni and cauliflower with four cheeses

Pasta with a wild mushroom cream sauce

Garlic prawns with lobster noodles

Salmon with French beans

Calamari with hot ratatouille

Steamed salmon with grilled vegetables

Lemon brioche turbot with a hint of horseradish

Pan-fried brill with red wine cockles

Cod with peas and ham stewed in butter

John Dory with red pepper, tomato and basil spaghetti

Roast chicken breasts with almond cream noodles

Sticky pork chops with sesame spinach

Pork chops with an apple tart topping

Lamb cutlets with crispy sage and capers

Burnt lamb chops with sweet peppers and onions

Fillet of beef with goulash noodles

Roast rabbit legs with sweetcorn and peas

coconut rice and peas with butternut squash

Basmati rice is normally used in this recipe, but here it's being made with arborio, leaving a looser and more risotto-like consistency, which suits a vegetarian main course a lot better.

Melt one knob of the butter in a large pan. Add the onion and squash and gently fry for a few minutes. Pour in 600ml (1 pint) of the stock, bring to a simmer and cook for 10 minutes before adding the rice, kidney beans, including the juice, and the coconut milk.

Stir and allow to cook gently for 15 to 20 minutes until the rice is tender. During the cooking time, a little extra stock may need to be added. The finished consistency should match that of a risotto.

Add the peas and remaining knob of butter. Season with salt and pepper. The butternut rice and peas is ready to serve.

serves four–six

2 large knobs of butter
1 large onion, finely
  chopped
1 butternut squash, roughly
  chopped
1–1.1 litres (1½–2 pints)
  vegetable stock
  (see page 13)
350g (12oz) arborio rice
410g (14½oz) tin of red
  kidney beans
400ml (14fl oz) tin of
  coconut milk
175g (6oz) frozen peas,
  defrosted
salt and pepper

watercress, leek and potato soup

This recipe provides you with four generous portions of hearty, supper soup or six or more large ladlefuls if there's another dish to follow. The soup can be left rustic and chunky or whizzed until smooth.

serves four–six

1 onion, halved and thinly sliced
2 medium potatoes, roughly chopped
2 tablespoons vegetable oil
a large knob of butter
900ml (1½ pints) vegetable stock (see page 13)
1 large or 2 medium leeks, thinly sliced
2 bunches of watercress, main stalks removed
salt and pepper

In a pan, gently cook the onion and potato in the oil and butter for 6 to 8 minutes without colouring. Add the stock, bring to the boil and simmer for 10 to 15 minutes until the potato is tender.

Drop in the leek, return to the boil and, after 5 minutes, chop the watercress and add it to the pan.

Simmer for a few minutes and season with salt and pepper. The soup is now ready to serve in a rustic style or whizzed in a blender until smooth.

more

- Accompany with some horseradish crème fraîche, made from a tablespoon of horseradish cream mixed with 3 tablespoons crème fraîche.

prawns, pancetta, pasta

serves four

400g (14oz) dried penne,
  spiralli or spaghetti
225g (8oz) pancetta cubes
2 cloves of garlic, chopped
25g (1oz) butter
350g (12oz) ready-to-eat
  peeled prawns
extra-virgin olive oil
sea salt and pepper
1 heaped tablespoon
  roughly chopped parsley

Cook the pasta in boiling salted water until tender, then drain.

Meanwhile, heat a large deep frying pan or wok. Once hot, fry the pancetta for a few minutes until golden. Add the garlic and butter, stirring for a further minute over a medium heat.

Scatter in the prawns and a trickle of olive oil and stir for a further minute or two before adding the cooked pasta. Toss all together well, seasoning with just a pinch of salt and a good twist of pepper. Sprinkle with the parsley and serve.

more

One or two extras can be added:

- a few dollops of crème fraîche stirred in for a creamy touch
- shavings or grated Parmesan cheese
- a large wedge of lemon on the side

pasta carbonara

serves four

olive oil
2 packets of sliced Parma
  ham, cut into 2cm (¾ inch)
  squares
150ml (5fl oz) double cream
4 egg yolks
salt and pepper
400–500g (14–18oz) dried
  pasta
a squeeze of lemon
75g (3oz) Parmesan
  cheese

Heat some olive oil in a large saucepan. Add the Parma ham and fry over a medium heat for a few minutes until the ham becomes crispy.

Mix together the cream and egg yolks and season with salt and pepper.

Meanwhile, cook the pasta until tender. Drain, return it to the hot saucepan and stir in the lemon juice with the egg yolks and cream mixture. The heat from the pasta will partially cook the cream sauce.

Check the seasoning and stir in the Parmesan and the Parma ham.

pasta with spinach and melting brie

Melt the butter in a large deep frying pan. Once sizzling, add the spinach leaves and turn in the pan for a minute until wilted. Season with the salt, pepper and nutmeg. Add the crème fraîche.

While making the sauce, cook the pasta until tender. Drain and add to the finished sauce before checking the seasoning.

Preheat the grill. Place the pasta in a large ovenproof dish and lay the Brie slices over the top. Place under the grill and warm the Brie until it melts into the pasta. Finish with a drizzle of olive oil and a twist of pepper.

serves four

a knob of butter
175g (6oz) washed and
 ready-to-eat baby spinach
salt and pepper
a pinch of freshly grated
 nutmeg
200ml (7fl oz) crème fraîche
400–500g (14–18oz) dried
 pasta
225g (8oz) Brie, very thinly
 sliced into lengths
olive oil

linguine and pesto frittata with asparagus, spinach, peas

serves four–six

225g (8oz) linguine,
  spaghetti or tagliatelle
olive oil, for cooking and
  drizzling
1 onion, sliced
1 bunch of asparagus
  (about 12 spears)
100g (4oz) washed and
  ready-to-eat baby spinach
  leaves
100g (4oz) frozen peas,
  defrosted
150ml (5fl oz) double cream
6 large eggs, beaten
2 heaped tablespoons
  pesto
4 heaped tablespoons
  freshly grated Parmesan
  cheese (optional)
salt and pepper

Preheat the oven to 190°C/375°F/gas 5. Cook the linguine in boiling salted water until tender. Meanwhile, heat an ovenproof frying pan with a tablespoon or two of olive oil. Gently fry the onion for 6 to 7 minutes until beginning to soften.

Cut the asparagus into 5cm (2 inch) pieces, discarding the woody base of each spear, and cook in boiling salted water for 2 to 3 minutes until tender. Drain, tipping them into a large bowl and mixing with the spinach and peas.

Pour over the cream and eggs and stir in the pesto, onion and drained linguine. Mix together well, adding the Parmesan, if using, and seasoning with salt and pepper.

Rewarm the frying pan with 2 tablespoons of the olive oil and pour in the linguine mixture. Shake the pan to spread the pasta and vegetables evenly, frying over a medium heat for 2 to 3 minutes to set the base. The frittata can now be finished off in the oven for 20 to 25 minutes or until set. Drizzle olive oil over the top before serving.

more

- Slices or chopped mozzarella can be scattered over the top during the frittata's last few minutes in the oven, softening and melting before serving.

parmesan risotto

serves four

olive oil
100g (4oz) butter
1 onion, finely chopped
350g (12oz) risotto rice
about 1–1.2 litres (1¾–2
  pints) vegetable or chicken
  stock (see page 13)
50g (2oz) Parmesan
  cheese
salt and pepper

Heat the olive oil and half the butter in a large shallow pan or deep frying pan. Add the onion and lightly fry, without colouring, for 6 to 8 minutes until softened.

Add the rice and stir for a minute, allowing the rice to be coated with the oil and butter without colouring. Heat the stock in a small saucepan.

Add a couple of ladlefuls of the gently simmering stock to the rice, stirring gently. Once the stock has been absorbed, add a further ladleful, stirring and adding more as it becomes absorbed.

Continue this process for 18 to 20 minutes, at which point the rice should be soft and creamy, but still maintaining a bite.

Add the remaining butter and Parmesan and season with salt and pepper. Adding the Parmesan can thicken the risotto, so if it becomes too thick, loosen with a little more stock.

more

- You can add half a glass of white wine just before the first ladleful of stock to give an edge to the dish. Vermouth can also be used and red wine risotto has now become very popular, the wine replacing half or all of the stock.
- The Parmesan can be replaced with a variety of cheeses. Mozzarella works very nicely and makes it slightly gooey. Gorgonzola, Fontina, Pecorino, Swiss Gruyère or a soft goat's cheese would all add their own personality.

broad bean, asparagus or courgette risotto

Cook broad beans, asparagus tips or chopped courgettes until just tender and add at the end of the cooking time.

mushroom risotto

Button and chestnut mushrooms are best sliced and wild mushrooms chopped. Add once the onions have softened.

ham risotto

Stir in slivers of Parma ham or cooked ham at the end of the cooking time.

leek risotto

Cook sliced leeks in a pan with some butter, then remove and leave to cool while the risotto is cooking. Add the leeks during the final couple of minutes of making the risotto to let them warm through and flavour the rice.

herb and lemon risotto

Add a squeeze of lemon and chopped herbs, like parsley, tarragon, chives or chervil, at the end of the cooking time.

tomato or pepper risotto

Simply chop them up and pop them into the pan as you cook the onion.

pancetta risotto

Fry diced pancetta until crispy and sprinkle over the cooked risotto.

pesto risotto

Add a few spoonfuls from a jar or make your own by mashing together basil leaves, a touch of garlic, pine nuts, olive oil and lots of Parmesan, stirring through the risotto just before serving.

macaroni and cauliflower with four cheeses

serves four

1 cauliflower, divided into
  small florets
350g (12oz) macaroni
350g (12oz) mixture of 4
  grated cheeses
  (Roquefort, Dolcelatte,
  Comté, Red Leicester,
  Emmental, Cheddar,
  Pecorino, Gruyère, Brie,
  Edam, Lancashire)
300ml (10fl oz) single or
  whipping cream
salt and pepper

Cook the cauliflower and macaroni together in boiling salted water until tender.

Meanwhile, mix together half your chosen four-cheese mixture with the cream. Drain the macaroni and cauliflower well, stir into the cheese cream and season with salt and pepper.

Preheat the grill. Place the macaroni in an ovenproof dish and sprinkle with the remaining cheese. Brown under the grill until the cheese is melted and bubbling.

pasta with a wild mushroom cream sauce

serves four

a knob of butter
1 onion, finely chopped
1 glass of white wine
25g (1oz) dried porcini or
  mixed wild mushrooms,
  soaked in 300ml (10fl oz)
  warm water (see page 20)
150ml (5fl oz) double cream
salt and pepper
a squeeze of lemon
400–500g (14–18oz) dried
  pasta
olive oil, for drizzling

Melt the butter in a saucepan, add the onion and gently fry for a few minutes until it begins to soften. Pour in the wine and boil until almost dry.

Roughly chop the mushrooms. Add the mushroom water and the mushrooms to the saucepan and boil until just a quarter of the liquid is left. Stir in the cream and simmer to a loose consistency. Season with salt and pepper and sharpen the sauce with a squeeze of lemon

While making the sauce, cook the pasta until tender. Drain and add to the finished sauce. Drizzle each portion with olive oil.

garlic prawns with lobster noodles

Cook the noodles in boiling salted water until tender. Warm the lobster bisque, adding the splash of Cognac, if using. Drain the noodles and stir into the lobster bisque with the chives.

Meanwhile, heat the olive oil in a large frying pan. Once hot, add the garlic and prawns, cooking them for a couple of minutes on each side before adding the butter and lime juice. The prawns are now ready to serve, drizzling them with the flavoured butter, offering the noodles straight from the pan.

serves four

350g (12oz) dried noodles
410ml (14½fl oz) tin or jar
   of lobster bisque
a splash of Cognac
   (optional)
1 tablespoon chopped
   chives
1–2 tablespoons olive oil
1 clove of garlic, crushed
12–16 large raw tiger
   prawns, peeled and
   deveined (see page 16)
50g (2oz) butter
1 lime, juiced

salmon with french beans

Season the salmon with the sea salt and pepper.

Heat a frying pan over a medium heat with a splash of olive oil and a knob of the butter. Once sizzling, gently cook the fillets for 5 to 6 minutes to a light golden brown before turning them in the pan. Remove the pan from the heat and keep to one side.

Meanwhile, put another knob of the butter and splash of water in a wok or another frying pan. Over a fairly hot heat and when the butter and water are bubbling, add the beans, seasoning with a twist of pepper. Stir for a few minutes until just tender before adding the pine nuts.

Arrange the salmon and beans on four plates. Heat the lemon juice in the wok or frying pan and, once warm, whisk in the remaining butter. Sprinkle a pinch of sea salt over the salmon and beans, drizzling with the lemon-flavoured butter.

serves four

4 x 175g (6oz) salmon
   fillets, skinned and
   pinboned (see page 14)
sea salt and pepper
olive oil
75g (3oz) cold chopped
   butter
225g (8oz) French beans,
   topped and tailed and
   thinly sliced at a slight
   angle
2 tablespoons pine nuts,
   toasted (see page 13)
juice of 1 lemon

calamari with hot ratatouille

serves four

450g (1lb) cleaned baby squid
90ml (3½fl oz) olive oil
1 tablespoon red wine vinegar
sea salt and pepper
2 tomatoes, peeled, deseeded and cut into cubes (see page 20)
1 tablespoon finely chopped chives
1 green pepper, thinly sliced
1 red pepper, thinly sliced
1 large clove of garlic, crushed
1 small or ½ a medium aubergine, cut into small pieces
2 small–medium courgettes, thinly sliced

Cut the squid into rings and cut the tentacles into smaller pieces if they are large in size.

To make the dressing, whisk together 3 tablespoons of the olive oil and the red wine vinegar, seasoning with salt and pepper before stirring in the tomatoes and chives.

Heat 2 tablespoons of the olive oil in a wok or large frying pan. Once hot, add the peppers, garlic, aubergine and courgettes. Fry for a couple of minutes until the vegetables are just beginning to soften.

Push the vegetables to one side of the wok or frying pan and add the remaining olive oil to the empty side. Add the squid rings and tentacles and fry for 30 seconds before mixing with the ratatouille. Cook together for a further minute, season with salt and pepper and spoon over the dressing.

more

- This dish eats particularly well with a spinach salad.
- The simple wok-fried ratatouille can be made without the squid and stirred into cooked noodles, couscous or rice for a filling meal.

steamed salmon with grilled vegetables

I love this contrast of flavours: tender, steamed salmon with vibrant, smoky vegetables. By the way, the vegetables can be purely your choice.

serves four

2 teaspoons red wine vinegar
1 tablespoon orange juice
a pinch of sugar
2 tablespoons olive oil, plus extra for drizzling
coarse sea salt and pepper
8 asparagus spears
2 small–medium courgettes, cut in half lengthways
2 red peppers, quartered and deseeded
1 small aubergine, cut into quarters lengthways
1 red onion, cut into 4 thick circles
4 x 175g (6oz) salmon fillets, skinned and pinboned (see page 14)
a large knob of butter

Whisk the red wine vinegar, orange juice and sugar together. Add the olive oil and season with salt and pepper.

Snap the woody end from each asparagus spear and discard. Lightly toss the asparagus spears with all the other vegetables in a drizzle of olive oil. Preheat a ridged griddle pan and grill the vegetables for 3 to 5 minutes on each side until they have reached a deep, grill-marked brown and are tender. Put the vegetables into a large bowl, season with a pinch of sea salt and drizzle with the dressing.

While grilling the vegetables, smear the salmon with the butter and sprinkle a little sea salt on top. Place in a steamer and cook for 6 to 8 minutes over rapidly simmering water before serving with the grilled vegetables.

more

- A large spoonful of mayonnaise or thick crème fraîche on the side, perhaps mixed with chopped herbs, is very tasty.

lemon brioche turbot with a hint of horseradish

Crumble the brioche slices into breadcrumbs, mix with the lemon zest and season with salt and pepper.

Season the turbot fillets and brush the skinned side only with the beaten egg before dipping into the crumbs to coat.

Warm the olive oil and the knob of butter in a frying pan and, once bubbling, gently fry the turbot, crumbed-side down, for 4 to 5 minutes until golden brown. Turn the fillets and continue to fry for a further minute or two before plating the fish.

Meanwhile, bring 6 tablespoons water to a simmer. Whisk in the chopped butter to emulsify and then add the horseradish to taste. Season with salt and pepper and the lemon juice and drizzle round the fish.

serves four

5–6 slices of brioche loaf, crusts on
grated zest of 1 small lemon
salt and pepper
4 x 150g (5oz) turbot fillets, skinned and pinboned (see page 14)
1 egg, beaten
2 tablespoons olive oil
50g (2oz) chopped butter, plus an extra knob
1–2 teaspoons horseradish cream
a squeeze of lemon juice

more
- A teaspoon of chopped chives could be stirred into the sauce.

pan-fried brill with red wine cockles

The brill and cockles need little more to accompany them than perhaps the buttered leek greens on page 458.

serves four

1kg (2¼lb) cockles, well washed
2 tablespoons red wine vinegar
6 tablespoons olive oil
1 level teaspoon Dijon mustard (optional)
coarse sea salt and pepper
4 x 150–175g (5–6oz) brill fillets, skinned and pinboned (see page 14)
flour, for dusting
a knob of butter

Place the washed cockles in a large pan, cover with a lid and cook for a few minutes until the shells have opened. Drain in a colander, saving the juices. Remove the cockles from the shells and keep to one side.

In a bowl, whisk together the red wine vinegar, 4 tablespoons of the olive oil and the Dijon mustard, if using. Stir in 2 to 3 tablespoons of the cockle cooking liquid and season with a twist of pepper and a pinch of salt, if needed.

Heat a large frying pan with the remaining olive oil. Lightly flour the brill, season and shallow fry for a few minutes until golden brown. Add the knob of butter and turn over the fish, basting it with the butter for a further minute or two.

Arrange the brill on plates, stir the cockles into the red wine vinaigrette and spoon around the fillets.

cod with peas and ham stewed in butter

You'll notice frozen peas are listed in the ingredients to allow this recipe to be enjoyed throughout the year. However, between late spring and the early days of autumn, wonderful fresh peas will be in season.

serves four

4 x 175g (6oz) cod fillets,
  skin on and pinboned
  (see page 14)
salt and pepper
flour, for dusting
oil, vegetable or olive
50g (2oz) butter, plus a
  knob for frying
450g (1lb) frozen peas
175g (6oz) piece of ham,
  cut into cubes
4 wedges of lemon

Pat the cod dry with kitchen paper, season with salt and pepper and lightly dust the skin with flour.

Heat some oil in a non-stick frying pan, place the fillets in the pan, skin-side down, and fry for 6 to 7 minutes until golden and crispy. Turn the fish in the pan, adding the knob of butter and cooking for a further minute.

While frying the fish, cook the peas in boiling salted water until tender, then drain away the majority of the water, leaving around 100ml (3½fl oz). Add the ham, warming it through before seasoning with salt and pepper. Stir in the remaining butter.

The crispy cod and peas are now ready to serve with a wedge of lemon.

more
- A little pinch of a chicken stock cube or an extra knob of butter can be stirred into the peas to enrich their flavour.
- Mashed potatoes mixed with buttery spring onions make the perfect accompaniment.

john dory with red pepper, tomato and basil spaghetti

I quite often enjoy this spaghetti as a supper on its own, but the sweet flavour is enhanced by the grilled fish, which adds a bitter edge.

Preheat the grill. Put the tomato quarters on to a baking tray, drizzling with olive oil and seasoning with salt and pepper. Place under the grill and cook for several minutes until softened and just beginning to colour. Once tender, spoon them into a blender and add the garlic, tomato juice and vinegar. Blitz until smooth before slowly pouring in the olive oil and mixing together.

Cook the spaghetti until tender. While cooking the pasta, warm 2 tablespoons of the olive oil in a large deep frying pan or braising pan. Once hot, add the peppers and red onion, frying until coloured and tender. Drain the pasta and mix it in well with the tomato dressing, peppers, red onion and basil.

Meanwhile, season the John Dory fillets with salt and pepper and lay on a greased baking tray, skin-side up, brushing with butter. Cook under the hot grill for 4 to 5 minutes until the skin colours and the fish is firmer but still tender to the touch. The John Dory and spaghetti are now ready to be served together.

serves four

4 tomatoes, quartered
100ml (3½fl oz) olive oil, plus extra for cooking
salt and pepper
1 clove of garlic, crushed
3 tablespoons tomato juice
1 tablespoon red wine vinegar
350g (12oz) spaghetti
2 large red peppers, cut into cubes
1 large red onion, chopped
8 basil leaves, chopped
4 x 150–175g (5–6oz) John Dory, fillets, skin on and pinboned (see page 14)
melted butter, for brushing

more

- The tomato dressing can be strained through a sieve for a smoother finish and Parmesan finely grated over the spaghetti.
- Mackeral, sea bass or tuna fillets also eat well with the spaghetti.

roast chicken breasts with almond cream noodles

serves four

4 chicken breasts, skin on
sea salt and pepper
olive oil
a knob of butter
400g (14oz) tagliatelle

for the sauce
50g (2oz) flaked almonds
2 shallots, finely chopped
1 glass of white wine
300ml (10fl oz) chicken
  stock (see page 13)
200ml (7fl oz) double cream

Preheat the oven to 180°C/350°F/gas 4.

To make the sauce, scatter the almonds on to a baking tray and toast in the oven until golden.

Boil together the shallots and white wine, reducing in volume until just a quarter of the liquid is left. Add the stock, stir in the cream and almonds (a few can be kept to sprinkle on top), then simmer for 5 to 10 minutes until slightly thickened. Remove from the heat and leave to cool for 10 minutes before liquidizing in a blender until smooth. To remove any slight grain caused by the almonds, strain through a fine sieve.

Meanwhile, season the chicken with sea salt and pepper. Heat a roasting tray with a splash or two of olive oil and fry the chicken, skin-side down for 5 to 7 minutes to a rich golden brown. Turn the breasts, add the butter and, once melted, baste the chicken and roast in the oven for 8 to 10 minutes until firm to the touch.

Once cooked, baste the chicken over and over with the butter and any juices to enrich its flavour.

Meanwhile, cook the tagliatelle until tender, then drain and stir in the almond cream sauce before serving with the chicken.

sticky pork chops with sesame spinach

Preheat the grill. Arrange the pork chops on the rack of a grill tray, seasoning with salt and pepper. Mix together well the redcurrant jelly, marmalade and Dijon mustard and spoon half the mixture over the chops. Cook the chops under the grill for 4 to 5 minutes before turning and covering with the remaining mixture. Grill for a further 4 to 5 minutes.

While grilling the pork, heat a large saucepan or wok and add the washed and well-drained spinach, stirring around the pan for a few minutes until wilted and tender. Add the butter and sesame seeds and mix with the spinach.

Arrange the sticky pork chops and spinach together on plates and serve.

serves four

4 pork chops
salt and pepper
2 tablespoons redcurrant
   jelly
2 tablespoons marmalade
1 tablespoon Dijon mustard
1kg (2¼lb) spinach, main
   stalks removed
a knob of butter
1 heaped tablespoon
   sesame seeds, toasted
   (see page 13)

pork chops with an apple tart topping

There is no pastry included here; the topping is made up purely of a chunky apple sauce and sliced apples arranged like an apple tart. The apple sauce recipe is given below, but using a quality bought product would make this recipe one of the easiest in the book.

serves four

7–8 Cox's apples
25g (1oz) caster sugar
juice of ½ lemon
4 pork chops
25g (1oz) butter, half of it
  melted
salt and pepper

Peel, core and roughly chop four of the apples and put into a saucepan. Add half the caster sugar, the lemon juice and 3 tablespoons water, cover with a lid and cook over a medium to low heat for 10–15 minutes until tender, stirring from time to time. The topping can be left very chunky or lightly whisked until smoother. Cover and keep warm.

Preheat the grill. Brush the pork chops with a little of the firm half of the butter and season with salt and pepper. Put the chops on a grill tray with a rack, place under the grill and cook for 4–5 minutes on each side.

While grilling the chops, peel, quarter and core the remaining apples. Cut into long thin slices, maintaining the shape of the apple. Spread the apple sauce over the chops and arrange the apple slices on top, slightly overlapping as you would for an apple tart. Brush or drizzle the chops with the melted butter, sprinkle over the remaining sugar and return to the grill. Cook for a few minutes until the apples are nicely toasted with a slightly burnt tinge around the edges.

more

- The lemon juice can be replaced with 1–2 tablespoons Calvados.
- The runner beans with chunky seasoning on page 453 eat very well with this dish.

lamb cutlets with crispy sage and capers

Lamb cutlets can be a little fatty and it is best to trim off a bit of the excess fat if you find this to be the case.

serves four

oil
1 bunch of sage leaves
salt and pepper
12 lamb cutlets
25–50g (1–2oz) softened
  butter
75ml (3fl oz) olive oil
1 tablespoon lemon juice
2 tablespoons capers

Heat a frying pan with 1cm (½ inch) oil and, once hot, fry the sage leaves, dropping in a small handful at a time. When the leaves are cooked and crispy, they will almost stop sizzling and become quite calm in the pan. Lift out and drain on kitchen paper, seasoning with a pinch of salt.

Preheat the grill. Place the lamb cutlets on a grill tray with a rack, brush with half the butter and season with salt and pepper. Cook under the grill for 3 to 5 minutes on each side, brushing with the remaining butter once turned.

Whisk together the olive oil, lemon juice and capers with a good twist of pepper. Arrange the cutlets on plates and pour any butter and juices from the grill tray into the caper dressing. Spoon the dressing over the lamb and sprinkle the crispy sage on top.

more
- A few tablespoons of chopped tomatoes can be added to the caper dressing for a sweeter touch.
- The lamb cutlets are wonderful with sweet fresh or frozen peas.

burnt lamb chops with sweet peppers and onions

Halve the peppers, cutting away the stalk and removing the seeds, and cut into strips. Meanwhile, heat a frying pan with the olive oil. Fry the onion over a medium heat until beginning to soften and colour. Season with salt and pepper and sprinkle over the sugar. Increase the heat and continue frying until the sugar begins to caramelize and the onion is a rich golden brown. Stir in the peppers.

Whisk the mint jelly and mint into the crème fraîche. Season with salt and pepper.

Heat another frying pan and, once very hot, season the chops with salt and pepper. Stand the chops upright on their fat-covered edge in the pan. As they heat up, some of the fat will melt, leaving a crispy burnt, bitter edge. Once well coloured, lay the chops in the pan and continue to cook over a high heat for a few minutes on each side, again to create a burnt edge.

Arrange the chops with the warm peppers and onion, offering the mint crème fraîche separately.

serves four

2 large red peppers, peeled (see page 20)
2 tablespoons olive oil
2 large onions, sliced
salt and pepper
2 teaspoons caster sugar
2 heaped teaspoons mint jelly
1 tablespoon chopped mint leaves
150ml (5fl oz) crème fraîche
8 lamb chops

more
- A simple green salad is all this dish needs to accompany it.

fillet of beef with goulash noodles

serves four

olive oil
1 large onion, finely
   chopped
2 cloves of garlic, crushed
1 large red pepper, cut into
   small cubes
1 teaspoon paprika
300ml (10fl oz) passata
3 tomatoes, peeled,
   deseeded and cut into
   cubes (see page 20)
salt and pepper
350g (12oz) linguine or
   tagliatelle
2 knobs of butter
4 x 150–175g (5–6oz) beef
   fillet steaks
2 teaspoons chopped
   chives
4 tablespoons sour cream

Heat a saucepan with some olive oil. Add the onion, garlic, pepper and paprika and stir over a medium heat for 6 to 7 minutes until they begin to soften. Pour the passata over the onions and bring to a gentle simmer. Allow the sauce to murmur softly for 10 to 15 minutes, adding the tomato during the final few minutes. Season with salt and pepper. Should the sauce become too thick, loosen with a few tablespoons of water.

Cook the noodles until tender, then drain, adding a drizzle of olive oil, a knob of butter and seasoning with salt and pepper.

Meanwhile, season the steaks with salt and pepper. Heat a frying pan with a bit more olive oil and cook the steaks over a high heat for 3 to 4 minutes on each side for rare to medium rare. Add the remaining butter and, once sizzling, baste the steaks before removing from the pan. Leave to rest for 1 to 2 minutes before serving.

The noodles can be left plain with the sauce spooned on top or stirred into the sauce before serving with the steaks. Mix the chives into the sour cream and drop a spoonful on top of the noodles.

roast rabbit legs with sweetcorn and peas

Preheat the oven to 190°C/375°F/gas 5.

Season the rabbit legs with salt and pepper.

Heat a frying pan with a tablespoon of the oil, lightly flour the rabbit legs and fry until golden brown.

Drizzle a roasting tray with the remaining vegetable oil. Add the onion slices, season and place a rabbit leg on top of each. Brush the legs with one of the knobs of butter, cover with foil and roast for 35 to 40 minutes. Remove the foil for the last 10 minutes and baste the legs with the juices in the tray.

Whisk together the sherry vinegar, maple syrup and walnut oil and season with salt and pepper.

Melt the remaining knob of butter in a frying pan, add the shallots and cook, without colouring, for a few minutes before adding the sweetcorn and peas. Once warm, stir in the sherry vinegar dressing.

Arrange the rabbit legs and onion slices on plates and spoon over the sweetcorn and peas.

serves four

4 large rabbit legs
salt and pepper
3 tablespoons vegetable oil
flour, for dusting
1 large onion, peeled and
  cut into 4 round slices
2 large knobs of butter
2 tablespoons sherry
  vinegar
1 tablespoon maple syrup
4 tablespoons walnut oil
2 shallots, finely chopped
1x400g tin of sweetcorn,
drained and rinsed
100g (4oz) frozen peas or
  petits pois, defrosted

more
- A heaped teaspoon of chopped parsley and tarragon can be added to the dressing.

Weekend eating/

This is the largest section of the book and it's where food takes its rightful place – at the dinner table with family and friends. Weekends should be about putting your feet up, but for me there's nothing more relaxing than enjoying good company over great food. This doesn't mean you have to be locked in the kitchen. Easy, pleasurable cooking is the aim here and simplicity and freshness are the keys that unlock this.

I've started the chapter with quick Saturday lunches and ended with light weekend suppers. Cooking and eating have a rhythm to them and if your weekend includes a roast and a Saturday-night dinner, you'll probably be craving lighter but savoury and tasty foods for your other meals, like butterflied prawns with sweet and sour papaya or a warm lentil, orange and watercress salad with grilled mackerel.

Saturday night entertaining includes more than a few showstoppers. Having friends round for dinner often demands a little extra effort but certainly doesn't mean you have to spend all day in the kitchen.

Virtually any of the dishes in this whole chapter can be served at any time of the weekend (or week!) - the beauty of this section shows off recipes to be enjoyed at any occasion, whether having friends round on a Saturday night, or family for Sunday lunch. So I've given you suggested times for when to cook, but don't feel beholden to these. Remember, cooking offers freedom and eating so often depends on your mood.

Weekend eating/

Saturday lunch

Irish stew broth

A bowl of cauliflower and Camembert

Three-mustard honey potato salad

Beetroot carpaccio with redcurrant walnut dressing

Sesame wild mushroom salad

Quick marinated aubergine and sweet pepper salad

Halloumi sticks with pear rings and mixed cress leaves

Leek, ham and Brie slice

Fennel with oysters and Parmesan shavings

Beef tomatoes and mozzarella with pine nuts and pesto crème fraîche

Pasta niçoise

Pizza tomato tart

Flat mushroom pastry with a watercress and cherry tomato salad

Butterflied prawns with sweet and sour papaya

Seared tuna with pissaladière toasts

Broken salmon with artichokes and asparagus

Grilled sardines with sweet potato and mango salsa

Pork steaks with lemon, honey and mustard apples

irish stew soup

Put the lamb, stock, onion and bouquet garni into a large saucepan. Bring to a simmer, cover partially with a lid and cook for 1¼ hours, skimming from time to time.

Add the potatoes and carrots to the pot and continue to simmer for 20 minutes. Add the cabbage and simmer for 10 minutes. Remove the bouquet garni, season with salt and pepper and scatter over the parsley.

The soup can now be ladled into bowls to serve.

serves four–six

450g (1lb) diced lean lamb
1 litre (1¾ pints) chicken
  stock (see page 13)
2 onions, sliced
1 bouquet garni
2 large potatoes, peeled
  and cut into chunks
2 carrots, peeled and sliced
½ small green cabbage,
  finely shredded
salt and pepper
1 heaped tablespoon
  coarsely chopped parsley

a bowl of cauliflower and camembert

Chunks of crusty bread for dunking in the soup and picking up melting Camembert complete this dish.

serves four

1 large cauliflower or 2
  small–medium, trimmed
  and divided into florets
½ vegetable stock cube
  (see page 13)
1 teaspoon Dijon mustard
500ml (18fl oz) milk
salt and pepper
100–150ml (3½–5fl oz)
  single cream (optional)
225g (8oz) Camembert,
  broken into pieces
olive oil
freshly grated nutmeg
  (optional)

Put the cauliflower florets, the stock cube, mustard and milk in a saucepan with the same amount of water. Simmer for 20 minutes until the cauliflower is tender.

Season with salt and pepper, saving a few of the cauliflower florets for garnish. Liquidize the soup in a blender until smooth.

Rewarm the soup with the cream, if using, and divide among the bowls. Finish with chunks of Camembert, the warm cauliflower florets, a drizzle of olive oil and a sprinkling of nutmeg, if using.

more
- Brie or a soft Gorgonzola are tasty alternatives to Camembert.

three-mustard honey potato salad

This salad can be taken on to another stage by binding with a few salad, watercress or fresh herb leaves and a sprinkling of shredded spring onion. If you happen to have smoked salmon, prawns or ham, all are perfect accompaniments, or even just a warm poached egg or two.

serves four

900g (2lb) new potatoes
sea salt and pepper
1 tablespoon clear honey
1 tablespoon white wine or
  red wine vinegar
1 tablespoon wholegrain
  mustard
1 teaspoon Dijon mustard
½ teaspoon English
  mustard
4 tablespoons olive oil

Cook the potatoes in boiling salted water for 20 to 25 minutes until tender. Drain and, while still warm, halve. Season with salt and pepper.

Meanwhile, in a bowl whisk together the honey, vinegar and mustards followed by the oil. Season with salt and pepper.

Add the warm potatoes, mixing together well to coat each potato.

more
- For a creamier finish, add a drizzling of crème fraîche or sour cream.

beetroot carpaccio with redcurrant walnut dressing

This recipe I've kept very simple by using precooked beetroots. Goat's cheese and walnuts could be added to the salad leaves, perhaps along with chopped chives.

Slice the beetroots thinly on a mandolin and arrange on plates, slightly overlapping them to cover the plates. Season with salt and pepper.

Microwave or gently warm together the redcurrant jelly and vinegar for 30 to 60 seconds. Once the jelly has melted whisk in the mustard followed by the oil. Season with salt and pepper.

Drizzle the dressing over the beetroot and arrange a small pile of salad leaves in the centre of each plate.

serves four

6 medium/large cooked and
  peeled beetroots
sea salt and pepper
a handful or two of rocket
  and watercress or mixed
  salad leaves

for the dressing
1 tablespoon redcurrant
  jelly
2 tablespoons red wine
  vinegar (preferably
  Cabernet Sauvignon)
1 level teaspoon Dijon
  mustard
4 tablespoons walnut or
  hazelnut oil
salt and pepper

sesame wild mushroom salad

Wild mushrooms are in season during the autumn and winter months, with one or two varieties showing their face during the spring and summer. Chestnut mushrooms would also be a good addition to this salad, adding another nutty flavour.

serves four

for the vinaigrette
1 tablespoon sesame oil
1 tablespoon groundnut oil
2 teaspoons sherry vinegar
1 tablespoon honey
salt and pepper

2 teaspoons sesame seeds,
  toasted (see page 13)
350g (12oz) mixed or one
  variety of wild mushrooms,
  rinsed and torn into bite-
  sized pieces
2 tablespoons sesame oil
sea salt and pepper
100g (4oz) watercress,
  main stalks removed
200g (8oz) washed and
  ready-to-eat baby spinach
  leaves

Whisk together the vinaigrette ingredients and season with salt and pepper.

Heat a frying pan and, once very hot, scatter in the mushrooms and sesame oil and season with salt and pepper. Stir for a minute or two, leaving a slight bite in the mushrooms.

Toss together the washed and well-drained watercress and the spinach in a bowl. Add the sesame seeds to the mushrooms and spoon over the leaves with the vinaigrette. Stir until the leaves begin to wilt before sharing the salad among plates or bowls.

more
- Cubes of Fontina or goat's cheese can be added to the mushrooms once fried and the cheese allowed to slightly soften.
- A splash of soy or Worcestershire sauce can be added to the vinaigrette for a tangy taste.

quick marinated aubergine and sweet pepper salad

This salad has scope for many additions. Chunks of feta, mozzarella slices, Parmesan shavings, basil leaves or chives would all be welcome.

To make the marinade, whisk together in a bowl the vinegar, honey and 100ml (3½fl oz) water.

Roll the aubergine slices in a tablespoon of oil and fry or grill for a few minutes on each side until tender. Season with salt and pepper and drop the slices into the marinade.

Cook the peppers in the same manner and also place in the marinade. Season again with salt and pepper and leave to cool until just warm.

Once warm, drain the marinade and whisk it with the remaining 2 tablespoons of olive oil. Place the aubergine and pepper on a plate and drizzle over the dressing.

serves two–four

3 tablespoons white wine vinegar
1 heaped teaspoon honey
2 aubergines cut into 5–10mm (¼–½ inch) slices
2 tablespoons olive oil
sea salt and pepper
2 large red peppers, cut into thick strips

halloumi sticks with pear rings and mixed cress leaves

serves four

1 tablespoon maple syrup, golden syrup or honey
1 tablespoon sherry vinegar
2 teaspoons wholegrain mustard
4 tablespoons olive oil
salt and pepper
2 Comice pears
2–3 handfuls of mixed watercress and mustard cress
1–2 tablespoons chopped walnuts or hazelnuts (optional)
225g (8oz) halloumi, cut into 16–20 square chunks

Whisk together the maple syrup, sherry vinegar, mustard and olive oil and season with salt and pepper.

Core the pears and slice thinly, preferably using a mandolin, into rings. Mix the rings with the cress and nuts, if using, and bind together with 2 to 3 tablespoons of the dressing.

Heat a large frying pan and dry fry the halloumi chunks until well coloured and beginning to soften. Add 3 tablespoons of dressing to the pan and roll the halloumi around as the dressing boils and reduces. Press a cocktail stick into each of the chunks and serve with the salad.

more

- The halloumi could be replaced with feta cheese, left natural in the salad.

leek, ham and brie slice

There are many soft-rind cheeses that can be used in place of the Brie. Try a Camembert or Coulommiers, a Sharpam from Devon or the Irish Cooleney.

serves four

a large knob of butter
3 leeks, sliced
salt and pepper
1x375g (13oz) sheet ready-
   rolled puff pastry
175g (6oz) piece of ham,
   cut into cubes
300–350g (10–12oz) Brie,
   cut into thin wedges
1 egg yolk
a splash of milk
olive oil, for brushing and
   drizzling

Melt the butter in a large saucepan and, once sizzling, add the leeks and cook over a medium heat, without colouring, until they start to soften. Season with salt and pepper, then drain and leave to cool.

Preheat the oven to 200°C/400°F/gas 6. Lightly brush a baking tray with oil, unroll the puff pastry and place on top. Using a fork, prick the base several times, leaving a clear 1cm (½ inch) border around the outside.

Add the ham to the leeks and spoon evenly across the pastry within the border. Arrange the Brie wedges across the top. Mix the egg yolk and milk together and brush around the border.

Bake for 20 to 25 minutes until the pastry is golden. Leave to cool slightly before drizzling with a little olive oil. Cut into slices to serve.

fennel with oysters and parmesan shavings

The oysters featured here are simply oyster mushrooms.

serves four

2 large fennel bulbs,
   trimmed and cored
2 tablespoons sherry
   vinegar
4 tablespoons olive oil
salt and pepper
225g (8oz) oyster
   mushrooms, torn into
   strips
Parmesan cheese

Slice the fennel as thinly as possible, preferably using a mandolin, and place in a large bowl before sprinkling with the vinegar and 3 tablespoons of the olive oil. Season with salt and pepper.

Heat a frying pan with the remaining olive oil. Once smoking, add the mushrooms, season and quickly toss just once or twice in the pan before spooning over the fennel.

Divide between plates or bowls and shave over the Parmesan using a vegetable peeler.

beef tomatoes and mozzarella with pine nuts and pesto crème fraîche

serves four

3 beef tomatoes, sliced
3 buffalo mozzarella, sliced
sea salt and pepper
2 tablespoons pine nuts,
  toasted (see page 13)
100ml (3½fl oz) crème
  fraîche
50g (2oz) pesto
a handful of basil leaves
olive oil

Arrange the sliced tomatoes and mozzarella on a large platter, season with salt and a twist of black pepper and sprinkle over the toasted pine nuts.

Whisk together the crème fraîche and pesto, then liberally drizzle it over the salad. Scatter the basil leaves and a few drops of olive oil over the top and the salad is ready to serve.

pasta niçoise

serves four

50g (2oz) fine French beans
200g (7oz) tin of tuna in oil,
  drained and flaked
225g (8oz) cherry tomatoes,
  quartered
10 black olives, stoned and
  quartered
4 spring onions, sliced
8 tablespoons olive oil
2 tablespoons tarragon
  vinegar
2 teaspoons Dijon mustard
1 clove of garlic, crushed
1 heaped teaspoon
  chopped tarragon
salt and pepper
400–500g (14–18oz) dried
  pasta

Cook the beans in a pan of boiling salted water for a few minutes until tender but still with a slight bite. Drain and place under cold running water. Cut the beans into 2cm (¾ inch) sticks.

In a large bowl, mix together the beans, tuna flakes, cherry tomatoes, black olives and spring onions.

Put the oil, vinegar, mustard, garlic, tarragon and some salt and pepper into a screw-top jar and give it a good shake.

While making the dressing, cook the pasta until tender. Drain and add to the tuna. Pour over the dressing and stir together before serving.

pizza tomato tart

Lightly oil a large baking tray. Place the pastry on the tray before cutting into a rough 30cm (12 inch) disc, discarding the trimmings. Using a fork, prick the pastry all over and refrigerate for 20 minutes.

Preheat the oven to 230°C/450°F/gas 8. Heat a tablespoon of the oil in a frying pan and fry the onion and garlic together for a few minutes until they begin to colour and soften. Season with salt and pepper, remove from the pan and leave to cool.

Sprinkle the onions over the pastry and place the tomatoes on top, flat-side up. Scatter over the olives and season with the sea salt and a twist of pepper. Bake the tart in the oven for 20 to 25 minutes until the pastry is crispy and the tomatoes softened with a golden brown tinge.

Brush the pastry border with a little of the olive oil, mixing the remaining with the balsamic vinegar, seasoning with salt and pepper. The dressing is now ready to be drizzled over the tart before serving.

serves two–four

3 tablespoons olive oil
225g (8oz) ready-rolled puff pastry, frozen or fresh
2 onions, sliced
1 small clove of garlic, crushed
sea salt and pepper
8–10 plum tomatoes, halved lengthways
6–8 pitted black olives, halved
1 teaspoon balsamic vinegar

more

- Grated mozzarella and/or Parmesan can be sprinkled over the tart during the final 5 minutes of baking.
- Torn basil leaves can also be scattered over the cooked tart.

flat mushroom pastry with a watercress and cherry tomato salad

serves four

1x375g (13oz) sheet
  ready-rolled puff pastry
flour, for dusting
600g (1lb 6oz) large button
  mushrooms
salt and pepper
3 tablespoons olive oil, plus
  extra for drizzling
4 knobs of butter, plus extra
  for greasing
1 tablespoon red wine
  vinegar
a squeeze of lemon juice
a pinch of sugar
1 large red onion, thinly
  sliced
1 bunch of watercress
10–12 cherry tomatoes,
  halved

Preheat the oven to 230°C/450°F/gas 8. Unroll the pastry, lightly dust the surface with flour and roll a touch thinner (approximately 2mm/⅛ inch). Cut out four 15cm (6 inch) discs, place on a lightly greased baking tray and refrigerate to firm.

Leaving the stalks on, slice the mushrooms 5mm (¼ inch) thick and season with salt and pepper. Arrange the large slices towards the edge of the pastry discs, scattering a few round mushroom ends in the centre to create a platform for the next layer. Repeat this a centimetre closer to the centre until reaching a pyramid point. Drizzle with a few drops of olive oil and top each with a knob of butter. Bake for 25 to 30 minutes until the mushrooms are flat and the pastry crispy.

Meanwhile, pour the remaining olive oil, red wine vinegar and lemon juice into a screw-top jar. Season with salt, pepper and the sugar and shake vigorously before using.

Mix together the red onion, watercress and cherry tomatoes with a few shakes of the dressing and serve the salad with the pastries.

butterflied prawns with sweet and sour papaya

serves four

16 raw tiger or king prawns,
  peeled, deveined and
  butterflied
  (see pages 16–17)
melted butter, for brushing
sea salt and pepper
50g (2oz) fresh red chillies,
  deseeded and roughly
  chopped
1 teaspoon caster sugar
1–2 tablespoons white wine
  vinegar
1 clove of garlic, finely
  crushed
1 tablespoon Thai fish
  sauce
3 tablespoons clear honey
juice of 1 lime
2 ripe papayas, peeled and
  cut into cubes

Butter a baking tray, then lay the prawns on their sides on top. Brush each with butter and sprinkle with a little salt and pepper.

Place the chillies in a food processor with all the remaining ingredients except the papaya and blend until puréed and smooth.

Preheat the grill. Cook the prawns for 2½ minutes until warm and tender.

While grilling the prawns, stir the sauce into the papaya, then divide the fruit between plates or bowls. The prawns can now be placed on top of the papaya to serve.

more

- Some chopped coriander leaves can be mixed in with the papaya.

seared tuna with pissaladière toasts

Pissaladière is an open, pizza-type onion tart from the south of France, flavoured with anchovies and black olives. The bread dough base is replaced here with simple toast.

Heat 2 tablespoons of olive oil and the butter together in a large frying pan. Add the onion and garlic and fry over a medium heat until tender and golden brown. Stir in the anchovies and olives, seasoning with salt and pepper.

Toast the sliced bread. Heat some more olive oil in a non-stick frying pan. Pat the tuna dry with kitchen paper, season with salt and pepper, then place the steaks in the pan and sear for 1 to 2 minutes on each side.

To serve, top each piece of toast with the pissaladière onions and a tuna steak.

serves four

olive oil
a knob of butter
4 large onions, thinly sliced
1 clove of garlic, finely chopped
8 anchovy fillets, chopped
8 pitted black olives, chopped
salt and pepper
4 thick slices of country loaf or ciabatta
4 x 150g (5oz) tuna steaks

more

- Mackerel is a good alternative fish to use in this dish.
- Fresh herbs can also be added to the onions, thyme working particularly well, while tomatoes, peppers and other 'pizza topping' ingredients can become part of the pissaladière.

broken salmon with artichokes and asparagus

Artichoke hearts packed in brine or oil are sold in jars and tins. They are also sold loose in delicatessens.

serves four

2 tablespoons lemon juice
½ teaspoon caster sugar
4 tablespoons extra-virgin olive oil, plus extra for brushing
salt and pepper
12 asparagus spears
6 artichoke hearts, quartered
a knob of butter
2 x 175g (6oz) salmon fillets, skinned and pinboned (see page 14)

Quickly mix together the lemon juice and caster sugar before whisking in the olive oil and seasoning with salt and pepper.

Snap away the woody end of each asparagus spear and discard.

Preheat a grill pan. Brush the spears with extra-virgin olive oil and grill for 5 to 6 minutes, turning them to colour on both sides. Season with salt and pepper, remove from the pan and cut each spear into two or three pieces.

The artichoke hearts can be served cold or you can quickly sauté then in olive oil to warm through.

Warm the butter in a frying pan and, once bubbling, season the salmon fillets and fry over a medium heat for 2 to 3 minutes, then turn over and fry for a further 1 to 2 minutes. Remove the salmon from the pan.

Scatter the artichoke hearts and asparagus on to plates with the salmon flesh, broken into chunks. Spoon over the lemon dressing and serve.

more

- The sweet lemon dressing on page 465 is a richer alternative to the one used above.

grilled sardines with sweet potato and mango salsa

When making a salsa, I prefer to chop the vegetables into 5–10mm (¼–½ inch) rough dice.

serves four

for the salsa
1 sweet potato, peeled and
  roughly chopped
1 mango, peeled and
  roughly chopped
½ small cucumber, peeled
  and roughly chopped
2 mild red chillies, very
  finely chopped
2 spring onions, thinly sliced
1 tablespoon chopped
  coriander leaves
3 tablespoons olive oil
juice of 1 large lime
salt and pepper

olive oil
sea salt and pepper
12 sardines, gutted and
  cleaned (see page 14)

Cook the sweet potato in boiling salted water for 3 to 4 minutes until tender, then drain. Spoon the sweet potato into a bowl and mix together with all the remaining chopped ingredients. Stir in the olive oil and lime juice and season with salt and pepper.

Preheat the grill. Lightly oil a baking tray and season with salt and pepper. Put the sardines on the tray, drizzle with olive oil and grill for a few minutes until golden brown on each side. Season with sea salt and a twist of pepper and arrange on plates with a spoonful of the sweet fiery salsa.

pork steaks with lemon, honey and mustard apples

Put the lemon zest, juice and honey into a saucepan with 2 tablespoons water and bring to a simmer. Add the apples and cook over a low to medium heat for 10 to 15 minutes until softened but still chunky. Stir in the mustard and keep warm.

Meanwhile, heat a grill pan. Once hot, season the pork steaks and stand them upright on their fat-covered edge in the pan. As they heat up, the fat is released and in 5 to 10 minutes you will have a crispy, golden brown edge. Once crispy, grill the steaks for a further 5 to 6 minutes on each side and serve with the apples.

serves four

grated zest and juice of ½ lemon
1 tablespoon honey
3 Bramley or 4 eating apples, peeled, cored and chopped
1 tablespoon wholegrain mustard
4 pork loin steaks
salt and pepper

more

- To accompany, why not offer the apple mascarpone salad on page 144?

Weekend eating/

Saturday night entertaining/

Starters
Mains
Puddings

Starters

Mushroom and goat's cheese tartlets

Savoury pear, stilton and chive cakes

Sautéed scallops with ginger spring greens and passion fruit hollandaise

Seared scallops and chilli-spiced cucumber

Lobster Caesar salad

Duck pancake rolls

Chicken livers with a sweet spinach and bacon salad

Sautéed snails, mushrooms and pasta with watercress sauce

Mains

Tiger prawns with leek and mozzarella risotto

Seared black bream with ginger, tomato and chilli pak choy

Pan-fried sea bass with bacon and caper cabbage

Toasted sea bass and oranges with basil yoghurt

Dover sole with a steak garnish

Monkfish with golden sultanas, onion and spinach

Roast monkfish 'Barnsley chops' with apple mint jelly and cider gravy

Roast monkfish in red wine with crème fraîche cabbage

Cod with new potatoes, baby spinach and cheddar cheese sauce

Chicken with porcini and chestnut mushrooms

Grilled chicken with carrot, celeriac and courgette cream

Baked chicken legs with Mediterranean vegetables

Roast duck with spinach and wild mushrooms

Braised lamb shanks with onions, tomatoes and pesto beans

Lamb 'osso buco'

Risotto Milanese

Braised pigs' cheeks with marmalade turnips

Seared calves' liver with caramelized grapes

Fillet of beef with red wine tomatoes

Cauliflower and mushroom curry

Puddings

Tiramisu bocker glory

Cracked summer berry meringue

Baked amaretti peaches

Mango cheesecake fool

Bailey's crème brûlée

Raspberry and white chocolate cream shortbreads

Chocolate brownie mousse

Liqueur-steeped summer fruits with lemon curd cream

Rice pudding with toasted honey plums

Toffee pie with grilled bananas

Apple jelly and cinnamon cream

Clotted cream panna cotta and strawberries

mushroom and goat's cheese tartlets

These have been kept very basic and simple, with just four main ingredients: the pastry, mushrooms, red onion and goat's cheese. Be warned – these appear to be very big starters, but they are an awful lot lighter than you think.

serves four

2 red onions, sliced
a knob of butter
sea salt and pepper
1 x 375g (13oz) sheet of
  ready-rolled puff pastry
4 flat mushrooms, stalks
  removed
4x1cm (½ inch) thick slices
  of goat's cheese loaf
1½ tablespoons sherry
  vinegar
2 tablespoons walnut oil
1 tablespoon groundnut oil
a handful or two of mixed
  salad leaves

Preheat the oven to 200°C/400°F/gas 6.

In a frying pan, quickly fry the onion in the butter until it softens, seasoning with salt and pepper.

Cut the pastry into four 11cm (4½ inch) squares.

Season the mushrooms with salt and pepper and place them cup-side up on the pastry squares. Spoon the onion on top and bake for 15 minutes before topping with the goat's cheese.

Season with a twist of pepper and a sprinkling of sea salt and continue to bake for a further 5 minutes until the cheese softens.

Meanwhile, whisk together the vinegar, walnut and groundnut oil and season with salt and pepper.

To serve, arrange a few salad leaves on top of each tartlet and sprinkle with the dressing.

savoury pear, stilton and chive cakes

These 'cakes' are simply a variation on Scotch pancakes and would also work well as a savoury dessert alternative or as a complete supper dish.

Sift the flour and salt into a bowl. Whisk in the eggs and milk to make a smooth batter, then stir in the chives.

Grease six 7–8cm (2½–3 inch) diameter rings (the kind used for frying eggs or making small tartlets) liberally with butter. Heat a non-stick frying pan with a trickle of oil and place the rings in the pan.

Divide half the batter among the rings and cook over a medium heat for 3 to 4 minutes until bubbles appear and the cakes begin to set. Lift the rings from the cakes, turn them over and cook for a further 2 to 3 minutes until a light golden brown. Keep warm while you cook the remaining batter.

Meanwhile, heat a second frying pan with a trickle of oil and the remaining butter. Once it begins to sizzle, add the pear and cook over a medium heat, turning from time to time, for 6 to 7 minutes until just tender.

Preheat the grill. Put the cakes on a baking tray, topping each one with a pear quarter and the Stilton. Grill the cakes, placing them not too close to the heat, just until the cheese softens and melts.

Arrange the cakes on six plates. Whisk together the walnut or olive oil, vinegar and honey. Season with salt and a twist of pepper and drizzle over the cakes. Scatter with a few salad leaves to garnish, if using.

serves six

225g (8oz) self-raising flour
½ teaspoon salt
2 eggs
200ml (7fl oz) milk
1 bunch of chives, finely
  chopped
25g (1oz) butter, plus extra
  for greasing
olive oil
3 pears, cored and
  quartered
225g (8oz) Stilton cheese,
  crumbled into chunks
chard, rocket or mixed
  leaves (optional)

for the dressing
4 tablespoons walnut or
  olive oil
2 tablespoons red wine
  vinegar
2 teaspoons honey
sea salt and pepper

sautéed scallops with ginger spring greens and passion fruit hollandaise

serves four

1 x quick hollandaise sauce
  (see page 464)
3 passion fruits (2 if large)
200g (7oz) spring greens,
  trimmed
2 teaspoons finely chopped
  or grated fresh ginger
2 large shallots, peeled and
  sliced
1 large knob of butter
sea salt and pepper
a pinch of sugar
olive oil
12 scallops, out of shell

Make the hollandaise sauce. Halve the passion fruits, scooping the seeds into a sieve over a bowl. With the back of a spoon, press and scrape all of the juices and pulp from the seeds. Add the juice to the hollandaise along with a spoonful of the seeds. Put the sauce to one side and keep warm.

Coarsely shred or tear the washed and well-drained spring greens into pieces. Blanch in boiling salted water for a few minutes until tender, then drain. Sauté the ginger and shallots in the butter until softened. Add the spring greens to warm through. Season with salt, pepper and a pinch of sugar.

Heat a few drops of olive oil in a frying pan and, once smoking, fry the scallops for 2 minutes, then turn and cook for a further 1 to 1½ minutes. Season with sea salt and pepper. The scallops are now ready to serve with the ginger spring greens and passion fruit hollandaise.

more

- For an alternative mayonnaise passion fruit sauce, whisk together 100g (4oz) mayonnaise and 50ml (2fl oz) crème fraîche with the sieved juice and seeds.

seared scallops and chilli-spiced cucumber

serves four

1 large cucumber, peeled
1 large fresh red chilli, deseeded and finely chopped
3 tablespoons groundnut or grapeseed oil
2 teaspoons soy sauce
1 teaspoon caster sugar
1 teaspoon white wine vinegar
sea salt and pepper
olive oil
12 scallops, out of shell
chive stalks (optional)

Slice the cucumber thinly on a mandolin into tagliatelle strips, discarding the central seed core.

Add the chilli to the oil. Quickly warm together the soy sauce, sugar and vinegar and, once the sugar has dissolved, whisk into the chilli oil, seasoning with a pinch of salt and a twist of pepper. Stir the dressing into the cucumber, checking for seasoning.

Halve each scallop to make two discs. Heat a frying pan with a drizzle of olive oil and, once very hot, cook the scallops for a minute or two until golden brown before removing from the pan.

Season each with one or two sea salt crystals. Divide the cucumber strips among four plates, drizzle with any remaining dressing and garnish with a chive stalk, if using, before serving with the scallop slices.

more

- Finely chopped chives or tarragon can be added to the tagliatelle or very thin, round slices of spring onion.
- Lime can be squeezed over the top of the scallops.

lobster caesar salad

Cut the lobster meat into pieces. Tear the salad leaves into a bowl, mixing with just enough Caesar dressing to coat, and toss with the lobster and papaya. Divide the salad among four plates or bowls.

Whisk together the orange juice and olive oil, season with salt and pepper, then drizzle over the salads.

serves four

1 large cooked lobster, shelled (see page 17)
3–4 little gem lettuces
1 x Caesar dressing (see page 464)
1 ripe papaya, peeled, deseeded and chopped
3 tablespoons orange juice
2 tablespoons olive oil
salt and pepper

more

- A thick slice or two of crusty bread, cut into cubes and pan-fried in olive oil and butter, creates crispy croutons to sprinkle over the salad. Why not also try some Parmesan shavings?

duck pancake rolls

The pancakes and hoisin sauce are both available at most supermarkets. If you're not keen on hoisin, sweet chilli or a sweet-and-sour sauce are good alternatives or you could offer all three.

serves four–six

4 duck legs
sea salt and pepper
1 bunch of spring onions
½ cucumber
vegetable oil
12 Peking duck pancakes
hoisin sauce

Season the duck legs with sea salt and pepper and place them in a bamboo steamer basket or on a wire rack. Pop the basket over a large saucepan of boiling water and cover with the lid. If using a wire rack, place it over a roasting tray of boiling water and cover with a similar-sized tray, topping up with water from a boiling kettle if needed. Steam for 1½ hours or until the duck is tender, then remove the legs from the steamer and pat dry with kitchen paper.

Meanwhile, cut the spring onions and cucumber into 7–8cm (3 inch) sticks, with the cucumber no more than 5mm (¼ inch) thick.

Heat about 5mm (¼ inch) of vegetable oil in a large frying pan. Once hot, put the duck legs, skin-side down, in the oil. Fry over a medium to hot heat for 10 to 15 minutes until completely crispy and deep golden brown. Turn the legs and fry for a further minute before draining on kitchen paper.

During the last 5 to 6 minutes of frying the duck, warm the pancakes over the steamer. Shred the duck with a couple of forks ready to arrive on the table with the warm pancakes, spring onion and cucumber sticks and the hoisin sauce.

chicken livers with a sweet spinach and bacon salad

This recipe is ideal as a starter or light lunch. The mincemeat is the kind we use for Christmas mince pies. Once puréed with the walnut oil, the spicy fruit flavour contrasts well with the peppery livers.

serves four

1 heaped tablespoon
  mincemeat
4 tablespoons walnut oil
8–12 chicken livers
4 rashers of streaky bacon
sea salt and pepper
olive oil
1–2 handfuls of washed and
  ready-to-eat baby spinach

Put the mincemeat, walnut oil and 4 tablespoons water into a food processor or blender and blitz to a smooth sauce, with dots of black raisin still visible. Trim the chicken livers and place them on kitchen paper to dry.

Preheat the grill. Lay the bacon rashers on a grill tray with a rack, place under the grill, not too close to the top, and cook until crispy.

Season the livers with a good twist of pepper. Heat some olive oil in a non-stick frying pan and fry the livers for just a few minutes until golden brown on both sides. Season with a sprinkling of sea salt, remove from the pan and leave to rest.

Spoon some of the dressing on to the plates and scatter over the spinach leaves and chicken livers. Drizzle a little more dressing over and top with a rasher of warm crispy bacon.

sautéed snails, mushrooms and pasta with watercress sauce

serves four

150ml (5fl oz) whipping
   cream
¼ chicken or vegetable
   stock cube (see page 13)
1 large bunch of watercress,
   chopped
salt and pepper
200g (7oz) tin of cooked
   snails (about 24 snails)
225g (8oz) dried pasta (any
   shape will do)
2 tablespoons olive oil
225g (8oz) small button or
   chestnut mushrooms,
   halved
2 shallots or 1 red onion,
   finely chopped
a large knob of butter

Bring the cream to the boil, crumbling in the stock cube. Add the watercress and simmer for 30 to 60 seconds before blending until smooth. Season with salt and pepper, strain and keep to one side.

Rinse the snails under hot water, drying on kitchen paper. Cook the pasta in boiling salted water.

Meanwhile, heat the olive oil in a large frying pan. Once smoking, sauté the snails, mushrooms and shallots for 4 to 5 minutes. Season with salt and pepper and stir in the butter. Drain the pasta and add to the pan along with a tablespoon or two of water. Stir everything together and divide among plates or bowls, quickly warming the watercress cream and drizzling a few tablespoons over each one.

more

- Try blitzing the watercress cream with a handheld blender until frothy before spooning over the pasta.
- Fresh herbs such as parsley, chives or chervil can be added to the snails.

tiger prawns with leek and mozzarella risotto

If tiger prawns are not available, a couple of handfuls of peeled prawns added to the risotto to warm through make for a tasty supper dish.

Soak four bamboo skewers in cold water for 20 minutes. Dry the prawns on kitchen paper, then pierce three to four on to each skewer. Refrigerate until needed.

Warm the olive oil and 25g (1oz) of the butter in a braising pan. Once bubbling, add the onion and leek, cooking for several minutes before stirring in the rice. Pour in the wine, simmering for a minute or two before adding a ladleful of the hot stock, stirring until absorbed. Repeat this process for about 20 minutes, stirring continuously until the rice is tender and creamy with a slight bite left in the centre. Season with salt and pepper and remove the pan from the heat.

Add the mozzarella, Parmesan, parsley, if using, and the remaining butter. Stir thoroughly, loosening with a little more stock if necessary (the quantity of stock listed is quite generous and not all may be needed), then cover with a lid and leave to rest.

Preheat the grill. Drizzle a baking tray with olive oil, season the prawn skewers with salt and pepper and lay on the tray. Brush each skewer with the knob of butter and grill for 2 minutes before turning and cooking for a further couple of minutes.

The risotto and prawns are now ready to serve. Arrange them together on plates or bowls, drizzling any juices over the prawns.

serves four

12–16 large raw tiger prawns, peeled and deveined (see page 16)
1 tablespoon olive oil, plus extra for drizzling
75g (3oz) butter, plus a large knob for brushing
1 large onion, chopped
1 leek, sliced
225g (8oz) arborio rice
1 glass of white wine
900ml (1½ pints) hot vegetable or chicken stock (see page 13)
salt and pepper
2 tablespoons grated mozzarella
2 tablespoons grated Parmesan cheese
1 heaped tablespoon chopped flat-leaf parsley (optional)

seared black bream with ginger, tomato and chilli pak choy

serves four

450g (1lb) pak choy, cut into
  halves or thin wedges
3 tablespoons olive oil
juice of 1 lime
1 teaspoon honey
1 fresh red chilli, sliced
  into rings (discard the
  seeds for a milder taste)
3–4cm (1¼–1½ inch) piece
  of fresh ginger, peeled and
  cut into very thin strips
2 spring onions, thinly sliced
3 plum tomatoes, peeled,
and diced (see page 20)
salt and pepper
4 x 175g (6oz) black bream
  fillets, pinboned
  (see page 14)
2 knobs of butter
1 tablespoon sesame seeds

Boil a saucepan of salted water and plunge in the pak choy. Stir once or twice and then drain.

Whisk together 2 tablespoons of the olive oil with the lime juice and honey, stirring in the chilli, ginger, spring onion and tomato. Season with salt and pepper.

Meanwhile, heat a frying pan with the remaining olive oil. Season the black bream with salt and pepper and fry, skin-side down, over a medium-high heat for 4 to 5 minutes. Add a knob of butter and once sizzling, turn the fish and remove the pan from the stove, basting the bream with the butter.

While frying the fish, heat a wok or frying pan. Sprinkle in the sesame seeds and once they are golden, add the remaining knob of butter and the pak choy. Season with salt and pepper and fry for a few minutes to heat through.

Arrange the pak choy on a plate, spooning the dressing over and around. Serve with the black bream.

pan-fried sea bass with bacon and caper cabbage

Dry the sea bass on kitchen paper, season with salt and pepper and lightly dust the skin with flour.

Heat a little olive oil in a non-stick frying pan. Place the bass in the pan, skin-side down, lightly pressing with a fish slice to ensure all the skin is frying and colouring. The sea bass will take 5 to 7 minutes to crisp before you can turn it and remove it from the heat. The residual warmth in the pan will continue the cooking process.

Meanwhile, plunge the cabbage into boiling salted water, cook until just tender but leaving a slight bite, then drain.

Meanwhile, in a separate pan, fry the bacon until golden. Add the cabbage, capers and the knob of butter and season with a twist of pepper.

Arrange the cabbage on plates with the sea bass. Pour the lemon juice into the sea bass frying pan along with a tablespoon of water. Once simmering, stir in the butter and trickle over and around the bass.

serves four

4 x 175g (6oz) sea bass
  fillets, skin on and
  pinboned (see page 14)
salt and pepper
flour, for dusting
olive oil
½ savoy cabbage, finely
  shredded
4 rashers of smoked bacon,
  roughly chopped
2 tablespoons small capers
50g (2oz) cold chopped
  butter, plus a knob
juice of ½ a lemon

more

- Chopped chives can be sprinkled into the cabbage or lemon butter adding an oniony bite.

toasted sea bass and oranges with basil yoghurt

serves four

150ml (5fl oz) natural
  yoghurt or sour cream
1 large bunch or a small pot
  of basil
salt
olive oil
4 x 175g (6oz) sea bass
  fillets, skin on and
  pinboned (see page 14)
sea salt
3 large oranges, segmented
  (see page 20)
demerara sugar, for
  sprinkling

Pour the yoghurt into a food processor or blender with the basil leaves. Blend until smooth, seasoning with a pinch of salt.

Preheat the grill. Oil a baking tray and arrange the sea bass fillets on top, skin-side up. Cut across the skin of the sea bass to score, brush with olive oil and season with a sprinkling of sea salt. Place under the grill, as close to the top as possible. Grill for just 2 to 3 minutes until golden brown and crispy, then move the tray to a lower shelf.

Place the orange segments on a baking tray, sprinkle with the sugar and place under the grill, leaving for just a minute to warm through. The sea bass, oranges and basil sauce are now ready to serve.

dover sole with a steak garnish

Meaty Dover sole easily copes with this steak garnish of grilled tomatoes, mushrooms and watercress. The traditional Béarnaise sauce has been changed to a butter, binding together all the flavours, and is a lot easier to make.

serves four

1 tablespoon finely chopped shallots or onion
2 tablespoons white wine vinegar
salt and pepper
150g (5oz) softened butter
a squeeze of lemon
1 heaped teaspoon chopped tarragon
4 x 450–550g (1–1¼lb) Dover soles, skinned
4 plum tomatoes, halved
sea salt
olive oil
225g (8oz) button mushrooms
4 sprigs of watercress

To make the Béarnaise butter, place the shallots, vinegar and a twist of pepper in a small saucepan. Allow to simmer until almost dry. Leave to cool. Mix the softened shallots with 100g (4oz) of the butter, adding the lemon juice and tarragon and seasoning with a pinch of salt.

Preheat the grill. Place the soles on a large greased baking tray along with the tomato halves. Brush with a little of the remaining butter, saving a small knob for the mushrooms, and season with sea salt and pepper. Place the tray under the grill and cook for 8 to 10 minutes until a rich golden brown and cooked through.

While grilling the fish and tomatoes, heat a frying pan with the olive oil and add the mushrooms and remaining knob of butter. Fry over a medium heat for a few minutes, turning them from time to time, until well coloured and tender.

Place the soles on large plates, garnishing with the tomatoes, mushrooms and watercress. Finish with a spoonful of Béarnaise butter on top.

monkfish with golden sultanas, onion and spinach

Pan-fry the onion in a little olive oil over a medium heat until softened. Increase the heat and continue to fry until a caramel golden brown.

Meanwhile, put the sultanas into a saucepan with the wine. Bring to a rapid simmer, allowing the wine to evaporate until it is a thick syrup. Mix the sultanas with the onion.

For the herb butter sauce, boil together the vinegar and 1 tablespoon of the lemon juice until just half the liquid is left. Add the cream and, once simmering, whisk in the butter, a little at a time. Season with salt and white pepper, loosening, if necessary, with the extra lemon juice or water. Keep warm to one side.

Heat 2 tablespoons of olive oil in a frying pan. Season the monkfish fillets and sear in the hot oil, cooking for 4 to 5 minutes on each side until golden brown.

Meanwhile, melt the butter in a large pan over a high heat. Add the spinach, seasoning with salt and pepper, and stir until wilted and tender before draining.

Divide the spinach and onion among four plates, topping the onion with the monkfish. Add the herbs to the butter sauce, pour around and serve.

serves four

2 onions, thinly sliced
olive oil
4 heaped tablespoons golden sultanas
200ml (7fl oz) sweet white wine
4 x 150–175g (5–6oz) monkfish fillets
salt and pepper
a knob of butter
600g (1lb 5oz) spinach, washed and stalks removed

for the herb butter sauce
1 tablespoon white wine vinegar
1–2 tablespoons lemon juice
2 tablespoons double cream
100g (4oz) cold unsalted butter, diced
salt and ground white pepper
1 heaped tablespoon mixed herbs (chives, tarragon, chervil, parsley)

roast monkfish 'barnsley chops' with apple mint jelly and cider gravy

These Barnsley chops are, as with lamb, two fillets connected by the central bone. To complete this meal, try the kale colcannon on page 454.

serves four

for the apple and mint jelly

2 green apples, peeled and chopped into 1cm (½ inch) cubes
600ml (1 pint) apple juice
a strip of lemon zest
50g (2oz) caster sugar
1–2 teaspoons white wine vinegar
3 leaves of gelatine, soaked in cold water (6g total weight)
1 teaspoon chopped mint

2 tablespoons vegetable oil
4 x 200g (7oz) monkfish 'Barnsley chops'
salt and pepper
flour, for dusting
300ml (10fl oz) cider
150ml (5fl oz) chicken stock (see page 13)
50g (2oz) butter, chopped
a pinch of sugar

Boil together the chopped apple, apple juice, lemon zest and sugar until only half the liquid is left. Remove from the heat and stir in enough vinegar to give a sharp bite. Add the soaked gelatine, stir and leave to cool. Once cold, add the mint and refrigerate for a few hours to set.

Preheat the oven to 200°C/400°F/gas 6.

Heat the oil in a large ovenproof frying pan. Season and lightly flour the monkfish and fry until golden brown on one side before turning and roasting in the oven for 8 to 10 minutes. Remove the fish from the pan and keep warm, pouring away any excess oil.

Boil the cider in the pan until just a third of the liquid is left. Add the stock and boil until just half the liquid is left. Whisk in the butter and season with salt, pepper and the sugar. The gravy is now ready to serve with the 'chops' and jelly.

roast monkfish in red wine with crème fraîche cabbage

serves four

olive oil
2 x 350g (12oz) monkfish
  fillets
a large knob of butter
5 tablespoons chicken stock
  (see page 13) or water
1 green cabbage, cut into
  thick slices
150ml (5fl oz) crème fraîche
salt and pepper
a pinch of freshly grated
  nutmeg
200ml (7fl oz) red wine
1 tablespoon light soft
  brown sugar

Preheat the oven to 200°C/400°F/gas 6. Heat the olive oil in a non-stick ovenproof frying pan. Pat the monkfish fillets dry with kitchen paper before placing in the pan. Fry for a few minutes, turning the fish to colour on all sides, then transfer the pan to the oven and roast for 10 more minutes.

While roasting the monkfish, heat the butter and stock together in a large saucepan. Once boiling, add the cabbage, cooking for several minutes until tender. Add the crème fraîche, boiling and stirring through the cabbage until slightly thickened. Season with salt, pepper and the nutmeg.

Remove the monkfish from the frying pan, keeping the fillets warm to one side. Add the red wine and sugar to the pan, boiling vigorously to a thick, sticky consistency. Return the monkfish to the pan, pouring in any juices that have been released, and continue to simmer, rolling the fillets until completely coated with the wine.

The monkfish can now be sliced in half, offering half a fillet per portion with the crème fraîche cabbage.

cod with new potatoes, baby spinach and cheddar cheese sauce

serves four

450g (1lb) new potatoes
salt and pepper
50g (2oz) butter
4 x 175g (6oz) cod fillets,
  skinned and pinboned
  (see page 14)
4 spring onions, thinly sliced
225g (8oz) washed and
  ready-to-eat baby spinach

for the cheese sauce
150ml (5fl oz) crème fraîche
150ml (5fl oz) milk or single
  cream
100–175g (4–6oz) Cheddar
  cheese, grated
1 level teaspoon English or
  Dijon mustard

Preheat the oven to 200°C/400°F/gas 6. Cook the potatoes in boiling salted water for 20 to 25 minutes until tender. Drain and leave to cool slightly before halving.

Lightly butter and season a small roasting tray before putting in the cod. Season with a little salt and, using half the butter, place a knob on top of each fillet. Pour approximately 5mm (¼ inch) water into the tin.

Bring to a simmer on top of the stove, then cover the cod with parchment or butter paper and poach in the oven for 8 to 10 minutes until tender.

Meanwhile, warm a large frying pan with the remaining butter. Once sizzling, fry the potato and spring onion over a medium heat to a light golden brown. Stir in the spinach and, once beginning to wilt, season with salt and pepper.

To make the cheese sauce, heat the crème fraîche and milk in a small saucepan to a gentle simmer, whisking in 100g (4oz) of the Cheddar and mustard until melted. For a richer and thicker sauce, stir in the remaining cheese.

Divide the potato and spinach among four plates or bowls, top each with a fillet of cod, offering the sauce on the side.

chicken with porcini and chestnut mushrooms

Porcini is the Italian word for cep mushrooms, available fresh during our autumn months. They are also available dried, as I'm using here. Chestnut mushrooms have become quite common on our shelves, their flavour adding a nutty edge.

Season the chicken breasts with salt and pepper and place them, skin-side down, in a preheated frying pan with a little olive oil and the knob of butter. Fry over a medium heat for 5 to 7 minutes on each side until cooked and golden brown. Lift from the pan and keep warm to one side.

Add the shallots, porcini and chestnut mushrooms to the pan, frying for a couple of minutes. Pour in 300ml (10fl oz) of the saved mushroom water. Boil until just half the liquid is left. Add the cream and return to a simmer, cooking the sauce until slightly thickened.

Season the sauce and add the lemon juice and parsley. Pop the chicken breasts back into the pan along with any juices and serve.

serves four

4 chicken breasts, skin on
salt and pepper
olive oil
a knob of butter
1 heaped tablespoon finely
  chopped shallots or onion
25g (1oz) sliced dried
  porcini mushrooms,
  soaked (see page 20)
100g (4oz) chestnut
  mushrooms, sliced
100–150ml (3½–5fl oz)
  double cream
juice of ½ lemon
1 tablespoon chopped
  flat-leaf parsley

grilled chicken with carrot, celeriac and courgette cream

serves four

2 medium/large carrots,
  peeled
1 small celeriac, peeled
2 large courgettes
salt and pepper
4 chicken breasts, skinless
  or skin on
3 tablespoons olive oil
1 tablespoon lemon juice

for the cream
1 small onion, halved and
  thinly sliced
100ml (3½fl oz) white wine
150ml (5fl oz) chicken stock
  (see page 13)
150ml (5fl oz) double cream
salt and pepper

Cut the vegetables into thin matchstick strips, approximately 6cm (2½ inches) long (using a mandolin makes this easier).

Put the carrot and celeriac in a pan of boiling salted water and simmer for a few minutes until tender. Add the courgette and simmer for a further minute before draining the vegetables from the pan.

To make the cream, return the pan to the heat, add the onion and wine, boiling until very little of the liquid is left. Pour in the stock and continue to boil, until just half the liquid is left. Add the cream, simmering until slightly thickened and season with salt and pepper.

Heat a ridged grill pan or frying pan. Brush the chicken liberally with olive oil, mixing any remaining with the lemon juice and seasoning with salt and pepper. Cook the breasts over a medium heat for 5 to 7 minutes on each side until just firm to the touch.

Meanwhile, warm the vegetable strips in just enough of the sauce to loosen before spooning on to four plates. Arrange the chicken on top of the vegetables, drizzling with the lemon-flavoured olive oil. Offer any remaining sauce on the side.

baked chicken legs with mediterranean vegetables

serves six

olive oil
salt and pepper
6 chicken legs
6 cloves of garlic, peeled
2 red onions, chopped
2 red peppers, roughly
   chopped
2 yellow peppers, roughly
   chopped
1 large aubergine, roughly
   chopped
4 courgettes, roughly
   chopped
300ml (10fl oz) passata
a handful of basil leaves

Preheat the oven to 200°C/400°F/gas 6.

Heat a roasting tray on top of the stove with a drop of olive oil. Season the chicken legs, add to the tray and colour to a golden brown. Turn over, add the garlic and roast in the oven for 15 minutes.

Add the onion, peppers and the aubergine and roast with the chicken for a further 30 minutes until nearly tender.

Add the courgette and return to the oven for 10 to15 minutes until the chicken legs are very moist and tender.

Season the vegetables with salt and pepper, stir in the passata, put on top of the heat and bring to a simmer.

Recheck for seasoning and sprinkle over the basil leaves. Serve with crusty bread to mop up the juices.

roast duck with spinach and wild mushrooms

Although the duck breasts are not actually roasted, simply pan-fried, the secret is to allow some of the duck fat to melt away, leaving a golden brown roasted colour and flavour.

Score the duck skin with a sharp knife. Season with salt and pepper and place, fat-side down, in a frying pan over a medium heat. As the fat begins to heat it will melt and crisp. Continue to colour the skin for 10 to 12 minutes before turning over and frying for a further 4 to 5 minutes to a pink stage. Remove the duck and keep warm.

Meanwhile, simmer the maple syrup until just 2 tablespoons are left. Whisk in the vinegar, groundnut and hazelnut oil and season with salt and pepper. While the duck is resting, fry the mushrooms in half the butter in a hot pan until just tender.

Heat a separate pan with the remaining butter and add the spinach, allowing the leaves to wilt before draining.

To serve, divide the spinach among four plates. Cut each breast into five to six slices and place on top of the spinach. Spoon over the wild mushrooms, drizzling with the maple syrup vinaigrette.

serves four

4 duck breasts, skin on
sea salt and pepper
4 tablespoons maple syrup
1½ tablespoons sherry
  vinegar
1½ tablespoons groundnut
  oil
1 tablespoon hazelnut oil
225g (8oz) wild mushrooms
  (girolles, trompettes, ceps,
  oyster mushrooms),
  trimmed
25g (1oz) butter
900g (2lb) spinach, main
  stalks removed

braised lamb shanks with onions, tomatoes and pesto beans

No friends coming round this weekend? Well, you'll find some in this pot.

serves two

vegetable oil
salt and pepper
2 small lamb shanks
2 large onions, sliced
1 teaspoon demerara sugar
a sprig of thyme
1 bay leaf
400g (14oz) tin of chopped
  tomatoes
1 glass of red wine
300ml (10fl oz) chicken
  stock (see page 13)
400g (14oz) tin of cannellini,
  borlotti, haricot or flageolet
  beans
a large knob of butter
2 tablespoons pesto sauce
  (from a jar)

Preheat the oven to 170°C/325°F/gas 3. Heat a small braising pot with a drizzle of oil. Season and fry the lamb shanks until completely coloured, before removing.

Pour away any excess fat from the pot and fry the onion. Once golden brown, add the sugar, thyme and bay leaf. Pour in the tomatoes, red wine and stock. Add the shanks, topping up with water, if necessary. Bring to a rapid simmer, cover with a lid and braise in the oven for 2 to 2½ hours until tender.

Drain and rinse the beans. Place the beans in a pan, cover with water and simmer for 5 minutes. Drain, leaving 2 to 3 tablespoons of water in the pan. Stir in the butter and pesto, season and serve with the shanks.

more

- During the final 30 to 40 minutes, add some cherry tomatoes to the pot and simmer with the lamb shanks.

lamb 'osso buco'

Osso buco is an Italian dish made with steaks taken from the hind shin of the calf, but here I'm using lamb. Translated, it means 'bone with a hole', referring to the hole found inside the circle of meat. It's said that tomatoes should not be included, however, I've added them here for their rich flavour and to help thicken the sauce. Classically, this osso buco is served with risotto Milanese, to be found on the opposite page.

serves four

2 tablespoons olive oil
4 x 300g (10oz)
  leg of lamb steaks
salt and pepper
2 tablespoons flour
1 large onion, chopped
3 plum tomatoes, halved,
  deseeded and chopped
300ml (10fl oz) white wine
150ml (5fl oz) fresh
  orange juice
400ml (14fl oz) tin of beef
  consommé or lamb stock
  (see page 13)
2 strips of orange zest
1 bay leaf
50g (2oz) butter

for the gremolata
2 heaped tablespoons
  chopped parsley
1 level tablespoon finely
  grated lemon zest
1 small clove of garlic, finely
  chopped

Preheat the oven to 170°C/325°F/gas 3.

Heat a large ovenproof pan with the olive oil. Season the lamb and lightly dust with flour. Brown well on both sides before removing from the pan.

Add the onion and cook over a medium heat for 10 minutes. Add the tomatoes and return the steaks, pouring in the wine, orange juice and consommé or stock. Add the orange zest and bay leaf and bring to a simmer. Cover with a lid and braise for 1½ to 2 hours until the meat is very tender.

Remove the meat from the pan and keep warm. Boil the sauce and reduce in volume by 100 to 150ml (3½ to 5fl oz) to strengthen the flavour. Whisk in the butter for a rich finish.

Mix together the gremolata ingredients and stir into the sauce, infusing for a minute before spooning the sauce over the lamb steaks and serving.

risotto milanese

This risotto is flavoured with saffron and usually served with osso buco (see opposite), but it works equally well on its own as a supper dish. For this recipe I've chosen carnaroli, the premier risotto rice, but arborio or vialone nano can also be used.

Bring the stock to a gentle simmer.

Melt half the butter in a heavy-based pan. Add the onion and cook gently for 6 to 7 minutes until softened.

Add the rice and stir to make sure the grains are coated in the butter. Mix the saffron into the wine, pour in and simmer until the wine has been totally absorbed.

Pour in one or two ladlefuls of hot stock and cook over a medium heat, stirring continuously. Once almost completely evaporated, add another ladleful and continue this process for 17 to 20 minutes. The risotto is ready when the rice grains are tender with the slightest of bites.

Stir in the remaining butter. Season and finish with a good sprinkling of Parmesan, offering any remaining on the side.

serves four
1.2 litres (2 pints) chicken
  or vegetable stock (see
  page 13)
100g (4oz) butter
1 onion, very finely chopped
350g (12oz) carnaroli rice
a generous pinch of saffron
  strands
150ml (5fl oz) white wine
salt and pepper
50g (2oz) Parmesan
  cheese, grated

more
- Veal or beef marrow can be added, melting it with the butter before cooking the onion. The marrow adds extra richness to the overall flavour.

braised pigs' cheeks with marmalade turnips

If pigs' cheeks are unavailable, follow the recipe using chunks of pork shoulder. Tagliatelle or linguine rolled in butter and herbs make a nice change from potatoes and vegetables.

serves four

salt and pepper
2 tablespoons plain flour
1kg (2¼lb) pigs' cheeks, trimmed
2 tablespoons vegetable oil
2 onions, chopped
4 strips of orange zest
juice from 1 orange
a sprig of thyme
1 bay leaf
1 bottle of red wine
400g (14oz) tin of beef consommé or stock (see page 13)
brown sugar (optional)
16–20 baby turnips, trimmed
2 tablespoons marmalade

Preheat the oven to 170°C/325°F/gas 3.

Season and flour the cheeks. Heat the oil in a braising pot and fry the cheeks until golden brown before removing from the pot. Add the onion, orange zest, juice, thyme, bay leaf and any remaining flour. Cook for a few minutes, add the red wine and boil until just half is left. Return the cheeks, top with the consommé or stock and bring to a simmer. Cover with a lid and braise for 2 hours until the cheeks are tender.

If the sauce is too thin, return the pot to the stove and rapidly simmer to thicken, checking the strength of the flavour as it simmers. If the sauce is too sharp, add a pinch or two of brown sugar. Once the sauce has thickened, keep warm to one side.

Meanwhile, cook the turnips in boiling salted water until tender before draining. Warm together the marmalade and 2 tablespoons water. If it's too thick, loosen with a drop more water. Roll the turnips in the sticky glaze and season, ready to serve with the braised cheeks.

seared calves' liver with caramelized grapes

These caramelized grapes have a double strength. If you serve them hot, their flavour is sweet and piquant. Cold, they become almost like pickled raisins and taste very good with pâtés. This dish eats particularly well with creamy mashed potatoes.

serves four

2 tablespoons vegetable oil
450g (1lb) white seedless grapes
2 heaped teaspoons light soft brown sugar
2 tablespoons brandy
2 tablespoons sherry vinegar
a few drops of balsamic vinegar
150ml (5fl oz) sweet white wine
salt and pepper
a knob of butter
4 x 175g (6oz) calves' liver steaks

Heat a large frying pan with a tablespoon of the vegetable oil. Pan-fry the grapes over a medium heat for 8 to 10 minutes until a rich golden brown. Add the sugar and cook until it dissolves and begins to caramelize. Pour in the brandy and simmer until almost completely evaporated.

Follow with the sherry and balsamic vinegar, boiling until just half the liquid is left. Pour in the wine and simmer to a syrupy, sauce-like consistency. Season and keep warm to one side.

To cook the liver, heat a frying pan with the remaining vegetable oil and the butter. Add the liver and cook for 3 to 4 minutes on each side, leaving a moist, pink centre. Season with salt and pepper. Serve the liver with the caramelized grapes spooned over the top.

more
- Chopped parsley or chives can be sprinkled over the dish.

fillet of beef with red wine tomatoes

This is superb with the bacon sauté new potatoes on page 451 and almost any green vegetable.

For the tomato sauce, heat the olive oil in a large frying pan. Fry the onion over a medium heat until golden brown. Add the sugar, frying for a few minutes before pouring in the red wine. Increase the heat and simmer until just a third of the liquid is left. Add the tomatoes and continue to boil. Season and keep warm to one side.

Preheat the oven to 220°C/425°F/gas 7.

Heat the olive oil in an ovenproof frying pan. Season the steaks and fry until they are well coloured. Add the butter and turn the steaks before placing in the oven for 4 to 5 minutes for rare or 7 to 8 minutes for medium. Remove from the oven and rest for 5 minutes.

To serve, top each of the steaks with the rich red wine tomato sauce.

serves four

2 tablespoons olive oil
salt and pepper
4 x 175g (6oz) fillet steaks
a knob of butter

for the red wine tomato sauce
2 tablespoons olive oil
2 onions, thinly sliced
a pinch of sugar
300ml (10fl oz) red wine
400g (14oz) tin of chopped
  tomatoes
salt and pepper

more
- A generous sprinkling of chopped tarragon stirred into the sauce provides a 'chasseur' style finish.

cauliflower and mushroom curry

A mild vegetarian curry perfect for a Saturday night. For a hotter finish, simply double the quantity of chilli powder.

serves four

1 small cauliflower, divided into florets
salt
1 bunch of spring onions, shredded
4 cloves of garlic, crushed
5cm (2 inch) nugget of fresh ginger, peeled and chopped
6 tablespoons vegetable oil
450g (1lb) large button mushrooms, halved
1 level tablespoon tomato purée
2 teaspoons ground coriander
⅛ teaspoon chilli powder
300ml (10fl oz) natural yoghurt
1 tablespoon mango chutney (optional)
1 heaped tablespoon chopped fresh coriander

Plunge the cauliflower into a large pan of boiling salted water and cook for a few minutes until tender, then drain.

Put the spring onions into a blender or small food processor with the garlic, ginger and 4 to 5 tablespoons of water and blend until smooth.

Heat half the oil in a frying pan and fry the mushrooms for 1 to 2 minutes until beginning to colour. Tip them into a bowl, wipe the pan clean and return to the stove.

Warm the remaining oil in the pan, pour in the blended onion purée and stir over a medium heat until lightly coloured. Add the tomato purée, ground coriander, ½ a teaspoon of salt and the chilli powder, cooking for a few minutes before adding the yoghurt and 300ml (10fl oz) of water. Add the mango chutney, if using, and whisk to blend the three together. After 5 minutes, add the cauliflower and mushrooms and gently simmer for a further 10 minutes.

Stir in the coriander and the curry is ready to eat.

more

- The tomato purée, ground coriander, salt and chilli powder could be replaced with 2 to 3 tablespoons Madras curry paste.

tiramisu bocker glory

serves four

500g (18oz) mascarpone
  cheese
4 heaped tablespoons sifted
  icing sugar
150ml (5fl oz) double cream
150ml (5fl oz) cold espresso
  coffee
4 tablespoons brandy
12 sponge fingers (savoiardi
  biscuits)
1 x warm chocolate sauce
  (see page 467) (optional)
cocoa powder or finely
  grated dark chocolate
  (optional)

Beat together the mascarpone and icing sugar until creamy.
Lightly whip the cream to a soft peak before folding into
the mascarpone.

In a separate bowl, mix together the coffee and brandy. Snap
each of the sponge fingers in half, dip eight pieces into the coffee
and arrange in four knickerbocker glory glasses or bowls. If using,
spoon a little cold chocolate sauce over each.

Using a piping bag the mascarpone can now be piped on top.
Layer up the sponge fingers, chocolate sauce and mascarpone
cream twice more, finishing with the mascarpone.

A dusting of cocoa powder or finely grated chocolate can be
sprinkled on top, if using.

cracked summer berry meringue

serves four

2 egg whites
175g (6oz) caster sugar
1 teaspoon cornflour,
  loosened with cold water
1 teaspoon lemon juice
oil, for greasing
225g (8oz) mixed summer
  berries, frozen and
  defrosted or fresh, hulled
1 tablespoon any berry jam,
  at room temperature
1–2 punnets of any fresh
  summer berries
clotted cream, to serve

Preheat the oven to 140°C/275°F/gas 1. In an electric mixer, whisk
the egg whites to a soft peak. Add a third of the caster sugar
and whisk until approaching the stiff peak stage. Add half of the
remaining sugar and continue to whisk until creamy. Add the
cornflour and lemon juice and whisk for a further minute.

Very lightly oil a sheet of parchment paper and place on a baking
tray. Spoon the meringue into four large mounds on the tray and
bake for 50 to 60 minutes until crispy. Remove from the oven and
allow to cool.

Put the 225g (8oz) of berries, the remaining sugar and jam into a
blender and blend until smooth. Strain into a bowl.

Arrange the meringues on plates and spoon the punnets of fresh
berries over and around. Drizzle with the sauce and complete with
a scoop of clotted cream.

baked amaretti peaches

A dollop of extra-thick cream melting over the top of this is heavenly, but I've also included a recipe for an amaretto zabaglione to drizzle over – purely optional.

Preheat the oven to 180°C/350°F/gas 4.

Put the amaretti biscuits in a bag and crush with a rolling pin. Mix the biscuits with the amaretto, ground almonds, egg yolks and sugar.

Fill each of the peach halves with the almond mix, completely covering the surface. Top each with a small knob of butter and place on a greased non-stick baking tray. Bake for 20 to 25 minutes or until completely tender. Dust lightly with icing sugar just before serving.

Meanwhile, whisk together the egg yolks, sugar, amaretto and 50ml (2fl oz) water in a large glass bowl. Ten minutes before the peaches are ready, place the bowl over a pan of gently simmering water. Using a balloon or electric hand whisk, whisk for 8 to 10 minutes until the zabaglione has thickened to a creamy, meringue stage.

Remove from the heat and drizzle the zabaglione over the peaches.

serves four

75g (3oz) amaretti biscuits
2 tablespoons amaretto liqueur (sweet sherry can be used)
50g (2oz) ground almonds
2 egg yolks
3 teaspoons caster sugar
4 peaches, halved and stones removed
25g (1oz) butter
icing sugar, for dusting

for the zabaglione
4 egg yolks
75g (3oz) caster sugar
75ml (3fl oz) amaretto liqueur

mango cheesecake fool

A packet of brandy snaps is quite handy to have in-house when making this pud, ready for dunking into the fool or crumbling over the top.

serves four–six

2 large ripe mangoes, peeled and roughly chopped
300g (10oz) cream cheese
3 heaped tablespoons caster sugar
150ml (5fl oz) double cream

Liquidize the mango in a blender until smooth.

Beat together the cream cheese and sugar in a bowl until soft and creamy.

In a separate bowl, lightly whip the cream to a soft peak stage.

Stir the mango purée into the cream cheese and fold in the cream. Spoon into one large bowl or individual glasses and the soft fool is ready to serve or can be refrigerated for 2 to 3 hours to firm.

bailey's crème brûlée

For a stronger Bailey's flavour, use 250ml (9fl oz) of Bailey's and 350ml (12fl oz) of cream.

serves six

8 egg yolks
50g (2oz) caster sugar
450ml (16fl oz) double or whipping cream
150ml (5fl oz) Bailey's
2 tablespoons demerara or caster sugar

Preheat the oven to 150°C/300°F/gas 2. Mix the egg yolks and caster sugar together in a bowl. Pour the cream and Bailey's into a saucepan and bring to the boil before whisking into the egg yolks and sugar.

Ladle the mixture into six 7.5cm (3 inch) ramekins. Place them in a deep tray and pour in boiling water from the kettle so it reaches halfway up the ramekins. Cover the tray with foil and bake for 30 to 35 minutes or until just set. To test, gently shake a ramekin. There should be a slight wobble in the centre of a set custard. Remove the ramekins from the tray and leave to cool. Refrigerate to chill.

Preheat the grill to very hot. Sprinkle the brûlées with sugar and place under the grill, watching carefully until the sugar caramelizes to a rich golden brown. Alternatively, a blowtorch can be used to caramelize the sugar.

raspberry and white chocolate cream shortbreads

This dessert can simply be presented with the raspberries, white chocolate cream and shortbreads all sat side by side. However, here I'm topping a couple of shortbread biscuits with the fruit and cream and stacking in a millefeuille style.

serves four

1 x white chocolate cream (see page 467), refrigerated for 10 to 15 minutes before using
20–24 raspberries per person

for the shortbreads
200g (7oz) butter, softened
100g (4oz) icing sugar
1 egg yolk
250g (9oz) plain flour

To make the shortbreads, cream together the butter, icing sugar and egg yolk. Sift the flour into the bowl and gently fold in. Clingfilm and refrigerate for 1 to 2 hours.

Preheat the oven to 180°C/350°F/gas 4.

Once rested, roll out the dough until just 2–3mm (⅛ inch) thick. Twelve circles, squares or rectangles can now be cut and placed on a non-stick baking tray. Bake for 12 to 15 minutes or until the shortbreads are lightly golden. Leave to cool.

Spoon or pipe the white chocolate cream on to eight of the biscuits, leaving a 5–10mm (¼–½ inch) border. Arrange the raspberries around the cream. Stack into four portions, topping with the remaining shortbreads.

more

- If you fancy a raspberry sauce to go with this, whiz 100g (4oz) raspberries and 25g (1oz) icing sugar in a blender until smooth. Strain through a sieve and serve.

chocolate brownie mousse

This recipe is quick to make and resembles a chocolate trifle. Any bought chocolate brownies are fine to use and the mousse is best eaten at room temperature.

Scatter the chocolate brownies in a pudding bowl.

Put the chocolate and half the cream in a bowl and place over a pan of simmering water, stirring occasionally until melted. Remove and leave to cool slightly.

Whip the remaining cream until soft peaks form and fold into the chocolate, a little at a time. Pour the mousse over the chocolate brownies. The soft mousse is now ready to eat or can be refrigerated for 1 to 2 hours until firm.

serves four

225g (8oz) chocolate
  brownies, cut into cubes
225g (8oz) dark chocolate,
  chopped
300ml (10fl oz) double
  cream

more

- The mousse can be topped with grated white chocolate.
- Cherries from a tin or jar can be added to the brownies to create a Black Forest flavour, then drizzled with kirsch.

liqueur-steeped summer fruits with lemon curd cream

Raspberries, strawberries, blackberries, blueberries, blackcurrants and redcurrants all suit this recipe. The steeping time here is just 15 to 20 minutes, but if you're prepared to wait an hour or two, it will be even better.

serves four

450g (1lb) mixed summer berries, hulled
3 tablespoons caster sugar
3 tablespoons raspberry or strawberry liqueur (crème de framboises or fraises or a fruit-flavoured eau-de-vie)
125ml (4½fl oz) double cream
5 tablespoons lemon curd, chilled

Put the fruits into a large bowl. Sprinkle with the sugar and liqueur and leave to steep for 15 to 20 minutes, stirring gently every 5 minutes to ensure all are coated and flavoured.

Whisk together the cream and lemon curd to a soft peak. The fruits and lemon curd cream are now ready to serve, drizzled with the sweet liqueur syrup.

rice pudding with toasted honey plums

This rice pudding is good served hot or cold with the toasted plums.

serves four

100g (4oz) short-grain
  pudding rice
900ml (1½ pints) milk
300ml (10fl oz) double
  cream
1–2 vanilla pods or a few
  drops of strong vanilla
  essence
50g (2oz) sugar
butter, for greasing
6 plums, halved and stoned
6 teaspoons honey

Put the rice into a sieve and pour over a kettle of boiling water to rinse. Place the rice in a saucepan and add the milk and cream. Split the vanilla pods in half lengthways. Scrape the seeds from the centre of each and add to the rice with the pods.

Bring the rice to the boil, then reduce the heat to a very gentle simmer and cook for 30 minutes, stirring from time to time. Add the sugar and continue to simmer for a further 10 minutes. Remove the vanilla pods.

About 10 to 15 minutes before serving, preheat the grill and grease a baking tray with butter and top with the plum halves, cut-side up. Drizzle ½ a teaspoon of the honey over each and cook under the grill, not too close to the heat, until tender and golden brown. The plums can now be served with the rice.

toffee pie with grilled bananas

This dessert is best served at room temperature.

Preheat the oven to 180°C/350°F/gas 4. Crush the biscuits to crumbs in a food processor or in a plastic bag with a rolling pin. Melt 100g (4oz) of the butter and half the golden syrup together in a small saucepan and stir in the crumbs until well coated. Press the biscuit mixture into the base of a 23cm (9 inch) loose-bottomed tart tin and bake for 10 minutes. Remove from the oven and leave to cool.

Gently heat the remaining butter and golden syrup, sugar and condensed milk together until the butter has melted. Bring to the boil, then reduce the heat to a simmer, stirring for 8 to 10 minutes until light caramel in colour. Pour the filling into the biscuit case and leave to set.

Quickly microwave the chocolate until melted, before pouring and spreading over the caramel and leave to firm.

Preheat the grill. Peel and slice the bananas in half lengthways and lay, cut-side up, on a baking tray, sprinkle liberally with sugar and grill until caramelized to a golden brown colour.

Divide up the pie and serve with the bananas.

serves six

225g (8oz) digestive
  biscuits
150g (5½oz) butter
4 tablespoons golden syrup
100g (4oz) caster sugar,
  plus extra for sprinkling
400ml (14fl oz) tin of
  condensed milk
200g (7oz) plain chocolate,
  chopped
3 bananas

apple jelly and cinnamon cream

serves four

300ml (10fl oz) sweet white
  wine
200ml (7fl oz) apple juice
100ml (3½fl oz) orange
  juice
juice of 1 small lemon
100g (3½oz) caster sugar
2 cloves
2 apples, coarsely chopped
5 leaves of gelatine, soaked
  in cold water (10g total
  weight)
150ml (5fl oz) double cream
25g (1oz) icing sugar
½ teaspoon cinnamon

Pour the wine, apple, orange and lemon juice into a saucepan, add the sugar and cloves and bring to the boil.

Add the chopped apple and simmer for a few minutes until tender. Squeeze the water from the gelatine leaves before stirring them into the pan until dissolved. Leave to cool. Strain the jelly through a sieve into a jug, gently pressing the apple to release any juices, and divide among glasses. Refrigerate to set.

Whip the cream with the icing sugar and cinnamon to a soft peak. The cream can be spooned or piped on to the apple jelly or served separately.

clotted cream panna cotta and strawberries

serves four–six

200ml (7fl oz) milk
75g (3oz) caster sugar
3 leaves of gelatine, soaked
  in cold water (6g total
  weight)
200ml (7fl oz) whipping
  cream
300ml (10fl oz) clotted
  cream
350g (12oz) strawberries
1 tablespoon room-
  temperature strawberry
  jam
1 teaspoon icing sugar

Boil the milk with the sugar, stirring until dissolved. Remove the pan from the heat and whisk in the gelatine leaves followed by the cream and clotted cream. Strain and divide the mixture among four to six small cups, glass bowls or ramekins. Refrigerate for a few hours to set.

Blend 100g (4oz) of the strawberries with the jam and icing sugar until smooth, then strain through a sieve.

Serve the panna cottas with the whole strawberries, spooning the sauce over the berries.

more

- Serve with the buttermilk mini scones featured on page 106 or the shortbread biscuits on page 294.

Sunday lunch

Beef

Beef 'coq au vin' stew

Beef and potatoes braised in Guinness

Roast veal with white onion and blue cheese potato gratin

Roast rib of beef

Roast beef trimmings: gravy; Yorkshire puddings; wild mushroom and garlic cream

Red wine beef with bacon crunch

Pork

Slow-roast pork with gorgonzola and apple cabbage

White pork and wild mushroom stew

Pork belly boulangère

Boiled pork pot

Pork belly potatoes and red cabbage roast

Boiled bacon collar with spicy sausage mash and peas gravy

Roast pork and trimmings: cider gravy; prune, leek and sage stuffing

Roast rack of pork with turnip and prune dauphinois

Lamb

Stout-glazed leg of lamb

Seven-hour leg of lamb with potatoes, carrots and onions

Roast leg of lamb and trimmings: mint sauce

Apricot and pine nut rack of lamb with soft onions

West country squab pie

Roast rump of lamb with pancetta champ and marjoram cream

Lamb goujons with curry mayonnaise and mint raita

Hogget cobbler with orange onions and sage scones

Lamb with beans, onions, tomatoes and tarragon

Lamb hotpot

Chicken, duck and game

Chicken, ham and mushroom pie

Roast chicken with gravy and trimmings: bacon and chipolatas; sage, onion and lemon stuffing; bread sauce

Roast paprika chicken

Roast chicken thighs with bacon, carrots, onions and potatoes

Roasted duck with red wine blackberries

Steamed duck with caramelized onions, olives and walnuts

Treacle duck breasts with creamy date parsnips

Roast partridge with toasted salsify and maple sherry gravy

Fish

Ham-wrapped trout with an English mustard sauce

Roast flat fish with parsley lemon butter and new potatoes lyonnaise

Roast monkfish with fennel, orange

and tarragon mussels

Cod poached in a tarragon broth

Roast halibut with buttery mussels and herbs

Puddings

Apple tart

Rhubarb and custard cheesecake

Prune and Armagnac bread and butter pudding

Baked apples with nutmeg custard pudding

Vanilla pear and peach salad

Pear macaroon crumble

Steamed plum pudding

Cognac peaches with pistachio brioche

Crème caramel

Spotted dick pudding with caramel golden syrup

Iced Jersey cream with lots of strawberries

beef 'coq au vin' stew

The classic coq au vin flavours of red wine, mushrooms, bacon and button onions all lend themselves to this beef stew as does the mashed potato featured on page 451.

serves four

900g (2lb) diced stewing or
  braising steak
salt and pepper
50g (2oz) butter
200g (7oz) cubes of
  pancetta
2 cloves of garlic, crushed
2 bay leaves
1 sprig of thyme
2 large carrots, sliced
20 button onions, peeled
225g (8oz) button
  mushrooms
2 tablespoons plain flour
1 tablespoon tomato purée
1 bottle of red wine
400ml (14fl oz) tin of beef
  consommé or stock
  (see page 13)
1 tablespoon chopped
  parsley

Preheat the oven to 170°C/325°F/gas 3. Season the beef with salt and pepper. Heat a large casserole dish with the butter and, once sizzling, fry the beef and pancetta until well coloured. Add the garlic, bay leaves, thyme, carrots, button onions and mushrooms. Cook for 2 to 3 minutes, then sprinkle in the flour and stir in the tomato purée.

Pour in the red wine and the beef consommé or stock. Bring to a simmer, skim, then cover with a lid. Cook in the oven for 2½ hours until the meat is tender.

Season if necessary with salt and pepper, then scatter over the parsley and serve.

beef and potatoes braised in Guinness

One of my favourites.

Preheat the oven to 170°C/325°F/gas 3.

Heat some oil in a large frying pan, add the onions and cook over a medium heat until tender and golden brown. Spoon the onions into a casserole dish.

Season the beef and toss in the flour. Heat a little more oil in the frying pan and fry the beef until well coloured on all sides, then add to the onions.

Pour the Guinness into the hot frying pan, and sprinkle in the sugar. Add the consommé or stock and simmer for a minute before pouring over the beef. Cover and cook in the oven for 1½ hours. Add a little water if necessary to keep the meat covered.

Add the potatoes and continue to cook for a further 1 to 1½ hours until the potatoes have absorbed and thickened the sauce and the beef is soft and tender.

more
- Serve the beef and potatoes with any green vegetable.

serves four

vegetable oil
3 large onions, sliced
salt and pepper
4 x 175–225g (6–8oz) pieces of chuck steak or braising beef
flour, for dusting
440ml (16fl oz) Guinness
1 tablespoon muscovado sugar
400ml (14fl oz) tin of beef consommé or stock (see page 13)
4 large potatoes, peeled and halved

roast veal with white onion and blue cheese potato gratin

Irish Cashel Blue or Gorgonzola blend beautifully with the onion and potatoes or, if you prefer a stronger taste, try Roquefort or Stilton.

serves six–eight

1.8kg (4lb) baking potatoes, peeled and thinly sliced
2 large onions, sliced
salt and pepper
175g (6oz) blue cheese
150ml (5fl oz) crème fraîche
60g (2½oz) butter, plus an extra knob
300ml (10fl oz) milk
3 tablespoons vegetable oil
1.35kg (3lb) boneless loin of veal
2 tablespoons maple syrup or honey
300ml (10fl oz) chicken stock (see page 13)

Preheat the oven to 180°C/350°F/gas 4. In a large bowl, mix together the potato and onion and season. In a food processor, blend together the blue cheese and crème fraîche.

Grease a large 30 x 23 x 6cm (12 x 9 x 2½ inch) baking dish with the knob of butter and fill with half the potato and onion. Spoon over half the blue cheese mix, top with the remaining potato and onion and finish with the blue cheese mix and 40g (1½oz) of the butter dotted across the top. Pour the milk over, cover with foil and bake for 1 hour. Remove the foil and continue to cook for 30 minutes until golden and tender.

Meanwhile, heat a large roasting tray with the vegetable oil and, once smoking, season the veal and fry, colouring on all sides. Roast for 30 to 35 minutes, turning the joint halfway through. Remove the veal, cover lightly and leave to rest.

Pour away any fat from the roasting tray and place over a medium heat. Pour in the maple syrup with the stock. Bring to the boil, simmering for a few minutes before whisking in the remaining butter. Strain through a fine sieve. Carve the veal, pouring any juices into the loose gravy before serving with the potato gratin.

roast rib of beef

serves six–eight

1 x 3-bone rib of beef
salt and pepper

Preheat the oven to 220°C/425°F/gas 7. Put the beef joint into a roasting tray and season liberally with salt and pepper. Roast in the oven for 15 minutes, then reduce the oven temperature to 190°C/375°F/gas 5. Continue to roast following the approximate cooking times stated below:

roasting times

medium rare	15 minutes per 450g (1lb)
medium	20 minutes per 450g (1lb)
well done	30 minutes per 450g (1lb)

To check the beef is cooked, pierce a skewer into the centre of the meat, leave for a few seconds, then remove and touch on your bottom lip. If it feels cold, the beef is not cooked; if warm, it is medium-rare to medium and if very hot, well done. Once cooked, remove the joint from the oven and roasting tray, cover with foil and leave to rest for at least 20 to 30 minutes.

The rib can now be removed from the bone and carved with ease.

gravy

serves six–eight

1 tablespoon plain flour
600ml (1 pint) beef stock
  (see page 13)
salt and pepper

To make the gravy, pour off most of the fat from the roasting tray, leaving about a tablespoon. Heat the tray on the stove, add the flour and stir over a medium heat until the flour begins to brown.

Stir in the stock, bring to the boil, then reduce to a simmer for a few minutes. Season with salt and pepper if needed, adding any released juices from the joint.

more

- A dash of Worcestershire sauce can help lift the flavour of your gravy.

yorkshire puddings

This Yorkshire pudding batter can be prepared and refrigerated up to 24 hours in advance to guarantee well-risen puddings.

serves six–eight

225g (8oz) plain flour
salt
3 eggs
1 egg white
300–400ml (10–14fl oz)
  milk
oil or dripping

Sift the flour and a pinch of salt into a large bowl. Add the eggs and egg white and whisk in 300ml (10fl oz) of the milk to make a thick batter. If the batter is rested, it may thicken. To loosen, simply whisk in some of the remaining milk.

Generously oil or grease 2 x 12-cup bun trays or 1 medium oven-proof dish, preferably non-stick. During the last 10 minutes of roasting the beef, place the trays or dish in the oven to heat.

Once the beef is resting, return the oven temperature to 220°C/425°F/gas 7. Fill the trays or dish with the batter until almost full and bake for 30 minutes. For very crispy puddings, cook for a further 10 minutes.

wild mushroom and garlic cream

This sauce is an alternative to gravy for roast beef, lamb, pork or chicken, creating a completely different flavour.

makes 400ml (14fl oz)

2 glasses of white wine
1 large clove of garlic,
  crushed
300ml (10fl oz) chicken or
  beef stock (see page 13)
200ml (7fl oz) double or
  whipping cream
225g (8oz) wild, chestnut,
  or button mushrooms,
  sliced
salt and pepper
1 tablespoon chopped
  chives

Boil together the wine and garlic until just a quarter of the liquid is left. Pour in the chicken or beef stock and boil until just half the liquid is left. Add the cream and mushrooms and simmer for 10 to 15 minutes. Season and add the chives just before serving.

red wine beef
with bacon crunch

Preheat the oven to 170°C/325°F/gas 3. Season the beef and dust with flour. Heat 2 tablespoons of oil in a large braising pot, searing the beef on all sides.

Pour away the oil left in the pot. Add the onions and fry until golden brown. Increase the heat, add the mushrooms and stir in the wine and sugar. Boil until just half the liquid is left.

Add the meat to the liquor, pour in the consommé or stock and top up with 400ml (14fl oz) water. Return to a simmer and add the bay leaves and thyme. Cover and braise for 2 hours before turning the joints. Return to the oven and cook for a further 1½ hours.

Meanwhile, put the bacon on a baking tray and cook in the oven for 10 minutes or until deep brown and crispy. Transfer to a wire rack. Once the beef is cooked, remove the joints, onions and mushrooms from the pot and keep warm. Strain the gravy and reboil, as it reduces by a third for a richer flavour. To thicken, add the loosened cornflower, little by little, to the consistency you prefer. Season with salt and pepper.

Cut the meat into chunky pieces and return to the sauce with the onions and mushrooms. Serve with the bacon sitting on top and sprinkled with the parsley, if using.

serves six

2kg (4½lb) feather blade of beef, divided into 2 pieces
salt and pepper
flour, for dusting
vegetable oil
450g (1lb) button onions
600g (1lb 5oz) button mushrooms
1 bottle of red wine
2 tablespoons soft brown or demerara sugar
2 x 400ml (14fl oz) tins of beef consommé or stock (see page 13)
2 bay leaves
2 sprigs of thyme
12 rashers of streaky bacon
1½ teaspoons cornflour (optional), loosened with a little cold water
a handful of roughly chopped curly parsley (optional)

slow-roast pork belly with gorgonzola and apple cabbage

Although it needs 3 hours' slow roasting, the beauty of this cut of pork is that it looks after itself. As the fat melts it bastes the meat, leaving the joint so soft it carves with a spoon.

serves four

1kg (2¼lb) belly of pork, skin scored
sea salt and pepper
vegetable oil
20 shallots, peeled
300ml (½ pint) chicken stock (see page 13)
a pinch of demerara sugar
1 small cabbage, quartered, cored and shredded
25g (1oz) butter
2 apples, grated
100g (4oz) room-temperature Gorgonzola, broken into pieces

Preheat the oven to 170°C/325°F/gas 3.

Season the meat side of the pork belly and place, skin-side up, on a wire rack over a roasting tray. Brush with oil, sprinkle with sea salt and roast for 3 hours before removing and leaving to rest.

Finely slice four of the shallots, placing the rest in a saucepan with the stock and sugar. Simmer the shallots until soft and the cooking liquor has reduced, leaving a nice shiny glaze. Meanwhile, boil the cabbage in salted water for a few minutes until tender. Melt the butter in a saucepan, add the sliced shallots and cook until they begin to soften. Add the apple, before stirring in the cabbage and seasoning. The Gorgonzola can now be stirred in, melting as it warms.

Cut the crackling from the belly, snapping it into large pieces. Carve the pork in thick slices, dividing it between plates with a spoonful of the cabbage and the shallots.

white pork and wild mushroom stew

While fresh wild mushrooms are only available during the autumn and winter months, good-quality dried wild mushrooms are available year-round.

serves four

50g (2oz) dried wild
  mushrooms
900g (2lb) diced pork
a large knob of butter
2 onions, finely chopped
salt and pepper
1 glass of white wine
150ml (5fl oz) double cream
a squeeze of lemon juice
1 heaped tablespoon
  roughly chopped chervil

Soak the mushrooms in 600ml (1 pint) warm water.

Put the pork into a large saucepan and cover with water. Bring to a simmer and cook for 5 minutes. Drain the meat and rinse under cold running water.

Return the pan to the stove and melt the butter. When sizzling, add the onion and cook over a medium heat until it begins to soften. Season the pork and return to the pan. Strain over the mushroom water, pour in the wine and bring to a gentle simmer. Cover with a lid, and cook for 1¾ hours until the meat is tender.

Add the drained mushrooms to the pan. Pour in the cream and return to a fairly rapid simmer until the sauce has slightly thickened. Check the seasoning and add a squeeze of lemon juice to taste. Scatter with the chervil and serve.

more
- Half a chicken stock cube can be sprinkled into the sauce to enrich the flavour.

pork belly boulangère

For a crunchier crackling, ask your butcher to score the skin.

Preheat the oven to 170°C/325°F/gas 3. Season the meat side of the pork belly and place, skin-side up, on a wire rack over a roasting tray. Brush with oil, sprinkle with sea salt and roast for 3 hours.

With the pork in the oven, mix the potatoes with the onions and spoon into a shallow baking dish or roasting tray large enough to sit beneath the pork and capture all of the released juices. Pour over the chicken stock.

After the first hour of roasting the pork, remove the roasting tray from beneath the meat and replace it with the tray of potatoes. Continue to roast for the final 2 hours. Once cooked, if the potatoes have only coloured slightly, simply place under a hot grill until golden brown.

Cut the crackling from the belly, snapping it into large pieces. Carve the pork in thick slices, dividing it among plates with the crackling and a generous spoonful of potatoes.

serves four

1kg (2¼ lb) pork belly
sea salt and pepper
oil, for brushing
4 large baking potatoes,
  peeled and thinly sliced
2 large onions, sliced
600ml (1 pint) chicken stock
  (see page 13)

more

- A couple of large crushed or sliced garlic cloves can be added to the potato and onion mix.

boiled pork pot

A complete meal in one pot. Traditionally served with sauerkraut, this recipe is with English buttered cabbage.

serves four

2 large onions, quartered
650g (1½lb) carrots, peeled
2 cloves of garlic, peeled
2 bay leaves
a few sprigs of thyme
450g (1lb) piece of pork shoulder
450g (1lb) piece of pork belly
½ bottle of dry white wine
1 chicken stock cube (see page 13)
450g (1lb) pork sausages
olive oil
450g (1lb) new potatoes
1 green cabbage, torn into bite-sized pieces
salt and pepper
50g (2oz) butter

Preheat the oven to 170°C/325°F/gas 3.

Put the onion, carrot, garlic, bay leaves, thyme, pork shoulder and belly into a large braising pot. Pour in the wine and enough water to cover the meat. Sprinkle over the stock cube and bring to the boil. Cover and braise for 2½ hours.

Remove the pot from the oven and skim off any excess fat. Quickly fry the sausages in a splash of olive oil until well coloured. Add the sausages to the pot with the new potatoes, cover and return to the oven for a further 45 minutes.

Cook the cabbage in boiling salted water for a few minutes until tender. Drain and return to the pan. Season with salt and pepper, stir in the butter and keep warm.

Once cooked, remove the meat and vegetables from the pot and place on a large platter, spooning over the cooking liquor and serve with the buttered cabbage.

more

- The cooking liquor can be boiled and reduced for a stronger flavour.

pork belly potatoes and red cabbage roast

Preheat the oven to 170°C/325°F/gas 3. Season the meat side of the pork belly, brushing the skin side with oil and sprinkle with the sea salt.

Season the potatoes and place them, cut-side down, in a large oiled roasting tray. Sit the pork belly on top and roast for 3 hours.

Meanwhile, prepare the red cabbage and cook in the oven for the last 2 hours of roasting the pork.

Once cooked, remove the pork and potatoes from the roasting tray and keep warm. Pour off the excess fat from the tray and return to the stove over a medium heat. Add the chicken stock and boil rapidly until just two thirds of the liquid is left. Stir in the butter and strain. Carve and serve the pork with the potatoes and red cabbage, drizzling with the buttery liquor.

serves six

1.5kg (3lb) piece of pork belly
salt and pepper
vegetable oil
sea salt
6 jacket potatoes, halved
1 x braised red cabbage (see page 13)
(14fl oz) chicken stock (see page 13)
a large knob of butter

boiled bacon collar with spicy sausage mash and peas

The bacon joint is often found presoaked, releasing excess salt content. If unavailable, simply soak in cold water for 24 hours before boiling.

serves six

1.5kg (3lb) boned and rolled bacon collar
2 onions, quartered
3 carrots, halved
3 sticks of celery, halved
1 chicken stock cube (see page 13)
1x mash potato recipe (see page 451)
olive oil
350g (12oz) chorizo sausage, peeled and cut into cubes
350g (12oz) frozen peas, defrosted
50g (2oz) butter

Rinse the bacon well and put into a large pan with the vegetables. Cover with water, sprinkling in the stock cube. Bring to the boil, and simmer for 2 hours, skimming from time to time. Remove from the heat and leave the bacon to rest in the liquid for 20 minutes.

Meanwhile, make the mashed potato. Heat a little olive oil in a frying pan. Once smoking, add the chorizo and fry for a few minutes until golden brown. Drain on kitchen paper before adding to the mash and keep warm.

Strain 400ml (14fl oz) of the bacon liquor into a saucepan, boiling until just three quarters of the liquid is left (any extra liquor can be refrigerated or frozen and used as a base for the bacon soup on page 398). Add the peas, simmering for a minute or two before stirring in the butter.

Carve the collar, offering one thick or two thinner slices per person. Serve with a generous spoon of spicy sausage mash and a ladleful of peas.

more
- The vegetables cooked with the bacon can be offered as a side dish.

roast pork

Generally leg, loin, shoulder or belly are the joints to choose when roasting pork. For this recipe I've chosen a joint from the leg. Pork needs 25 to 30 minutes cooking per 450g (1lb) with an additional 25 to 30 minutes.

serves four–six

2kg (4½lb) boned and
  rolled joint of pork
oil
sea salt

Preheat the oven to 200°C/400°F/gas 6.

Place the joint on a wire rack over the top of a roasting tray to protect the base of the meat from drying out. Brush the skin lightly with oil and sprinkle with salt. Roast the pork for 2½ hours. Basting the joint is not necessary because pork has enough fat to keep the meat moist as it cooks.

To check the pork is cooked, insert a skewer into the thickest part. Any juices released should be totally clear. Take the pork off the rack and keep warm while resting for 30 minutes before carving. The pork is now ready to serve with a piece of the crispy crackling.

cider gravy

serves four–six

1 tablespoon plain flour
300ml (10fl oz) sweet cider
300ml (10fl oz) chicken
  stock (see page 13)
salt and pepper

While the pork is resting, pour away the fat from the roasting tray (it can be used for roasting potatoes). Place the tray on top of the stove over a medium heat. Stir in the flour and cook for a minute before whisking in the cider and stock a little at a time. Bring the gravy to a simmer and cook for a few minutes, seasoning before straining and serving.

prune, leek and sage stuffing

serves four–six

450g (1lb) pork sausages
12 prunes, roughly chopped
1 small–medium leek, sliced
75g (3oz) fresh white
  breadcrumbs
10 sage leaves, chopped
1 egg
salt and pepper
a knob of butter

Slit the sausages lengthways and remove the skins.

In a large bowl, beat all the ingredients together and season with salt and pepper.

Spoon the mixture into a buttered baking dish or small roasting tin and bake in the oven alongside the pork during the last 45 minutes of roasting.

roast rack of pork with turnip and prune dauphinois

It's best to ask for the pork to be French trimmed, as per a rack of lamb. Also, if possible, have the chine bone removed so you can cut between the ribs with ease.

Preheat the oven to 190°C/375°F/gas 5.

Cover the rack bones with foil and season the underside of the rack with salt and pepper. Place in a roasting tray and brush with a little oil, seasoning the skin with sea salt.

Rub a large, deep ovenproof dish with the garlic, brushing with half the butter. Season the turnip and mix with the cream and spoon half in the dish. Top with the prunes and finish with the remaining turnip. Cook the pork and dauphinois in the oven for 15 minutes before reducing the temperature to 150°C/300°F/gas 2 and baking for a further 60 minutes. Remove the dauphinois from the oven and keep warm to one side. Increase the oven temperature to 220°C/425°F/gas7 and continue to roast the pork for a further 20 minutes for a crispy crackling finish before removing from the tray.

Drain and discard any excess fat from the pork tray and warm on top of the stove, adding the honey. As the honey begins to caramelize, add the stock and return to a simmer.

Cook gently for a few minutes, seasoning if needed. Whisk in the butter before straining through a fine sieve. The pork is now ready to serve with the turnip and prune dauphinois.

serves six–eight

1 rack of pork (6–8 bones), French trimmed
sea salt and pepper
vegetable oil
1 tablespoon honey
300ml (10fl oz) chicken stock (see page 13)
25–50g (1–2oz) butter

for the turnip and prune dauphinois

1 large clove of garlic, peeled and halved
25g (1oz) butter
salt and ground white pepper
1kg (2¼lb) peeled turnips, thinly sliced
600ml (1 pint) double cream (½ cream and ½ milk can also be used)
300g (10oz) prunes

stout-glazed leg of lamb

serves four

1.75kg (4lb) leg of lamb
olive oil
salt and pepper
300ml (10fl oz) stout
3 heaped tablespoons soft
  brown sugar
300ml (10fl oz) lamb,
  chicken or beef stock
  (see page 13)

Preheat the oven to 200°C/400°F/gas 6. Brush the leg with olive oil and season with salt and pepper.

Place the leg in a roasting tray or large ovenproof pan and cook for 1 hour 15 minutes for medium rare, 1 hour 30 minutes for medium, 1 hour 45 minutes for medium well and 2 hours for well done. Add the stout and sugar during the final 30 minutes of cooking and baste from time to time.

Remove the leg from the tray and skim off the fat. Bring the juices in the tray to the boil and simmer to a thick, sticky consistency before rolling the leg in the glaze to coat. Remove the lamb from the tray and leave to rest for 15 to 20 minutes.

Heat any remaining glaze left in the pan until sizzling. Add the stock and bring to a simmer, then season and strain.

Carve the lamb and serve with the gravy.

more

- For a thicker gravy, whisk in 1–2 teaspoons of cornflour loosened with a little cold water.
- 1–2 tablespoons of redcurrant jelly can be added to the gravy for a fruitier flavour.

seven-hour leg of lamb with potatoes, carrots and onions

This is a Sunday lunch to be served in the evening.

serves four

4 small onions, peeled
3 cloves of garlic, peeled
  and halved
2–3 sprigs of thyme
2 bay leaves
2.25kg (5lb) leg of lamb
sea salt and pepper
1 bottle of white wine
600ml (1pint) chicken stock
  (see page 13)
8 carrots, peeled
4 potatoes, peeled and
  quartered
4 plum tomatoes, peeled,
  deseeded and cut into
  cubes (see page 20)

Preheat the oven to 150°C/300°F/gas 2. Cut each onion into three thick rings and put into a roasting tray with the garlic, thyme and bay leaves. Season the lamb, place on top and roast for 30 minutes.

Remove the lamb from the oven and pour away any fat released into the pan. Ladle half the wine and stock over the leg. Return to the oven and bake for a further 3½ hours. Add the carrots, potato, tomato and remaining wine and stock to the roasting tray. Cover the joint with foil and return to the oven for the final 3 hours.

The lamb is now moist, tender and falling off the bone and ready to serve with the potato, carrots and onion, finishing with the tomato and garlic-flavoured juices.

more

- If all the cooking liquor evaporates, simply loosen with a ladleful or two of water.

roast leg of lamb

serves four

1.75kg (4lb) leg of lamb
olive oil
salt and pepper
300ml (10fl oz) lamb,
  chicken or beef stock
  (see page 13)
2 tablespoons redcurrant
  jelly

Preheat the oven to 200°C/400°F/gas 6. Brush the leg with olive oil and season with salt and pepper.

Place the leg in a roasting tray and cook and baste for 1 hour 15 minutes for medium rare, 1 hour 30 minutes for medium, 1 hour 45 minutes for medium well and 2 hours for well done. Remove the leg from the tray and leave to rest for 15 to 20 minutes.

Pour off the fat from the roasting tray and heat the remaining juices until sizzling. Add the stock and bring to a simmer. Whisk in the redcurrant jelly until melted, then season with salt and pepper.

Carve the lamb, offering the gravy as it is or straining it before serving.

more

- For rosemary and garlic roast lamb, make some incisions in the flesh side of the leg and insert a sprig of rosemary and a thick slice of garlic in each.

mint sauce

serves two–four

3 teaspoons caster sugar
3 tablespoons mint leaves,
  chopped
4 tablespoons malt or white
  wine vinegar

Mix together the caster sugar with 1 tablespoon of boiling water and stir until the sugar has dissolved.

Stir in the mint and vinegar and leave to infuse for 30 minutes before serving.

apricot and pine nut rack of lamb with soft onions

Preheat the oven to 220°C/425°F/gas 7. Heat a roasting tray on the stove. Season and place the lamb in, fat-side down. Fry for a few minutes until well browned, then seal the racks on the meat side before removing from the tray. Pour away most of the fat, leaving a tablespoon in the pan.

Roughly chop the pine nuts and mix with the breadcrumbs, lemon thyme, parsley, apricots and melted butter, seasoning with salt and pepper. Press the crumbs on to the fat side of each rack, then return to the roasting tray, crumb-side up.

For a pink finish, roast the racks for 15 to 20 minutes. Remove from the tray and keep the racks warm while they rest.

Return the roasting tray to the stove, add the onion and fry for 5 to 10 minutes until the onions have softened, absorbing any juices and roasted crumbs left in the tray. Season with salt and pepper.

Halve the racks or divide into cutlets and serve with the soft onions.

serves four

2 racks of lamb (6–8 bones
    per rack), French trimmed
salt and pepper
1 heaped tablespoon pine
    nuts, toasted
    (see page 13)
4 thick slices of white bread,
    crumbed
1 heaped teaspoon
    chopped lemon thyme
1 tablespoon chopped
    parsley
6 dried apricots, roughly
    chopped
40g (1½oz) melted butter
2 large onions, thinly sliced

west country squab pie

An easy-to-make pie from the West Country that doesn't actually contain any squab or wild pigeon but was traditionally made with neck of mutton, here replaced with lamb neck fillets. Classically the pie is served with clotted cream.

serves four

900g (2lb) lamb neck fillets,
  cut into 16 pieces
salt and pepper
1 onion, sliced
1 leek, sliced
8 prunes
2 Cox's apples, peeled,
  cored and sliced into
  wedges
2 thick slices of white bread,
  crumbled
½ teaspoon ground allspice
a generous pinch of nutmeg
350g (12oz) ready-rolled
  shortcrust or puff pastry
1 beaten egg

Preheat the oven to 200°C/400°F/gas 6. Season the lamb before mixing in a 1.8 litre (3 pint) pie dish with the onion, leek, prunes and apples. Stir in the breadcrumbs, allspice and nutmeg.

Roll the pastry 4cm (1½ inches) larger than the pie dish, cutting off a thin strip from around the edge. Moisten the rim of the dish with water and press the thin strip of pastry on it before brushing with the beaten egg. Top the pie dish with the rolled pastry, pressing the edges together. Brush the egg over the top and pierce a hole in the centre. Any pastry trimmings can be used to decorate the top. Leave to rest for 20 minutes.

Bake for 20 minutes, then lower the oven temperature to 170°C/325°F/gas 3 and bake for a further 1¼ hours, the meat, vegetables and fruit creating their own gravy within the pie. Should the pastry begin to colour and brown too quickly, cover with a piece of foil to prevent it from burning.

roast rump of lamb with pancetta champ and marjoram cream

Champ, of course, is the classic Irish dish of buttery mashed potatoes with spring onions.

serves four

for the pancetta champ
675g (1½lb) floury
   potatoes, peeled and
   quartered
sea salt and ground white
   pepper
1 bunch of spring onions,
   thinly sliced
50g (2oz) butter
100–150ml (3½–5fl oz)
   double cream or milk
225g (8oz) pancetta cubes

4 x 150–175g (5–6oz)
   rumps of lamb, trimmed
300ml (10fl oz) chicken
   stock (see page 13)
3 generous sprigs of
   marjoram
4–5 tablespoons double
   cream
a squeeze of lemon juice

Cook the potatoes in boiling salted water for 20 to 25 minutes until tender. Drain well before mashing until smooth. Melt the butter in a frying pan. Once sizzling, stir in the spring onions and cook until soft. Fold them into the mash with the cream. Quickly fry the pancetta until golden before stirring into the champ and seasoning.

Meanwhile, preheat the oven to 200°C/400°F/gas 6. Heat a roasting pan on top of the stove. Season the rumps and fry, fat-side down, to a golden brown before turning and roasting in the oven for 10 to 12 minutes, leaving a pink centre. Leave to rest.

Meanwhile, boil the stock with 2 sprigs of the marjoram until just half of the liquid is left. Add the cream, simmer for a few minutes, then add the lemon juice and any juices released from the lamb. Season and strain through a fine sieve or blitz with a hand blender for a light, frothy finish.

Carve the lamb and serve on a spoonful of the pancetta champ, sprinkling with leaves from the remaining marjoram sprig and trickling with the sauce.

lamb goujons with curry mayonnaise and mint raita

Here I'm featuring one of the cheaper cuts, the breast of lamb. It needs a few hours to cook, but is well worth waiting for.

Preheat the oven to 150°C/300°F/gas 2. Place the lamb, onion, carrot, garlic and rosemary in an ovenproof braising pot or dish. Cover with water, season and bring to a simmer on top of the stove. Cover with a lid and bake for 3 hours until tender.

Remove the lamb from the pot and leave until just warm before pulling the bones from the meat. Place the lamb between two baking trays with the top one weighted and refrigerate for a few hours or overnight to set before cutting into finger-sized strips.

Mix together the breadcrumbs, lemon zest and parsley and season. Dip the lamb fingers in the egg and then breadcrumb firmly so they are well covered.

Heat a few centimetres of vegetable oil in a deep pan. Fry a handful of lamb goujons at a time until golden brown and crispy. Drain on kitchen paper and keep warm while frying the rest. Once all cooked, the goujons are ready for dunking in the sauces.

serves four

1 breast of lamb
1 large onion, chopped
2 carrots, chopped
2 cloves of garlic, peeled and halved
a sprig of rosemary
salt and pepper
100g (4oz) fresh white breadcrumbs
grated zest of 1 lemon
2 tablespoons chopped parsley
2 eggs, beaten
vegetable oil
1 x curry mayonnaise (see page 465)
1 x mint raita (see page 465)

hogget cobbler with orange onions and sage scones

Lamb becomes hogget on its first birthday, hogget being the stage between lamb and mutton.

serves six–eight

1.8kg (4lb) diced shoulder
  of hogget
salt and pepper
1 heaped tablespoon plain
  flour
vegetable oil
450g (1lb) button onions,
  peeled
1 tablespoon tomato purée
1 teaspoon demerara sugar
grated zest of 1 orange
300ml (10fl oz) orange juice
600ml (1 pint) lamb or beef
  stock (see page 13)

for the sage scones

225g (8oz) plain flour, plus
  extra for dusting
15g (⅔oz) baking powder
50g (2oz) butter, chopped
1 tablespoon chopped sage
  leaves
150ml (5fl oz) buttermilk
1 egg, beaten
sea salt

Preheat the oven to 170°C/325°F/gas 3.

Season the hogget and roll in the flour. Heat 3 tablespoons of oil in a braising pot and fry the meat until well coloured. Add the button onions, tomato purée, sugar, orange zest, juice and stock, topping up with a little water, if needed. Bring to a simmer, cover and braise in the oven for 2½ hours.

Meanwhile, sift the flour and baking powder into a bowl. Rub in the butter until it resembles fine crumbs, and stir in the sage. Pour in the buttermilk and mix to a smooth dough. Clingfilm and refrigerate for at least 1 hour to rest.

After 2 hours of braising the hogget, roll out the scone dough on a floured surface until 1–1.5cm (½–¾ inch) thick. Cut into six to eight 6cm (2½ inch) discs, brushing each one with the beaten egg.

Remove the lid from the braising pot, place the scones on the top and increase the oven temperature to 200°C/400°F/gas 6. Bake until the scones have risen and are golden brown. The dish is now ready to serve.

lamb with beans, onions, tomatoes and tarragon

serves four–six

900g (2lb) lamb neck fillets,
   cut into large chunks (2–3
   per person)
sea salt and pepper
1 heaped tablespoon flour
olive oil
3 onions, sliced
4 cloves of garlic, chopped
450g (1lb) tomatoes, cut
   into chunks
½ bottle of red wine or
   300ml (10fl oz) water
1 x 400g (14oz) tin of
   tomatoes
2 x 400g (14oz) tins of
   haricot beans, drained and
   rinsed
1 chicken stock cube
   (see page 13)
4 generous sprigs of
   tarragon

Preheat the oven to 170°C/325°F/gas 3.

Season the lamb chunks with sea salt and pepper and dust with flour. Heat 3 tablespoons of olive oil in a large braising pot and fry the lamb, colouring well. Add the onion and garlic and continue to fry until softened.

Stir in the tomatoes, red wine or water, tinned tomatoes (including all the juices), haricot beans, stock cube, 2 sprigs of the tarragon and about 300ml (10fl oz) water to just cover the meat. Bring to a simmer, cover and braise in the oven for 2½ hours until tender.

Once cooked, transfer the pot on to the stove, remove the lid and skim any excess fat from the top. Should the sauce be too thin, rapidly simmer until thickened with a stronger flavour.

Chop the remaining tarragon, add to the pot and check for seasoning before serving.

lamb hotpot

This is a complete meal baked under the same roof: lamb chops, potatoes, carrots and onions.

Preheat the oven to 180°C/350°F/gas 4. Heat a frying pan with 2 tablespoons of the oil, season the chops and fry until well coloured.

Brush a deep casserole dish with some of the butter. Scatter half the potatoes across the base, followed by half the onions, carrots, and chops, sprinkling them with the rosemary. Cover with the remaining carrots, onions and chops, arranging the potatoes on top.

Pour over the stock, cover with a lid and bake for 2 hours. Remove the lid and brush the potatoes with the remaining melted butter. Increase the oven temperature to 200°C/400°F/gas 6 and bake for a further 15 to 20 minutes until the potatoes are golden brown.

serves four

vegetable oil
8 large lamb chops
salt and pepper
25g (1oz) melted butter
4 potatoes, peeled and
  sliced
3 onions, sliced
4 carrots, sliced
1 large sprig of rosemary,
  finely chopped
600ml (1 pint) chicken stock
  (see page 13)

chicken, ham and mushroom pie

serves six

butter, for greasing
12 chicken thighs, skinned
  and boned
salt and pepper
2 onions, finely sliced
350g (12oz) small button
  mushrooms
225g (8oz) piece of cooked
  ham, broken into bite-
  sized pieces
1 bay leaf
2 sprigs of thyme
100ml (3½fl oz) chicken
  stock (see page 15)
350g (12oz) ready-rolled
  shortcrust or puff pastry
1 egg, beaten

Preheat the oven to 220°C/425°F/gas 7. Lightly butter a deep 1.8 litre (3 pint) pie dish.

Halve the chicken thighs and season with salt and pepper. Mix in the pie dish with the onion, mushrooms and ham. Add the bay leaf, thyme sprigs and chicken stock.

Cut the pastry 4cm (1½ inches) larger than the pie dish. Moisten the rim of the dish with water and, using some of the pastry trimmings, cut a strip to press around the edge. Brush the pastry rim with egg, lay the pastry sheet over the top, trimming and pressing the edges together. Brush the beaten egg over the top and pierce a hole in the centre. Any remaining pastry trimmings can be used to decorate the pie. Leave the pie to rest for 15 to 20 minutes.

Bake the pie for 15 minutes, then lower the temperature to 170°C/325°F/gas 3 and continue to bake for a further 45 minutes, covering with aluminium foil if colouring too quickly. The succulent chicken pie is now ready to serve.

roast chicken with gravy

serves four

1.6–1.8kg (3½–4lb)
  chicken
25g (1oz) softened butter
salt and pepper
300ml (10fl oz) chicken
  stock (see page 13)

Preheat the oven to 200°C/400°F/gas 6. Brush the chicken with the butter and season.

Place the chicken in a roasting tray, breast-side down, and roast for 40 minutes, basting from time to time. Turn the bird breast-side up, baste liberally and roast for a further 20 minutes. To see if the bird is cooked, pierce the thigh with a skewer and check that the juices run clear. Transfer the bird on to a plate, breast-side down, and leave to rest for 15 minutes.

Pour away any fat from the roasting tray before returning to the stove. Once sizzling, pour in the stock, stirring to loosen the sticky juices from the base of the tray. Simmer for a few minutes, seasoning before straining through a sieve. Carve the chicken into thick pieces to retain maximum moistness and serve with the gravy.

more

- The gravy can be thickened by whisking in 1–2 teaspoons cornflour, loosened with a little cold water, and simmering for a few minutes before serving.

bacon and chipolatas

serves four

4–8 rashers of streaky
  bacon or pancetta
8–12 chipolatas

The bacon can be fried or grilled until crispy and served alongside the chicken. Alternatively, lay the bacon over the chicken's breast while roasting to help maintain succulence. If trying this method, the bird should be roasted breast-side up for the entire time.

The chipolatas can be added to the roasting tray during the last 20 minutes of cooking.

sage, onion and lemon stuffing

Mix together in a bowl the onion, sausage meat, lemon zest and juice, sage, breadcrumbs and egg, seasoning with salt and pepper.

Preheat the oven to 200°C/400°F/gas 6. Put the stuffing into a buttered dish and roast for 30 to 40 minutes. The stuffing can also be placed in the cavity formed by gently releasing the skin at the neck end of the chicken. Replace the skin over the stuffing and secure with a small skewer or cocktail stick before roasting.

serves four

1 large onion, finely chopped
100g (4oz) sausages, skinned
finely grated zest and juice of 1 lemon
1 tablespoon chopped sage
100g (4oz) fresh white breadcrumbs
1 beaten egg
salt and pepper
butter, for greasing

bread sauce

Stud the onion halves with the cloves. Place the studded onions and bay leaf in the milk and bring to a simmer. Remove the pan from the heat, cover with a lid and leave to infuse for 1 hour.

When ready to serve, remove the onions and bay leaf. Stir in the breadcrumbs and warm over a low heat for 5 to 10 minutes until the sauce thickens.

Add the butter and cream and season with the salt, pepper and nutmeg.

serves four

1 small onion, peeled and halved
2 cloves
1 bay leaf
300ml (10fl oz) milk
50g (2oz) fresh white breadcrumbs
a knob of butter
2 tablespoons double cream
salt and pepper
a pinch of grated nutmeg

roast paprika chicken

serves four

1.6–1.8kg (3½–4lb)
  chicken
50g (2oz) softened butter
salt
1 lemon, halved
1 tablespoon paprika

Preheat the oven to 200°C/400°F/gas 6. Brush the chicken all over with the butter and season with salt. Squeeze over the lemon juice, then dust the chicken with paprika.

Place the chicken in a roasting tray, breast-side up, and roast for 1 hour, basting from time to time. To see if the bird is cooked, pierce the thigh with a skewer and check that the juices run clear. Transfer the bird on to a plate breast-side down, pour over the juices from the tray and leave to rest for 15 minutes.

Carve the chicken into thick pieces to retain maximum moistness, then spoon the juices over the meat.

more

- 1–2 spoonfuls of sour cream added to the juices blends very well with the paprika.

roast chicken thighs with bacon, carrots, onions and potatoes

Preheat the oven to 200°C/400°F/gas 6.

Heat a large earthenware dish or roasting tray and dry-fry the bacon until well coloured. Add the red onion, potatoes, carrots and herbs. Season and roast in the oven for 10 to 15 minutes.

Meanwhile, season the chicken thighs. Warm a splash of olive oil in a frying pan and, once smoking, fry the thighs, skin-side down, to a golden brown. Turn the pieces over and cook for a further minute. Remove the vegetables from the oven, add the thighs to the dish and continue cooking for a further 30 to 35 minutes before adding the butter.

Spoon the chicken, bacon and vegetables on to four plates. Whisk the vinegar and mustard, if using, into the buttery juices left in the dish and drizzle over the roast.

serves four

225g (8oz) piece of streaky
  bacon, divided into 4
  chunks
2 red onions, each cut into
  8 wedges
500g (18oz) new potatoes,
  halved
12 small peeled Chantenay
  carrots or 4 large peeled
  carrots, cut into chunks
a few sprigs of thyme
a few sage leaves
sea salt and pepper
8 chicken thighs, skin on
olive oil
2 knobs of butter
1–2 tablespoons red wine
  vinegar (optional)
1–2 teaspoons Dijon or
  wholegrain mustard
  (optional)

roasted duck with red wine blackberries

In this recipe, the legs and breasts are carved off the duck to serve, but if you have poultry shears, they can be used to serve each person half a duck.

serves four

2 x 1.5kg (3lb 5oz) ducks
salt and pepper
2 glasses of fruity red wine
2 teaspoons soft brown or
  demerara sugar
5 tablespoons blackberry
  jam or jelly
175g (6oz) blackberries
50g (2oz) butter

Preheat the oven to 220°C/425°F/gas 7. Place the ducks in a roasting tray and sprinkle with salt before roasting for 20 minutes.

Reduce the oven temperature to 180°C/350°F/gas 4. Baste the birds and continue to roast for a further 1 hour 40 minutes, basting from time to time.

Remove the ducks from the tray and rest for 10 to 15 minutes. To serve, cut the legs and the breasts from each duck, offering one of each per person.

Meanwhile, boil the wine with the sugar in a saucepan until just two-thirds of the liquid is left. Stir in the jam and gently warm through until it has completely melted.

Add the blackberries and butter, simmering until the fruits have softened, before seasoning. Spoon the sauce over the duck and serve.

more
- Mashed or sauté potatoes (see page 451) work well with this dish.

steamed duck with caramelized onions, olives and walnuts

This recipe will serve two to four depending on whether you want to serve half or quarter a duck each.

serves two–four

1.6–1.8kg (3½–4lb) duck
sea salt and pepper
8 tablespoons olive oil
4 medium onions, sliced
2 teaspoons demerara
  sugar
100g (4oz) green olives,
  pitted and halved
50g (2oz) walnuts, chopped
2 tablespoons sherry
  vinegar
vegetable oil

Prick the duck with a fork and season with salt and pepper. Steam the duck in a bamboo steamer or on a wire rack over a large saucepan of rapidly simmering water, covered with a pot, for 2 to 2½ hours, keeping the water topped up from time to time. Once cooked, remove from the steamer and allow the duck to rest for 5 to 10 minutes.

Meanwhile, heat 2 tablespoons of the olive oil in a large frying pan, add the onion and fry until a rich, deep golden brown. Sprinkle in the sugar and season, stir in the olives and walnuts and keep warm.

Whisk together the remaining olive oil and the sherry vinegar, and season with ¼ teaspoon of salt and a twist of pepper.

Cut the legs and breasts from the duck, remove the skin and quickly shred into strips. Fry the strips in a little vegetable oil until golden and crispy. Serve with the duck and caramelized onions, spooning over the dressing.

treacle duck breasts with creamy date parsnips

Although not essential, the wrinkled, toffee-like medjool dates are the best to use for this dish. I've also included a rich sauce, which isn't strictly needed as the date parsnips are very moist, but does add a tasty extra.

serves four

900g (2lb) parsnips, peeled
    and quartered
100g (4oz) dates, halved
    and stoned
milk
salt and ground white
    pepper
4 duck breasts
vegetable oil
150ml (5fl oz) Madeira or
    red wine
400ml (14fl oz) tin of game
    or beef consommé or
    chicken stock
    (see page 13)
1–2 teaspoons cornflour,
    loosened with water
1 tablespoon black treacle

Cut away and discard the woody core from each of the parsnip quarters and place the parsnips in a saucepan with the dates, topping with milk to cover. Simmer for 15 to 20 minutes until the parsnips are completely tender. Purée the parsnips and dates in a blender until smooth, adding a little milk if needed to loosen before seasoning.

Preheat the oven to 220°C/425°F/gas 7. Season the duck breasts and heat a tablespoon of the oil in a roasting tray. Place the breasts, skin-side down, in the oil and fry over a medium heat for 8 to 10 minutes, until golden brown. Turn and finish cooking in the oven for 7 to 8 minutes. Remove from the tray and leave to rest.

Meanwhile, boil the Madeira in a small saucepan until almost dry. Pour in the consommé and simmer for a few minutes. Whisk in the cornflour, a little at a time, until a sauce consistency is reached.

Preheat the grill. Loosen the treacle with a little water, arrange the duck breasts on a baking tray and brush lightly with the treacle. Grill until the treacle begins to sizzle, brushing each breast once more, then serve whole or cut into three to four slices with the hot creamy date parsnips and the sauce.

roast partridge with toasted salsify and maple sherry gravy

Peel the salsify, cut each into three or four sticks and place in a bowl of cold water with half the lemon juice. Cook the salsify in boiling salted water with the remaining lemon juice for 10 to 12 minutes until just tender, drain and keep to one side.

Preheat the oven to 200°C/400°F/gas 6. Heat the oil in an ovenproof frying pan, season the partridges and fry until completely golden brown. Roast, breast-side up, for 12 to 15 minutes (or up to 20 minutes for well done). Remove the birds from the pan and keep warm.

For the gravy, pour any excess fat from the pan before adding the maple syrup and sherry, bubbling to a syrupy consistency. Add the chicken stock and boil until just two-thirds is left. Season and whisk in the 50g (2oz) of butter before straining.

Meanwhile, preheat the grill. Lay the salsify on a baking tray, brush with a knob of butter and season. Toast under the grill until golden brown.

Cook the cabbage in boiling salted water for a few minutes until tender, drain and season, rolling in the remaining knob of butter. Remove the legs and breasts from the birds and serve with the salsify, cabbage and maple sherry gravy.

serves four

8 salsify sticks
juice of 1 lemon
2 tablespoons vegetable oil
4 oven-ready partridges
salt and pepper
2 large knobs of butter
½ green cabbage, cut into
   bite-sized pieces

for the maple sherry gravy
2 tablespoons maple syrup
100ml (3½fl oz) dry sherry
300ml (10fl oz) chicken
   stock (see page 13)
50g (2oz) butter

more
- An extra dot or two of maple syrup can be drizzled over the legs before serving.

ham-wrapped trout with english mustard sauce

serves four

20–24 sage leaves
4 trout
salt and pepper
4 slices of Parma ham
olive oil
2 teaspoons English
  mustard
1 teaspoon clear honey
3 teaspoons red wine
  vinegar
4 teaspoons mayonnaise
5 tablespoons walnut or
  groundnut oil
a large knob of butter

Preheat the oven to 250°C/475°F/gas 9.

Place five to six sage leaves inside each fish and season. Wrap a slice of Parma ham around the centre of the fish, brushing the trout liberally with olive oil.

Heat a roasting tray or large frying pan and brush with olive oil. Once hot, place in the trout carefully, transferring the tray to the oven and roasting for 10 to 12 minutes until cooked through.

Meanwhile, whisk together in a bowl the mustard, honey, vinegar and mayonnaise. Continue to whisk while drizzling in the walnut or groundnut oil. The consistency should be just thin enough to pour without being runny. If it is too thick, loosen with 1–2 teaspoons of water. Season with a pinch of salt.

Lift the trout on to the plates, returning the baking tray to the stove. Once hot, melt the knob of butter into the trout juices and spoon over the fish. Drizzle the sauce over or serve separately.

more
- Should English mustard be a little too fiery for your taste buds, replace with wholegrain or Dijon mustard.

roast flat fish with parsley lemon butter and new potatoes lyonnaise

serves four–six

1kg (2¼lb) new potatoes
1.5–2kg (3–4½lb) turbot, brill, plaice or flounder, cleaned and scaled
olive oil
sea salt and pepper
50g (2oz) butter, plus 1 large extra knob
3–4 tablespoons duck or goose fat
2 large onions, sliced
juice of 1 lemon
2 tablespoons coarsely chopped parsley

Cook the new potatoes in boiling salted water for 20 to 25 minutes until tender. Drain and cool before slicing.

Preheat the oven to 220°C/425°F/gas 7.

Meanwhile, score through the dark skin around the fish close to the fins. This makes the fins easier to remove once cooked. Oil a large baking tray and season. Lay the fish on the tray, white skin-side down and brush with olive oil. Break the knob of butter into pieces and scatter over the top before seasoning. Roast for 20 to 30 minutes until the fish is tender throughout.

While roasting the fish, heat half the duck fat in a large frying pan and sauté the onion until golden brown, then remove from the pan. Add the remaining fat and fry the potato over a fierce heat until crispy. Spoon the onion into the potatoes and season with salt and pepper.

Melt the 50g of butter and whisk together with the lemon juice. Season and stir in the parsley before spooning it over the fish.

The fish and Lyonnaise potatoes are now ready to serve.

more

- The potatoes are sautéed in duck or goose fat, but this can be replaced with olive oil or butter.

roast monkfish with fennel, orange and tarragon mussels

This recipe is wonderful served with the garlic-flavoured aïoli sauce on page 464.

Put the mussels into a large saucepan with the wine. Cover with a lid and cook over a high heat for 6 to 8 minutes, shaking the pan and stirring the mussels until all have opened. Strain in a colander, saving all the cooking juices except the last couple of tablespoons, which tend to be gritty. Remove the cooked mussels from their shells, discarding any that have not opened.

Warm half the olive oil in a saucepan, add the onion, fennel and finely grated zest from one of the oranges. Cook for 5 to 6 minutes before straining 300ml of the mussel juices over. Add the bay leaf and one sprig of tarragon, simmering until the vegetables are tender, allowing the liquid to reduce slightly to increase the flavour.

Preheat the oven to 200°C/400°F/gas 6. Heat the remaining olive oil in a roasting tray. Once hot, season the monkfish fillets and fry for a few minutes, turning the fish to colour on all sides. Add the knob of butter, basting the fillets before roasting in the oven for 8 to 10 minutes.

Segment both oranges (see page 20), halving the segments before adding to the sauce with the mussels. Once warm, stir in the butter, finishing with torn tarragon leaves from the remaining sprig. Arrange the monkfish in warm bowls and spoon the mussel liquor around.

serves four

675g (1½lb) mussels, cleaned (see page 17)
1 glass of white wine
4 tablespoons olive oil
1 onion, sliced
2 fennel bulbs, trimmed and sliced
2 oranges
1 bay leaf
2 large sprigs of tarragon
4 x 100g (4oz) monkfish fillets
salt and pepper
50g (2oz) butter, plus an extra knob

cod poached in a tarragon broth

The tarragon broth in this recipe is similar to a court bouillon, an aromatic vegetable stock used for cooking fish. Here the cod and vegetables are cooked together in the broth to create the complete dish.

serves four

2 carrots, thinly sliced
1 onion, sliced into rings
2 sticks of celery, thinly sliced
1 small leek, thinly sliced
1 bay leaf
1 sprig of thyme
a few black peppercorns
salt and pepper
150ml (5fl oz) orange juice
4 x 175g (6oz) cod fillets, skinned and pinboned (see page 14)
a generous squeeze of lemon
1 teaspoon chopped tarragon

Put the vegetables, bay leaf, thyme, peppercorns and a pinch of salt into a large saucepan. Cover with 300ml (10fl oz) water and allow to simmer for a few minutes until the vegetables are tender. Add the orange juice, boiling until just half the liquid is left.

Season the cod with salt and pepper and place on top of the vegetables. Cover the pan and simmer very gently for 8 to 10 minutes until the fish is firm to the touch and cooked through.

Lift the fillets on to large plates or bowls. Add the lemon juice and tarragon to the broth, taste for seasoning and spoon with the vegetables over and around the cod.

roast halibut with buttery mussels and herbs

In this recipe, halibut is roasted on the bone. Halibut can be quite huge, so speak to your fishmonger and have a fish split down the middle, taking just half.

serves six

2kg (4½lb) half halibut on
  the bone
sea salt and pepper
1 glass of white wine
1.5kg (3¼ lb) mussels,
  cleaned (see page 17)
75g (3oz) butter,
  plus extra for greasing
a squeeze of lemon juice
1 heaped tablespoon
  chopped chives
1 heaped tablespoon
  chopped chervil
1 heaped tablespoon
  chopped tarragon
1 heaped tablespoon
  chopped flat-leaf parsley

Preheat the oven to 190°C/375°F/gas 5.

Pour 50ml (2fl oz) of water in a buttered roasting tray large enough to hold the halibut and mussels. Season the halibut, place in the tin, baking, white skin-side up, for 20 minutes.

Add the wine and mussels and bake for a further 6 to 8 minutes or until the mussels have opened.

Remove from the oven and carefully transfer the halibut on to a large warm platter. Scatter the mussels around, discarding any that haven't opened.

Place the roasting tray over a high heat and bring the liquid to a rapid simmer. If a lot of juices have been left in the tray, boil and allow to reduce in volume for a richer flavour before whisking in the butter. Check for seasoning, finish with a squeeze of lemon and the herbs and pour the sauce over the halibut and mussels.

more
- Serve the fish with plenty of steamed new potatoes.

apple tart

This recipe is based on a classic French apple tart, with blackberry jam spread over the tart base to provide a bit more of a 'blackberry and apple' British touch.

Preheat the oven to 200°C/400°F/gas 6.

Lightly grease and flour a 23–25cm (9–10 inch) loose-bottomed tart ring.

Roll out the pastry on a lightly floured surface into a circle large enough to line the tin, easing it into the bottom and corners. Prick the base with a fork and refrigerate for 20 minutes.

Meanwhile, peel and core six of the apples and cut into chunks. Sprinkle with a little lemon juice, mixing it through well. Place the apples and sugar in a saucepan over a low to medium heat and cook for 12 to 15 minutes, stirring occasionally, until tender, then drain.

Line the pastry case with greaseproof paper. Fill with baking beans and blind bake for 15 minutes. Remove the beans and return the tart case to the oven for a further 5 minutes. Remove from the oven and leave to cool. Once cool, spread the blackberry jam over the base of the tart.

Reduce the oven temperature to 190°C/375°F/gas 5.

Peel, core and very thinly slice the remaining apples, squeezing over a few dots of lemon juice. Spread the cooked apples into the tart case. Arrange the raw apple slices on top in a circular fashion and bake for 25 to 30 minutes. Leave to cool slightly before removing from the tin. The tart can be served warm or cold and dusted lightly with icing sugar, if using.

serves six–eight

butter, for greasing
flour, for dusting
275–350g (10–12oz) ready-made sweet shortcrust pastry
9 firm, crisp eating apples
½ a lemon
25g (1oz) caster sugar
3 heaped tablespoons blackberry jam
icing sugar, for dusting (optional)

rhubarb and custard cheesecake

The thin, bright sticks of rhubarb available between autumn and spring are the best to use, offering a rich colour and sweet flavour.

serves eight–ten

225g (8oz) digestive biscuits, finely crushed
100g (4oz) melted butter
450g (1lb) rhubarb, plus 6 extra sticks, cut into 1cm (½ inch) pieces
200g (7oz) light soft brown sugar
juice of ½ a lemon
3 leaves of gelatine, soaked in cold water (6g total weight)
450g (1lb) cream cheese
250ml (9fl oz) ready-made custard, chilled
100ml (5fl oz) double cream, lightly whipped
3 tablespoons caster sugar

Mix together the crushed biscuits and melted butter, pressing the mixture into the base of a 22–25cm (9–10 inch) loose-bottomed cake tin. Refrigerate to set.

Put 450g of the rhubarb and brown sugar into a saucepan and stir over a medium heat until thick and mushy. Add the lemon juice and soaked gelatine and liquidize in a blender to a smooth purée.

Add the cream cheese and custard, blending until smooth. Transfer the mixture to a large bowl and fold in the whipped cream. Pour the rhubarb cream on to the biscuit base and refrigerate for 2 to 3 hours to set before serving.

Meanwhile, put the remainder of the chopped rhubarb into a saucepan with 3 tablespoons of caster sugar. Cook over a medium heat for several minutes until the rhubarb becomes tender, then leave to cool before spooning on top of the cheesecake.

more

- 1–2 drops of grenadine can also be added to the rhubarb purée for a richer colour.

prune and armagnac bread and butter pudding

Prune and Armagnac ice cream and tart are French classics and here these flavours have been borrowed to introduce into one of our greats. For the richest of flavours, it's best to pre-soak the prunes in the Armagnac for several hours

serves six

175g (6oz) ready-to-eat
  prunes, halved
5 tablespoons Armagnac
1 vanilla pod, split
  lengthways, or a few drops
  of vanilla extract
400ml (14fl oz) double
  cream
400ml (14fl oz) milk
8 egg yolks
175g (6oz) caster sugar,
  plus extra for glazing
12 medium slices of white
  bread, buttered and crusts
  cut off
butter, for greasing

Preheat the oven to 170°C/325°F/gas 3. Butter a 1.5–1.8 litre (2½–3 pint) pudding dish. Soak the prunes in the Armagnac.

Whisk together the egg yolks and sugar. Put the vanilla pod or extract into a saucepan with the cream and milk and bring to the boil, before whisking into the egg yolks. Remove the vanilla pod and leave to slightly cool. Drain the prunes in a sieve over the cream, stirring in the Armagnac.

Cut the bread into triangular halves and arrange eight in the base of the dish. Top with half the prunes and cover with six triangles of bread. Scatter over the remaining prunes, arranging the final slices of bread slightly overlapping on top.

Pour over the warm custard and leave to stand for 20 to 30 minutes. Place the dish in a roasting tray, three-quarters filled with warm water. Cover with buttered foil and bake for 20 to 30 minutes until just beginning to set. Remove the pudding from the tray and leave to stand for 10 to 15 minutes before sprinkling extra sugar liberally on top.

Preheat the grill. To glaze, pop under the grill and colour to a crunchy caramelized finish. A blowtorch can also be used.

baked apples with nutmeg custard pudding

This dessert needs to be made several hours in advance. The nutmeg custard pudding is precooked and set before serving cold with the hot apples.

Preheat the oven to 140°C/275°F/gas 1. Boil the cream in a small pan. Whisk together the eggs and sugar in a bowl and pour in the cream, whisking continuously. Pour the custard into an ovenproof dish and sprinkle liberally with nutmeg.

Place in a deep tray and pour in boiling water from the kettle so it reaches halfway up the dish. Bake for 30 to 40 minutes until the custard is just set and has a slight quiver when gently shaken. Remove the pudding from the oven and tray and leave to cool. Refrigerate to chill.

Preheat the oven again to 190°C/375°F/gas 5. Lightly grease a baking tray with butter and arrange the apple halves, cut-side up, on the tray. Spoon over the golden syrup and scatter on the brown sugar. Add a knob of butter on top of each apple half and bake for 15 to 20 minutes until tender.

Divide the apples among the plates, spoon any syrup on top and accompany with a large spoonful of the nutmeg custard pudding.

serves four

600ml (1 pint) whipping
  cream
3 eggs
100g (4oz) caster sugar
freshly grated nutmeg
2 large dessert apples,
  cored and cut in half
  lengthways
1 tablespoon golden syrup
1 tablespoon light soft
  brown sugar
25g (1oz) butter

more
- A tablespoon of Calvados can be mixed into the syrup for extra apple punch.

vanilla pear and peach salad

Seeds from the vanilla pod are used here to provide the spice flavour. If unavailable, simply replace with a splash or two of vanilla extract or essence.

serves four

4 ripe pears, peeled, cored and cut into cubes
4 ripe peaches, stoned and cut into cubes
juice of 1 lemon or 2 limes
2 teaspoons icing sugar
1 vanilla pod, split and the seeds loosened

Place the fruit in a bowl with the lemon or lime juice and the icing sugar. Stir in the vanilla seeds, adding the scraped-out pods too.

Refrigerate for 2 to 3 hours, stirring very gently just before serving.

more
- Serving with extra thick cream helps smooth the rich vanilla fruit flavour.
- Fresh raspberries sprinkled over the top.

pear macaroon crumble

Almond macaroons are easily available to buy and add a different taste to this crumble with their crispy edge and chewy centre.

serves six

1kg (2¼ lb) ripe pears, peeled, cored and cut into large chunks
125g (4½ oz) caster sugar
juice of 1 lime
200g (7oz) plain flour
100g (4oz) cold butter, cut into cubes
12 macaroons, broken into small pieces

Preheat the oven to 190°C/375°F/gas 5. Put the pears, 25g (1oz) of the sugar and the lime juice into a large saucepan and cook for a few minutes until softened. Spoon the pears and cooking juices into a 1.5–1.8 litre (2½ –3 pint) pudding dish.

Sift the flour and place in a food processor with the butter, blitzing until the mixture resembles fine breadcrumbs. Add the remaining sugar and mix again for a few seconds. Stir in the macaroon pieces.

Sprinkle the crumbs over the fruit without pressing down. Bake in the oven for 20 to 25 minutes until golden brown.

steamed plum pudding

serves four–six

100g (4oz) butter chopped, plus extra for greasing
175g (6oz) self-raising flour
100g (4oz) caster sugar
2 tablespoons golden syrup
salt
grated zest of 1 lemon
2 eggs
1 egg yolk
milk, to loosen
8 plums, quartered
40g (1½oz) caster sugar
1–2 teaspoons grenadine (optional)

Grease and lightly flour a 900ml (1½ pint) pudding basin.

Sift the flour into a bowl and add the butter, sugar, 1 tablespoon of golden syrup, a pinch of salt, the lemon zest, eggs and egg yolk. Using an electric hand whisk, beat all the ingredients together until soft and creamy. If too thick, loosen with a few tablespoons of milk.

Spoon the remaining golden syrup into the pudding basin and place eight plum quarters on top. Fill with the pudding mixture and cover with greaseproof paper or well-greased foil, with a fold in the centre to create space for the rising sponge. Steam over boiling water for 1½ to 1¾ hours, topping up with hot water from the kettle, if necessary.

Meanwhile, put the remaining quartered plums and the sugar into a saucepan, adding 5 tablespoons water. Bring to a simmer and cook gently for 5 to 6 minutes until the plums have softened. Stir in the grenadine, if using, to enrich the red plum syrup.

Remove the paper from the pudding and turn out on to a large plate, spooning the soft syrupy plums over the top. Serve with custard, ice cream or pouring cream.

cognac peaches with pistachio brioche

Peach schnapps can be used in place of Cognac, or you can totally forget the alcohol and leave the peaches just sweetened.

Preheat the grill. Put the brioche slices on a baking tray and toast on one side only.

Mix the pistachios with 50g (2oz) of the butter and the icing sugar. Turn the brioche over on the tray and spread with the pistachio butter.

Heat a large non-stick frying pan, add the remaining butter and, once it starts to foam, tip in the peaches. Sprinkle with the caster sugar and pan-fry for a few minutes to soften. Pour in the Cognac (once warmed it will ignite, so do be careful) and stir just once or twice.

Meanwhile, return the brioche slices under the grill and toast to a golden brown. Serve the peaches scooped on to the toasts, drizzling with any pan juices.

serves four

4 thick slices of brioche loaf
1 heaped tablespoon
  chopped pistachios
75g (3oz) butter, softened
1 heaped tablespoon icing
  sugar
4 peaches, each cut into 6
  wedges
1 tablespoon caster sugar
2 tablespoons Cognac

more

- Jersey cream has the richest of flavours and will complement the quite powerful peaches perfectly.

crème caramel

This is best made 24 hours in advance, providing plenty of time for the pudding to set.

serves six

1 vanilla pod, split
  lengthways
500ml (18fl oz) full cream
  milk
225g (8oz) caster sugar
2 eggs
4 egg yolks

Very lightly grease a 900ml (1½ pint) ovenproof dish or 6 x 150ml (5fl oz) individual moulds or ramekins.

Scrape the seeds from the vanilla pod into a small saucepan with the milk and pod and bring to the boil. Remove from the heat and leave to infuse for 15 to 20 minutes.

Meanwhile, put half the sugar in a small heavy-based saucepan. Add water to level with the sugar and gently simmer, allowing it to cook to a rich golden caramel. Pour enough caramel into the dish or moulds to cover the base and leave to set.

Preheat the oven to 150°C/300°F/gas 2.

In a large bowl, beat together the remaining sugar, eggs and egg yolks. Boil the milk again before stirring it into the eggs. Strain through a sieve and pour into the dish or moulds.

Place the dish or moulds in a deep roasting tray and fill with enough hot water to reach two thirds up the sides. Cook for 1½ hours if using one large dish or 40 to 45 minutes for individual moulds. To see if the custard is ready, insert a small knife into the centre and check the knife is clean when removed.

Allow the crème caramel to cool before refrigerating for a minimum of 6 to 8 hours, preferably overnight. To remove the crème caramel from the dish, run a small knife around the edge, place a plate on top and carefully turn over to release.

spotted dick pudding with caramel golden syrup

serves four–six

300g (10oz) plain flour,
  plus extra for dusting
a pinch of salt
15g (½oz) baking powder
½ teaspoon mixed spice
150g (5oz) shredded suet
100g (4oz) soft brown sugar
150g (5oz) currants
finely grated zest of 1 lemon
250–300ml (9–10fl oz) milk
butter, for greasing

**for the caramel golden
syrup**
5 tablespoons golden syrup
1 tablespoon black treacle

Sift the flour, salt, baking powder and mixed spice together into a large bowl. Mix in the suet, sugar, currants and lemon zest and then stir in 250ml (9fl oz) milk, adding a little more if necessary to create a soft dough.

On a lightly floured surface, roll the dough into a cylinder 20–30cm (8–12 inches) long and wrap it in buttered clingfilm or greaseproof paper. Steam over rapidly simmering water for 2 hours, topping up with hot water from the kettle, if necessary.

Meanwhile, warm together the golden syrup and black treacle (the black treacle creates the caramel flavour in the syrup).

Slice the spotted dick, pouring over the caramel golden syrup.

more

- This pudding eats wonderfully with fresh custard, cream or vanilla ice cream.

iced jersey cream with lots of strawberries

This is purely an ice cream made from Jersey cream and milk.

serves four–six

300ml (10fl oz) full-fat
  Jersey milk
300ml (10fl oz) Jersey
  cream
6 egg yolks
150g (5oz) caster sugar
650g (1½lb) strawberries,
  hulled
1 tablespoon strawberry
  jam
icing sugar, to taste

Bring the milk and cream to the boil.

Meanwhile, beat the egg yolks and sugar together until thick and creamy. Pour the boiled milk into the mix, whisking continuously, then pour the custard mix back into the saucepan and stir continuously. Cook over a low heat until the custard thickens, coating the back of a spoon.

Remove the custard from the heat and leave to cool before churning in an ice-cream machine until thickened and frozen.

Whiz 150g (5oz) of the strawberries with the jam in a blender until smooth, adding a teaspoon or two of icing sugar to sweeten, if needed. Strain the sauce through a sieve.

The iced Jersey cream, strawberries and strawberry sauce are ready to scoop and drizzle into bowls.

more

- To accompany? Perhaps the shortbread biscuits on page 294.
- If an ice-cream machine is unavailable, simply freeze the mixture in a bowl, stirring from time to time until completely frozen. For a creamier finish, place the ice cream in a food processor and blitz until smooth. Pour back into the bowl and re-freeze until set.

Weekend eating/

Light weekend suppers/

Fish
Meat
Vegetarian

Fish

Seared halibut with a blood orange and courgette salad

Swiss cheese halibut with spinach and mushrooms

Mozzarella monkfish steaks with tomato and basil

Warm lentil, orange and watercress salad with grilled mackerel

Sweet sharp herrings with potato, cucumber and horseradish salad

Steamed sea bass with crispy seaweed and cucumber

Smoked haddock and spinach tart with Emmental

Foil-baked bass with garlic, parsley and lemon

Pan-fried brill with capers, lemon and mash

Mussels with leeks and Gorgonzola

Curried mussels and noodle broth

Meat

Chicken with wholegrain mustard asparagus

Honey, lemon and thyme roast chicken

Pork stroganoff

Grilled gammon with pear mayonnaise and chicory

Rump steak with oven-baked garlic chips

Steak au poivre burger

Sirloin steak with hot red wine and mustard vinaigrette

Bacon soup

Vegetarian

Asparagus vichyssoise

Aubergine caviar pasta with rocket and parmesan

Potatoes stuffed with stilton, leek and mushrooms

Baked ratatouille peppers with melting goat's cheese

Potato, leek and gouda gratin

Asparagus and mushroom pudding with melting fontina

Leek and gruyère quiche

Spring and summer vegetables with fresh herbs

seared halibut with a blood orange and courgette salad

serves four

4 x 175g (6oz) halibut fillets,
  skinned and pinboned
  (see page 16)
salt and pepper
flour, for dusting
olive oil
a knob of butter
a squeeze of lemon juice

for the salad

4 small or 2 medium/large
  courgettes
3 blood oranges,
  segmented (see page 20)
1 red onion, thinly sliced
a handful of basil leaves

for the dressing

200ml (7fl oz) fresh orange
  juice
½ teaspoon caster sugar
50ml (2fl oz) olive or walnut
  oil
salt and pepper

To make the dressing, boil the orange juice along with the sugar until just 100ml (4fl oz) of liquid is left. Once cool, whisk in the oil and season.

With a Y-shaped potato peeler, peel the courgettes lengthways into long, thin strips. Pat dry the halibut on kitchen paper. Season with salt and pepper and lightly dust with flour.

Heat 2 to 3 tablespoons olive oil in a non-stick frying pan and fry the fillets over a medium heat for 5 to 8 minutes. Turn the fillets in the pan, adding the butter. Once sizzling, add the lemon juice and baste the fish for a minute before removing the pan from the heat.

Meanwhile, mix together the courgette strips, orange segments, onion and basil. Add a few tablespoons of the dressing and gently stir it all together.

Divide the salad and halibut among the plates and drizzle with the remaining dressing.

swiss cheese halibut with spinach and mushrooms

Chestnut mushrooms have a slightly nutty bite, which partners the spinach very well. During the autumn months, wild mushrooms make a wonderful alternative.

serves four

4 x 175g (6oz) halibut fillets, skinned
salt and pepper
flour, for dusting
olive oil
50g (2oz) butter
225g (8oz) chestnut mushrooms, sliced
400g (14oz) washed and ready-to-eat baby spinach
4 slices Gruyère cheese

Preheat the oven to 200°C/400°F/gas 6. Dry the halibut fillets, season and lightly dust each in flour. Heat 2 tablespoons of olive oil in a non-stick ovenproof frying pan and fry the fillets, skinned-side down, for several minutes until golden brown. Turn them over and transfer the pan to the oven, roasting for 5 to 6 minutes.

Meanwhile, melt half the butter in a large pan and fry the mushrooms for 1 to 2 minutes until tender. Add the spinach leaves, season and stir until the leaves begin to wilt.

Preheat the grill. Place the slices of Gruyère cheese on top of the halibut fillets. Place under the grill until the cheese begins to soften and melt.

Spoon the spinach and mushrooms on to the plates, whisking the remaining butter into any juices left in the pan. Trickle the butter over the spinach, placing the halibut on top.

mozzarella monkfish steaks with tomato and basil

To cook the tomatoes, gently simmer 3 tablespoons of the olive oil and the garlic together in a saucepan for 2 minutes before stirring in the honey. Add the tomatoes and heat gently until they are just warm and softening. Season and keep to one side.

Pat dry the monkfish with kitchen paper and season with salt and pepper, lightly dusting each piece in flour. Heat the remaining olive oil in a large non-stick frying pan. Once hot, place the monkfish in the pan and fry for 2 to 3 minutes on each side, before transferring them to a baking tray.

Preheat the grill. Sit a slice of mozzarella on top of each monkfish steak and pop under the grill until the mozzarella softens.

Add the basil to the warm tomatoes, spooning them into large bowls or plates with the mozzarella monkfish steaks.

serves four

5–6 tablespoons olive oil
1 clove of garlic, crushed
½ teaspoon honey
6 large, ripe plum tomatoes, deseeded and cut into small cubes
salt and pepper
8 x 50–75g (2–3oz) monkfish fillet steaks
flour, for dusting
2 buffalo mozzarella, each sliced into 4
1 tablespoon chopped basil

warm lentil, orange and watercress salad with grilled mackerel

serves four

75g (3oz) Puy lentils
4 mackerel fillets, pinboned
  (see page 14)
a large knob of butter
sea salt and pepper
2 teaspoons red wine
  vinegar
1 teaspoon wholegrain
  mustard
3 tablespoons olive or
  walnut oil
2 oranges, segmented with
  juices reserved
  (see page 20)
1 small red onion, thinly
  sliced
1 large bunch of watercress,
  torn into sprigs

Rinse the lentils in cold water. Put into a saucepan and cover generously with cold water. Bring to the boil and simmer for 35 to 40 minutes until completely tender. Drain and keep warm.

Preheat the grill, lightly butter a baking tray and sprinkle with salt and pepper. Place the mackerel skin-side up on the tray, brush with the remaining butter and season with sea salt.

Whisk the vinegar, mustard and olive oil together with the reserved orange juice from the segments and season.

Halve the orange segments and mix together with the warm lentils, red onion and watercress and loosen with the dressing before arranging on plates. Grill the mackerel for 4 to 5 minutes until golden brown and place the fillets on top of the salad.

sweet sharp herrings with potato, cucumber and horseradish salad

serves four

450g (1lb) new potatoes
4 tablespoons olive oil
a squeeze of lemon
salt and pepper
½ cucumber, peeled,
  halved and sliced
100ml (3½fl oz) white wine
2 tablespoons white wine
  vinegar
1 tablespoon demerara
  sugar
1 small onion, sliced
2 large herrings,
  filleted and pinboned
  (see page 14)
4 heaped tablespoons
  crème fraîche
2 tablespoons horseradish
  cream

Cook the new potatoes in boiling salted water for 20 minutes until tender. Drain, slice into three or four pieces, drizzle with half the olive oil and the lemon juice and season with salt and pepper.

Meanwhile, place the cucumber in a colander, mix with a generous pinch of salt and leave to drain. After 20 minutes, rinse and pat dry with kitchen paper.

Bring the white wine, white wine vinegar, sugar and onion to the boil. Place the herring fillets in an ovenproof dish and pour the white wine liquor over. Warm the dish, returning the liquor to a simmer. Cover with a lid, remove from the heat and leave to stand for a few minutes.

Stir together the potato, cucumber, crème fraîche and horseradish and season. Arrange the potato salad on plates with the warm herrings and onion. Mix 2 to 3 teaspoons of the cooking liquid with the remaining olive oil and drizzle it over the herrings.

steamed sea trout with crispy seaweed and cucumber

Here, the crispy 'seaweed' is simply imitated by spring greens.

serves four

for the vinaigrette
1 heaped teaspoon sesame
  seeds, toasted
  (see page 13)
juice of 1 orange
1 teaspoon honey
1 tablespoon light soy
  sauce
2 tablespoons sesame oil
2 tablespoons groundnut or
  walnut oil
salt and pepper

1 lemon, quartered
1 small head of spring
  greens
1 small cucumber, peeled
vegetable oil
salt and pepper
2 pinches of caster sugar
4 x 150–175g (5–6oz) sea
  trout fillets, skinned and
  pinboned (see page 14)
2 large knobs of butter, plus
  extra for greasing
sea salt

To make the vinaigrette, put all the ingredients in a screw-top jar, adding a few drops of lemon juice from one of the lemon quarters. Season with salt and pepper and shake vigorously before using.

Separate the spring green leaves, cutting away any thick stalks. Quickly rinse the leaves under cold water, dry them on kitchen paper and finely shred. Separate the shreds on to kitchen paper.

Cut the cucumber into 7cm x 5mm (3 x ¼ inch) sticks, discarding the seeds, and place in a bowl. Pour in enough boiling water from a kettle to cover and leave to stand for a minute before draining.

Heat 2 centimetres of vegetable oil in a wok or saucepan. Fry a handful of the greens, removing once crispy and crinkled. Drain on kitchen paper and keep warm while frying the remainder. Mix a generous pinch of salt with the sugar and scatter over the 'crispy seaweed'.

Lightly butter and season a square of greaseproof paper. Lay the sea trout on top, dotting with half the butter and a few sea salt flakes. Steam over rapidly simmering water for 5 to 6 minutes until just springy to the touch.

Meanwhile, warm the cucumber sticks in the remaining knob of butter, season and spoon on to plates. Drizzle liberally with the vinaigrette and top with the sea trout and a pile of crispy seaweed.

smoked haddock and spinach tart with emmental

Preheat the oven to 200°C/400°F/gas 6.

Lightly butter and flour a 20cm (8 inch) round tart tin and place on a baking tray. Roll out the dough on a lightly floured surface and line the tin. Any excess pastry can be left overhanging. Refrigerate for 15 minutes before lining with greaseproof paper and filling with baking beans. Bake for 15 minutes. Remove the greaseproof paper and baking beans and return to the oven for a further 5 minutes. Remove the pastry case from the oven, trimming away the pastry from around the top. Lower the oven temperature to 180°C/350°F/gas 4.

Put the smoked haddock into a saucepan with the cream and milk. Bring to a simmer and cook for 4 to 5 minutes. Remove the fish from the pan and leave to cool slightly before separating into flakes. Keep the cooking cream to one side.

Place the spinach in a large saucepan and cook over a medium heat until wilted. Drain in a colander and leave to cool.

Sprinkle half the Emmental in the base of the pastry case, scatter the haddock flakes and spinach on top and finish with the remaining cheese. Whisk together the eggs, egg yolk, saved cream and a twist of pepper. Pour the mixture into the pastry case and bake for 30 to 35 minutes until the filling has just set. The quiche can be served warm or at room temperature.

serves four–six

butter, for greasing
flour, for dusting
225–275g (8–10oz) ready-made shortcrust or puff pastry
300g (11oz) fillet of smoked haddock, skinned
150ml (5fl oz) double or whipping cream
50ml (2fl oz) milk
225g (8oz) ready-to-eat spinach leaves
100g (4oz) Emmental cheese, grated
2 eggs
1 egg yolk
pepper

foil-baked bass with garlic, parsley and lemon

Very simple and quick, the bass needs little accompaniment. Perhaps serve with a bowl of leaves, fresh spinach or just good crusty bread to mop up the buttery juices.

serves four

2 large cloves of garlic, crushed
100g (4oz) butter
1 heaped tablespoon chopped parsley
sea salt and pepper
4 x 150–175g (5–6oz) sea bass fillets, skin on and pinboned (see page 14)
juice of 1 lemon

Preheat the oven to 200°C/400°F/gas 6. Heat a large baking tray in the oven.

Mix together the garlic, butter and parsley, seasoning with salt and pepper.

Scoop a dollop of butter on top of four squares of aluminium foil (large enough to encase the fillets). Season the sea bass and place skin-side up on the butter. Squeeze the lemon juice over the fish before wrapping and sealing the foil tightly.

Put the foil bags on the preheated tray and bake for 7 to 8 minutes. To serve, present the bags on plates ready to cut open and enjoy the garlic and citrus aroma and succulent fish.

pan-fried brill with capers, lemon and mash

For me, this is a complete meal, but if you want veg to go with it, steamed spinach is probably your best bet.

serves four

1 x mash (see page 451)
2 tablespoons olive oil
4 x 150–175g (5–6oz) brill fillets, skinned and pinboned (see page 14)
salt and pepper
100ml (3½fl oz) white wine
200ml (7fl oz) chicken stock (see page 13)
1 lemon, halved
2 tablespoons small capers
50g (2oz) butter
1 heaped tablespoon chopped flat-leaf parsley

Make the mash and keep warm to one side.

Heat a frying pan with the olive oil. Season the fish and fry, skinned-side down, for 1 to 2 minutes until golden. Transfer to a plate and keep to one side.

Pour away any remaining oil in the pan and return it to the stove. Increase the heat, pour in the wine and boil until there are just a few tablespoons left. Add the stock and return to the boil, evaporating until just half the liquid is left.

Squeeze in the juice of ½ the lemon, adding extra for a sharper taste. Add the capers and stir in the butter for a silky consistency. Season and return the brill to the pan, fried-side up. Simmer gently for 1 minute and sprinkle with the parsley. Serve the brill with the creamy mashed potatoes.

mussels with leeks and gorgonzola

Put the mussels into a large saucepan with the white wine. Cover with a lid and cook over a high heat for 6 to 8 minutes, shaking the pan and stirring the mussels until they have opened. Strain in a colander, saving all the cooking juices except the last couple of tablespoons, which tend to be gritty. Remove the cooked mussels from their shells, discarding any that have not opened.

Melt the knob of butter in a saucepan and add the leeks. Cover and simmer gently for a few minutes until tender. Pour the mussel cooking juices over and return to a gentle simmer, then stir in the Gorgonzola and butter. Add the lemon juice and season with a twist of pepper.

Stir the mussels into the leeks before dividing between bowls. Serve with lots of crusty bread.

serves four

2kg (4½lb) mussels, cleaned (see page 17)
1 glass of white wine
50g (2oz) butter, plus a large knob
2 small–medium leeks, thinly sliced into rings
50g (2oz) Gorgonzola or any blue cheese, crumbled
a squeeze of lemon juice
pepper

more

- 175g (6oz) sliced mushrooms can also be added with the leeks.
- 1 tablespoon chopped herbs, such as parsley, tarragon or chives, can be added to the leeks.

curried mussels and noodle broth

Rice noodles, Chinese egg noodles and vermicelli all suit this recipe. Simply follow the instructions on the packet.

serves four

1 glass of white wine
1kg (2¼lb) mussels, cleaned (see page 17)
a large knob of butter
2 onions, sliced
2 teaspoons mild or medium curry paste
a pinch of saffron strands, soaked in 2 tablespoons water (optional)
100ml (3½fl oz) double cream or crème fraîche
150g (5oz) noodles (see above)
1 mango, peeled and chopped
1 tablespoon coarsely chopped chervil
1 tablespoon finely chopped chives
4 wedges of lime (optional)

In a large saucepan, bring the wine to the boil with 300ml (10fl oz) water. Add the mussels, cover with a lid and cook over a high heat for 6 to 8 minutes, stirring the mussels until they have opened. Strain in a colander, saving all the cooking juices except the last few tablespoons, which tend to be gritty. Remove the cooled mussels from their shells, discarding any that have not opened.

Melt the butter in a large wide pan. Once foaming, fry the onion for a few minutes without colouring. Add the curry paste and continue to gently fry for a further 5 minutes. Add the saffron, if using, and pour in the saved mussel cooking juices through a fine sieve. Stir in the cream and simmer for 10 to 15 minutes.

Cook the noodles in boiling salted water until tender, then drain and add to the curry sauce with the mussels, mango and herbs. Serve with the lime for a citrus squeeze.

chicken with wholegrain mustard asparagus

Preheat the oven to 200°C/400°F/gas 6. Season the chicken thighs with salt and pepper. Heat a roasting tray on top of the stove with 25g (1oz) of the butter. Once it begins to sizzle, lay in the chicken, skin-side down, and fry over a medium heat for a few minutes to a golden brown. Turn the thighs and bake in the oven for 20 minutes, basting from time to time.

Snap the woody end from each asparagus spear, cut the spears in three, drop into a large pan of boiling salted water and cook for several minutes until tender. Spoon the spears into a shallow pan along with 4–5 tablespoons of their cooking water and bring to a simmer, stirring in the mustard and remaining butter.

Remove the chicken from the oven and squeeze over the lemon juice. Arrange in a large serving dish, pouring any lemony juices into the mustard butter asparagus and spooning the lot over and around the chicken.

serves four

12 chicken thighs, skin on
salt and pepper
75g (3oz) butter
12–16 asparagus spears
1 tablespoon wholegrain
  mustard
juice of ½ lemon

honey, lemon and thyme roast chicken

Here's a dish with little work but lots of flavour. Ideal for a weekend supper.

serves four

1.6–1.8kg (3½–4lb)
  chicken
a large knob of butter
sea salt and pepper
finely grated zest of 1 lemon
1 level tablespoon thyme
  leaves
4 tablespoons clear honey

Preheat the oven to 200°C/400°F/gas 6.

Rub the chicken all over with butter and season liberally. Place the chicken in a roasting tray and roast for 40 minutes. Remove the bird from the oven and pour any juices into a bowl.

Mix together the lemon zest, thyme and honey and pour over the chicken before returning it to the oven. Every 5 minutes or so, baste, then after 20 minutes, baste once more and turn off the oven, leaving the chicken to rest there for 15 minutes.

Remove the chicken from the roasting tray and heat all the honey and juices in the tray with a little water to loosen, if necessary.

Meanwhile, remove the legs from the chicken, separating the thigh and drumstick, and carve the breast into thick slices. Divide the chicken on to four plates, spooning over the honey, lemon and thyme juices.

pork stroganoff

Pork fillet is the same tender, lean joint as beef fillet. If unavailable, thin strips of pork loin can also be used.

serves four

a knob of butter
1 onion, sliced
100g (4oz) button
  mushrooms, sliced
350g (12oz) pork fillet, cut
  into thin strips
salt
a pinch of cayenne pepper
a pinch of paprika
2–3 tablespoons brandy
1 teaspoon Dijon mustard
100–150ml (3½–5fl oz)
  sour cream or crème
  fraîche

Melt the knob of butter in a wok or large frying pan. Once sizzling, add the onion and mushrooms and fry for a few minutes until softened.

Season the pork fillet strips with salt, cayenne pepper and paprika. Scatter the strips into the pan, increasing the heat and cooking for several minutes with the onion and mushrooms.

Pour in and flambé the brandy in the pan. Stir in the Dijon mustard before adding the sour cream, seasoning with more salt, cayenne pepper and paprika, if needed.

more

- A red pepper cut into thin strips can be added and fried with the onion and mushroom until tender.
- Serve with rice or mash (see page 451).

grilled gammon with pear mayonnaise and chicory

The pear-flavoured mayonnaise is an alternative to the regular pairing of gammon and apple, but if you do fancy apple, simply take a small jar of smooth apple sauce and whisk with 1–2 tablespoons mayonnaise.

serves four

2 large ripe pears, peeled, quartered and roughly chopped
a knob of butter
a squeeze of lime juice
3 tablespoons mayonnaise
2 small chicory heads
1 bag of washed and ready-to-eat watercress
12 walnut halves, quartered
1 teaspoon clear honey
1 tablespoon sherry vinegar
2 tablespoons walnut oil
2 tablespoons sunflower or groundnut oil
salt and pepper
4 x 175g (6oz) gammon steaks
olive oil

Put the pears into a saucepan with the butter and lime juice. Cook over a low heat for a few minutes until tender and beginning to purée, then whisk in a blender until smooth. Leave to cool. Once cold, stir in the mayonnaise.

Separate the chicory leaves and mix together with the watercress and walnuts in a bowl. To make the dressing, whisk the honey, sherry vinegar and the two oils, seasoning with salt and pepper.

Preheat a ridged grill pan or grill. Using scissors, snip a few times around the gammon rinds to prevent the steaks from curling as they cook. Brush each with olive oil and season with a twist of pepper. Grill the steaks for 3 to 4 minutes on each side.

Drizzle the dressing over the salad leaves and serve with the steaks and pear mayonnaise.

more

- A couple of tablespoons of crème fraîche or sour cream can be added to the salad dressing.

rump steak with oven-baked garlic chips

Preheat the oven to 200°C/400°F/gas 6.

Leaving the skin on, cut the potatoes into thick chips. Dry the potatoes well on kitchen paper. Place in a bowl and coat with the olive oil before scattering over a large baking tray. Bake for 25 minutes, then turn them over and sprinkle with the garlic slices. Continue to cook for a further 20 to 25 minutes until crisp and golden brown. Season with salt before serving.

Once the chips have reached their last 10 minutes of cooking, heat a ridged grill pan or frying pan until very hot. Brush the steaks with olive oil and season. Fry the steaks for 2 to 3 minutes before turning, and frying for a further 2 to 3 minutes for medium rare. Remove the steaks from the pan and allow to rest for a few minutes before serving with the garlic chips.

serves four

900g (2lb) potatoes
4 tablespoons olive oil, plus extra for brushing
2 cloves of garlic, thinly sliced
salt and pepper
4 x 225g (8oz) rump steaks

steak au poivre burger

Here these burgers are served just like steak with a green peppercorn cream sauce.

serves four

1 large onion, finely
  chopped
1 egg
675g (1½ lb) lean minced
  beef
salt and pepper
oil
a knob of butter
2 tablespoons green
  peppercorns, lightly
  crushed
2–3 slugs of brandy
1 teaspoon Dijon mustard
150ml (5fl oz) whipping
  cream
a squeeze of lemon

Mix the onion and egg into the beef, seasoning with salt and pepper. Divide the mixture into four, shaping and pressing each into a burger.

Heat some oil and butter in a frying pan. Once sizzling, cook the burgers for 6 to 7 minutes on each side for medium. Remove from the pan and keep warm to one side.

Pour off any excess fat and spoon in the green peppercorns. Add the brandy along with the mustard and cream. Simmer for a couple of minutes until the sauce has thickened and season with a pinch of salt and a squeeze of lemon.

The sauce is now ready to spoon over the burgers.

more

- Any juices released from the burgers can be added to the sauce.
- A heaped teaspoon of chopped parsley can be added to the sauce or sprinkled on top.

sirloin steak with hot red wine and mustard vinaigrette

Heat a frying pan and brush each of the steaks with a little olive oil. Season the steaks with salt and pepper and place them in the pan. Fry for a few minutes before adding the butter then turning the steaks and continuing to fry for a further 2 to 3 minutes for medium rare. Remove from the pan and leave to rest.

Spoon the shallots into the frying pan, reducing the heat slightly. Stir for a minute or two, pour in the vinegar and simmer until almost dry. Stir in the mustard and olive oil.

Pour any juices released from the steaks into the vinaigrette, then spoon the dressing over the steaks and serve.

serves two

2 x 225–275g (8–10oz) sirloin steaks
3 tablespoons olive oil, plus extra for brushing
salt and pepper
a knob of butter
1 heaped tablespoon finely chopped shallots
2 tablespoons red wine vinegar
1 teaspoon Dijon mustard

bacon soup

This recipe is a follow-on from the boiled bacon collar on page 320, taking advantage of any leftovers. A poached egg (see page 18) added to each bowl enriches the dish. Don't forget lots of crusty bread for dunking.

serves two–four

600ml (1 pint) bacon
  cooking liquor
  (see page 320)
100–150ml (3½–5fl oz)
  double or whipping cream
boiled bacon collar, roughly
  chopped or broken into
  pieces (see page 320)
pepper

Bring the bacon liquor to the boil. Add the cream and bacon pieces and simmer for 5 minutes. Finish with a twist of pepper before dividing among bowls.

more

- Before adding the bacon to the soup, a quick blitz with a hand blender gives a frothy finish.

asparagus vichyssoise

A perfect cold soup for a warm, sunny day.

serves four–six

16 asparagus spears
25g (1oz) butter
1 onion, sliced
2 leeks, trimmed and
  shredded
2 potatoes, peeled and cut
  into cubes
900ml (1½ pints) vegetable
  stock (see page 13)
150ml (5fl oz) single cream
salt and pepper
freshly grated nutmeg

Cut the tips of the asparagus into 4cm (1½ inch) lengths, slicing the stalks finely, discarding the woody ends.

Melt the butter in a large saucepan and add the onion, leek and potato. Stir and allow to bubble gently for a minute or two before pouring in the stock. Bring to a simmer and cook for 20 minutes. Add the sliced asparagus stalks and the cream and simmer for a further 10 minutes until all the vegetables are tender.

Season with the salt and pepper and a little nutmeg. Liquidize the soup until smooth and pour into a bowl. Allow to cool before refrigerating to chill.

Cook the asparagus tips in a pan of boiling salted water for several minutes until tender, then plunge into iced water. Once cold, dry on kitchen paper.

To serve, divide the soup among the bowls and scatter with the asparagus tips.

more
• Half the cream can be saved and used to drizzle over the soup just before serving.

aubergine caviar pasta with rocket and parmesan

Preheat the oven to 200°C/400°F/gas 6.

To make the caviar, score the aubergine flesh in a criss-cross fashion. Insert the garlic slices into the cuts and season with sea salt.

Put the aubergines, cut-side up, on a large sheet of foil on a baking tray, drizzle with olive oil and wrap the foil to seal.

Bake for 20 minutes before reducing the oven temperature to 150°C/300°F/gas 2 and continuing to bake for 50 minutes until completely softened.

Unwrap the aubergines, scraping the flesh from the skin into a food processor. Blend until completely smooth then transfer to a saucepan. Warm and whisk in 150ml (5fl oz) of the crème fraîche, adding the remaining for a creamier finish. To loosen to a thick pouring consistency, stir in some stock, a little at a time, and season.

Cook the pasta in boiling salted water until tender. Drain and add to the aubergine sauce, stirring in the rocket. Using a potato peeler, finish with shavings of Parmesan and a trickle of olive oil.

serves four

for the aubergine caviar
2 large aubergines, halved
  lengthways
2 cloves of garlic, sliced
sea salt and pepper
olive oil
150–250ml (5–9fl oz) crème
  fraîche
vegetable stock, to loosen
  (see page 13)

400g (14oz) dried penne,
  macaroni or bucatini
a handful or two of rocket
  leaves
Parmesan cheese, for
  shaving

potatoes stuffed with stilton, leek and mushrooms

serves four

sea salt and pepper
4 large baking potatoes
50g (2oz) butter, plus an
 extra knob
100g (4oz) button
 mushrooms, quartered
1 large leek, sliced
100g (4oz) cream cheese,
 at room temperature
100–175g (4–6oz) stilton
 cheese

Heat the oven to 200°C/400°F/gas 6. Lightly sprinkle the baking tray with sea salt. Prick the potatoes and place on top, baking for 1¼ to 1½ hours until cooked through.

Meanwhile, melt the knob of butter in a large pan and, once sizzling, add the mushrooms and fry for 1 to 2 minutes until they begin to soften and colour. Stir in the leek and continue to cook for a further 2 minutes until tender, then season with salt and pepper.

Halve the potatoes, scooping out the flesh into a bowl and saving the skins. Fork lightly to a crumbly texture, season and stir in the 50g of butter and the cream cheese before folding in the leek and the mushrooms.

Fill the skins with the mixture, place the potatoes back on the tray and crumble the Stilton over the top. Bake in the oven until the cheese has melted.

more

- It is not essential to use Stilton; there are so many blue cheeses, and Gorgonzola works particularly well. As an alternative to blue cheese, try grated Cheddar or Gruyère.

baked ratatouille peppers with melting goat's cheese

These rustic peppers are fabulous to eat, particularly with a slice of focaccia bread and a tossed salad.

serves four

sea salt and pepper
4 red peppers, halved lengthways, leaving stalks intact, and deseeded
4 tablespoons olive oil, plus extra for greasing
1 aubergine, cut into large cubes
2 courgettes, cut into large cubes
1 large onion, chopped
2 large cloves of garlic, chopped
4 plum tomatoes, roughly chopped
8 thick slices of goat's cheese

Preheat the oven to 170°C/325°F/gas 3.

Season the peppers and place on a greased baking tray.

Heat the olive oil in a large frying pan and fry the aubergine, courgette, onion and garlic over a medium heat for 5 to 6 minutes until just beginning to soften. Season with salt and pepper.

Stir the tomatoes into the vegetables and divide the ratatouille into the peppers. Bake for 50 to 60 minutes until tender.

Once cooked, top each of the peppers with the goat's cheese and increase the oven temperature to 190°C/ 375°F/gas 5. Cook for a further 5 to 6 minutes until the cheese has melted. Divide among plates or bowls, drizzling with any juices left on the tray.

potato, leek and gouda gratin

In between the layers of potato and leek are slices of Gouda cheese, which enrich the whole dish. Truffle Gouda can also be used. It's very expensive, but it does take the dish up to a different level.

Preheat the oven to 180°C/350°F/gas 4.

Heat the butter in a large frying pan. Once bubbling, add the onion and leek and cook, without colouring, for 7 to 8 minutes until beginning to soften. Season with salt and pepper.

Brush the base of a deep 20cm (8 inch) gratin dish with butter. Slice the potatoes thinly and scatter a layer in the gratin dish. Season and spoon over a few dollops of leek and onion along with some Gouda cheese. Repeat the layers, finishing with potato.

Pour the stock over the top and cover with aluminium foil. Bake for 45 minutes before removing the foil, brushing the top with butter and continuing to bake for 20 minutes until golden. The gratin is best left to stand for 10 minutes before serving, allowing any extra stock to be absorbed by the potatoes.

serves two–four

50g (2oz) butter, plus extra
  for brushing
1 large onion, sliced
450g (1lb) leeks, white part
  only, sliced 5mm (¼ inch)
  thick
salt and pepper
6 large waxy potatoes,
  peeled
300g (10oz) Gouda cheese,
  sliced or grated
300ml (10fl oz) warm
  vegetable stock
  (see page 13)

asparagus and mushroom pudding with melting fontina

The 'pudding' is a savoury batter that encases the vegetables as they bake. Fontina is an Italian cow's milk cheese that has a delicate nutty flavour. Once melted it becomes earthier, with a hint of mushroom.

serves four

350g (12oz) small new
  potatoes
12 asparagus spears
a large knob of butter,
  plus extra for greasing
450g (1lb) mixed wild or
  chestnut mushrooms,
  quartered if large
salt and pepper
4 eggs
25g (1oz) plain flour
200ml (7fl oz) crème fraîche
50ml (2fl oz) milk
1 teaspoon thyme leaves
100g (4oz) Fontina cheese,
  rind removed and cheese
  cut into cubes
hazelnut or walnut oil, for
  drizzling (optional)

Cook the new potatoes in boiling salted water for approximately 20 minutes until cooked through. When cool, cut in half.

Preheat the oven to 190°C/375°F/gas 5. Snap the woody end from each asparagus spear, cut the spears in half and drop into a large pan of boiling salted water, cooking for several minutes until tender. Plunge into iced water and dry on kitchen paper.

Heat the butter in a large frying pan and, once sizzling, add the mushrooms, turning them in the pan quickly before draining and leaving to cool. Mix the asparagus, mushrooms and new potatoes in a 23cm (9 inch) buttered flan or earthenware dish and season with salt and pepper.

Crack the eggs into a food processor and blend with the flour, crème fraîche, milk, thyme and a pinch of salt and pepper until smooth.

Pour the mix over the vegetables and bake for 35 to 40 minutes until golden brown and just set. During the last 5 to 10 minutes of cooking, scatter the Fontina cheese over the top to melt. Leave to rest for 5 minutes, drizzling with a little hazelnut or walnut oil, if using.

leek and gruyère quiche

Preheat the oven to 200°C/400°F/gas 6 and butter a 20cm (8 inch) loose-bottomed tart tin.

Roll out the pastry on a lightly floured surface and line the tart tin, leaving any excess pastry overhanging. Line the pastry case with greaseproof paper, fill with baking beans and refrigerate for 20 minutes. Bake blind for 15 to 20 minutes, then allow to cool. Remove the greaseproof paper and baking beans and trim away the excess pastry. Lower the oven temperature to 170°C/325°F/gas 3.

Meanwhile, heat the butter and olive oil together in a large frying pan. Once sizzling, fry the onion for 5 to 6 minutes before adding the leek. Fry for a further minute or two, before spreading on a tray to cool.

Beat the eggs with the extra egg yolk and then add the cream or milk. Stir in the cheese and the onion and leek and season with salt and a pinch of cayenne pepper.

Pour the filling into the pastry case and bake for 35 to 40 minutes until just set. Leave to rest for 20 minutes before serving just warm.

serves four–six

a large knob of butter, plus extra for greasing
175g (6oz) fresh or frozen ready-made shortcrust pastry
flour, for dusting
1 tablespoon olive oil
1 large onion, sliced
1 large leek, finely shredded
2 eggs
1 egg yolk
150ml (5fl oz) double cream or milk
100g (4oz) Gruyère cheese, grated
salt
a pinch of cayenne pepper

spring and summer vegetables with fresh herbs

Serve this as a vegetable accompaniment or a vegetarian main course.

serves four

12 new potatoes
12 baby turnips
12 baby carrots
12 button onions, peeled
2–3 baby leeks, cut into
　4cm (1½ inch) pieces
75g (3oz) peas, shelled
75g (3oz) broad beans,
　shelled
50g butter, chopped
sea salt and pepper
1 heaped teaspoon
　chopped chives
1 heaped teaspoon
　chopped chervil
1 heaped teaspoon
　chopped parsley

Cook the new potatoes in boiling salted water for 20 to 25 minutes until tender, drain and keep warm.

Scrape, peel or leave the skin on the turnips and carrots, keeping 1cm (½ inch) of the centre stalk. In about 900ml (1½ pints) boiling water, cook the turnips until just tender with a slight bite. Lift the turnips from the water and keep to one side. Repeat this cooking method with the carrots and then all the vegetables, cooking each separately until tender, allowing the water to reduce in volume as the vegetables cook.

Once all the vegetables are cooked, whisk the butter into the remaining cooking liquor, season and stir in the herbs.

Microwave the potatoes and vegetables in a bowl to reheat before pouring over the herb butter to finish.

Special occasions/

My focus here is on the big three – Valentine's, Easter and Christmas – although, of course, the recipes are just suggestions and can be swapped around or made for any special birthday or anniversary dinner.

The traditional foods we eat at Easter and Christmas are right at the heart of these celebrations, so this chapter includes braised shoulder of lamb with rosemary, carrots and onions and little steamed Simnel puddings for Easter and Christmassy whipped Stilton with figs and watercress and mince pie turnovers. However, never be afraid to use the best of the season's produce in new ways. A glazed mandarin tart may be all that's needed to add a fresh touch to the most established and well loved of Christmas lunches.

I've included a couple of exquisite canapés to hand round at a drinks party. Of course, looks are important, but flavour is still central. Canapés should never be wimpy, and these can stand up to a punchy fruit cocktail, but equally make an elegant companion for a glass of chilled champagne.

Special occasions/

Valentine's

Charentais melon and avocado with passion fruit vinaigrette

Baked Vacherin cheese

Toasted ginger figs

Pan-fried white fish with buttery grapes and chervil

Baked lemon halibut with leek and shrimp cream

Veal cutlets with white wine chestnut mushrooms

Easter

Easter turkey steaks with apple and prune stuffing

Braised shoulder of lamb with rosemary, carrots and onions

Duck, bacon and onion quiche

Braised beef chuck with carrots and baked potatoes

Potato, pumpkin, white leek and goat's cheese gratin

Hot chocolate fondants

Toffee apple crumble

Steamed simnel pudding

Christmas

Crispy Camembert with cranberry sauce

Roast turkey with pistachio and golden sultana stuffing

Roast hand of pork with baked black pudding apples

Glazed mandarin tart

Mince pie turnovers

Passion fruit brûlée

Christmas Pudding

Risotto rice pudding with cognac sultanas

Whipped Stilton with figs and watercress

Prawn rarebits

Pork and duck sausage rolls

charentais melon and avocado with passion fruit vinaigrette

Halve the passion fruits and scoop the pulp into a small saucepan, whisking in the orange juice and sugar, simmering until just half to a third of the liquid is left and slightly syrupy. Remove from the heat, whisking in the raspberry vinegar and chosen oil. Season with salt and pepper.

Cut the melon half into three wedges and carefully cut away the skin with a sharp knife. The wedges can now be thinly sliced. Cut the avocado into similar-sized slices.

Lay the melon and avocado together on the plate or allow each to cover a separate half. Just before serving, drizzle liberally with the passion fruit vinaigrette.

serves two

2 passion fruits
juice of 1 orange
1 tablespoon caster sugar
1 tablespoon raspberry
  vinegar
2 tablespoons olive or
  walnut oil
salt and pepper
½ a small Charentais
  melon, seeds removed
1 ripe avocado, halved and
  peeled

baked vacherin cheese

Simply baked, this wonderful cheese provides an instant fondue, ready for dipping things like hot boiled new potatoes, crusty bread, Parma ham, gherkins, cherry tomatoes and spring onions, or whatever else you fancy. All are perfect for this cheese

serves two

1 small Vacherin cheese, approximately 12cm (4½ inches) in diameter

Preheat the oven to 180°C/350°F/gas 4. Wrap the Vacherin while still in its lidded box in foil and bake for 20 minutes.

Remove the foil and lid from the box of cheese. Cut around the border and remove the top of the cheese crust to reveal the warm, melting Vacherin fondue.

toasted ginger figs

serves two

2 tablespoons caster sugar
⅓ teaspoon ground ginger
4–5 figs, halved
100ml (3½fl oz) double cream

Preheat the grill.

Put the figs, cut-side up, on a baking tray. Mix together the sugar and ginger, before sprinkling liberally over the figs.

Place beneath the grill, not too close to the top, and cook for 6 to 8 minutes until toasted with a tinged edge, offering the cream ready to drizzle over.

pan-fried white fish with buttery grapes and chervil

Baby leaf spinach can be served along with this dish.

serves two

olive oil
2 x 150–175g (5–6oz)
  turbot, halibut, hake or cod
  fillets, skinned and
  pinboned (see page 14)
salt and pepper
25 (1oz) cold butter,
  chopped, plus 2 knobs
150g (5oz) seedless white
  grapes, halved
a squeeze of lemon juice
1 tablespoon finely chopped
  chervil

Heat a frying pan with 2 tablespoons of olive oil. Once hot, season the fish with salt and pepper and place in the pan, skinned-side down. Fry over a medium heat for 5 to 6 minutes until golden. Add a knob of butter and, once sizzling, turn the fish, basting with the butter. Remove from the heat, leaving the fish in the pan for a further 1 to 2 minutes to continue the cooking.

Meanwhile, warm a saucepan with the remaining knob of butter. Add the grapes and gently fry until they begin to soften. Season, adding the lemon juice and 1 tablespoon water. Stir in the chopped butter and warm through until melted before stirring in the chervil.

Serve the fish with the buttery grapes and chervil spooned over.

baked lemon halibut with leek and shrimp cream

Preheat the oven to 200°C/400°F/gas 6. Using a knob of the butter, lightly grease a small baking dish and season.

Put the halibut fillets, skinned-side up, in the dish and drizzle with half the lemon juice and 5 tablespoons water. Sprinkle over a pinch of salt and cover with greaseproof paper. Bring to a gentle simmer on top of the stove before baking in the oven for 6 to 8 minutes until just lightly springy to the touch.

Meanwhile, melt half the remaining butter in a large pan, add the leek and season with salt and pepper. Cover and cook over a moderate heat for a few minutes, stirring until just beginning to soften. Add the shrimps and crème fraîche and allow to gently bubble.

Spoon the leek and shrimps on to two plates and top with the halibut. Quickly place the baking dish on top of the stove over a rapid heat and squeeze in the remaining lemon juice while stirring in the last of the butter before spooning over and around the fish.

serves two

50g (2oz) butter
salt and pepper
2 x 150–175g (5–6oz)
  halibut fillets, skinned and
  pinboned (see page 14)
juice of 1 lemon
1 large leek, shredded
50g (2oz) cooked and
  peeled shrimps
75–100ml (3–3½fl oz)
  crème fraîche or double
  cream

veal cutlets with white wine chestnut mushrooms

A beef sirloin or fillet steak would work equally well here.

serves two

2 x 300g (10oz) veal cutlets
salt and pepper
a knob of butter
1 large shallot or ½ small
  onion, finely chopped or
  sliced
175g (6oz) chestnut
  mushrooms, thickly sliced
½ glass of white wine
100ml (3½fl oz) whipping
  cream or crème fraîche

Heat a frying pan and season the veal cutlets before frying for 6 to 8 minutes on their fat-side (the fat surrounding the cutlets) until well coloured. Lay the cutlets down in the pan and continue frying for 3 to 4 minutes on each side for a pink finish. Remove from the pan and keep warm.

Drain away any fat left in the pan, return it to the heat and add a knob of butter along with the chopped shallot. Fry for a few minutes until softened, then add the mushrooms and allow to colour before pouring in the white wine and cream. Bring to a simmer, season and return the veal to the pan to quickly warm through.

Put the cutlets on plates and spoon the creamy mushrooms on top.

more

- A handful of defrosted petits pois can be added to the sauce before the cutlets, giving a sweet flavour.

easter turkey steaks with apple and prune stuffing

Order the turkey steaks, cut from a large turkey breast, from your local butcher. The gravy is taken from the roast partridge recipe on page 349.

serves six

for the stuffing
450g (1lb) pork sausage
  meat
1 onion, finely chopped
2 apples, peeled and
  roughly diced
100g (4oz) ready-to-eat
  prunes, chopped
finely grated zest of 1 lemon
1 egg
salt and pepper
2 tablespoons sage and
  onion dried stuffing mix

6–8 slices of Parma ham
vegetable oil
salt and pepper
6 x 175–200g (6–7oz)
  turkey steaks
1 large knob of butter
1 x maple sherry gravy
  (see page 349)

Beat together the sausage meat, onion, apple, prunes, lemon zest and egg. Season and fold in the stuffing mix. On a lightly floured surface, roll the stuffing into a 5–6cm (2–2½ inch) diameter sausage. Lay six Parma ham slices, slightly overlapping, on a chopping board, sit the sausage on top and roll up, using the other two slices if not completely covered. Grease a sheet of foil, top with the sausage and wrap up, twisting at each end to tighten. Refrigerate for an hour or two to firm.

Preheat the oven to 200°C/400°F/gas 6. Roast the foil-wrapped stuffing on a baking tray for 25 to 30 minutes.

Heat a couple of large frying pans with a drizzle of the oil. Season the turkey steaks and fry for 7 to 8 minutes until golden brown on each side. Remove the steaks from the pan and keep warm while making the gravy.

Unroll the stuffing from the foil and divide into six, serving each piece with a turkey steak and the gravy.

braised shoulder of lamb with rosemary, carrots and onions

Preheat the oven to 150°C/300°F/gas 2.

Heat a deep braising pot on top of the stove with 2 to 3 tablespoons of vegetable oil. Season the shoulder and fry until well coloured. Remove the joint from the pot, absorbing any fat left in the pot with kitchen paper.

Put the carrots and onion in the pot with the sprigs of rosemary, top with the lamb and pour in the stock or water. Bring to a simmer, cover and braise in the oven for 3½ to 4 hours, turning the lamb once or twice. Once cooked, remove the shoulder from the pot and keep warm. Pour the cooking liquor into another pan, skimming off any excess fat.

Meanwhile, heat the braising pot on top of the stove and, once sizzling, add the honey, lemon and rosemary leaves to the vegetables, rolling them in the honey until they become glossy and sticky.

Spoon the vegetables on to plates and carve the lamb into thick, steak-like portions, drizzling with the lamb liquor.

serves four–six

vegetable oil
2kg (4½lb) shoulder of
  lamb, boned and rolled
salt and pepper
2–3 whole peeled carrots
  per person
3 onions, peeled and
  quartered
2 sprigs of rosemary, plus 2
  teaspoons rosemary
  leaves
1 litre (1¾ pints) chicken
  or lamb stock or water
  (see page 13)
2 tablespoons honey
juice of 1 lemon

more
- The lamb cooking liquor can be thickened with a little water-loosened cornflour if prefered.

duck, bacon and onion quiche

Tins or jars of duck confit are available in some supermarkets and most delicatessens. Those with a gross weight of 750g (1½lb) will give you up to 400g (14oz) duck meat. This quiche is perfect for an Easter Sunday supper.

serves four–six

butter, for greasing
flour, for dusting
175g (6oz) ready-made
  shortcrust pastry
6 rashers of streaky bacon,
  cut into cubes
1 onion, sliced
3 eggs
250ml (9fl oz) double cream
  or milk
salt and pepper
750g (1½lb) tin or jar of
  duck confit (see above)

Preheat the oven to 200°C/400°F/gas 6. Butter a 20 x 3.5cm (8 x 1½ inch) loose-bottomed flan tin.

Roll the pastry on a lightly floured surface and line the flan tin, leaving any excess pastry overhanging. Line the pastry case with greaseproof paper and baking beans. Refrigerate for 20 minutes. Blind bake for 15 to 20 minutes, remove the beans and greaseproof paper and bake for a further 5 minutes. Cut away the excess pastry and allow to cool. Lower the oven temperature to 170°C/325°F/gas 3.

Heat a large frying pan and dry fry the bacon for a few minutes until well coloured. Add the onion and cook for a further 4 to 5 minutes before draining on kitchen paper.

Break the eggs into a bowl and beat together with the cream. Stir in the cooled bacon and onion and season with salt and pepper.

Open the tin or jar of duck confit and drain the meat in a sieve, keeping the fat for a later use (it is lovely for roasting meat or for crispy roast potatoes). Remove the skin from the duck, break the meat into pieces and add to the egg mixture.

Pour the egg mixture into the pastry case and bake for 25 to 30 minutes or until just set. Remove the quiche from the oven and leave to rest for 15 minutes before serving.

braised beef chuck with carrots and baked potatoes

An easy, slow-cooked alternative to lamb for an Easter lunch.

serves six–eight

salt and pepper
2kg (4½lb) piece of beef
  chuck
flour, for dusting
2 tablespoons vegetable oil
1 bottle of red wine
2 tablespoons demerara
  sugar
2 tablespoons tomato purée
2 x 400g (14oz) tins of beef
  consommé
1kg (2¼lb) carrots, peeled
  and cut into 5cm (2 inch)
  pieces
2 onions, quartered
6 large jacket potatoes
sea salt
1–2 teaspoons cornflour,
  loosened with a little cold
  water (optional)
25g (1oz) butter

Preheat the oven to 170°C/325°F/gas 3. Season the beef and dust with flour.

Heat the oil in a large, deep braising pot and fry the beef until well coloured on all sides. Add the red wine, demerara sugar and tomato purée, then the beef consommé and enough cold water to cover. Bring to a simmer, cover and braise in the oven for 2 hours. Add the carrots and onions and continue cooking for a further 2 hours.

Meanwhile, prick the potatoes with a fork, sprinkle sea salt on a baking tray and place the potatoes on top. Bake during the last 1½ hours of braising the beef.

Lift the beef, carrot and onion into a clean pot and keep warm. Skim and boil the cooking liquor until just half is left. If too thin, whisk in the loosened cornflour, a little at a time, to thicken. Season and strain the gravy over the beef and carrots.

Halve the baked potatoes, top each with a small knob of butter and season with sea salt. Break the meat into large chunks and spoon over the potatoes with the carrots, onions and gravy.

potato, pumpkin, white leek and goat's cheese gratin

A vegetarian option for Easter lunch, the goat's cheese is melted on top of the gratin so can be omitted if preferred.

Preheat the oven to 170°C/325°F/gas 3. Lightly grease a large (about 25cm/10 inch) earthenware or ovenproof dish with butter. Put a layer of potato and a few leeks in the base, season and sprinkle with a few thyme leaves, then top with a layer of pumpkin. Continue with the layers, finishing with either pumpkin or a combination of potato and pumpkin.

Stir the garlic into the cream and pour over the top. Cover with buttered foil and bake for 1 hour, until tender.

Remove the foil from the potatoes and pierce with a knife. If still slightly firm, continue to bake for 10 to 15 minutes.

The gratin can now be coloured under a preheated grill, before topping with the crumbled goat's cheese, and warming beneath the grill until beginning to soften.

serves four–six

butter, for greasing
450g (1lb) potatoes, peeled and thinly sliced
2 leeks, white part only, sliced
salt and pepper
1 teaspoon thyme leaves
750g (1½lb) pumpkin, peeled and thinly sliced
2 cloves of garlic, finely crushed
600ml (1 pint) double cream
175–225g (6–8oz) goat's cheese

more

- The green leek tops can be used in the buttered leek greens recipe on page 458, which will also taste delicious served with this dish.

hot chocolate fondants

A delicious end to Easter lunch, it is a good idea to have vanilla, chocolate or coffee ice cream in your freezer to serve with the fondants.

serves six

150g (5oz) butter, plus extra
  for greasing
cocoa powder, for dusting
150g (5oz) dark chocolate,
  chopped
3 eggs
3 egg yolks
5 tablespoons caster sugar
3 tablespoons plain flour

Preheat the oven to 200°C/400°F/gas 6. Liberally butter six 150ml (5fl oz) ramekins, dusting each with the cocoa powder.

Melt the butter and chocolate together in a bowl set over a pan of gently simmering water. Once melted, remove from the heat and keep warm.

Using an electric hand whisk, beat together the eggs, egg yolks and sugar until pale and thick and almost the consistency of soft peak cream.

Pour the mixture into the warm chocolate and sift the flour over the top before folding the three together. Spoon the mixture into the ramekins and bake for 9 to 10 minutes.

Remove the puddings from the oven and leave to rest for 1 minute before serving in the ramekins or carefully turning them out on to plates.

toffee apple crumble

The toffee in this crumble is created as the fudge begins to melt amongst the apples, encouraging them to soften.

serves four

200g (7oz) plain flour
100g (4oz) butter, cut into cubes
50g (2oz) caster sugar
50g (2oz) pecan nuts, roughly chopped (optional)
5 large crisp eating apples
150g (5oz) fudge, roughly chopped

Preheat the oven to 190°C/375°F/gas 5. Sift the flour and place in a food processor with the butter, blitzing until the mixture resembles breadcrumbs, as coarse or as fine as you wish. Stir in the sugar and pecan nuts, if using.

Peel, core and quarter the apples, then slice each quarter into three or four pieces. Butter a 1.8 litre (3 pint) pudding dish and fill with the apple and fudge. Sprinkle the crumble over the top.

Bake for 35 to 40 minutes, then leave to rest for 5 to 10 minutes before serving. Thick pouring cream is the perfect accompaniment.

steamed simnel pudding

Simnel is a fruitcake layered with marzipan, traditionally served at Lent or Easter. I've taken all the flavours and transferred them into an easy steamed pudding, which can be made in the microwave. A jug of warm custard completes the dish.

serves six

100g (4oz) butter, plus extra for greasing
200g (7oz) self-raising flour, plus extra for dusting
100g (4oz) caster sugar
2 eggs
1 egg yolk
50g (2oz) sultanas
50g (2oz) currants
25g (1oz) glace cherries, chopped
25g (1oz) candied peel, chopped
75g (3oz) marzipan, cut into small cubes

Lightly butter and flour a 1.2 litre (2 pint) pudding basin or six 150ml (5fl oz) moulds. Put the butter, sugar, eggs, egg yolk and flour into a food processor and blend until smooth. Remove the blade from the machine and fold in the fruits and the marzipan. Spoon the mixture into the basin and cover with a lid or clingfilm pierced with the point of a knife.

Steam the pudding over boiling water for 1 hour 45 minutes or 40–45 minutes for individual puddings. Top up the water level from the kettle as necessary during cooking.

The pudding can also be cooked in a microwave. For a 500-watt oven, cook a large pudding on high for 5 to 6 minutes, or until a skewer pushed into the centre of the sponge comes out clean. For every 100 watts above this setting, take 15 seconds off the cooking time. Individual puddings will take approximately 2½ to 3 minutes.

crispy camembert with cranberry sauce

It's important the Camembert wedges are cooked direct from the refrigerator. This will prevent the cheese from over melting as it fries. This dish is so simple and tasty, it needs no more than a sprig of watercress to garnish.

serves four–six

grated zest of 1 lemon
6 heaped tablespoons white
  breadcrumbs
a handful of curly parsley,
  chopped
coarse sea salt and pepper
1 egg
a splash of milk
1 chilled Camembert, cut
  into 6–8 wedges
flour, for dusting
sunflower oil

for the cranberry sauce
450g (1lb) fresh cranberries
125–150g (4–5oz) caster or
  jam sugar
juice of 2 oranges
2 teaspoons very finely
  chopped shallots
5 tablespoons port
a pinch of salt
1 tablespoon redcurrant jelly

To make the cranberry sauce, place all of the ingredients, except the redcurrant jelly, in a saucepan. Bring to a simmer and cook over a moderate heat for 10 to 15 minutes, stirring from time to time. Once the berries are tender, add the redcurrant jelly and mix well. Cook for a further 1 to 2 minutes, then remove from the heat.

Stir the lemon zest into the breadcrumbs with the parsley and season.

Whisk the egg and milk in a bowl. Lightly flour the Camembert wedges before dipping in the egg and rolling in the breadcrumbs to coat, then refrigerate.

Heat a few inches of oil in a wok or deep-fat fryer to 180°C (350°F). Deep-fry the Camembert for a few minutes until golden. The cheese wedges can also be quickly pan-fried on each side in just a few millimetres of oil. Carefully remove and drain on kitchen paper.

The warm crispy Camembert is now ready to serve with the homemade cranberry sauce, finishing with a squeeze of lemon juice and a drizzle of olive oil.

roast turkey with pistachio and golden sultana stuffing

The size of the turkey listed is 6.5kg (14lb), offering a generous six to eight portions. To roast, it will take about 4 hours, but if you're roasting potatoes and vegetables with it, cook for a further 30 to 40 minutes. The stuffing can be made up to 48 hours in advance.

serves six–eight

for the stuffing
2 onions, finely chopped
1 large knob of butter
2 chicken breasts, chopped
450g (1lb) pork sausage
    meat
150g (5oz) unsweetened
    chestnut purée
2 eggs
finely grated zest of 2
    oranges
75g (3oz) shelled pistachios,
    chopped
75g (3oz) golden sultanas,
    chopped
50g (2oz) white
    breadcrumbs
salt and pepper

6.5kg (14lb) fresh oven-
    ready turkey
50g (2oz) softened butter
salt and pepper

for the gravy
15g (½oz) plain flour
juice of 2 oranges
600ml (1 pint) chicken stock
    (see page 13)
1 large knob of butter
salt and pepper

Preheat the oven to 200°C/400°F/gas 6.

For the stuffing, cook the onion in the butter without colouring until softened, then leave to cool. Blitz together in a food processor the chicken, sausage meat, chestnut purée and eggs until well combined. Spoon into a large bowl and stir in the cooked onion, orange zest, pistachios, sultanas and breadcrumbs. Season with salt and pepper.

Fill the neck of the turkey with the stuffing, securing the skin beneath with one to two cocktail sticks, and refrigerate. Any remaining stuffing can be baked in an ovenproof dish during the final hour of roasting the bird.

Sit the turkey in a roasting tray, brush the bird with the butter and season with salt and pepper. Roast the turkey for 30 minutes, then reduce the oven temperature to 180°C/350°F/gas 4 and roast for a further 3½ hours, basting every 30 minutes, covering with foil once golden brown to prevent over-colouring. To check the turkey is cooked, pierce the thigh with a skewer. Once the juices run clear the bird is ready to remove from the tray and keep warm.

Pour away the fat from the roasting tray, add the flour and cook for a minute or two before pouring in the orange juice and chicken stock. Simmer for 5 to 10 minutes, add the knob of butter, season and strain.

The turkey is ready to carve and serve with a spoonful of stuffing and a trickle of gravy. Crispy rashers of bacon and chipolata sausages add a classic garnish.

roast hand of pork with baked black pudding apples

An alternative to turkey, the 'hand' is a joint just below the shoulder and is a very succulent and economical slow roast.

serves six–eight

2.7–3.6kg (6–8lb) hand of
  pork
vegetable oil
salt and pepper
sea salt
4 onions
2 tablespoons honey
300ml (10fl oz) apple juice
600ml (1 pint) chicken stock
  (see page 13)

for the baked apples
450g (1lb) pork sausages
1 onion, finely chopped
1 tablespoon chopped fresh
  sage
2 slices of white bread,
  crumbed
1 egg
225g (8oz) black pudding,
  diced
6–8 green apples

Preheat the oven to 150°C/300°F/gas 2. Score the pork skin, brush lightly with vegetable oil and season with table salt and sea salt. Cut the top and bottom off the onions, slice in half and place in a roasting tray, cut-side up. Sit the pork on the onions, pour in 150ml (5fl oz) water and roast for 5 to 6 hours, topping up with water if needed during the first 4 to 5 hours.

Meanwhile, cut, peel and discard the skins from the sausages, mixing the meat with the onion, sage, breadcrumbs and egg, then fold in the black pudding.

Cut the tops from the apples and keep to one side. Remove the core and scoop out some of the flesh to make room for the stuffing. Fill each one with the stuffing, finishing with an apple top, and place on a baking tray. Any remaining stuffing can be cooked in a separate dish. Bake the apples and extra stuffing for the final 45 minutes of roasting the pork.

Once cooked, remove the pork and onions from the roasting tray and keep warm. Pour away any excess pork fat and place the tray over a fierce heat. Once sizzling, add the honey and apple juice and boil quickly to a syrupy consistency before adding the stock. Bubble until just two-thirds of the liquid is left before straining through a fine sieve.

Snap the pork crackling from the joint and serve with the tender meat, the black pudding apples, the soft centres from the onions and the honey apple gravy.

glazed mandarin tart

An alternative Christmas pud.

serves eight

175–225g (6–8oz) ready-made sweet shortcrust pastry
flour, for dusting
butter, for greasing
600ml (1 pint) fresh mandarin juice (squeezed from approximately 15–18 mandarins)
grated zest of 2 mandarins
6 eggs
100g (4oz) caster sugar
150ml (5fl oz) double cream
icing sugar, for glazing (optional)

Preheat the oven to 200°C/400°F/gas 6. Roll out the pastry on a lightly floured surface large enough to line a 20 x 3.5cm (8 x 1½ inch) greased loose-bottomed flan case and place on a baking tray.

Line the flan case with the pastry, leaving any excess overhanging. Line with greaseproof paper and fill with baking beans. Refrigerate for 20 minutes. Bake blind for 15 to 20 minutes, and then remove the baking beans and the greaseproof paper and cook for a further 5 minutes. Trim away any overhanging pastry and leave to cool. Lower the oven temperature to 150°C/300°F/gas 2.

Boil the mandarin juice and zest together rapidly until there is just 175ml (6fl oz) left. Leave to cool.

Beat together the eggs and sugar and stir in the cooled mandarin juice and the cream. Pour the filling into the pastry case and carefully place in the oven. Bake for 40 to 50 minutes until just set with a slight wobble in the centre. Remove from the oven and leave to cool before removing from the flan case.

Each slice of tart can be dusted liberally with icing sugar, if using, and glazed with a blowtorch or under the grill for a rich caramel top.

mince pie turnovers

makes twelve

flour, for dusting
375g (13oz) ready-rolled
  puff pastry
1 egg, beaten
1 jar of mincemeat
caster sugar, for sprinkling

Unroll the pastry on to a lightly floured surface and roll out 2.5cm (1 inch) wider. Cut out 12 x 10cm (4 inch) discs and refrigerate for 5 to 10 minutes to firm. Once firm, brush a little beaten egg around the border of each, spoon a heaped teaspoon of mincemeat into the centre and fold the pastry over into a crescent shape, pressing the edges together to seal. Place on a greaseproof-lined baking tray and refrigerate for a further 5 to 10 minutes.

Preheat the oven to 200°C/400°F/gas 6. Brush the pastries with the beaten egg and bake for 15 to 20 minutes until golden and crispy. Once cooked, remove from the oven and sprinkle with caster sugar.

The mince pie turnovers can be served warm or cold.

passion fruit brûlée

A light end to a Christmas lunch.

serves six

12 passion fruit, to yield
  approximately 200ml
  (7fl oz) passion fruit juice
orange juice (optional)
8 egg yolks
75g (3oz) caster sugar, plus
  extra for glazing
400ml (14fl oz) double
  cream

Preheat the oven to 150°C/300°F/gas 2.

Halve the passion fruit, scoop the flesh into a blender and blitz to lightly crush but not purée the seeds, releasing the maximum amount of juice before straining. Top up to 200ml with orange juice if necessary.

Whisk the egg yolks and sugar together in a bowl. Bring the cream and passion fruit juice to the boil, and then pour on to the sweet egg yolks, stirring all the time.

Divide the mixture into six ramekins and place in a roasting tray. Fill the tray halfway up the ramekins with boiling water from the kettle.

Bake for 35 to 40 minutes until just set. To test, gently shake a ramekin – there should be a slight wobble in the centre. Remove the ramekins from the water, leave to cool, then refrigerate to chill.

Just before serving, sprinkle 1 to 2 teaspoons of sugar on top of each brûlée to cover. Caramelize with a blowtorch or under a very hot grill.

christmas pudding

This recipe makes three 900g (2lb) Christmas puddings and is best made several months or at least weeks in advance, giving time for the flavours to mature and enrich.

makes three puddings

225g (8oz) plain flour, for dusting
1 teaspoon baking powder
225g (8oz) fresh white breadcrumbs
225g (8oz) shredded suet
100g (4oz) ground almonds
500g (18oz) dark soft brown sugar
1 teaspoon ground mixed spice
½ teaspoon grated nutmeg
½ teaspoon ground cinnamon
175g (6oz) ready-to-eat prunes, chopped
175g (6oz) grated carrots
750g (1½lb) mixed currants, raisins, sultanas
50g (2oz) chopped mixed peel
2 apples, peeled, cored and roughly chopped
juice and grated zest of 1 lemon
juice and grated zest of 1 orange
5 eggs
225ml (8fl oz) rum
4 tablespoons black treacle
4 tablespoons golden syrup
300ml (10fl oz) stout
butter, for greasing

Sift the flour and baking powder into a large bowl, add the breadcrumbs, suet, ground almonds, brown sugar, spices, prunes, carrot, dried fruits, mixed peel, apple and lemon and orange zest. Beat the eggs into the mix with the lemon and orange juice, rum, treacle, golden syrup and stout. The mix should now be refrigerated for a week before steaming.

Butter and lightly flour three 900ml (2lb) pudding basins. Fill each three-quarters full with the mixture, cover with greaseproof paper or foil and tie on firmly. Steam over boiling water for 6 hours, topping up from time to time with water from the kettle.

Once cooked, leave the puddings to cool before refrigerating or storing in a cold dark place for several weeks or months.

To serve, the puddings will need to be steamed for 1½ to 2 hours to completely heat through.

more

- A splash or two of rum, brandy or Grand Marnier will give a home-made or good-quality bought custard a Christmas lift.

risotto rice pudding with cognac sultanas

This rice pudding is made with arborio rice, hence its title, although the method is very much that of a classic rice pudding. The Cognac-soaked sultanas are stirred in and the dish is finished off with a knob of butter, just as you would a risotto.

serves four

75g (3oz) golden sultanas
3–4 tablespoons Cognac
700ml (1¼ pints) milk
300ml (10fl oz) double
  cream
finely grated zest of 1 small
  orange
1 vanilla pod, split
  lengthways
100g (4oz) arborio rice
50g (2oz) caster sugar
a large knob of butter

Put the sultanas and brandy in a small saucepan and gently bring to a simmer. Remove the pan from the heat and keep to one side.

Pour the milk and cream into a saucepan and add the orange zest and vanilla pod. Bring to the boil before adding the rice and sugar. Simmer very gently over a low heat, stirring slowly, for 30 to 35 minutes until the rice is completely cooked through and creamy.

Remove the vanilla pod from the rice and stir in the sultanas. Add the knob of butter and the 'risotto' is ready to serve.

more

- The rice pudding can be served hot or cold. If cold, why not accompany with fresh orange segments.

whipped stilton with figs and watercress

Crumble the Stilton into a small food processor and whip with 125ml (4½fl oz) of the crème fraîche until creamy. The remaining crème fraîche can be added for a softer finish. The whipped Stilton can be eaten at room temperature or chilled for a firmer texture.

Put the redcurrant jelly, vinegar and port, if using, into a bowl and whisk until smooth. Stir in the oil and season with salt and pepper.

Present the Stilton either scrolled like ice cream or simply dolloped on to plates. Arrange the figs alongside, topped with sprigs of watercress and walnuts, if using. Drizzle with the redcurrant dressing and sprinkle with a little sea salt and a twist of pepper.

serves four

225g (8oz) Stilton cheese
125–150ml (4½–5fl oz)
  crème fraîche
6 figs, quartered
1 bunch of watercress, torn
  into sprigs
1 heaped tablespoon
  chopped walnuts (optional)
sea salt and pepper

for the dressing
1 tablespoon redcurrant
  jelly
1 tablespoon red wine
  vinegar
1 tablespoon port (this can
  be replaced with vinegar)
4 tablespoons walnut or
  olive oil
sea salt and pepper

more
- Slices of walnut, raisin or granary bread all accompany the whipped Stilton and figs very well.

prawn rarebits

This cheese sauce is instantly created with cream and can also be used to top chicken breasts, baked potatoes or even to make a quick lobster thermidor. Just replace the Worcestershire sauce with lemon juice, spoon over the cooked lobster and brown under the grill.

serves four–six as bites

4–6 thick slices of French bread
melted butter, for brushing
1 teaspoon English mustard
a dash of Worcestershire sauce
150ml (5fl oz) double or whipping cream
75g (3oz) grated Cheddar cheese
75g (3oz) grated Gruyère cheese
175g (6oz) cooked and peeled prawns

Preheat the grill. Brush both sides of each bread slice with butter and toast the top and bottom to a golden brown under the grill.

In a large bowl, stir the mustard and Worcestershire sauce into the cream. Loosely fold in the cheese and prawns, then spoon the mixture on to the toasts.

Place under the grill, not too close to the top, and toast until the cheese has melted. The rarebits are now ready to serve.

more

- Extra mustard can be added for a stronger taste.

pork and duck sausage rolls

These are also great for a brunch, lunch or afternoon tea.

makes 12–18 rolls approximately

1x400g (14oz) tin of duck confit
450g (1lb) pork sausage meat
2 eggs
a handful of fresh breadcrumbs
50g (2oz) semi-dried cranberries, chopped (optional)
salt and pepper
375g (13oz) ready-rolled puff pastry
flour, for dusting

Preheat the oven to 200°C/400°F/gas 6.

Drain the fat from the duck confit (this can be refrigerated and used for roasting potatoes). Remove the duck skin and roughly chop the meat.

In a bowl, beat the sausage meat, 1 egg, the breadcrumbs and cranberries, if using, together. Season and fold in the duck meat.

Unroll the puff pastry on a large chopping board and cut across the width to divide it into three. Beat the remaining egg and lightly brush each piece.

Separate the sausage meat into three balls and, on a lightly floured surface, roll into three long cylinders. Place each cylinder close to the edge of a pastry sheet and roll to cover. Once sealed, cut away any excess pastry, divide each one into six or more pieces and, if you want, score the tops with the back of a small knife. Place on a baking tray and refrigerate for 10 to 15 minutes.

Brush the sausage rolls with the remaining beaten egg and bake for 25 to 30 minutes until golden brown.

more

- Here are a few extras you could add to the mix: 1–2 tablespoons chopped shallots, chopped thyme or grated orange zest.

I've put the all-important side dishes together here to make it easy for you to match a main recipe in the book with potatoes, perhaps some Lyonnaise or creamy mash, or a bowlful of vegetables, from orange curd carrots to buttered leek greens. Where a main and side dish are just meant for each other, I've tried to point this out in the recipe, but I find it impossible to resist vibrant, burstingly sweet produce and I always pick what's in season and garden-fresh.

And never be afraid to let vegetables be the star of the show. A simple piece of grilled fish with a squeeze of lemon and butter makes a very agreeable partner for wonderful purple sprouting broccoli, while grilled lamb cutlets would be an irresistible side for my parsnip and onion fritters or the warm crème frâiche brussels tops. Many of these recipes can quite easily be served as a vegetarian main and if I had a vegetarian coming for Sunday lunch, I might still do my roast but make an extra large dish of kale colcannon or a sweet potato bake for everyone to happily spoon into.

Potatoes & vegetables/

Sauté potatoes

Bacon sauté new potatoes

Mash

Gratin dauphinois

Asparagus with an orange mascarpone dressing

Nutmeg raisin spinach

Mixed roast veg

Runner beans with chunky seasoning

Broccoli with Caesar dressing

Chicory caramelized with honey

Kale colcannon

Brussels sprouts with pecan nuts and maple butter

Warm crème fraîche brussels tops

Purple sprouting broccoli

Orange curd carrots

Parsnip and onion fritters

Buttered leek greens

Sweet potato bake

Braised red cabbage

sauté potatoes

Any variety of potato can be used for sautéing. Potatoes with a waxy texture maintain their shape, while floury ones become crumbly and crispy when fried. New potatoes also sauté very well. An addition of a couple of sliced and fried onions turn the saute into Lyonnaise potatoes.

Cook the potatoes in their skins in boiling salted water for 20 minutes until tender. Peel and cut into 5mm (¼ inch) thick slices.

Heat a non-stick frying pan, with a generous drizzle of the oil. Place a layer of potatoes in the pan and fry until golden brown.

Turn the potatoes once and add a small knob of the butter and season with a pinch of salt. Transfer to an ovenproof dish and keep warm in a low oven while you fry the remainder. Once all sautéed, sprinkle with the parsley, if using, before serving.

serves four

600g (1lb 5oz) new potatoes
8 rashers of streaky bacon, cut into strips
25g (1oz) butter
coarse sea salt and pepper
1 heaped tablespoon chopped flat-leaf parsley (optional)

bacon sauté new potatoes

Cook the potatoes in boiling salted water for 20 minutes until tender. Drain and cool before slicing in half lengthways.

Fry the bacon over a high heat until golden, then add the potatoes and fry them until golden, adding the butter to help colour and enrich the flavour. Season with salt and pepper and sprinkle with parsley, if using.

serves four

600g (1lb 5oz) new potatoes
8 rashers of streaky bacon, cut into strips
25g (1oz) butter
sea salt and pepper
1 heaped tablespoon chopped flat-leaf parsley (optional)

mash

Cook the potatoes in a pan of boiling, salted water until tender. Drain well, replace the lid and shake vigorously to break up the potatoes.

Mash the potatoes using a potato masher or ricer. Add the butter and milk or cream, a little at a time, until the potatoes are soft, light and creamy. Season with salt and ground white pepper. For a slightly spicy edge, add some freshly grated nutmeg.

serves four–six

900g (2lb) Desirée, King Edwards or Maris Piper potatoes
50g (2oz) cold butter
150ml warm milk or cream
salt and ground white pepper
freshly grated nutmeg (optional)

gratin dauphinois

serves four–six

5 potatoes
500ml (18fl oz) double or
  whipping cream
salt and pepper
freshly grated nutmeg
1 clove of garlic, halved
butter, for greasing

Preheat the oven to 150°C/300°F/gas 2. Peel and slice the potatoes thinly (preferably using a mandolin). Do not put the potatoes into water as this will remove the starch needed to thicken the cream.

Place the slices in a bowl, pour in the cream and season with salt, pepper and a pinch of grated nutmeg. Carefully mix together without breaking up the potatoes.

Rub the base and sides of an earthenware dish with the garlic clove halves and brush the dish with butter. Layer the creamy potatoes into the dish evenly and cover with buttered foil.

Bake for 40 minutes, remove the foil and continue to bake for a further 20 to 30 minutes until golden and tender. Leave the potatoes to rest for 10 to 15 minutes before serving.

asparagus with an orange mascarpone dressing

serves four

100ml (3½fl oz) half-fat
  crème fraîche
50g (2oz) mascarpone
  cheese
2 large oranges
salt and pepper
24 asparagus spears

Mix together the crème fraîche and mascarpone until smooth. Finely grate a teaspoon of orange zest before halving and juicing the oranges. Boil the juice and zest together in a pan until just a quarter of the liquid remains. Stir the zesty juice into the mascarpone and season.

Snap the woody end from each asparagus spear, drop the spears into a large pan of boiling salted water and cook for several minutes until tender. Drain, season and drizzle the dressing over the spears or offer separately as a dip.

nutmeg raisin spinach

serves four

50g (2oz) butter
50g (2oz) raisins
900g (2lb) spinach, washed
  and stalks removed
¼ teaspoon freshly grated
  nutmeg
salt and pepper

Warm the butter and raisins together in a large saucepan, gently simmering for a few minutes to soften the fruit.

Increase the heat and add the spinach leaves. As they begin to wilt, add the nutmeg and season with salt and pepper, mixing together well before serving.

mixed roast veg

Preheat the oven to 180°C/350°F/gas 4. Pour the oil into a roasting tray, scatter and roll the vegetables in the oil and season with salt and pepper.

Roast the vegetables for 50 to 60 minutes, turning occasionally, until tender and golden brown. Brush with butter before serving.

serves four

3 tablespoons vegetable oil
4 carrots, peeled
4 parsnips, peeled
4 small onions, peeled
1 small swede, peeled and
  quartered
salt and pepper
a large knob of butter

runner beans with chunky seasoning

The chunky seasoning is coarse sea salt and green peppercorns, the two replacing the usual table salt and pepper.

Top and tail the beans, pull away the strings from the sides and cut at an angle into thin strips. Plunge the beans into a pan of boiling salted water and cook for a few minutes until tender. Drain well.

Melt the butter in a saucepan with the green peppercorns and, once sizzling, add the beans. Stir over a medium heat for 1 to 2 minutes, season with a sprinkling of sea salt and serve.

serves four

675g (1½lb) runner beans
25g (1oz) butter
1 tablespoon green
  peppercorns in brine,
  chopped
sea salt

broccoli with caesar dressing

Put the mayonnaise, crème fraîche, garlic, mustard, capers, lemon juice, Tabasco and Worcestershire sauces and a pinch of salt into a food processor or blender and blitz to a smooth purée.

Drop the broccoli florets into a pan of boiling salted water and cook for 3–5 minutes until tender. Drain the florets, season with salt and pepper and place in a serving dish.

Spoon the dressing over the broccoli and top with the Parmesan or offer separately.

serves four–six

50ml (2fl oz) mayonnaise
100ml (3½fl oz) crème
  fraîche
1 small clove of garlic,
  crushed
1 teaspoon Dijon mustard
1 teaspoon capers
1 tablespoon lemon juice
a dash of Tabasco
a dash of Worcestershire
  sauce
salt and pepper
900g (2lb) broccoli, divided
  into florets
25–50g (1–2oz) Parmesan
  cheese, grated or shaved

chicory caramelized with honey

serves four

4 medium/large or 6 small
  chicory heads
juice of 1 lemon
2 tablespoons olive oil
salt and pepper
1 tablespoon clear honey
a knob of butter

Halve the chicory, removing any brown outside leaves. Drizzle half the lemon juice over the chicory and cook in boiling salted water for 5 to 6 minutes. Remove and leave to slightly cool.

Heat a large frying pan with the olive oil. Squeeze any excess water from the chicory halves before placing them cut-side down in the oil and seasoning. Fry over a medium heat until golden before adding the honey and remaining lemon juice. Continue to cook for a few minutes until the honey begins to caramelize. Turn the chicory and cook for a further minute or two before removing from the pan, seasoning with salt and pepper and arranging in a serving dish.

Stir the butter into any honey remaining in the pan and drizzle over the chicory halves.

kale colcannon

Jersey milk is smoothed into the mash, giving it a creamy flavour without becoming too heavy.

serves four

675g (1½lb) floury potatoes,
  peeled and quartered
75g (3oz) butter
150–200ml (5–7fl oz)
Jersey full-cream milk,
  warmed
salt and ground white
  pepper
a pinch of freshly grated
  nutmeg
450g (1lb) curly kale
1 bunch of spring onions,
  shredded

Cook the potatoes in boiling salted water for 20 to 25 minutes until tender, then drain well and mash until smooth. Stir in 50g (2oz) of the butter and the warm Jersey milk and season with salt, pepper and nutmeg.

Meanwhile, remove the stalks from the kale and chop the leaves into bite-sized pieces or strips. Cook in boiling salted water for a few minutes or until tender before draining.

Warm the remaining butter in a pan and, once foaming, add the spring onion and kale, stirring once or twice before mixing with the mash.

brussels sprouts with pecan nuts and maple butter

serves four–six

500g (18oz) Brussels
  sprouts
25g (1oz) butter
50g (2oz) pecan nuts,
  coarsely chopped
sea salt and pepper
1–2 tablespoons maple
  syrup

Remove any loose or damaged outside leaves from the sprouts. Plunge the sprouts into a deep pan of boiling salted water and cook for 3 to 4 minutes until tender with a crisp bite, then drain.

Melt the butter in a frying pan and, once foaming, add the pecan nuts, stirring once or twice before adding the sprouts. Fry for a further minute and season with salt and pepper before trickling with a tablespoon of the maple syrup, adding the extra if preferred. Roll the sprouts in the butter and syrup until well coated.

warm crème fraîche brussels tops

Brussels tops are the green leaves at the top of the stem the sprouts grow on.

serves four

4–6 Brussels tops, trimmed
  from stem and rinsed
sea salt and pepper
a knob of butter
100ml (3½fl oz) crème
  fraîche
¼–½ teaspoon English
  mustard

Cook the Brussels tops for a few minutes in a large pan of boiling salted water, then drain in a colander.

Heat a large frying pan or wok. Melt the butter, add the leaves and season with sea salt and a twist of black pepper.

Mix the crème fraîche and mustard together and spoon it among the warm leaves, creating a ripple effect.

purple sprouting broccoli

serves four

500g (18oz) purple
  sprouting broccoli
salt and pepper
25g (1oz) butter

Trim any tough stalks from the base of the broccoli and cook in boiling salted water for just a few minutes until tender but leaving a slight bite. Drain off the water, leaving just a tablespoon or two in the pan.

Season with salt and pepper before lifting the broccoli on to a plate. Whisk the butter into the cooking liquor and drizzle liberally over the broccoli.

orange curd carrots

Orange curd rolled around cooked carrots leaves not only a glossy shine but a piquant sweet orange bite.

serves four

675g (1½lb) baby
  Chantanais or large
  sliced carrots
2 heaped tablespoons
  orange curd
salt and pepper

Cook the carrots in boiling salted water until tender. Once cooked, drain off the water, leaving about 2 tablespoons in the pan. Gently stir in the orange curd until completely melted, glazing every carrot, before seasoning.

parsnip and onion fritters

The perfect accompaniment to grilled lamb cutlets or roast duck breast. For preparing the vegetables, you can use either a hand-held grater or a food processor.

serves four

2kg (4½lb) large parsnips,
  peeled and coarsely
  grated
2 onions, coarsely grated
2 large eggs, beaten
salt and pepper
vegetable oil

Mix together the parsnip, onion and egg, season with salt and pepper and divide the mix into eight to twelve piles.

Heat a few tablespoons of the oil in a large frying pan. Once hot, put the piles of fritter mix into the pan, four to six at a time, and lightly press into cakes. Fry over a low to medium heat for 5 to 6 minutes until golden, then carefully turn over and repeat the same frying time.

Transfer on to a baking tray and keep warm while the remainder of the fritters are fried.

buttered leek greens

serves four

50g (2oz) butter
500g (18oz) green leek
  tops, finely shredded and
  washed
sea salt and pepper

Melt the butter in a large wide pan. Add the leek, cover with a lid and cook over a medium heat until the butter starts to bubble. Stir the leeks, replace the lid and cook for a further few minutes until soft. Season with salt and pepper and serve.

sweet potato bake

serves four–six

1kg (2¼lb) sweet potatoes (orange or white)
2 onions, sliced
½ teaspoon ground ginger
50g (2oz) butter
salt and pepper
300ml (10fl oz) vegetable or chicken stock (see notes page 13)
walnut or olive oil, for drizzling

Preheat the oven to 190°C/375°F/gas 5.

Peel and cut the sweet potato into 2–3mm (⅛ inch) slices. Mix the sliced onions with the ground ginger.

Using a knob of the butter, grease a 1.5 litre (2½ pint) baking dish. In alternate layers, stack the sweet potato and onion, seasoning and adding a knob of butter between each, finishing with sweet potato.

Pour over the stock until just below the top layer and bake for 50 to 60 minutes until tender with a crisp, golden brown edge. Trickle with the chosen oil before serving.

braised red cabbage

serves four–six

1 small red cabbage or half a large, thinly sliced
3 pears or apples, peeled, cored and cut into cubes
1 large onion, sliced
500ml (18fl oz) red wine
2 tablespoons honey
a knob of butter
salt and pepper

Preheat the oven to 170°C/325°F/gas 3.

Put all the ingredients into a braising pot and season with salt and pepper. Bring to a simmer, cover with parchment paper and a lid and cook in the oven for 2 hours until the cabbage is tender and the red wine is syrupy.

If the cooking liquor is too thin, simply boil and reduce.

Sauces/

Quick hollandaise sauce
Aïoli sauce
Caesar dressing
Curry mayonnaise
Mint raita
Sweet lemon dressing
Red wine mustard dressing
Cream vinaigrette
Roast gravy
Fresh vanilla custard
Warm chocolate sauce
White chocolate cream

All finished sauce quantities in this section are approximate

quick hollandaise sauce

makes 250ml (9fl oz)

175g (6oz) butter
3 egg yolks
juice of 1 small lemon
salt
a pinch of cayenne or
  ground white pepper

Melt the butter in a small saucepan or place in a bowl, cover with clingfilm and microwave.

Place the egg yolks and lemon juice in a blender and, while at maximum speed, slowly add the melted butter, continuing to blend until thick and creamy.

Season with salt and cayenne pepper, stirring in an extra squeeze of lemon to finish it off, if needed.

Keep warm until ready to serve.

aïoli sauce

makes 150ml (5fl oz)

a pinch of saffron strands
  (optional)
2 cloves of garlic, crushed
salt and pepper
2 egg yolks
1 teaspoon Dijon mustard
2 teaspoons lemon juice
  or white wine vinegar
150ml (5fl oz) olive oil

Moisten the saffron strands, if using, in a tablespoon of cold water.

Put the garlic, egg yolk, mustard and lemon juice into a food processor and blend at full speed. The olive oil can now be trickled into the yolk mixture, continually pouring in a thin stream until completely mixed together. Season with salt and pepper, stirring in the saffron strands and water to finish.

caesar dressing

makes 200ml (7fl oz)

150g (5oz) mayonnaise
2 tablespoons lemon juice
1 small clove of garlic,
  crushed
1 teaspoon Dijon mustard
1 teaspoon capers
a dash of Worcestershire
  sauce
2 tinned anchovy fillets,
  chopped (optional)
a dash of Tabasco sauce
  (optional)

Put all the ingredients, including the anchovies and Tabasco sauce, if using, in a small food processor or blender and blitz until smooth.

Loosen with a few tablespoons of water, if needed, to give a double cream consistency.

curry mayonnaise

Simply whisk all the ingredients together.

makes 200ml (7fl oz)

100g (4oz) mayonnaise
50ml (2fl oz) crème fraîche
  or sour cream
1 heaped tablespoon 'no-
  cook' medium curry paste
1 heaped teaspoon mango
  chutney

mint raita

Stir all the ingredients together in a bowl, seasoning with a pinch of salt and pepper to finish.

makes 200ml (7fl oz)

200ml (7fl oz) Greek
  yoghurt
juice of 1 lime
1 tablespoon chopped mint
2 tablespoons peeled and
  grated cucumber
salt and pepper

sweet lemon dressing

Boil the sugar, lemon juice, zest and lemon grass, if using, with 50ml (2fl oz) water and simmer for several minutes.

Remove from the heat and leave to infuse for 20 to 30 minutes before straining. Whisk together with the olive oil and season with salt and pepper, then pour into a screw-top jar ready for shaking when needed.

The dressing can be kept in an airtight container in the refrigerator for several weeks. In fact, if you add the lemon grass, the longer the dressing is left to infuse, the better the flavour becomes.

Drizzle the dressing over fish, chicken or salads.

makes 200ml (7fl oz)

50g (2oz) caster sugar
juice of 2 lemons
1 strip of lemon zest
1 stem of lemon grass,
  finely shredded (optional)
150ml (5fl oz) olive oil
salt and pepper

red wine mustard dressing

makes 200ml (7fl oz)

2 teaspoons Dijon mustard
2 tablespoons red wine
  vinegar
a pinch of sugar
2 tablespoons mayonnaise
5 tablespoons walnut oil
5 tablespoons groundnut oil
2 teaspoons double cream
  or crème fraîche (optional)
salt and pepper

Mix together the mustard, red wine vinegar, sugar and mayonnaise.

Slowly whisk in the two oils. Add the cream, if using, and season with salt and pepper.

If the dressing is too thick, loosen with a tablespoon or two of water.

The dressing can be kept refrigerated in a screw-top jar for up to 2 weeks.

cream vinaigrette

makes 250ml (9fl oz)

2 teaspoons white wine
  vinegar
2 tablespoons lemon juice
2 tablespoons groundnut or
  grape seed oil
6 tablespoons hazelnut or
  walnut oil
6 tablespoons double
  cream
sea salt and pepper

Stir together the vinegar and lemon juice in a small bowl, add the two oils and whisk slowly into the cream before serving.

Season with salt and pepper.

The vinaigrette can be stored in a screw-top jar or squeezy bottle in the refrigerator for up to 5 days (depending on the age of the cream).

roast gravy

makes 450ml (15fl oz)

1 teaspoon butter
  (or roasting fat)
2 teaspoons plain flour
150ml (5fl oz) red wine
300ml (10fl oz) beef, lamb
  or chicken stock or
  consommé (see page 13)
salt and pepper

Melt the butter in a saucepan (or used roasting tray). Once melted, stir in the flour, cooking gently for a few minutes. Add the tomato purée, red wine and stock and bring to a simmer, cooking the gravy to your preferred consistency.

Season with salt and pepper, if needed, before straining and serving.

fresh vanilla custard

Boil together the milk, double cream and split vanilla pod.

Meanwhile, in a large bowl whisk the sugar and egg yolks together until pale and creamy.

Whisk half the boiled vanilla cream into the egg mixture, before adding to the remaining cream in the pan. Cook over a gentle heat, stirring continuously until thickened, coating the back of the spoon.

Strain and the custard is ready to serve.

makes 600ml (1 pint)

200ml (7fl oz) milk
300ml (10fl oz) double
  cream
1 vanilla pod, halved
  lengthways
50g (2oz) caster sugar
6 egg yolks

warm chocolate sauce

Put the chocolate and double cream in a bowl and place over a pan of gently simmering water or microwave until the chocolate has melted.

Remove the bowl from the heat and stir until silky smooth, adding the butter, if using, for an even glossier finish.

makes 250ml (9fl oz)

100g (4oz) chopped dark
  chocolate
150ml (5fl oz) double cream
a knob of butter (optional)

white chocolate cream

In a small saucepan, bring 100ml (3½fl oz) of the cream to the boil. Add the chocolate, stirring until completely melted. Pour the chocolate cream into a bowl and leave to cool.

Whip the remaining cream to soft peaks and fold in the cooled chocolate. If too loose, continue to whisk to a soft peak.

The cream is now ready to serve as a complete dessert, particularly with summer red berries, or simply alongside fruit or biscuits.

serves four–six

300ml (10fl oz) double
  cream
225g (8oz) white chocolate,
  finely chopped or grated

index

afternoon tea 94
  high tea and treats 96–115
  teatime for children 116–47
aïoli sauce 464
almonds
  blackberry and almond tart 100
  roast chicken breasts with
    almond cream noodles 218
amaretti biscuits, baked amaretti
  peaches 291
anchovies, crisp liver slices with
  anchovy gremolata butter 195
apples
  apple jelly and cinnamon cream
    300
  apple mascarpone salad with
    warm sausage chunks 144
  apple tart 357
  baked apples with nutmeg
    custard pudding 361
  black pudding and bacon with
    honey apples and yoghurt
    rocket 47
  black pudding with blue cheese,
    celery and apple salad 48
  broken feta cheese salad with
    apples and pears 73
  charcuterie board with celeriac
    coleslaw 45
  Easter turkey steaks with apple
    and prune stuffing 420
  fennel, asparagus, grapefruit
    and apple 76
  fresh tuna with mango, apple,
    orange and curry vinaigrette
    184
  grilled mackerel with Calvados
    apples 62
  pork chops with an apple tart
    topping 220
  pork steaks with lemon, honey
    and mustard apples 249
  quick-fry monkfish and curry
    dip with banana, cucumber
    and apple 181
  roast hand of pork with baked
    black pudding apples 434
  roast monkfish 'Barnsley chops'
    with apple mint jelly and cider
    gravy 270
  slow-roast pork belly with
    Gorgonzola and apple
    cabbage 314
  spiced lamb with mango, apple
    and cucumber salad 190
  toffee apple crumble 428
apricot and pine nut rack of
  lamb with soft onions 329
Armagnac, prune and Armagnac
  bread and butter pudding 360
artichokes, broken salmon with
  artichokes and asparagus
  246
asparagus
  asparagus with an orange
    mascarpone dressing 452
  asparagus and ham glazed with
    Cheddar and Parmesan 84
  asparagus and mushroom
    pudding with melting Fontina
    406
  asparagus vichyssoise 400
  broken salmon with artichokes

and asparagus 246
chicken with wholegrain
  mustard asparagus 389
fennel, asparagus, grapefruit
  and apple 76
linguine and pesto frittata with
  asparagus, spinach, peas 204
risotto 207
aubergines
  aubergine caviar pasta with
    rocket and Parmesan 401
  aubergine, red onion and
    mozzarella bake 170
  quick marinated aubergine and
    sweet pepper salad 235
avocados
  avocado and courgette salad
    with lime 79
  Charentais melon and avocado
    with passion fruit vinaigrette
    413
  crunchy fish strips with an
    avocado dip 127

bacon
  bacon butty 28
  bacon and egg risotto 44
  bacon and egg salad 63
  bacon and onion potatoes 25
  bacon, potato and cheese
    frittata 124
  bacon sauté new potatoes 451
  bacon soup 398
  baked potatoes with sour cream,
    chives and bacon 122
  black pudding and bacon with
    honey apples and yoghurt
    rocket 47
  boiled bacon collar with spicy
    sausage mash and peas 320
  chicken and bacon sticks 138
  chicken livers with a sweet
    spinach and bacon salad 260
  and chipolatas 340
  duck, bacon and onion quiche
    422
  fried bacon pieces with spinach
    and prawns 84
  full English breakfast 32
  pan-fried sea bass with bacon
    and caper cabbage 265
  pea pancakes and grilled
    bacon 41
  red wine beef with bacon crunch
    313
  roast chicken thighs with bacon,
    carrots, onions and potatoes
    343
Bailey's crème brûlée 292
baked amaretti peaches 291
baked apples with nutmeg
  custard pudding 361
baked chicken legs with
  Mediterranean vegetables
  278
baked lemon halibut with leek and
  shrimp cream 417
baked potatoes with sour cream,
  chives and bacon 122
baked ratatouille peppers with
  melting goat's cheese 404
baked Vacherin cheese 414
balsamic vinegar, pesto linguine
  with balsamic tomatoes 151
bananas
  banana, pecan and honey
    cakes with espresso butter
    cream 108
  grilled gingerbread slice with

crushed banana and yoghurt
  36
quick-fry monkfish and curry
  dip with banana, cucumber
  and apple 181
sweet sesame mackerel with
  banana chutney 88
thick banana and coconut
  smoothie 38
toffee pie with grilled
  bananas 299
barbecued spare ribs 138
basil
  crispy Parmesan chicken with
    basil tomatoes 132
  John Dory with red pepper,
    tomato and basil spaghetti
    217
  mozzarella monkfish steaks with
    tomato and basil 377
  pasta with tomato, mozzarella
    and basil 123
  stir-fried chicken with tomatoes,
    basil and crispy Parmesan
    185
  tiger prawns and tomatoes with
    basil and garlic mayonnaise
    175
  toasted sea bass and oranges
    with basil yoghurt 266
bass see sea bass
bean sprouts, courgette and bean
  sprout stir-fry 160
beans
  braised lamb shanks with
    onions, tomatoes and pesto
    beans 280
  lamb with beans, onions,
    tomatoes and tarragon 336
  pasta niçoise 240
  runner beans with chunky
    seasoning 453
  salmon with French beans 209
  three bean salad 74
Béarnaise butter, Dover sole with
  a steak garnish 268
beef
  beef 'coq au vin' stew 306
  bittersweet beef fillet leaves 192
  Bolognese 134
  braised beef chuck with carrots
    and baked potatoes 424
  fillet of beef with goulash
    noodles 224
  fillet of beef with red wine
    tomatoes 287
  and potatoes braised in
    Guinness 307
  red wine beef with bacon
    crunch 313
  roast rib of beef 310
  roast veal with white onion and
    blue cheese potato gratin 308
  rump steak with home-made
    oven-baked garlic chips 395
  seared beef with Provençal
    tomatoes and mustard
    watercress 194
  seared calves' liver with
    caramelized grapes 286
  sirloin steak with hot red wine
    and mustard vinaigrette 397
  steak au poivre burger 396
  steak Diane 90
  steak sandwich with bittersweet
    fried onions 160
  surf 'n' turf 158
  T-bone steak with melting
    Roquefort cherry tomatoes
    162

tomato soup, spaghetti and
  meatballs 118
veal cutlets with white wine
  chestnut mushrooms 418
beef tomatoes and mozzarella
  with pine nuts and pesto
  crème fraîche 240
beer
  beef and potatoes braised in
    Guinness 307
  stout-glazed leg of lamb 324
beetroot carpaccio with
  redcurrant walnut dressing
  233
berries
  cracked summer berry
    meringue 290
  see also blackberries;
    blackcurrants; raspberries;
    strawberries
bittersweet beef fillet leaves 192
black bream, seared black bream
  with ginger, tomato and chilli
  pak choy 264
black pepper lamb steak with
  pomegranates 189
black pudding
  black pudding and bacon with
    honey apples and yoghurt
    rocket 47
  black pudding with blue
    cheese, celery and apple
    salad 48
  full English breakfast 32
  roast hand of pork with baked
    black pudding apples 434
blackberries
  apple tart 357
  blackberry and almond tart 100
  roasted duck with red wine
    blackberries 344
blackcurrants, venison sausages
  with red wine onions and
  blackcurrants 196
blood oranges, seared halibut
  with a blood orange and
  courgette salad 374
blue cheese
  black pudding with blue
    cheese, celery and apple
    salad 48
  dressing 63
  roast veal with white onion and
    blue cheese potato gratin 308
boiled bacon collar with spicy
  sausage mash and peas 320
boiled eggs 19
  home-made salad cream with
    broken new potatoes, eggs
    and red onions 64
boiled pork pot 318
Bolognese 134
bowl of broccoli with a
  Gorgonzola swirl 132
a bowl of cauliflower and
  Camembert 200
braised beef chuck with carrots
  and baked potatoes 424
braised lamb shanks with onions,
  tomatoes and pesto beans
  280
braised pigs' cheeks with
  marmalade turnips 284
braised red cabbage 460
braised shoulder of lamb with
  rosemary, carrots and onions
  421
bread and butter pudding, prune
  and Armagnac bread and

butter pudding 360
bread sauce 341
breakfast 22, 24–39
bream, seared black bream with
ginger, tomato and chilli pak
choy 264
Brie
leek, ham and Brie slice 238
pasta with spinach and melting
Brie 203
brill
pan-fried brill with capers,
lemon and mash 386
pan-fried brill with red wine
cockles 214
brioche
Cognac peaches with pistachio
brioche 365
lemon brioche turbot with a hint
of horseradish 213
British sausage soup 167
broad beans, risotto 207
broccoli
bowl of broccoli with a
Gorgonzola swirl 162
with Caesar dressing 453
purple sprouting 456
broken feta cheese salad with
apples and pears 73
broken salmon with artichokes
and asparagus 246
broth
cod poached in a tarragon
broth 354
curried mussels and noodle
broth 388
brownies
chocolate brownie gypsy
pudding 146
chocolate brownie mousse 295
brunch 22, 40–67
bruschettas, courgette soup with
tomato and red onion
bruschetta 71
Brussels tops, warm crème
fraîche Brussels tops 456
buffalo mozzarella, grilled buffalo
mozzarella with garlic, lemon
and courgettes 80
burgers, steak au poivre burger
396
burnt lamb chops with sweet
peppers and onions 223
buttered leek greens 458
butterflied prawns with sweet and
sour papaya 244
buttermilk mini scones 106
butternut squash
butternut squash soup 72
coconut rice and peas with
butternut squash 199
butters
cod with peas and ham stewed
in butter 216
crisp liver slices with anchovy
gremolata butter 195
Dover sole with hot lemon
butter 153
Dover sole with a steak garnish
268
herb butter sauce 269
pasta with chicken, sage and
onion butter 82
roast chicken with goat's cheese
and fresh herb butter 93
roast flat fish with parsley
lemon butter and new
potatoes Lyonnaise 352

cabbage
boiled pork pot 318
braised red cabbage 460
pan-fried sea bass with bacon
and caper cabbage 265
pork belly potatoes and red
cabbage roast 319
roast monkfish in red wine with
crème fraîche cabbage 272
slow-roast pork belly with
Gorgonzola and apple
cabbage 314
Caesar dressing 464
broccoli with Caesar dressing
453
Caesar salad, lobster Caesar
salad 257
cakes
banana, pecan and honey
cakes with espresso butter
cream 108
black cherry Victoria sponge
cake 110
hazelnut cake with Frangelico
cream 103
see also cheesecake
calamari with hot ratatouille 210
Calvados, grilled mackerel with
Calvados apples 62
calves' liver, seared calves' liver
with caramelized grapes 286
Camembert
a bowl of cauliflower and
Camembert 230
crispy Camembert with
cranberry sauce 430
cannellini beans, three bean
salad 74
capers
grilled plaice with chives and
capers 156
lamb cutlets with crispy sage
and capers 222
pan-fried brill with capers,
lemon and mash 386
pan-fried sea bass with bacon
and caper cabbage 265
caramel
chocolate and caramel
shortbread 104
crème caramel 366
honeycomb caramel slice 114
spotted dick pudding with
caramel golden syrup 368
carbonara, pasta carbonara 202
carpaccio
beetroot carpaccio with
redcurrant walnut dressing
233
cured ham with a carpaccio
sauce 51
carrots
braised beef chuck with carrots
and baked potatoes 424
braised shoulder of lamb with
rosemary, carrots and onions
421
grilled chicken with carrot,
celeriac and courgette cream
276
orange curd carrots 458
roast chicken thighs with bacon,
carrots, onions and potatoes
343
seven-hour leg of lamb with
potatoes, carrots and onions
326
cauliflower
a bowl of cauliflower and

Camembert 230
macaroni and cauliflower with
four cheeses 208
and mushroom curry 288
celeriac
charcuterie board with celeriac
coleslaw 45
grilled chicken with carrot,
celeriac and courgette cream
276
celery, black pudding with blue
cheese celery, and apple
salad 48
cep mushrooms see porcini
champ
crushed champ kippers with
wilted watercress 61
roast rump of lamb with
pancetta champ and
marjoram cream 332
charcuterie board with celeriac
coleslaw 45
Charentais melon and avocado
with passion fruit vinaigrette
413
charred squid with passion fruit,
pineapple and sesame leaves
92
Cheddar cheese
asparagus and ham glazed with
Cheddar and Parmesan 84
Cheddar cheese and onion
Scotch pancakes 120
cod with new potatoes, baby
spinach and Cheddar cheese
sauce 274
cheese
apple mascarpone salad with
warm sausage chunks 144
asparagus and ham glazed with
Cheddar and Parmesan 84
asparagus and mushroom
pudding with melting Fontina
406
asparagus with an orange
mascarpone dressing 452
aubergine caviar pasta with
rocket and Parmesan 401
aubergine, red onion and
mozzarella bake 170
bacon, potato and cheese
frittata 124
baked ratatouille peppers with
melting goat's cheese 404
baked Vacherin cheese 414
beef tomatoes and mozzarella
with pine nuts and pesto
crème fraîche 240
black pudding with blue cheese
celery, and apple salad 48
bowl of broccoli with a
Gorgonzola swirl 162
a bowl of cauliflower and
Camembert 230
broken feta cheese salad with
apples and pears 73
Cheddar cheese and onion
Scotch pancakes 120
cod with new potatoes, baby
spinach and Cheddar cheese
sauce 274
crispy Camembert with
cranberry sauce 430
crispy Parmesan chicken with
basil tomatoes 132
fennel with oysters and
Parmesan shavings 238
Gorgonzola, Parma ham and
rocket pasta 82

grilled buffalo mozzarella
with garlic, lemon and
courgettes 80
halloumi sticks with pear rings
and mixed cress leaves 236
ham, cheese and onion
spaghetti 123
hot potato salad with melting
raclette 78
leek and Gruyère quiche 407
leek, ham and Brie slice 238
macaroni and cauliflower with
four cheeses 208
macaroni cheese 126
mozzarella monkfish steaks with
tomato and basil 377
mushroom and goat's cheese
tartlets 252
mussels with leeks and
Gorgonzola 387
open spinach and ricotta ravioli
with pine nuts and Parmesan
168
Parmesan risotto 206
pasta with spinach and melting
Brie 203
pasta with tomato, mozzarella
and basil 123
pesto linguine with balsamic
tomatoes 151
potato, leek and Gouda gratin
405
potato, pumpkin, white leek and
goat's cheese gratin 425
potatoes stuffed with Stilton,
leek and mushrooms 402
prawn rarebits 444
raspberry mascarpone oat
pud 146
Red Leicester mushrooms 66
roast chicken with goat's cheese
and fresh herb butter 93
roast veal with white onion and
blue cheese potato gratin 308
savoury pear, Stilton and chive
cakes 253
smoked haddock-topped
eggs with melting Lancashire
cheese 26
stir-fried chicken with tomatoes,
basil and crispy Parmesan
185
Swiss cheese halibut with
spinach and mushrooms 376
T-bone steak with melting
Roquefort cherry tomatoes
162
tiger prawns with leek and
mozzarella risotto 263
tiramisu bocker glory 290
warm chorizo and goat's cheese
salad with raspberry
vinaigrette 46
Wensleydale patties 130
whipped Stilton with figs and
watercress 443
cheesecake
mango cheesecake fool 292
rhubarb and custard
cheesecake 358
white chocolate cheesecake
109
cherries, black cherry Victoria
sponge cake 110
cherry tomato soup 72
chervil, pan-fried white fish with
buttery grapes and chervil
416

chestnut mushrooms
  chicken with porcini and
    chestnut mushrooms 275
  Swiss cheese halibut with
    spinach and mushrooms 376
  veal cutlets with white wine
    chestnut mushrooms 418
chicken
  baked chicken legs with
    Mediterranean vegetables
    278
  chicken and bacon sticks 138
  chicken and chorizo sausage
    stew 186
  chicken, ham and mushroom
    pie 338
  chicken livers with a sweet
    spinach and bacon salad 260
  chicken skewers with peanut
    sauce 142
  crispy Parmesan chicken with
    basil tomatoes 132
  grilled chicken with carrot,
    celeriac and courgette cream
    276
  honey, lemon and thyme roast
    chicken 390
  pasta with chicken, sage and
    onion butter 82
  with porcini and chestnut
    mushrooms 275
  roast chicken breasts with
    almond cream noodles 218
  roast chicken with goat's cheese
    and fresh herb butter 93
  roast chicken with gravy 340
  roast chicken thighs with bacon,
    carrots, onions and potatoes
    343
  roast paprika chicken 342
  sticky lemon chicken 132
  stir-fried chicken with tomatoes,
    basil and crispy Parmesan
    185
  with wholegrain mustard
    asparagus 389
chicory
  caramelized with honey 454
  grilled gammon with pear
    mayonnaise and chicory 394
  red and white chicory salad with
    a rhubarb vinaigrette 75
children's teatime 116–47
chillies
  lemon and chilli sesame pork
    with mangetout 188
  seared black bream with ginger,
    tomato and chilli pak choy
    264
  seared scallops and chilli-
    spiced cucumber 256
chipolatas
  bacon and chipolatas 340
  sautéed kidneys and chipolatas
    with mushrooms and garlic
    toasts 52
chips
  fish and chips for two 177
  grilled Portobello mushroom
    steaks, chips and tomatoes
    152
  rump steak with home-made
    oven-baked garlic chips 395
chives
  baked potatoes with sour
    cream, chives and bacon 122
  grilled plaice with chives and
    capers 156
  prawn and cucumber
    sandwiches with chive cream

and a tomato dressing 98
  savoury pear, Stilton and chive
    cakes 253
chocolate
  chocolate brownie gypsy
    pudding 146
  chocolate brownie mousse 295
  chocolate and caramel
    shortbread 104
  chocolate and nut pancakes
    with maple syrup 34
  hot chocolate fondants 426
  raspberry and white chocolate
    cream shortbreads 294
  warm chocolate sauce 467
  white chocolate cheesecake
    109
  white chocolate cream 467
  white chocolate cream with
    mango sauce 147
chorizo sausages
  boiled bacon collar with spicy
    sausage mash and peas 320
  chicken and chorizo sausage
    stew 186
  warm chorizo and goat's cheese
    salad with raspberry
    vinaigrette 46
Christmas pudding 440
chutney, sweet sesame mackerel
  with banana chutney 88
cider
  cider gravy 322
  roast monkfish 'Barnsley chops'
    with apple mint jelly and cider
    gravy 270
cinnamon, apple jelly and
  cinnamon cream 300
clafoutis, raspberry clafoutis 104
clotted cream panna cotta and
  strawberries 302
cobbler, hoggett cobbler with
  orange onions and sage
  scones 334
cockles, pan-fried brill with red
  wine cockles 214
coconut
  coconut rice and peas with
    butternut squash 199
  thick banana and coconut
    smoothie 38
cod
  cod with new potatoes, baby
    spinach and Cheddar cheese
    sauce 274
  cod with peas and ham stewed
    in butter 216
  cod poached in a tarragon
    broth 354
coffee, banana, pecan and
  honey cakes with espresso
  butter cream 108
Cognac
  Cognac peaches with pistachio
    brioche 365
  risotto rice pudding with
    Cognac sultanas 442
colcannon, kale colcannon 454
coleslaw, charcuterie board with
  celeriac coleslaw 45
courgettes
  avocado and courgette salad
    with lime 79
  courgette and bean sprout
    stir-fry 160
  courgette soup with tomato and
    red onion bruschetta 71
  grilled buffalo mozzarella
    with garlic, lemon and

courgettes 80
  grilled chicken with carrot,
    celeriac and courgette cream
    276
  John Dory with sautéed honey
    sesame courgettes 178
  risotto 207
  seared halibut with a blood
    orange and courgette salad
    374
crab 17
  crab salad with crispy poached
    egg 60
  crab and spinach omelette with
    lobster cream 180
cracked summer berry meringue
  290
cranberries, crispy Camembert
  with cranberry sauce 430
cream vinaigrette 466
creamed mushrooms with fresh
  herbs 172
crème brûlée
  Bailey's crème brûlée 292
  passion fruit brûlée 438
crème caramel 366
crème fraîche
  beef tomatoes and mozzarella
    with pine nuts and pesto
    crème fraîche 240
  roast monkfish in red wine with
    crème fraîche cabbage 272
  warm crème fraîche Brussels
    tops 456
cress
  halloumi sticks with pear rings
    and mixed cress leaves 236
  see also watercress
crisp liver slices with anchovy
  gremolata butter 195
crispy Camembert with cranberry
  sauce 430
crispy Parmesan chicken with
  basil tomatoes 132
crushed champ kippers with
  wilted watercress 61
cucumber
  prawn and cucumber
    sandwiches with chive cream
    and a tomato dressing 98
  quick-fry monkfish and curry
    dip with banana, cucumber
    and apple 181
  seared scallops and chilli-
    spiced cucumber 256
  spiced lamb with mango, apple
    and cucumber salad 190
  steamed sea trout with crispy
    seaweed and cucumber 382
  sweet sharp herrings with
    potato, cucumber and
    horseradish salad 380
Cumberland sausage and red
  onion tart 42
cured ham with a carpaccio
  sauce 51
curly kale, kale colcannon 454
curry
  cauliflower and mushroom
    curry 288
  curried mussels and noodle
    broth 388
  curry mayonnaise 465
  fresh tuna with mango, apple,
    orange and curry vinaigrette
    184
  lamb goujons with curry
    mayonnaise and mint raita
    333

quick curried prawns 176
  quick-fry monkfish and curry
    dip with banana, cucumber
    and apple 181
custard
  baked apples with nutmeg
    custard pudding 361
  fresh vanilla custard 467
  rhubarb and custard
    cheesecake 358

dates, treacle duck breasts with
  creamy date parsnips 348
desserts see puddings
Dover sole
  with hot lemon butter 153
  with a steak garnish 268
dressings see sauces
duck
  duck, bacon and onion quiche
    422
  duck pancake rolls 258
  pork and duck sausage rolls
    446
  quick seared duck à l'orange
    164
  roast duck with spinach and
    wild mushrooms 279
  roasted duck with red wine
    blackberries 344
  steamed duck with caramelized
    onions, olives and walnuts
    346
  treacle duck breasts with
    creamy date parsnips 348

Easter turkey steaks with apple
  and prune stuffing 420
eggs 18–19
  bacon and egg risotto 44
  bacon and egg salad 63
  bacon, potato and cheese
    frittata 124
  crab salad with crispy poached
    egg 60
  crab and spinach omelette with
    lobster cream 180
  eggs, tomatoes and mushrooms
    30
  fried egg, tomatoes and
    mushrooms 32
  home-made salad cream with
    broken new potatoes, eggs
    and red onions 64
  leeks and red onions with a
    warm poached egg 66
  linguine and pesto frittata with
    asparagus, spinach, peas 204
  omelette 25
  pasta carbonara 202
  ratatouille omelette 126
  red wine and mushroom
    poached eggs on toast 62
  scrambled egg mushroom
    muffins 34
  smoked haddock, poached egg
    and sorrel hollandaise 58
  smoked haddock-topped
    eggs with melting Lancashire
    cheese 26
  smoked salmon and poached
    egg muffins 56
  zabaglione 291
Emmental cheese, smoked
  haddock and spinach tart
  with Emmental 383
espresso, banana, pecan and
  honey cakes with espresso
  butter cream 108

Eton mess, strawberry Eton mess with raspberry sauce 147

fennel
fennel, asparagus, grapefruit and apple 76
fennel with oysters and Parmesan shavings 238
red mullet with fennel and olives 154
roast monkfish with fennel, orange and tarragon mussels 353
feta cheese, broken feta cheese salad with apples and pears 73
fiery mushrooms on toast 83
figs
toasted ginger figs 414
whipped Stilton with figs and watercress 443
fillet of beef with goulash noodles 224
fillet of beef with red wine tomatoes 287
fish 14, 16
baked lemon halibut with leek and shrimp cream 417
broken salmon with artichokes and asparagus 246
cod with new potatoes, baby spinach and Cheddar cheese sauce 274
cod with peas and ham stewed in butter 216
cod poached in a tarragon broth 354
crunchy fish strips with an avocado dip 127
crushed champ kippers with wilted watercress 61
Dover sole with hot lemon butter 153
Dover sole with a steak garnish 268
fish cake fingers 128
fish and chips for two 177
foil-baked bass with garlic, parsley and lemon 384
glazed horseradish tuna with spring onion potatoes 54
golden oatmeal herrings 55
grilled kipper and granary fried bread 27
grilled mackerel with Calvados apples 62
grilled plaice with chives and capers 156
grilled sardines with sweet potato and mango salsa 248
grilled tuna with a niçoise salsa 87
ham-wrapped trout with English mustard sauce 350
John Dory with red pepper, tomato and basil spaghetti 217
John Dory with sautéed honey sesame courgettes 178
lemon brioche turbot with a hint of horseradish 213
monkfish with golden sultanas, onion and spinach 269
mozzarella monkfish steaks with tomato and basil 377
pan-fried brill with capers, lemon and mash 386
pan-fried brill with red wine

cockles 214
pan-fried sea bass with bacon and caper cabbage 265
pan-fried white fish with buttery grapes and chervil 416
pasta niçoise 240
potted mackerel 90
quick-fry monkfish and curry dip with banana, cucumber and apple 181
red mullet with fennel and olives 154
roast flat fish with parsley lemon butter and new potatoes Lyonnaise 352
roast halibut with buttery mussels and herbs 356
roast monkfish 'Barnsley chops' with apple mint jelly and cider gravy 270
roast monkfish with fennel, orange and tarragon mussels 353
roast monkfish in red wine with crème fraîche cabbage 272
salmon cutlets with minted leeks and peas and a sweet lemon dressing 86
salmon skewers with pistachio lime yoghurt 182
seared black bream with ginger, tomato and chilli pak choy 264
seared halibut with a blood orange and courgette salad 374
seared tuna with pissaladière toasts 245
smoked haddock, poached egg and sorrel hollandaise 58
smoked haddock and spinach tart with Emmental 383
smoked haddock-topped eggs with melting Lancashire cheese 26
smoked salmon and poached egg muffins 56
smoked salmon, trout and mackerel open sandwiches 97
steamed salmon with grilled vegetables 212
steamed sea trout with crispy seaweed and cucumber 382
sweet sesame mackerel with banana chutney 88
sweet sharp herrings with potato, cucumber and horseradish salad 380
Swiss cheese halibut with spinach and mushrooms 376
toasted sea bass and oranges with basil yoghurt 266
tuna steak with red wine mushrooms 156
warm lentil, orange and watercress salad with grilled mackerel 378
warm salmon on brown bread 57
flans, orange flan, strawberries and orange curd cream 102
flat mushroom pastry with a watercress and cherry tomato salad 242
foil-baked bass with garlic, parsley and lemon 384
fondants, hot chocolate fondants 426

Fontina cheese, asparagus and mushroom pudding with melting Fontina 406
fool, mango cheesecake fool 292
Frangelico, hazelnut cake with Frangelico cream 103
French beans
pasta niçoise 240
salmon with French beans 209
three bean salad 74
fresh tuna with mango, apple, orange and curry vinaigrette 184
fresh vanilla custard 467
fried bread, grilled kipper and granary fried bread 27
fried eggs 19
bacon and egg salad 63
fried egg, tomatoes and mushrooms 32
frittata
bacon, potato and cheese frittata 124
linguine and pesto frittata with asparagus, spinach, peas 204
fritters, parsnip and onion fritters 458
full English breakfast 32
vegetarian 30

game, roast partridge with toasted salsify and maple sherry gravy 349
gammon
grilled gammon with pear mayonnaise and chicory 394
warm gammon and pineapple with English leaves 50
garlic
aïoli sauce 464
foil-baked bass with garlic, parsley and lemon 384
garlic prawns with lobster noodles 209
grilled buffalo mozzarella with garlic, lemon and courgettes 80
rump steak with home-made oven-baked garlic chips 395
sautéed kidneys and chipolatas with mushrooms and garlic toasts 52
tiger prawns and tomatoes with basil and garlic mayonnaise 175
wild mushroom and garlic cream 312
ginger
sautéed scallops with ginger spring greens and passion fruit hollandaise 254
seared black bream with ginger, tomato and chilli pak choy 264
toasted ginger figs 414
gingerbread, grilled gingerbread slice with crushed banana and yoghurt 36
glazed horseradish tuna with spring onion potatoes 54
glazed mandarin tart 436
goat's cheese
baked ratatouille peppers with melting goat's cheese 404
mushroom and goat's cheese tartlets 252
potato, pumpkin, white leek and goat's cheese gratin 425
roast chicken with goat's cheese

and fresh herb butter 93
warm chorizo and goat's cheese salad with raspberry vinaigrette 46
golden oatmeal herrings 55
golden sultanas
monkfish with golden sultanas, onion and spinach 269
risotto rice pudding with Cognac sultanas 442
roast turkey with pistachio and golden sultana stuffing 432
golden syrup, spotted dick pudding with caramel golden syrup 368
Gorgonzola
bowl of broccoli with a Gorgonzola swirl 162
Gorgonzola, Parma ham and rocket pasta 82
mussels with leeks and Gorgonzola 387
slow-roast pork belly with Gorgonzola and apple cabbage 314
Gouda cheese, potato, leek and Gouda gratin 405
goulash, fillet of beef with goulash noodles 224
grapefruit 20
fennel, asparagus, grapefruit and apple 76
grapes
pan-fried white fish with buttery grapes and chervil 416
seared calves' liver with caramelized grapes 286
gratin
gratin dauphinois 452
potato, leek and Gouda gratin 405
potato, pumpkin, white leek and goat's cheese gratin 425
roast veal with white onion and blue cheese potato gratin 308
gravy 310
cider gravy 322
roast chicken with gravy 340
roast gravy 466
roast monkfish 'Barnsley chops' with apple mint jelly and cider gravy 270
roast partridge with toasted salsify and maple sherry gravy 349
roast turkey with pistachio and golden sultana stuffing 432
gremolata
crisp liver slices with anchovy gremolata butter 195
lamb 'osso buco' 282
grilled buffalo mozzarella with garlic, lemon and courgettes 80
grilled chicken with carrot, celeriac and courgette cream 276
grilled gammon with pear mayonnaise and chicory 394
grilled gingerbread slice with crushed banana and yoghurt 36
grilled kipper and granary fried bread 27
grilled mackerel with Calvados apples 62
grilled plaice with chives and capers 156

grilled Portobello mushroom steaks, chips and tomatoes 152
grilled sardines with sweet potato and mango salsa 248
grilled tuna with a niçoise salsa 87
Gruyère cheese
    leek and Gruyère quiche 407
    Swiss cheese halibut with spinach and mushrooms 376
Guinness, beef and potatoes braised in Guinness 307
gypsy pudding, chocolate brownie gypsy pudding 146

haddock
    fish and chips for two 177
    smoked haddock, poached egg and sorrel hollandaise 58
    smoked haddock and spinach tart with Emmental 383
    smoked haddock-topped eggs with melting Lancashire cheese 26
halibut
    baked lemon halibut with leek and shrimp cream 417
    roast halibut with buttery mussels and herbs 356
    seared halibut with a blood orange and courgette salad 374
    Swiss cheese halibut with spinach and mushrooms 376
halloumi sticks with pear rings and mixed cress leaves 236
ham
    asparagus and ham glazed with Cheddar and Parmesan 84
    chicken, ham and mushroom pie 338
    cod with peas and ham stewed in butter 216
    cured ham with a carpaccio sauce 51
    Gorgonzola, Parma ham and rocket pasta 82
    ham, cheese and onion spaghetti 123
    ham risotto 207
    ham-wrapped trout with English mustard sauce 350
    leek, ham and Brie slice 238
    pasta carbonara 202
haricot beans
    lamb with beans, onions, tomatoes and tarragon 336
    see also cannellini beans
hazelnuts, hazelnut cake with Frangelico cream 103
herbs
    creamed mushrooms with fresh herbs 172
    herb butter sauce 269
    herb and lemon risotto 207
    roast chicken with goat's cheese and fresh herb butter 93
    roast halibut with buttery mussels and herbs 356
    salmon with a salted tomato and herb salad 85
    seared beef with Provençal tomatoes and mustard watercress 194
    spring and summer vegetables with fresh herbs 408
herrings 14
    golden oatmeal herrings 55

sweet sharp herrings with potato, cucumber and horseradish salad 380
hoggett cobbler with orange onions and sage scones 334
hollandaise sauce
    quick 464
    sautéed scallops with ginger spring greens and passion fruit hollandaise 254
    smoked haddock, poached egg and sorrel hollandaise 58
home-made salad cream with broken new potatoes, eggs and red onions 64
honey
    banana, pecan and honey cakes with espresso butter cream 108
    black pudding and bacon with honey apples and yoghurt rocket 47
    chicory caramelized with honey 454
    honey, lemon and thyme roast chicken 390
    John Dory with sautéed honey sesame courgettes 178
    pork steaks with lemon, honey and mustard apples 249
    rice pudding with toasted honey plums 298
    three-mustard honey potato salad 232
honeycomb caramel slice 114
horseradish
    glazed horseradish tuna with spring onion potatoes 54
    lemon brioche turbot with a hint of horseradish 213
    sweet sharp herrings with potato, cucumber and horseradish salad 380
hot chocolate fondants 426
hot potato salad with melting raclette 78
hotpot, lamb hotpot 337

iced Jersey cream with lots of strawberries 370
Irish stew soup 229

jelly, apple jelly and cinnamon cream 300
Jersey cream, iced Jersey cream with lots of strawberries 370
John Dory
    John Dory with red pepper, tomato and basil spaghetti 217
    John Dory with sautéed honey sesame courgettes 178

kale colcannon 454
kidneys
    lemon and parsley crusted lambs' kidneys 165
    sautéed kidneys and chipolatas with mushrooms and garlic toasts 52
kippers
    crushed champ kippers with wilted watercress 61
    grilled kipper and granary fried bread 27

lamb
    apricot and pine nut rack of lamb with soft onions 329

with beans, onions, tomatoes and tarragon 336
    black pepper lamb steak with pomegranates 189
    braised lamb shanks with onions, tomatoes and pesto beans 280
    braised shoulder of lamb with rosemary, carrots and onions 421
    burnt lamb chops with sweet peppers and onions 223
    hoggett cobbler with orange onions and sage scones 334
    hotpot 337
    Irish stew soup 229
    lamb cutlets with creamy mint peas 130
    lamb cutlets with crispy sage and capers 222
    lamb goujons with curry mayonnaise and mint raita 333
    lemon and parsley crusted lambs' kidneys 165
    lamb 'osso buco' 282
    roast leg of lamb 328
    roast rump of lamb with pancetta champ and marjoram 332
    seven-hour leg of lamb with potatoes, carrots and onions 326
    spiced lamb with mango, apple and cucumber salad 190
    stout-glazed leg of lamb 324
    West Country squab pie 330
Lancashire cheese, smoked haddock-topped eggs with melting Lancashire cheese 26
leeks
    baked lemon halibut with leek and shrimp cream 417
    buttered leek greens 458
    leek and Gruyère quiche 407
    leek risotto 207
    leek, ham and Brie slice 238
    leeks and red onions with a warm poached egg 66
    mussels with leeks and Gorgonzola 387
    potato, leek and Gouda gratin 405
    potato, pumpkin, white leek and goat's cheese gratin 425
    potatoes stuffed with Stilton, leek and mushrooms 402
    prune, leek and sage stuffing 322
    salmon cutlets with minted leeks and peas and a sweet lemon dressing 86
    tiger prawns with leek and mozzarella risotto 263
    watercress, leek and potato soup 200
lemon curd
    lemon meringue tartlets 112
    liqueur-steeped summer fruits with lemon curd cream 296
lemon sole, crunchy fish strips with an avocado dip 127
lemons
    Dover sole with hot lemon butter 153
    foil-baked bass with garlic, parsley and lemon 384
    grilled buffalo mozzarella with garlic, lemon and

courgettes 80
    herb and lemon risotto 207
    honey, lemon and thyme roast chicken 390
    lemon brioche turbot with a hint of horseradish 213
    lemon and chilli sesame pork with mangetout 188
    lemon and parsley crusted lambs' kidneys 165
    pan-fried brill with capers, lemon and mash 386
    pork steaks with lemon, honey and mustard apples 249
    roast flat fish with parsley lemon butter and new potatoes 352
    sage, onion and lemon stuffing 341
    salmon cutlets with minted leeks and peas and a sweet lemon dressing 86
    sticky lemon chicken 132
    sweet lemon dressing 465
lentils, warm lentil, orange and watercress salad with grilled mackerel 378
limes
    avocado and courgette salad with lime 79
    salmon skewers with pistachio lime yoghurt 182
linguine
    linguine and pesto frittata with asparagus, spinach, peas 204
    pesto linguine with balsamic tomatoes 151
liqueur-steeped summer fruits with lemon curd cream 296
liver
    chicken livers with a sweet spinach and bacon salad 260
    crisp liver slices with anchovy gremolata butter 195
    seared calves' liver with caramelized grapes 286
lobster 17
    crab and spinach omelette with lobster cream 180
    garlic prawns with lobster noodles 209
    lobster Caesar salad 257
lyonnaise potatoes
    roast flat fish with parsley lemon butter and new potatoes lyonnaise 352

macaroni
    macaroni and cauliflower with four cheeses 208
    macaroni cheese 126
macaroons, pear macaroon crumble 364
mackerel
    grilled mackerel with Calvados apples 62
    potted mackerel 90
    smoked salmon, trout and mackerel open sandwiches 97
    sweet sesame mackerel with banana chutney 88
    warm lentil, orange and watercress salad with grilled mackerel 378
mandarins, glazed mandarin tart 436
mangetout, lemon and chilli sesame pork with

mangetout 188
mangoes
  fresh tuna with mango, apple,
    orange and curry vinaigrette
    184
  grilled sardines with sweet
    potato and mango salsa 248
  mango cheesecake fool 292
  spiced lamb with mango, apple
    and cucumber salad 190
  white chocolate cream with
    mango sauce 147
maple syrup
  Brussels sprouts with pecan
    nuts and maple butter 456
  chocolate and nut pancakes
    with maple syrup 34
  roast partridge with toasted
    salsify and maple sherry
    gravy 349
marjoram, roast rump of lamb
    with pancetta champ and
    marjoram cream 332
marmalade, braised pigs' cheeks
    with marmalade turnips 284
mascarpone cheese
  apple mascarpone salad with
    warm sausage chunks 144
  asparagus with an orange
    mascarpone dressing 452
  raspberry mascarpone oat
    pud 146
  tiramisu bocker glory 290
mash 451
mayonnaise
  crunchy fish strips with an
    avocado dip 127
  curry mayonnaise 465
  grilled gammon with pear
    mayonnaise and chicory 394
  lamb goujons with curry
    mayonnaise and mint raita
    333
  tiger prawns and tomatoes with
    basil and garlic mayonnaise
    175
meatballs, tomato soup, spaghetti
    and meatballs 118
Mediterranean vegetables, baked
    chicken legs with
    Mediterranean vegetables
    278
melon, Charentais melon and
    avocado with passion fruit
    vinaigrette 413
meringues
  cracked summer berry
    meringue 290
  lemon meringue tartlets 112
  strawberry Eton mess with
    raspberry sauce 147
milanese, risotto milanese 283
mince pie turnovers 438
mint
  lamb cutlets with creamy mint
    peas 130
  lamb goujons with curry
    mayonnaise and mint raita
    333
  mint raita 465
  mint sauce 328
  roast monkfish 'Barnsley chops'
    with apple mint jelly and cider
    gravy 270
  salmon cutlets with minted leeks
    and peas and a sweet lemon
    dressing 86
mixed roast veg 453
monkfish

with golden sultanas, onion and
    spinach 269
mozzarella monkfish steaks with
    tomato and basil 377
quick-fry monkfish and curry
    dip with banana, cucumber
    and apple 181
roast monkfish 'Barnsley chops'
    with apple mint jelly and cider
    gravy 270
roast monkfish in red wine with
    crème fraîche cabbage 272
moules marinières 174
mousse, chocolate brownie
    mousse 295
mozzarella
  aubergine, red onion and
    mozzarella bake 170
  beef tomatoes and mozzarella
    with pine nuts and pesto
    crème fraîche 240
  grilled buffalo mozzarella with
    garlic, lemon and courgettes
    80
  mozzarella monkfish steaks with
    tomato and basil 377
  pasta with tomato, mozzarella
    and basil 123
  tiger prawns with leek and
    mozzarella risotto 263
muffins
  scrambled egg mushroom
    muffins 34
  smoked salmon and poached
    egg muffins 56
mushrooms 20
  asparagus and mushroom
    pudding with melting Fontina
    406
  cauliflower and mushroom
    curry 288
  chicken, ham and mushroom
    pie 338
  chicken with porcini and
    chestnut mushrooms 275
  creamed mushrooms with fresh
    herbs 172
  Dover sole with a steak garnish
    268
  eggs, tomatoes and mushrooms
    30
  fennel with 'oysters' and
    Parmesan shavings 238
  fiery mushrooms on toast 83
  flat mushroom pastry with a
    watercress and cherry tomato
    salad 242
  fried egg, tomatoes and
    mushrooms 32
  grilled Portobello mushroom
    steaks, chips and tomatoes
    152
  mushroom and goat's cheese
    tartlets 252
  mushroom risotto 207
  oyster mushrooms and spinach
    pancakes 67
  pasta with a wild mushroom
    cream sauce 208
  potatoes stuffed with Stilton,
    leek and mushrooms 402
  Red Leicester mushrooms 66
  red wine and mushroom
    poached eggs on toast 62
  roast duck with spinach and wild
    mushrooms 279
  sautéed kidneys and chipolatas
    with mushrooms and garlic
    toasts 52
  sautéed snails, mushrooms

and pasta with watercress
    sauce 262
scrambled egg mushroom
    muffins 34
sesame wild mushroom salad
    234
Swiss cheese halibut with
    spinach and mushrooms 376
tuna steak with red wine
    mushrooms 156
veal cutlets with white wine
    chestnut mushrooms 418
white pork and wild mushroom
    stew 316
wild mushroom and garlic
    cream 312
mussels 17
  curried mussels and noodle
    broth 388
  moules marinières 174
  mussels with leeks and
    Gorgonzola 387
  roast halibut with buttery
    mussels and herbs 356
  roast monkfish with fennel,
    orange and tarragon mussels
    353
mustard
  chicken with wholegrain
    mustard asparagus 389
  ham-wrapped trout with English
    mustard sauce 350
  pork steaks with lemon, honey
    and mustard apples 249
  red wine mustard dressing 466
  seared beef with Provençal
    tomatoes and mustard
    watercress 194
  sirloin steak with hot red wine
    and mustard vinaigrette 397
  three-mustard honey potato
    salad 232

niçoise
  grilled tuna with a niçoise
    salsa 87
  pasta niçoise 240
noodles
  curried mussels and noodle
    broth 388
  fillet of beef with goulash
    noodles 224
  garlic prawns with lobster
    noodles 209
  roast chicken breasts with
    almond cream noodles 218
nutmeg
  baked apples with nutmeg
    custard pudding 361
  nutmeg raisin spinach 452
nuts 13

oatmeal
  golden oatmeal herrings 55
  raspberry mascarpone oat
    pud 146
olives
  red mullet with fennel and
    olives 154
  steamed duck with caramelized
    onions, olives and walnuts
    346
omelette 25
  bacon, potato and cheese
    frittata 124
  crab and spinach omelette with
    lobster cream 180
  linguine and pesto frittata with
    asparagus, spinach, peas 204

ratatouille omelette 126
smoked haddock-topped
    eggs with melting Lancashire
    cheese 26
onions
  apricot and pine nut rack of
    lamb with soft onions 329
  bacon and onion potatoes 25
  braised lamb shanks with
    onions, tomatoes and pesto
    beans 280
  braised shoulder of lamb with
    rosemary, carrots and onions
    421
  burnt lamb chops with sweet
    peppers and onions 223
  Cheddar cheese and onion
    Scotch pancakes 120
  duck, bacon and onion quiche
    422
  ham, cheese and onion
    spaghetti 123
  hoggett cobbler with orange
    onions and sage scones 334
  lamb with beans, onions,
    tomatoes and tarragon 336
  monkfish with golden sultanas,
    onion and spinach 269
  parsnip and onion fritters 458
  pasta with chicken, sage and
    onion butter 82
  roast chicken thighs with bacon,
    carrots, onions and potatoes
    343
  sage, onion and lemon stuffing
    341
  sage and onion porkies 117
  sausage sandwich with sweet
    and sour tomatoes and onions
    33
  seven-hour leg of lamb with
    potatoes, carrots and onions
    326
  steak sandwich with bittersweet
    fried onions 160
  steamed duck with caramelized
    onions, olives and walnuts
    346
  sticky sausage and onions 136
  sweet potatoes and onions 30
  venison sausages with red wine
    onions and blackcurrants 196
  see also red onions; spring
    onions; white onions
open spinach and ricotta ravioli
    with pine nuts and Parmesan
    168
orange curd
  orange curd carrots 458
  orange flan, strawberries and
    orange curd cream 102
oranges 20
  asparagus with an orange
    mascarpone dressing 452
  fresh tuna with mango, apple,
    orange and curry vinaigrette
    184
  glazed mandarin tart 436
  hoggett cobbler with orange
    onions and sage scones 334
  orange flan, strawberries and
    orange curd cream 102
  quick seared duck a l'orange
    164
  roast monkfish with fennel,
    orange and tarragon mussels
    353
  seared halibut with a blood
    orange and courgette salad
    374

oranges – *cont.*
strawberry and orange smoothie 38
toasted sea bass and oranges with basil yoghurt 266
warm lentil, orange and watercress salad with grilled mackerel 378

oyster mushrooms
fennel with oysters and Parmesan shavings 238
oyster mushrooms and spinach pancakes 67

pak choy, seared black bream with ginger, tomato and chilli pak choy 264
pan-fried brill with capers, lemon and mash 386
pan-fried brill with red wine cockles 214
pan-fried sea bass with bacon and caper cabbage 265
pan-fried white fish with buttery grapes and chervil 416
pancakes 120
Cheddar cheese and onion Scotch pancakes 120
chocolate and nut pancakes with maple syrup 34
duck pancake rolls 258
oyster mushrooms and spinach pancakes 67
pea pancakes and grilled bacon 41
savoury pear, Stilton and chive cakes 253
sweetcorn pancakes 30

pancetta
Bolognese 134
fried bacon pieces with spinach and prawns 84
pancetta risotto 207
prawns, pancetta, pasta 202
roast rump of lamb with pancetta champ and marjoram cream 332

panna cotta, clotted cream panna cotta and strawberries 302
papaya, butterflied prawns with sweet and sour papaya 244
paprika, roast paprika chicken 342
Parma ham
Gorgonzola, Parma ham and rocket pasta 82
pasta carbonara 202

Parmesan cheese
asparagus and ham glazed with Cheddar and Parmesan 84
aubergine caviar pasta with rocket and Parmesan 401
crispy Parmesan chicken with basil tomatoes 132
fennel with oysters and Parmesan shavings 238
open spinach and ricotta ravioli with pine nuts and Parmesan 168
Parmesan risotto 206
pesto linguine with balsamic tomatoes 151
stir-fried chicken with tomatoes, basil and crispy Parmesan 185

parsley
foil-baked bass with garlic, parsley and lemon 384
lemon and parsley crusted

lambs' kidneys 165
roast flat fish with parsley lemon butter and new potatoes Lyonnaise 352

parsnips
parsnip and onion fritters 458
treacle duck breasts with creamy date parsnips 348

partridge, roast partridge with toasted salsify and maple sherry gravy 349

passion fruit
Charentais melon and avocado with passion fruit vinaigrette 413
charred squid with passion fruit, pineapple and sesame leaves 92
passion fruit brûlée 438
sautéed scallops with ginger spring greens and passion fruit hollandaise 254

pasta
aubergine caviar pasta with rocket and Parmesan 401
garlic prawns with lobster noodles 209
Gorgonzola, Parma ham and rocket pasta 82
ham, cheese and onion spaghetti 123
John Dory with red pepper, tomato and basil spaghetti 217
linguine and pesto frittata with asparagus, spinach, peas 204
macaroni and cauliflower with four cheeses 208
macaroni cheese 126
open spinach and ricotta ravioli with pine nuts and Parmesan 168
pasta carbonara 202
pasta with chicken, sage and onion butter 82
pasta niçoise 240
pasta with spinach and melting Brie 203
pasta with tomato, mozzarella and basil 123
pasta with a wild mushroom cream sauce 208
pesto linguine with balsamic tomatoes 151
prawns, pancetta, pasta 202
roast chicken breasts with almond cream noodles 218
sautéed snails, mushrooms and pasta with watercress sauce 262
tomato soup, spaghetti and meatballs 118

pastry
flat mushroom pastry with a watercress and cherry tomato salad 242
honeycomb caramel slice 114
leek, ham and Brie slice 238
pork and duck sausage rolls 446
see also flans; pies; quiche; tartlets; tarts; turnovers

patties, Wensleydale patties 130
peaches
baked amaretti peaches 291
Cognac peaches with pistachio brioche 365
vanilla pear and peach salad 362

peanuts, chicken skewers with peanut sauce 142
pears
broken feta cheese salad with apples and pears 73
charcuterie board with celeriac coleslaw 45
grilled gammon with pear mayonnaise and chicory 394
halloumi sticks with pear rings and mixed cress leaves 236
pear macaroon crumble 364
savoury pear, Stilton and chive cakes 253
vanilla pear and peach salad 362

peas
boiled bacon collar with spicy sausage mash and peas 320
coconut rice and peas with butternut squash 199
cod with peas and ham stewed in butter 216
lamb cutlets with creamy mint peas 130
linguine and pesto frittata with asparagus, spinach, peas 204
pea pancakes and grilled bacon 41
pork and peas risotto 140
roast rabbit legs with sweetcorn and peas 225
see also mangetout

pecan nuts
banana, pecan and honey cakes with espresso butter cream 108
Brussels sprouts with pecan nuts and maple butter 456
chocolate and nut pancakes with maple syrup 34

pepper
black pepper lamb steak with pomegranates 189
steak au poivre burger 396

peppers 20
baked ratatouille peppers with melting goat's cheese 404
burnt lamb chops with sweet peppers and onions 223
John Dory with red pepper, tomato and basil spaghetti 217
pepper risotto 207
quick marinated aubergine and sweet pepper salad 235

pesto
beef tomatoes and mozzarella with pine nuts and pesto crème fraîche 240
braised lamb shanks with onions, tomatoes and pesto beans 280
linguine and pesto frittata with asparagus, spinach, peas 204
pesto linguine with balsamic tomatoes 151
pesto risotto 207

pies
chicken, ham and mushroom pie 338
toffee pie with grilled bananas 299
West Country squab pie 330

pigs' cheeks, braised pigs' cheeks with marmalade turnips 284
pine nuts 13
apricot and pine nut rack of lamb with soft onions 329

beef tomatoes and mozzarella with pine nuts and pesto crème fraîche 240
open spinach and ricotta ravioli with pine nuts and Parmesan 168

pineapple
charred squid with passion fruit, pineapple and sesame leaves 92
warm gammon and pineapple with English leaves 50

pissaladière, seared tuna with pissaladière toasts 245
pistachios
Cognac peaches with pistachio brioche 365
roast turkey with pistachio and golden sultana stuffing 432
salmon skewers with pistachio lime yoghurt 182

pizza tomato tart 241
plaice, grilled plaice with chives and capers 156
plums
rice pudding with toasted honey plums 298
steamed plum pudding 364

poached eggs 18
bacon and egg risotto 44
crab salad with crispy poached egg 60
eggs, tomatoes and mushrooms 30
leeks and red onions with a warm poached egg 66
red wine and mushroom poached eggs on toast 62
smoked haddock, poached egg and sorrel hollandaise 58
smoked salmon and poached egg muffins 56

pollack, fish cake fingers 128
pomegranates, black pepper lamb steak with pomegranates 189
porcini
chicken with porcini and chestnut mushrooms 275
pasta with a wild mushroom cream sauce 208

pork
barbecued spare ribs 138
boiled pork pot 318
braised pigs' cheeks with marmalade turnips 284
lemon and chilli sesame pork with mangetout 188
pork belly boulangère 317
pork belly potatoes and red cabbage roast 319
pork chops with an apple tart topping 220
pork and duck sausage rolls 446
pork and peas risotto 140
pork steaks with lemon, honey and mustard apples 249
roast hand of pork with baked black pudding apples 434
roast pork 322
roast rack of pork with turnip and prune dauphinois 323
slow-roast pork belly with Gorgonzola and apple cabbage 314
sticky pork chops with sesame spinach 219
stroganoff 392
white pork and wild mushroom

stew 316
see also bacon; gammon; ham;
    sausages
porridge, raspberry mascarpone
    oat pud 146
Portobello mushrooms, grilled
    Portobello mushroom steaks,
    chips and tomatoes 152
potatoes
    bacon and onion potatoes 25
    bacon, potato and cheese
        frittata 124
    bacon sauté new potatoes 451
    baked potatoes with sour
        cream, chives and bacon 122
    beef and potatoes braised in
        Guinness 307
    boiled bacon collar with spicy
        sausage mash and peas 320
    braised beef chuck with carrots
        and baked potatoes 424
    cod with new potatoes, baby
        spinach and Cheddar cheese
        sauce 274
    crab salad with crispy poached
        egg 60
    crushed champ kippers with
        wilted watercress 61
    glazed horseradish tuna with
        spring onion potatoes 54
    gratin dauphinois 452
    grilled Portobello mushroom
        steaks, chips and tomatoes
        152
    home-made salad cream with
        broken new potatoes, eggs
        and red onions 64
    hot potato salad with melting
        raclette 78
    kale colcannon 454
    Lyonnaise 451
    mash 451
    pan-fried brill with capers,
        lemon and mash 386
    pork belly boulangère 317
    pork belly potatoes and red
        cabbage roast 319
    potato, leek and Gouda gratin
        405
    potato, pumpkin, white leek and
        goat's cheese gratin 425
    roast chicken thighs with bacon,
        carrots, onions and potatoes
        343
    roast flat fish with parsley
        lemon butter and new
        potatoes Lyonnaise 352
    roast rump of lamb with
        pancetta champ and
        marjoram cream 332
    roast veal with white onion and
        blue cheese potato gratin 308
    rump steak with home-made
        oven-baked garlic chips 395
    sauté 32, 451
    seven-hour leg of lamb with
        potatoes, carrots and onions
        326
    stuffed with Stilton, leek and
        mushrooms 402
    sweet sharp herrings with
        potato, cucumber and
        horseradish salad 380
    three-mustard honey potato
        salad 232
    watercress, leek and potato
        soup 200
potted mackerel 90
prawns 16
    butterflied prawns with sweet

and sour papaya 244
    fried bacon pieces with spinach
        and prawns 84
    garlic prawns with lobster
        noodles 209
    prawn and cucumber
        sandwiches with chive cream
        and a tomato dressing 98
    prawn rarebits 444
    prawns, pancetta, pasta 202
    quick curried prawns 176
    surf 'n' turf 158
    tiger prawns with leek and
        mozzarella risotto 263
    tiger prawns and tomatoes with
        basil and garlic mayonnaise
        175
prunes
    Easter turkey steaks with apple
        and prune stuffing 420
    prune and Armagnac bread and
        butter pudding 360
    prune, leek and sage stuffing
        322
    roast rack of pork with turnip
        and prune dauphinois 323
puddings
    apple jelly and cinnamon cream
        300
    apple tart 357
    Bailey's crème brûlée 292
    baked amaretti peaches 291
    baked apples with nutmeg
        custard pudding 361
    chocolate brownie gypsy
        pudding 146
    chocolate brownie mousse 295
    Christmas pudding 440
    clotted cream panna cotta and
        strawberries 302
    Cognac peaches with pistachio
        brioche 365
    cracked summer berry
        meringue 290
    crème caramel 366
    glazed mandarin tart 436
    hot chocolate fondants 426
    iced Jersey cream with lots of
        strawberries 370
    liqueur-steeped summer fruits
        with lemon curd cream 296
    mango cheesecake fool 292
    mince pie turnovers 438
    passion fruit brûlée 438
    pear macaroon crumble 364
    prune and Armagnac bread and
        butter pudding 360
    raspberry mascarpone oat
        pud 146
    raspberry and white chocolate
        cream shortbreads 294
    rhubarb and custard
        cheesecake 358
    rice pudding with toasted honey
        plums 298
    risotto rice pudding with
        Cognac sultanas 442
    spotted dick pudding with
        caramel golden syrup 368
    steamed plum pudding 364
    steamed Simnel pudding 428
    strawberry Eton mess with
        raspberry sauce 147
    tiramisu bocker glory 290
    toasted ginger figs 414
    toffee apple crumble 428
    toffee pie with grilled bananas
        299
    vanilla pear and peach salad
        362

white chocolate cream with
        mango sauce 147
    pumpkin, potato, pumpkin, white
        leek and goat's cheese gratin
        425
    purple sprouting broccoli 456

quiche
    duck, bacon and onion quiche
        422
    leek and Gruyère quiche 407
quick curried prawns 176
quick-fry monkfish and curry
    dip with banana, cucumber
    and apple 181
quick hollandaise sauce 464
quick marinated aubergine and
    sweet pepper salad 235
quick seared duck à l'orange 164

rabbit, roast rabbit legs with
    sweetcorn and peas 225
raclette, hot potato salad with
    melting raclette 78
raisins, nutmeg raisin spinach 452
raita, lamb goujons with curry
    mayonnaise and mint raita
    333
rarebits, prawn rarebits 444
raspberries
    raspberry clafoutis 104
    raspberry mascarpone oat
        pud 146
    raspberry sauce 294
    raspberry and white chocolate
        cream shortbreads 294
    strawberry Eton mess with
        raspberry sauce 147
    warm chorizo and goat's cheese
        salad with raspberry
        vinaigrette 46
ratatouille
    baked ratatouille peppers with
        melting goat's cheese 404
    calamari with hot ratatouille 210
    ratatouille omelette 126
ravioli, open spinach and
    ricotta ravioli with pine nuts
    and Parmesan 168
red and white chicory salad with a
    rhubarb vinaigrette 75
red cabbage
    braised red cabbage 460
    pork belly potatoes and red
        cabbage roast 319
Red Leicester mushrooms 66
red mullet with fennel and olives
    154
red onions
    aubergine, red onion and
        mozzarella bake 170
    courgette soup with tomato and
        red onion bruschetta 71
    Cumberland sausage and red
        onion tart 42
    home-made salad cream with
        broken new potatoes, eggs
        and red onions 64
    leeks and red onions with a
        warm poached egg 66
red peppers
    baked ratatouille peppers with
        melting goat's cheese 404
    burnt lamb chops with sweet
        peppers and onions 223
    John Dory with red pepper,
        tomato and basil spaghetti
        217
    quick marinated aubergine and

sweet pepper salad 235
red wine
    beef 'coq au vin' stew 306
    fillet of beef with red wine
        tomatoes 287
    pan-fried brill with red wine
        cockles 214
    red wine beef with bacon
        crunch 313
    red wine and mushroom
        poached eggs on toast 62
    red wine mustard dressing 466
    roast monkfish in red wine with
        crème fraîche cabbage 272
    roasted duck with red wine
        blackberries 344
    sirloin steak with hot red wine
        and mustard vinaigrette 397
    tuna steak with red wine
        mushrooms 156
    venison sausages with red wine
        onions and blackcurrants 196
redcurrants, beetroot carpaccio
    with redcurrant walnut
    dressing 233
rhubarb
    red and white chicory salad with
        a rhubarb vinaigrette 75
    rhubarb and custard
        cheesecake 358
ribs, barbecued spare ribs 138
rice
    coconut rice and peas with
        butternut squash 199
    rice pudding with toasted honey
        plums 298
    risotto rice pudding with
        Cognac sultanas 442
ricotta, open spinach and
    ricotta ravioli with pine nuts
    and Parmesan 168
risotto 206–7
    bacon and egg risotto 44
    Milanese 283
    pork and peas risotto 140
    risotto rice pudding with
        Cognac sultanas 442
    tiger prawns with leek and
        mozzarella risotto 263
roast beef
    gravy 310
    roast rib of beef 310
    Yorkshire puddings 312
roast chicken
    bacon and chipolatas 340
    with goat's cheese and fresh
        herb butter 93
    honey, lemon and thyme roast
        chicken 390
    roast chicken breasts with
        almond cream noodles 218
    roast chicken with gravy 340
    roast chicken thighs with bacon,
        carrots, onions and potatoes
        343
    roast paprika chicken 342
    sage, onion and lemon stuffing
        341
roast duck
    roast duck with spinach and
        wild mushrooms 279
    roasted duck with red wine
        blackberries 344
roast flat fish with parsley
    lemon butter and new
    potatoes Lyonnaise 352
roast gravy 466
roast halibut with buttery mussels
    and herbs 356

roast lamb
  mint sauce 328
  roast leg of lamb 328
  roast rump of lamb with
    pancetta champ and
    marjoram cream 332
roast monkfish
  with fennel, orange and tarragon
    mussels 353
  in red wine with crème fraîche
    cabbage 272
  roast monkfish 'Barnsley chops'
    with apple mint jelly and cider
    gravy 270
roast partridge with toasted salsify
  and maple sherry gravy 349
roast pork 322
  cider gravy 322
  prune, leek and sage stuffing
    322
  roast hand of pork with baked
    black pudding apples 434
  roast rack of pork with turnip
    and prune dauphinois 323
roast rabbit legs with sweetcorn
  and peas 225
roast turkey with pistachio and
  golden sultana stuffing 432
roast veal with white onion and
  blue cheese potato gratin 308
roast veg, mixed 453
rocket
  aubergine caviar pasta with
    rocket and Parmesan 401
  black pudding and bacon with
    honey apples and yoghurt
    rocket 47
  Gorgonzola, Parma ham and
    rocket pasta 82
Roquefort cheese, T-bone steak
  with melting Roquefort cherry
  tomatoes 162
rosemary, braised shoulder of
  lamb with rosemary, carrots
  and onions 421
rump steak with home-made
  oven-baked garlic chips 395
runner beans
  with chunky seasoning 453
  three bean salad 74

sage
  hoggett cobbler with orange
    onions and sage scones 334
  lamb cutlets with crispy sage
    and capers 222
  prune, leek and sage stuffing
    322
  sage, onion and lemon stuffing
    341
  sage and onion porkies 117
salad cream, home-made salad
  cream with broken new
  potatoes, eggs and red
  onions 64
salad leaves
  bittersweet beef fillet leaves 192
  warm gammon and pineapple
    with English leaves 50
salads
  apple mascarpone salad with
    warm sausage chunks 144
  avocado and courgette salad
    with lime 79
  bacon and egg salad 63
  black pudding with blue cheese
    celery, and apple salad 48
  broken feta cheese salad with
    apples and pears 73

charcuterie board with celeriac
  coleslaw 45
chicken livers with a sweet
  spinach and bacon salad 260
crab salad with crispy poached
  egg 60
fennel, asparagus, grapefruit
  and apple 76
flat mushroom pastry with a
  watercress and cherry tomato
  salad 242
fresh tuna with mango, apple,
  orange and curry vinaigrette
  184
halloumi sticks with pear rings
  and mixed cress leaves 236
home-made salad cream with
  broken new potatoes, eggs
  and red onions 64
hot potato salad with melting
  raclette 78
lobster Caesar salad 257
quick-fry monkfish and curry
  dip with banana, cucumber
  and apple 181
quick marinated aubergine and
  sweet pepper salad 235
red and white chicory salad with
  a rhubarb vinaigrette 75
salmon with a salted tomato and
  herb salad 85
scallop salad 174
seared halibut with a blood
  orange and courgette salad
  374
sesame wild mushroom salad
  234
spiced lamb with mango, apple
  and cucumber salad 190
sweet sharp herrings with
  potato, cucumber and
  horseradish salad 380
three bean salad 74
three-mustard honey potato
  salad 232
warm chorizo and goat's cheese
  salad with raspberry
  vinaigrette 46
warm gammon and pineapple
  with English leaves 50
warm lentil, orange and
  watercress salad with grilled
  mackerel 378
salmon
  broken salmon with artichokes
    and asparagus 246
  salmon cutlets with minted leeks
    and peas and a sweet lemon
    dressing 86
  salmon with French beans 209
  salmon with a salted tomato and
    herb salad 85
  salmon skewers with pistachio
    lime yoghurt 182
  smoked salmon and poached
    egg muffins 56
  smoked salmon, trout and
    mackerel open sandwiches
    97
  steamed salmon with grilled
    vegetables 212
  warm salmon on brown bread
    57
salsas
  grilled sardines with sweet
    potato and mango salsa 248
  grilled tuna with a niçoise
    salsa 87
salsify, roast partridge with
  toasted salsify and maple

sherry gravy 349
sandwiches
  bacon butty 28
  prawn and cucumber
    sandwiches with chive cream
    and a tomato dressing 98
  sausage sandwich with sweet
    and sour tomatoes and onions
    33
  smoked salmon, trout and
    mackerel open sandwiches
    97
  steak sandwich with bittersweet
    fried onions 160
  warm salmon on brown bread
    57
sardines 14
  grilled sardines with sweet
    potato and mango salsa 248
satay, chicken skewers with
  peanut sauce 142
sauces
  aïoli sauce 464
  asparagus with an orange
    mascarpone dressing 452
  beetroot carpaccio with
    redcurrant walnut dressing
    233
  bread sauce 341
  Caesar dressing 464
  cod with new potatoes, baby
    spinach and Cheddar cheese
    sauce 274
  crispy Camembert with
    cranberry sauce 430
  cured ham with a carpaccio
    sauce 51
  curry mayonnaise 465
  fresh vanilla custard 467
  ham-wrapped trout with English
    mustard sauce 350
  herb butter sauce 269
  mint raita 465
  mint sauce 328
  prawn and cucumber
    sandwiches with chive cream
    and a tomato dressing 98
  quick hollandaise sauce 464
  raspberry sauce 294
  red wine mustard dressing 466
  red wine tomato sauce 287
  roast gravy 466
  sautéed scallops with ginger
    spring greens and passion
    fruit hollandaise 254
  sautéed snails, mushrooms
    and pasta with watercress
    sauce 262
  smoked haddock, poached egg
    and sorrel hollandaise 58
  sweet lemon dressing 465
  warm chocolate sauce 467
  white chocolate cream 467
  white chocolate cream with
    mango sauce 147
  wild mushroom and garlic
    cream 312
  see also vinaigrette
sausages
  apple mascarpone salad with
    warm sausage chunks 144
  bacon and chipolatas 340
  boiled bacon collar with spicy
    sausage mash and peas 320
  British sausage soup 167
  chicken and chorizo sausage
    stew 186
  Cumberland sausage and red
    onion tart 42
  full English breakfast 32

pork and duck sausage rolls
  446
sage and onion porkies 117
sausage sandwich with sweet
  and sour tomatoes and onions
  33
sautéed kidneys and chipolatas
  with mushrooms and garlic
  toasts 52
sticky sausage and onions 136
tomato soup, spaghetti and
  meatballs 118
venison sausages with red wine
  onions and blackcurrants 196
warm chorizo and goat's cheese
  salad with raspberry
  vinaigrette 46
sauté potatoes 32, 451
  bacon sauté new potatoes 451
sautéed kidneys and chipolatas
  with mushrooms and garlic
  toasts 52
sautéed scallops with ginger
  spring greens and passion
  fruit hollandaise 254
sautéed snails, mushrooms and
  pasta with watercress sauce
  262
savoury pear, Stilton and chive
  cakes 253
scallops
  sautéed scallops with ginger
    spring greens and passion
    fruit hollandaise 254
  scallop salad 174
  seared scallops and chilli-
    spiced cucumber 256
scones
  buttermilk mini scones 106
  hoggett cobbler with orange
    onions and sage scones 334
Scotch pancakes
  Cheddar cheese and onion
    Scotch pancakes 120
  savoury pear, Stilton and chive
    cakes 253
scrambled eggs 18
  scrambled egg mushroom
    muffins 34
sea bass
  foil-baked bass with garlic,
    parsley and lemon 384
  pan-fried sea bass with bacon
    and caper cabbage 265
  toasted sea bass and oranges
    with basil yoghurt 266
sea trout, steamed sea trout with
  crispy seaweed and
  cucumber 382
seafood 16–17
  baked lemon halibut with leek
    and shrimp cream 417
  butterflied prawns with sweet
    and sour papaya 244
  calamari with hot ratatouille 210
  charred squid with passion
    fruit, pineapple and sesame
    leaves 92
  crab salad with crispy poached
    egg 60
  crab and spinach omelette with
    lobster cream 180
  curried mussels and noodle
    broth 388
  fried bacon pieces with spinach
    and prawns 84
  garlic prawns with lobster
    noodles 209
  lobster Caesar salad 257

moules marinières 174
mussels with leeks and
Gorgonzola 387
pan-fried brill with red wine
cockles 214
prawn and cucumber
sandwiches with chive cream
and a tomato dressing 98
prawn rarebits 444
prawns, pancetta, pasta 202
quick curried prawns 176
roast halibut with buttery
mussels and herbs 356
roast monkfish with fennel,
orange and tarragon mussels
353
sautéed scallops with ginger
spring greens and passion
fruit hollandaise 254
scallop salad 174
seared scallops and chilli-
spiced cucumber 256
surf n' turf 158
tiger prawns with leek and
mozzarella risotto 263
tiger prawns and tomatoes with
basil and garlic mayonnaise
175
seared beef with Provençal
tomatoes and mustard
watercress 194
seared black bream with ginger,
tomato and chilli pak choy
264
seared calves' liver with
caramelized grapes 286
seared halibut with a blood orange
and courgette salad 374
seared scallops and chilli-spiced
cucumber 256
seared tuna with pissaladière
toasts 245
sesame seeds 13
charred squid with passion
fruit, pineapple and sesame
leaves 92
John Dory with sautéed honey
sesame courgettes 178
lemon and chilli sesame pork
with mangetout 188
sesame wild mushroom salad
234
sticky pork chops with sesame
spinach 219
sweet sesame mackerel with
banana chutney 88
seven-hour leg of lamb with
potatoes, carrots and onions
326
sherry, roast partridge with
toasted salsify and maple
sherry gravy 349
shortbreads
chocolate and caramel
shortbread 104
raspberry and white chocolate
cream shortbreads 294
shrimps, baked lemon halibut with
leek and shrimp cream 417
Simnel pudding, steamed 428
sirloin steak with hot red wine and
mustard vinaigrette 397
slow-roast pork belly with
Gorgonzola and apple
cabbage 314
smoked haddock
smoked haddock, poached egg
and sorrel hollandaise 58
smoked haddock and spinach
tart with Emmental 383

smoked haddock-topped
eggs with melting Lancashire
cheese 26
smoked salmon
smoked salmon and poached
egg muffins 56
smoked salmon, trout and
mackerel open sandwiches
97
smoothies
strawberry and orange smoothie
38
thick banana and coconut
smoothie 38
snails, sautéed snails, mushrooms
and pasta with watercress
sauce 262
sole
crunchy fish strips with an
avocado dip 127
Dover sole with hot lemon
butter 153
Dover sole with a steak garnish
268
sorrel, smoked haddock, poached
egg and sorrel hollandaise 58
soup
asparagus vichyssoise 400
bacon soup 398
bowl of broccoli with a
Gorgonzola swirl 162
a bowl of cauliflower and
Camembert 230
British sausage soup 167
butternut squash soup 72
cherry tomato soup 72
courgette soup with tomato and
red onion bruschetta 71
Irish stew soup 229
tomato soup, spaghetti and
meatballs 118
watercress, leek and potato
soup 200
sour cream, baked potatoes with
sour cream, chives and bacon
122
spaghetti
ham, cheese and onion
spaghetti 123
John Dory with red pepper,
tomato and basil spaghetti
217
tomato soup, spaghetti and
meatballs 118
spare ribs, barbecued spare
ribs 138
spiced lamb with mango, apple
and cucumber salad 190
spinach
charred squid with passion
fruit, pineapple and sesame
leaves 92
chicken livers with a sweet
spinach and bacon salad 260
cod with new potatoes, baby
spinach and Cheddar cheese
sauce 274
crab and spinach omelette with
lobster cream 180
fried bacon pieces with spinach
and prawns 84
linguine and pesto frittata with
asparagus, spinach, peas 204
monkfish with golden sultanas,
onion and spinach 269
nutmeg raisin spinach 452
open spinach and ricotta ravioli
with pine nuts and
Parmesan 168
oyster mushrooms and spinach

pancakes 67
pasta with spinach and melting
Brie 203
roast duck with spinach and
wild mushrooms 279
smoked haddock and spinach
tart with Emmental 383
sticky pork chops with sesame
spinach 219
Swiss cheese halibut with
spinach and mushrooms 376
spotted dick pudding with caramel
golden syrup 368
spring greens
sautéed scallops with ginger
spring greens and passion
fruit hollandaise 254
steamed sea trout with crispy
seaweed and cucumber 382
spring onions
crushed champ kippers with
wilted watercress 61
glazed horseradish tuna with
spring onion potatoes 54
roast rump of lamb with
pancetta champ and
marjoram cream 332
spring and summer vegetables
with fresh herbs 408
sprouts, Brussels sprouts with
pecan nuts and maple butter
456
squash see butternut squash
squid
calamari with hot ratatouille 210
charred squid with passion
fruit, pineapple and sesame
leaves 92
steak
bittersweet beef fillet leaves 192
rump steak with home-made
oven-baked garlic chips 395
sirloin steak with hot red wine
and mustard vinaigrette 397
steak au poivre burger 396
steak Diane 90
steak sandwich with bittersweet
fried onions 160
surf 'n' turf 158
T-bone steak with melting
Roquefort cherry tomatoes
162
steamed duck with caramelized
onions, olives and walnuts
346
steamed plum pudding 364
steamed salmon with grilled
vegetables 212
steamed sea trout with crispy
seaweed and cucumber 382
steamed Simnel pudding 428
stew
beef 'coq au vin' stew 306
chicken and chorizo sausage
stew 186
Irish stew soup 229
white pork and wild mushroom
stew 316
sticky lemon chicken 132
sticky pork chops with sesame
spinach 219
sticky sausage and onions 136
Stilton cheese
potatoes stuffed with Stilton,
leek and mushrooms 402
savoury pear, Stilton and chive
cakes 253
whipped Stilton with figs and
watercress 443
stir-fried chicken with tomatoes,

basil and crispy Parmesan
185
stocks 13
stout-glazed leg of lamb 324
strawberries
clotted cream panna cotta and
strawberries 302
iced Jersey cream with lots of
strawberries 370
orange flan, strawberries and
orange curd cream 102
strawberry Eton mess with
raspberry sauce 147
strawberry and orange smoothie
38
stroganoff, pork stroganoff 392
stuffing
Easter turkey steaks with apple
and prune stuffing 420
prune, leek and sage stuffing
322
roast turkey with pistachio and
golden sultana stuffing 432
sage, onion and lemon stuffing
341
sultanas
monkfish with golden sultanas,
onion and spinach 269
risotto rice pudding with
Cognac sultanas 442
roast turkey with pistachio and
golden sultana stuffing 432
summer berries, cracked summer
berry meringue 290
summer fruits, liqueur-steeped
summer fruits with lemon curd
cream 296
surf 'n' turf 158
sweet lemon dressing 465
sweet peppers see peppers
sweet potatoes
grilled sardines with sweet
potato and mango salsa 248
sweet potato bake 460
sweet potatoes and onions 30
sweet sesame mackerel with
banana chutney 88
sweet sharp herrings with potato,
cucumber and horseradish
salad 380
sweetcorn
roast rabbit legs with sweetcorn
and peas 225
sweetcorn pancakes 30

T-bone steak with melting
Roquefort cherry tomatoes
162
tagliatelle, roast chicken breasts
with almond cream noodles
218
tarragon
cod poached in a tarragon
broth 354
lamb with beans, onions,
tomatoes and tarragon 336
roast monkfish with fennel,
orange and tarragon mussels
353
tartlets
lemon meringue tartlets 112
mushroom and goat's cheese
tartlets 252
tarts
apple tart 357
blackberry and almond tart 100
Cumberland sausage and red
onion tart 42
glazed mandarin tart 436
pizza tomato tart 241

tarts – *cont.*
smoked haddock and spinach tart with Emmental 383
thick banana and coconut smoothie 38
three bean salad 74
three-mustard honey potato salad 232
thyme, honey, lemon and thyme roast chicken 390
tiger prawns
butterflied prawns with sweet and sour papaya 244
garlic prawns with lobster noodles 209
with leek and mozzarella risotto 263
quick curried prawns 176
surf 'n' turf 158
tiger prawns and tomatoes with basil and garlic mayonnaise 175
tiramisu bocker glory 290
toasted ginger figs 414
toasted sea bass and oranges with basil yoghurt 266
toffee apple crumble 428
toffee pie with grilled bananas 299
tomatoes 20
beef tomatoes and mozzarella with pine nuts and pesto crème fraîche 240
braised lamb shanks with onions, tomatoes and pesto beans 280
cherry tomato soup 72
courgette soup with tomato and red onion bruschetta 71
crispy Parmesan chicken with basil tomatoes 132
Dover sole with a steak garnish 268
eggs, tomatoes and mushrooms 30
fillet of beef with red wine tomatoes 287
flat mushroom pastry with a watercress and cherry tomato salad 242
fried egg, tomatoes and mushrooms 32
grilled Portobello mushroom steaks, chips and tomatoes 152
John Dory with red pepper, tomato and basil spaghetti 217
lamb with beans, onions, tomatoes and tarragon 336
lemon and parsley crusted lambs' kidneys 165
mozzarella monkfish steaks with tomato and basil 377
pasta with tomato, mozzarella and basil 123
pesto linguine with balsamic tomatoes 151
pizza tomato tart 241
prawn and cucumber sandwiches with chive cream and a tomato dressing 98
salmon with a salted tomato and herb salad 85
sausage sandwich with sweet and sour tomatoes and onions 33
seared beef with Provençal tomatoes and mustard watercress 194

seared black bream with ginger, tomato and chilli pak choy 264
stir-fried chicken with tomatoes, basil and crispy Parmesan 185
T-bone steak with melting Roquefort cherry tomatoes 162
tiger prawns and tomatoes with basil and garlic mayonnaise 175
tomato risotto 207
tomato soup, spaghetti and meatballs 118
treacle duck breasts with creamy date parsnips 348
trout
ham-wrapped trout with an English mustard sauce 350
smoked salmon, trout and mackerel open sandwiches 97
steamed sea trout with crispy seaweed and cucumber 382
tuna
fresh tuna with mango, apple, orange and curry vinaigrette 184
glazed horseradish tuna with spring onion potatoes 54
grilled tuna with a niçoise salsa 87
pasta niçoise 240
seared tuna with pissaladière toasts 245
tuna steak with red wine mushrooms 156
turbot, lemon brioche turbot with a hint of horseradish 213
turkey
Easter turkey steaks with apple and prune stuffing 420
roast turkey with pistachio and golden sultana stuffing 432
turnips
braised pigs' cheeks with marmalade turnips 284
roast rack of pork with turnip and prune dauphinois 323
turnovers, mince pie turnovers 438

Vacherin cheese, baked 414
vanilla
fresh vanilla custard 467
vanilla pear and peach salad 362
veal
roast veal with white onion and blue cheese potato gratin 308
seared calves' liver with caramelized grapes 286
veal cutlets with white wine chestnut mushrooms 418
vegetables 20
baked chicken legs with Mediterranean vegetables 278
mixed roast 453
spring and summer vegetables with fresh herbs 408
steamed salmon with grilled vegetables 212
see also individual vegetables
vegetarian full English breakfast 30
venison sausages with red wine onions and blackcurrants 196

vichyssoise, asparagus vichyssoise 400
Victoria sponge cake, black cherry Victoria sponge cake 110
vinaigrette
Charentais melon and avocado with passion fruit vinaigrette 413
charred squid with passion fruit, pineapple and sesame leaves 92
cream vinaigrette 466
fresh tuna with mango, apple, orange and curry vinaigrette 184
red and white chicory salad with a rhubarb vinaigrette 75
sirloin steak with hot red wine and mustard vinaigrette 397
warm chorizo and goat's cheese salad with raspberry vinaigrette 46
see also sauces

walnuts
beetroot carpaccio with redcurrant walnut dressing 233
charcuterie board with celeriac coleslaw 45
steamed duck with caramelized onions, olives and walnuts 346
warm chocolate sauce 467
warm chorizo and goat's cheese salad with raspberry vinaigrette 46
warm crème fraîche Brussels tops 456
warm gammon and pineapple with English leaves 50
warm lentil, orange and watercress salad with grilled mackerel 378
warm salmon on brown bread 57
watercress
crushed champ kippers with wilted watercress 61
Dover sole with a steak garnish 268
flat mushroom pastry with a watercress and cherry tomato salad 242
sautéed snails, mushrooms and pasta with watercress sauce 262
seared beef with Provençal tomatoes and mustard watercress 194
warm lentil, orange and watercress salad with grilled mackerel 378
watercress, leek and potato soup 200
whipped Stilton with figs and watercress 443
Wensleydale patties 130
West Country squab pie 330
whipped Stilton with figs and watercress 443
white chocolate
raspberry and white chocolate cream shortbreads 294
white chocolate cheesecake 109
white chocolate cream 467
white chocolate cream with mango sauce 147
white onions, roast veal with white onion and blue cheese potato

gratin 308
white pork and wild mushroom stew 316
white wine, veal cutlets with white wine chestnut mushrooms 418
wild mushroom and garlic cream 312
wine *see* red wine; white wine

yoghurt
black pudding and bacon with honey apples and yoghurt rocket 47
grilled gingerbread slice with crushed banana and yoghurt 36
mint raita 465
salmon skewers with pistachio lime yoghurt 182
toasted sea bass and oranges with basil yoghurt 266
Yorkshire puddings 312

zabaglione 291

acknowledgements

Recipes are created from a gathering of ingredients, blending them all together, making sure the finished dish shows off their very best strengths. Writing this book has followed much the same process. The 'ingredients' come from the team listed below, without whom these colourful pages would not exist.

So, a very special thank you to Lindsey Evans, Wayne Tapsfield, Adam Gray, Tom Weldon, John Hamilton, Richard Bravery, Lottie Davies, Kay Halsey, Sarah Hulbert, Lisa Harrison, Abby Fawcett, Anna Burges-Lumsden, Robbie Kadhim, Lucinda Kaizik, Karen Taylor, Robert Allison and all at Penguin and Rhodes Restaurants.

Plus, with love, to my wife, Jennie, and sons Samuel and George, for tasting and critiquing where necessary.

**Sega
Dreamcast:
Collected
Works**

Simon Parkin

Read-Only
Memory

Contents

One
Confidential Mission 4

Two
What Dreams Are Made Of 10

Three
Five Thousand Names in a Hat 18

Four
Arrival 26

Five
Borders Down 32

Six
To Make Friends and Influence People 40

Seven
A Phantasy Online 54

Eight
Loss of a Dream Maker 62

Nine
Insert Credit to Continue 70

Ten
Dream On 86

Eleven
Hardware Development   94

Twelve
Hardware Showcase   106

Thirteen
Game Production Artwork   126

Fourteen
Making Shenmue   212

Fifteen
Making Space Channel 5   222

Sixteen
Making Crazy Taxi   228

Seventeen
Making Jet Set Radio   234

Eighteen
Making Segagaga   240

Nineteen
Making Rez   250

Twenty
In-Game Artwork   258

Confidential Mission

On a spring morning in 1998, a number of Japanese national newspapers printed a gruesome photograph: a battlefield, littered with the bodies of slain samurai. Alongside the image, the provocative text: 'Has Sega been defeated for good?'

Never before had a videogame company staged such a melodramatic and public mea culpa. And yet, it was a reasonable question.

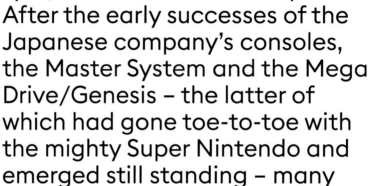

After the early successes of the Japanese company's consoles, the Master System and the Mega Drive/Genesis – the latter of which had gone toe-to-toe with the mighty Super Nintendo and emerged still standing – many believed that Sega had lost its way. A cluster of add-ons and incremental upgrades to its videogame consoles had bewildered and impoverished all but the most attentive and deep-pocketed consumer.

Then, the Saturn, the company's first major system since the Mega Drive/Genesis, was hamstrung by last-minute technical revisions, implemented in response to the announcement of Sony's PlayStation, a muscular newcomer to the console business that was built with a keen focus on the future: 3D graphics. The Saturn, by contrast

4

a gloriously powerful 2D machine, had entered the 32-bit era equipped for the wrong battle. For all its niche charms (and make no mistake, the Saturn is home to a number of bright and timeless jewels), consumers, retailers and, soon enough, third-party game developers dismissed the machine as an anachronism, and Sega with it.

In the late 1990s, Sega was over-staffed and under-equipped, a company that had lost both its focus and its identity. It had also lost a significant part of its fortune. For the financial year leading to March 1998, Sega's consumer division reported losses of $242 million. Had Sega been defeated for good? It was a reasonable question. Another, just as fair, but more painful than the first, also hung in the air: who even cares?

The following day, a second advertisement ran in the same Japanese newspapers, in the same position on the page. This time, the image showed one of the beleaguered samurai rising to his feet, ready, perhaps, to fight again. The question had been asked and the answer had sounded back clearly from those men and women who had pledged their talents and hopes to Sega: we care. We care.

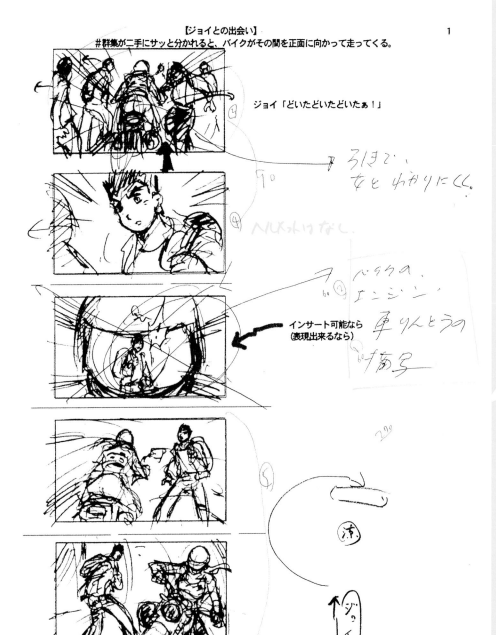

【ジョイとの出会い】 1
#群集が二手にサッと分かれると、バイクがその間を正面に向かって走ってくる。

ジョイ「どいたどいたどいたぁ！」

インサート可能なら
(表現出来るなら)

Shenmue, storyboard, 1999

Tetsuya Mizuguchi, head of United Game Artists

I think it was early 1996 that I first heard about the project that would become the Dreamcast. At that time, I was working on the arcade side of the business. In the middle of the production of *Sega Rally 2*, Hayao Nakayama, Sega's co-founder and, at that time, chairman, called me up. He told me that the company was planning to build new hardware. It was to be a very important project for Sega. He told me that Sega needed a much wider portfolio of games. The Sega Saturn had been too niche. Finally, he asked if I would join the project.

Bernie Stolar, president and COO, Sega of America

In the winter of 1996, my boss at PlayStation, Steve Race, got fired. Micki Shohoff, who ran Sony North America, was also let go. It was obvious what was happening: despite PlayStation's success in the US, Sony no longer wanted the original team there; they wanted the Japanese office to have full control. Kaz Hirai from Sony Music was brought in to take things over. I had a strong intuition that I would be on their replacement list sooner or later. Around that time, Nakayama asked me to become president of Sega of America. The company needed a new hardware system because the systems that they had – all eight of them, no less – were not selling. The Saturn was not being supported by Sega the way it should have been. The console was just too far gone, too expensive and too difficult to develop games for to salvage. The company was nearly bankrupt. It needed a new console and it needed it quick.

Tetsuya Mizuguchi, head of United Game Artists

I asked Nakayama-san for a month to think about his offer. I already had 20 people working on my team. It was a great team: we had made *Sega Rally*, *Sega Touring Car Championship* and, most recently, the sequel to *Sega Rally*. I needed to talk with my team first. Also, I needed to think about my future. There was no *Rez*, no *Space Channel 5* at this point. I was just a person who made racing games for amusement arcades. So I took the month to talk with friends and colleagues. They argued it was a great opportunity that I should definitely take. We can make arcade games by ourselves, they said. Well, after that, even though it was not clear what I would be doing, I agreed to join the Dreamcast team.

Bernie Stolar, president and COO, Sega of America

The year before Dreamcast launched, Sega had lost close to $1 billion. Sega management had greatly overextended themselves. I took Sega from about 300 people down to around 90 people. It was the hardest decision. We had to do what we had to do though, otherwise we would have gone bankrupt. Sega had become a bloated mess with no real sense of direction. It was either a bunch of people lost their jobs or everyone did. That's a tough no-win situation. Of course, all the armchair executives started to chime in...

Tetsu Katano, programmer, *Sonic Adventure*

I was asked to give feedback on what kind of specs we wanted to see in the new system so I got back to them with some suggestions. It was a time that was filled with hope and positivity. Personally, when I saw how things were shaping up, I thought to myself, 'We can win with this!'

There was no time to relax though, because, at the end of the day, success in the videogame industry always depends on the quality of the software.

Masayoshi Kikuchi, director, *Jet Set Radio*

Contrary to what you might think, in Japan, at least, there was quite a vibrant atmosphere in the office before development on the Dreamcast started. The Sega Saturn was selling well in Japan, and lots of its games had sold hundreds of thousands of copies, which was the first time for the consumer product department in Sega. Even so, when the Dreamcast was announced, I was excited and had high expectations. I knew that the level of detail we could put into our games would be dramatically higher and then we heard that it would also be able to connect to the internet. I couldn't wait to get to work on it.

Hideki Sato, head of console R&D, Sega

The challenge of the Dreamcast was to take our already-wide user base and see if we could enlarge it further. In that sense, the Dreamcast represents a recapitulation for us of 20 years of determination, and a commitment to challenge ourselves and move forward in the home videogame console market.

Keiji Okayasu, game director, *Shenmue*

Of course, there were high expectations as it was Sega's own hardware, but we had some worries that the development environment might dramatically change as there were lots of new features, such as the modem system, the Microsoft operating system and memory cards that used LCD screens.

Kenji Kanno, director, *Crazy Taxi*

Since I was in the arcade division, I didn't feel any pressure from the home console side of things; it really had nothing to do with me and the arcade business was growing at that time. I was conscious that we were the ones who had to set the company alight.

Naoto Ohshima, designer, *Sonic Adventure*

Following Sega's company motto, 'Creativity is life', people were constantly taking a chance on something new and nobody had ever got yelled at for failing. Therefore, in the game teams at least, there was no pressure.

8

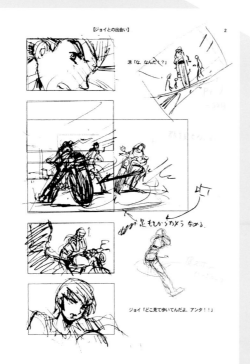

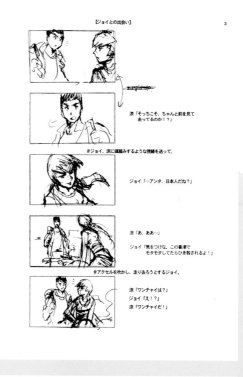

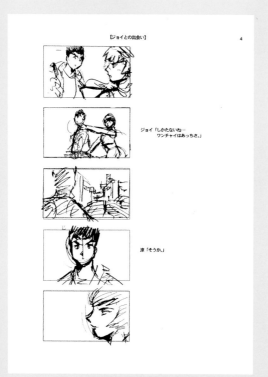

Shenmue, storyboard, 1999

What Dreams Are Made Of

Even within Sega's Haneda HQ, many blamed the Saturn's commercial failure on the machine's arcane technological specifications. Three years earlier, in late 1993, Sony had shown off early PlayStation development kits to key game developers around the world. When word of the machine's tech specs circulated, Sega's executives panicked. The company's president – the equivalent of chief executive in Japanese companies – at the time, Hayao Nakayama, instructed Sega's R&D division to beef up its forthcoming Saturn, the design of which was all but settled, adding a new CPU and graphics processor. The result was a Frankenstein of a machine, with difficult-to-programme dual processors and attendant reams of documentation that intimidated all but the most experienced coders. (Yu Suzuki once said that only a handful of Sega programmers was ever able to get the most out of the machine.)

For its PlayStation, Sega's new rival Sony was pitching savvy advertising campaigns, especially in Japan and the UK, at an older, design-conscious audience, snubbing the teenage-boy-in-blackened-bedroom market.

146

10

It worked. Overnight, the PlayStation became the cooler choice, a videogame system that could be carried past adolescence into adulthood. For the programmers and engineers, Sony's console was also a far more appetising choice, having arrived, in stark contrast to the Saturn, with user-friendly development kits and wide-ranging support.

Sega's past mistakes would not be repeated. This was the pledge made by two of the new top executives in the company – Bernie Stolar, poached from the original PlayStation launch team to head up Sega of America, and, in 1997, Shoichiro Irimajiri, Sega of Japan's new president. Described as a 'flashy, well-liked senior executive' by the *New York Times*, he joined the company from the car manufacturer Honda.

Work began on two distinct designs from two distinct teams, one based in America (their system was codenamed 'Black Belt'), the other in Japan (theirs was known as 'Dural'). Tatsuo Yamamoto led the American team, which based its design on an American-made graphics processor made by 3dfx. Hideki Sato, who had led the design of the ill-fated Saturn, led the Japanese team, basing its design around a chip made by the Japanese company NEC. Reportedly, Sega's management had all but decided to go with the American design when, during an investor call, 3dfx revealed details about Sega's unannounced console. The indiscretion may have cost 3dfx a fortune; thereafter, Sega switched to Sato's design and the Japanese-made chip.

The graphics processor was just the first of many forward-looking components that made the Dreamcast such an extraordinary machine. A built-in 56k modem would enable the system to connect to a bespoke online portal known as SegaNet and, with the right software, allow players to meet in digital kingdoms to go on adventures together.

The removable memory cards, known as VMUs, would feature small LCD screens and work as clock calendars, even allowing rudimentary minigames to be played on the move. Proprietary GD-ROM discs would be used for the games, a data storage format that could hold more information than a CD-ROM and that were much harder to pirate. Under the hood, Sega's new console, still without a name, was the technological manifestation of a new, company-wide style, focus and direction: clean, tidy and forward facing.

Jet Set Radio/Jet Grind Radio, character production artworks, 1999

What Dreams Are Made Of

Hideki Sato, head of Sega's console R&D

We ended up with two contenders for the Dreamcast's graphics engine: the American 3dfx chip, and NEC's PowerVR 2. The 3dfx chip was of an orthodox, typical construction, while the PowerVR 2 showed the way to the next generation of graphics. At the end of a long series of debates and comparisons, we chose the PowerVR 2. Its high quality graphics were 100 times more powerful than the Sega Saturn and other previous consoles. Furthermore, NEC also planned to help support Dreamcast development by incorporating the same graphics chip in its own line of personal computers. The collaboration with Microsoft and Windows CE was likewise for the same purpose – to make game development easier.

Tetsuya Mizuguchi, head of United Game Artists

Sega Rally 2, which was the game I had worked on prior to the launch of Dreamcast, was actually built on the Model 3 arcade board. Its successor, the NAOMI, which was very similar to the Dreamcast hardware, was not finished yet. Sega's engineers were very familiar with the Model 3. They were able to bring all of that experience and knowledge into the design of the NAOMI and Dreamcast.

Yu Suzuki, head of Sega AM2

Dreamcast was created using techniques gained from developing arcade machines. I have no doubt that the machine had superior structure and specs as a distributed processing machine. Of course, I was both excited and nervous when I exchanged opinions with people from each section, picturing a finalised version of the machine.

Bernie Stolar, president and COO, Sega of America

Dreamcast came about at a time when we were switching from Model 3 arcade hardware to NAOMI. I was disappointed with the fact that the Dreamcast would not really be able to support ports from both arcade units. I had wanted ports of several licensed units, including the *Star Wars* trilogy and *The Lost World: Jurassic Park* series. I felt these would be very popular, especially in the American market. Anyway, NAOMI and Dreamcast were developed in tandem, definitely with the thought that many of the games such as *Crazy Taxi* and *House of the Dead 2* would be ported from the arcade to console. We also licensed the NAOMI architecture to Capcom, Namco and Taito.

Hideki Sato, head of Sega's console R&D

We researched the possibility of using DVDs, but the costs were still too high. If we were to use that media for games, we'd have to research authoring issues as well. All that would have taken too much time, so we did not adopt DVDs. Our next idea was to include a rewriteable CD-ROM drive. We didn't go with that idea, but it ultimately led us to adopt a new technology, the GD-ROM, which was a natural extension of the CD-ROM's technology, with double the storage capacity.

Bernie Stolar, president and COO, Sega of America

More money could have been spent on the machine, I said this from the beginning. There were three things that I wanted in Dreamcast: an online network, for multi-player and digital downloads, DVD support, and internal storage. I had to argue for everything. At one point, I had to ensure the modem didn't get dropped from the US version. Online was most important to me. So, I chose that over DVD and internal storage because my plan was to add those later. With regards to internal storage, I also began discussions with an early DVR company about releasing a cable box with the ability to download our games, especially Dreamcast titles, as the plan was to deliver Genesis, Master System and even Saturn games as well, similar to the way LodgeNet worked in hotels. I also pushed hard for a dual joystick controller, similar to what we did at PlayStation. There's a reason the DualShock is still used to this day. I chose online functionality over DVD playback and internal storage, because I was forced to pick one of the three due to budget limitations. I would have preferred, obviously, to include all three from the get-go or, at the very least, online play with a DVD drive.

Greg Zeschuk, CEO, Bioware

We found [the Dreamcast] powerful and reasonably well documented. It had better graphics, sound and architecture than anything that came before it, and some of its features are still better than many of the current and upcoming consoles. If the winner of the console wars was based on merit, I believe the Dreamcast would still be around. It truly was a wonderful system to work on.

Pete Hawley, programmer, Lionhead

It was a great machine to work for. Some would argue that the libraries and dev tools were a little confusing but, generally, it was a good machine to work on once you'd made that choice. Sega's third-party dev support was excellent too.

Scot Bayless, senior producer, Sega of America

As good as Dreamcast was, it's a classic example of solving last year's problem. Everything about it seemed to be aimed at countering the things that made PlayStation so successful. It was well-executed, feature-rich and pretty much ticked every check box against Sony's console, but PS2 was about to shift the paradigm once again.

John Metcalfe, vice president, Videologic

The Dreamcast is very similar in performance to the PlayStation 2, but I believe it offered two key benefits: it's much cheaper to make than a PlayStation 2, and it's relatively easy to program, largely thanks to the tiling architecture, which enables the main memory to be used efficiently for texture storage, and hardware support for compressed textures, rather than PS2's small on-chip RAM. This meant that developers could achieve stunning visuals with much less effort than on PS2. Other benefits include translucency sorting, which takes a big problem away from developers, and Dreamcast's ability to render at 640×480 in 60Hz and send the output to a TV after flicker-filtering, which results in fewer jaggies than a PS2. Finally, the Dreamcast also had superior support for the PAL 50Hz format.

16

Jet Set Radio/Jet Grind Radio, production artwork, 1999

Five Thousand Names in a Hat

By the end of the 1990s, with Sega's reputation in tatters and just 3% of the market share, the company had ceded any advantage it had once enjoyed to its competitors. It was time for a new image and, for this forthcoming system, a new kind of name. 'Black Belt' and 'Dural', the codenames used to refer to the console while it was in development, were considered, variously, to be too Japanese, too obscure, too masculine or too niche. Sega wanted a breezier name for its great new hope, something with mass appeal, something that shrugged off the image the company had cultivated in the early 1990s of black plastic wraparound shades and pubescent boys punching the air in reeking bedrooms.

Sony, with its PlayStation, had for the first-time marketed videogames to an older, trendier kind of customer, and Sega wanted, if not some of that fashionable aura, then at the very least a shot at appealing to some of that broader market. 'Katana', 'Dragon' and, amusingly, 'Guppy' were all considered, then summarily rejected, for the new machine. Sega needed something that expanded its horizons, not one that narrowed them.

155

18

There was also the question of aesthetics. The decision was made to build the new console, not in the black plastic that had typified many of the company's previous machines, but in cleaner white colours. Under the guidance of the branding company InterBrand, the decision was initially made to drop the word Sega from the hardware (Irimajiri's management team ultimately opted for a compromise: a greyed-out Sega logo quietly positioned on the front of the machine), and instead use what the company hoped would become an iconic swirl as the system's logo (orange for Japan and the US; a less striking blue for Europe).

A decision about the name had to be reached. More than 5,000 names were considered, but none felt quite right to Sega's management. Finally, according to numerous former Sega employees, the late Kenji Eno, who had composed the music for Tetsuya Mizuguchi's *Sega Rally 2*, as well as directing his own games, such as *D2* at WARP, suggested 'Dreamcast', which was an elegant, elegiac portmanteau that implied that this was a machine designed to both catch visions of the future, and also to transmit reveries.

154

19

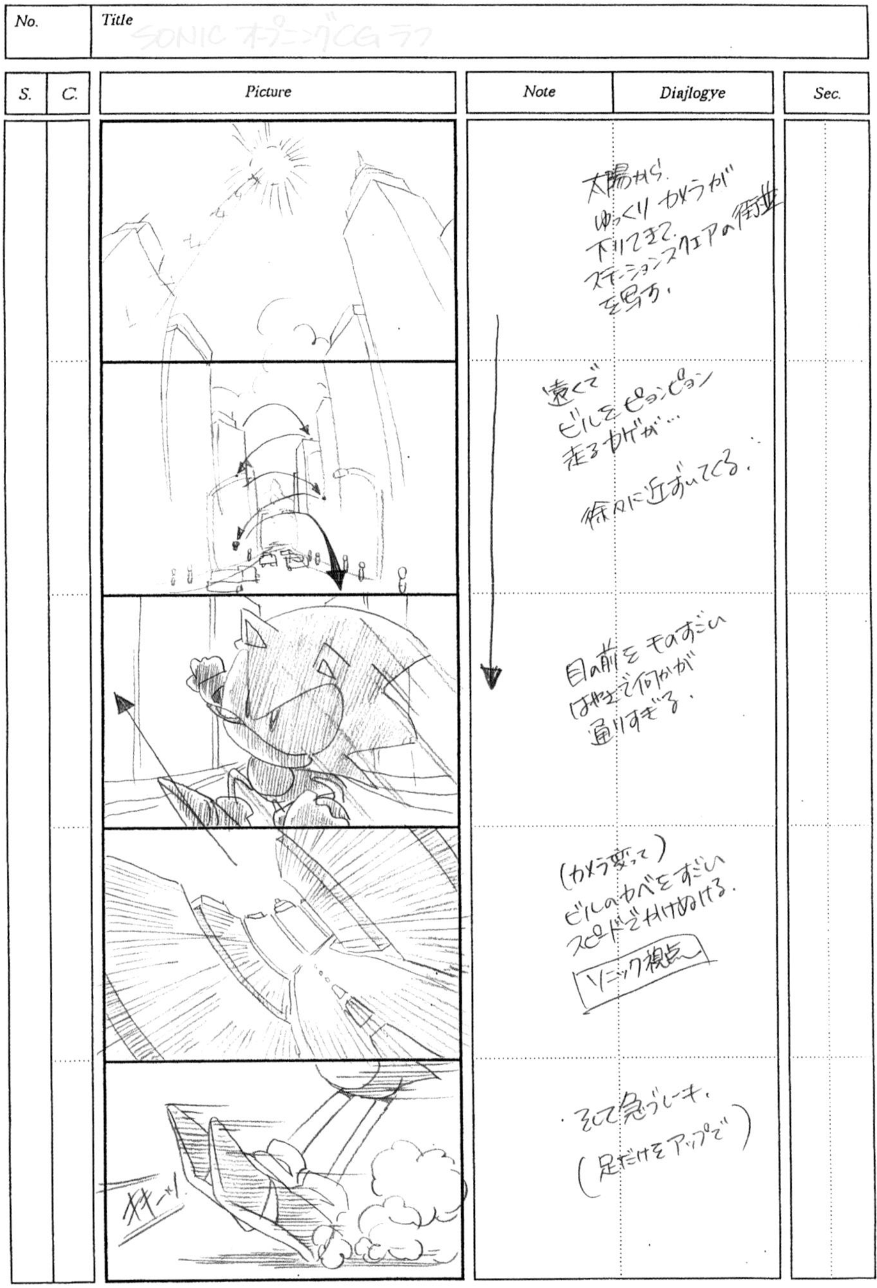

No.	Title	S.	C.	Picture	Note	Diajlogye	Sec.

Title: SONIC オープニングCG ラフ

太陽から、
ゆっくりカメラが
下りてきて、
ステーションスクエアの街並
を写す。

遠くで
ビルをピョンピョン
走るカゲが…

徐々に近ずいてくる。

目の前をモのすごい
はやさで何かが
通りすぎる。

(カメラ変って)
ビルのカベをすごい
スピードでかけぬける。
ソニック視点

・そして急ブレーキ。
(足だけをアップで)

SEGA

Sonic Adventure, cutscene storyboard, 1998

Five Thousand Names in a Hat

Tadashi Takezaki, head of marketing, Sega of Japan

We did our best to make the console approachable to a mass audience, from the system's design and colouring to the name itself.

Bernie Stolar, president and COO, Sega of America

I believe it was called 'Dural' and later 'Katana' at one point. I first heard the word 'Dreamcast' around May 1998.

Tetsuya Mizuguchi, head of United Game Artists

I was there in the meeting when the name was finally chosen. Shoichiro Irimajiri-san, the new CEO of the company, was there, sitting around a table with all of the other executives, and the heads of each of Sega's R&D departments. There were also a few key game directors, like Kenji Eno [*Enemy Zero*, *Sega Rally 2*, *D2*] and Yoot Saito [*Seaman*]. There were lots of potential names: 'Black Belt', 'Katana'.

Sega spokesperson and fact-checker for this book

Who came up with the name? Due to various confidentiality issues and third-party involvement, we have been advised to skip this question.

Tetsuya Mizuguchi, head of United Game Artists

'Dreamcast' was Kenji Eno's idea.

Takayuki Kawagoe, producer, *Jet Set Radio*

'Black Belt' and 'Katana' were used as the codenames. My initial reaction [to the name 'Dreamcast'] was that it sounded too cute for a system. But, after the person who named it explained to me the reasoning behind it, I was convinced.

Brian Bacino, creative director, Foote, Cone & Belding

Honestly? We were actually kinda bummed at first. The name 'Dreamcast' sounded so light and childlike. We had been working on the campaign long before the name showed up. Bernie Stolar came to us in 1996–97 and told us something was coming that was going to absolutely change the world of videogaming. He talked about early artificial intelligence and the ability of the console to learn the player's moves and react accordingly. He also talked about how gamers would play each other from all around the world over the internet. We imagined it to be totally badass and competitive – it was codenamed 'Katana'. In comparison, 'Dreamcast' sounded like a toddler's game to us at the time, but that was the name Japan decided on, so game on.

Yu Suzuki, head of Sega AM2

I thought the name was not bad at all. We needed to change the image as most of the machines had space-related names such as Saturn.

Masayoshi Kikuchi, director, *Jet Set Radio*

21   The name sounded fresh and unconventional to me at that time. I could imagine it will be well received by both men and women of all ages.

Tetsuya Mizuguchi, head of United Game Artists

I loved the name. Out of all the various choices, I wanted 'Dreamcast'. The others were too Japanese, too niche. 'Dreamcast' has a wider appeal, and it doesn't only say 'videogames' to me, which I was happy about. At the same time, we made the decision on the 'swirl' logo. We also decided to make the plastic white, rather than black. It was to signal the change in direction for Sega. It was a very good choice, I think.

No.	Title			
S.	C.	Picture	Note	Diajlogye	Sec.

ゆっくりカメラが
上がっていき。
ソニックの全身が写る

ここも ずいぶん
変ったなぁ

街のガヤガヤした
様子をゆっくりなめる。

街並を見渡せる高台。

ソニックの後ろから、
何者かが、せまってくる。

ふりかえって
あわてるソニック。

カオスがソニックの
頭をふみ台にして。
JUMPする。

（ スローモーション ）

立ち去る、カオス。

ソニックは突然の事。
に、どうしようする。

何だ!?

SEGA

Sonic Adventure, cutscene storyboard, 1998

Five Thousand Names in a Hat

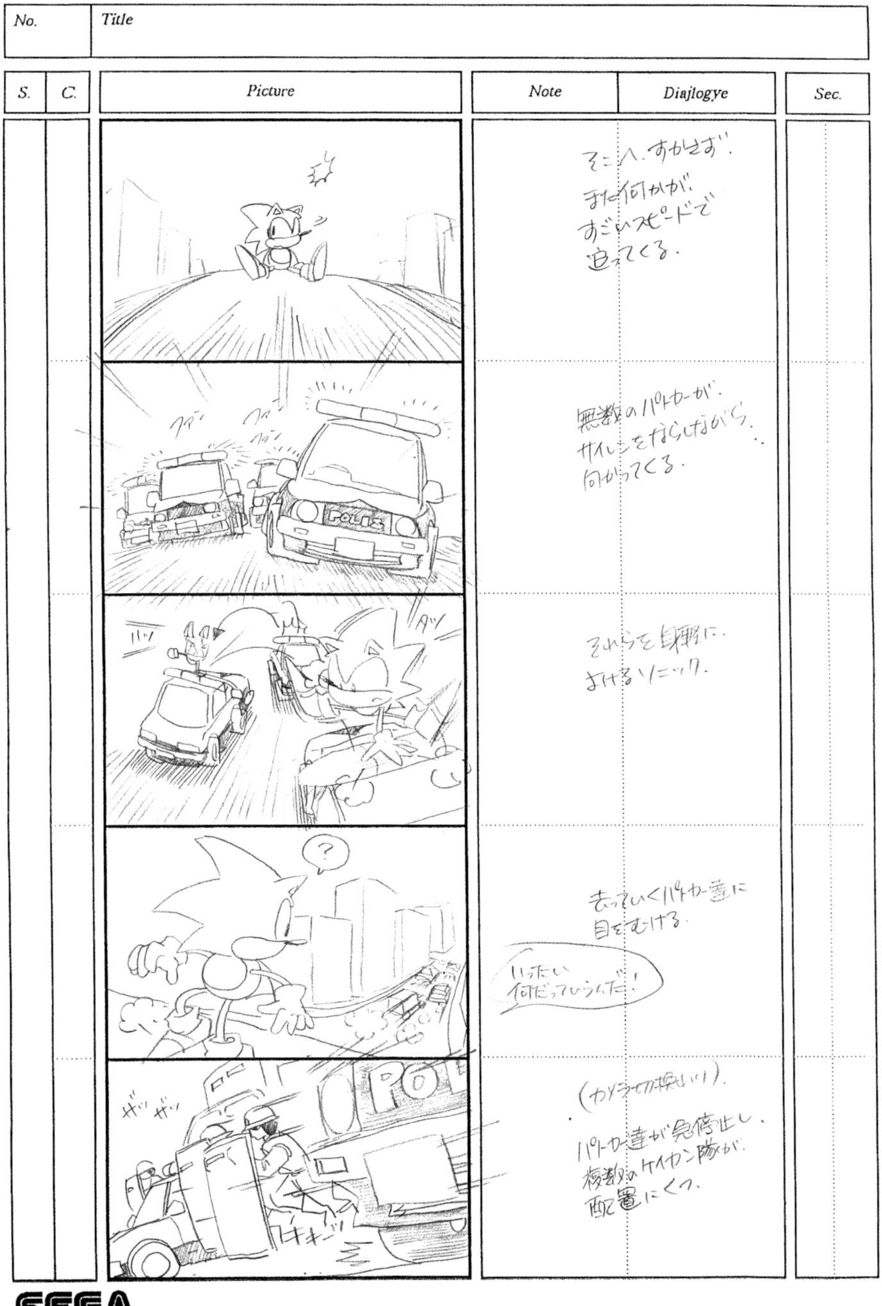

No.	Title			

S.	C.	Picture	Note	Diajlogye	Sec.
			そこへ、すかさず、また何かが、すごいスピードで追ってくる。		
			無数のパトカーが、サイレンをならしながら、向かってくる。		
			それらを自然に、よけるソニック。		
			去っていくパトカー達に目をむける。	いったい何だっていうんだ！	
			(カメラでか揺らい)。パトカー達が急停止し、複数のケイカン隊が配置につく。		

23

SEGA

Sonic Adventure, cutscene storyboard, 1998

Sonic Adventure, cutscene storyboard, 1998

Five Thousand Names in a Hat

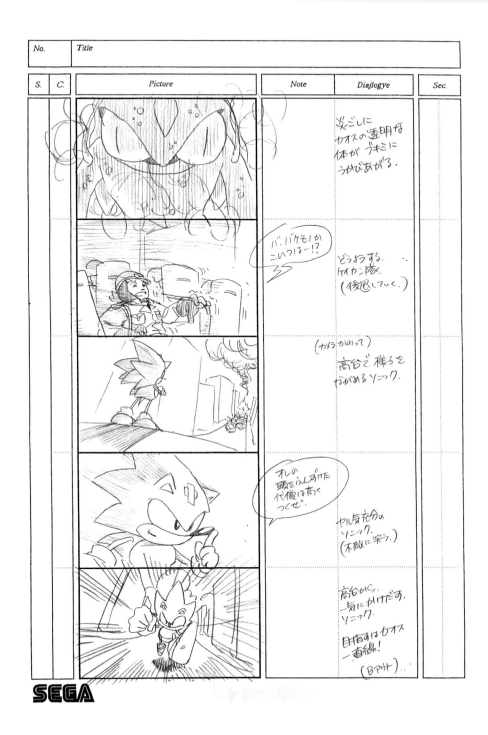

25

Sonic Adventure, cutscene storyboard, 1998

Arrival

On 27 November 1998, six months after the publication of the striking newspaper advertisement showing the Japanese samurai rising up, the Dreamcast launched in Japan. When the day arrived, last-minute issues sought to ruin all the months of careful planning and preparation. The hotly contested graphics chip that sat at the heart of the console was first delayed and then, when it came to manufacturing, was in grimly short supply. 'We have had some trouble modifying the PowerVR 2 for the Sega machine, which had led to the delay of the total development schedule of the new chip,' admitted Hajime Kinoshita, who was an investor relations manager for NEC at the time. 'For that reason, NEC's shipment of the new chips to Sega is behind schedule.'

The knock-on effect of NEC's inability to deliver, for which Sega reportedly threatened the company with a lawsuit, was a costly delay, pushing the launch back by a week and vastly affecting the number of consoles that Sega was able to ship to retailers. In fact, almost all Japanese units had been pre-ordered and reserved weeks and months earlier. As such, the Dreamcast

172

26

was effectively sold out before launch day, frustrating both retailers and those consumers who had not gone through the rather arcane and confusing pre-order process. Much to the dismay of Sega's CEO Shoichiro Irimajiri, just 140,830 Dreamcasts were sold in the three days following the console's Japanese launch (with a further 9,000 given away for promotional purposes), which was less than 75% of the target he had set the company. By contrast, Sony sold 600,000 PlayStation 2s in the first 24 hours of its launch.

It was a disastrous debut for a system that was supposed to right the administrative wrongs of Sega's recent past, and did nothing to convince the retail industry that the Dreamcast was going to be a well-organised, money-making success. Retailers did not hide their dismay. One said, at the time, 'The [Dreamcast] debut has been one of the most chaotic, frustrating and disappointing premieres we have ever witnessed. It was poorly planned, mismanaged, and has given grief to everyone involved.' One American journalist likened the Japanese launch of the Dreamcast to the hapless American launch of Sega's Saturn a few years earlier, writing that retailers were similarly 'confused and alienated', consumers had 'trouble finding' a system to buy for weeks afterwards, and concluding that Sega had 'rushed the Dreamcast to market'.

Arguably, the Japanese launch came too early in terms of software support as well. Just four games were available for the system – *July*, *Pen Pen TriIcelon*, *Virtua Fighter 3tb*, and *Godzilla Generations* – none of which particularly showed off the Dreamcast's considerable capabilities. Of these, *Virtua Fighter 3tb* proved the most successful, selling almost as many copies as the Dreamcast itself, but, as a port of an arcade game designed for the Model 3 hardware rather than the Dreamcast's arcade-based cousin NAOMI, it was broadly based on old technologies. Out of the gates, Dreamcast's vision of the future was looking decidedly anachronistic.

Even after the console's arrival, the problems continued. Sega's initial plan to release one game every week for four weeks following the launch – *Blue Stinger* followed by *Geist Force*, then *Sonic Adventure* and, finally, a quartet of games headed by the RPG *Evolution* – fell apart. Half the games were delayed until the following year. *Geist Force* was cancelled entirely and *Sonic*

173

28

Adventure, the first fully 3D game to feature Sega's mascot and undeniably the system's killer app, slipped by a fortnight.

Issues with the Japanese launch were costly, and not only in terms of sullying the Dreamcast's name before it had a chance to build a reputation. While Sega spent an estimated US$50–80 million on hardware development, the company had earmarked no less than US$300 million on marketing and worldwide promotion (a sum that Irimajiri, who previously worked for the Japanese car giant Honda, compared to the investment needed to design and launch a new automobile). But Japan, where the relative success of the Saturn had done little to reverse the company's declining fortunes, was not Sega's primary focus. Better to mess up the Japanese launch and to use those lessons to ensure that, come 9.9.99, the date of the American launch, everything went smoothly.

29

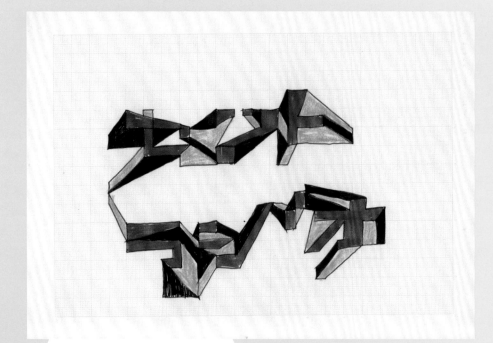

Jet Set Radio/Jet Grind Radio, logotype production artworks, grAphic tAkorA, 1999

Arrival

Keiji Okayasu, game director, *Shenmue*

On the day of the Japanese launch, I was working in the office as usual. If I remember correctly, there were not that many systems shipped due to a shortage of chips. Yes, that's right, there had been a delay in the chip's development. But even so, I was surprised and relieved when I heard that the hardware sold out right away.

Takayuki Kawagoe, producer, *Jet Set Radio*

I remember watching how it all played out in one of the mass retailers in Shibuya. The volume of shipments for the launch day was pretty small, so I remember being disappointed and not feeling like we had lived up to the users' expectations.

Hideki Naganuma, composer, *Jet Set Radio*

I was probably in the office working as normal but I can't remember where exactly I was when the machine was launched. I bought the machine out of my own pocket on the launch day or the day after in a shop. I, for one, was very happy.

Tetsu Katano, programmer, *Sonic Adventure*

I was in Japan working on *Sonic Adventure* when the Dreamcast launched over here. *Sonic Adventure* was one of the three projects that I have done in my life where I really worked my hardest and went the extra mile. Mainly I was thinking, 'Great, we still have a month left. Let's do this.'

Hideki Naganuma, composer, *Jet Set Radio*

I liked its cool design and the fact that it was compact, but in a good way, in that it felt unexpectedly hefty. I was a fan of the Saturn's games even before joining Sega so I was expecting people to be even more excited for the Dreamcast. I didn't have any particular concerns but if I had to choose, I did wonder if the Dreamcast would be able to beat Sony's console.

Tetsuya Mizuguchi, head of United Game Artists

I was in Shibuya for the launch event. But to be honest, I was so focused on *Space Channel 5* that I couldn't enjoy myself. Development of *Space Channel 5* was fully underway, and I was going crazy trying to ensure we would have the game finished on time.

Jake Kazdal, artist, *Rez*

The Dreamcast launched two months prior to my moving to Tokyo to join Tetsuya Mizuguchi's newly formed internal studio, United Game Artists. The atmosphere was electric. Mizuguchi-san was so excited about what we were doing, and his enthusiasm was infectious. The whole team was dedicated and incredibly talented. The ghosts of Sega's past weren't a problem for that group.

31

Borders Down

Compared to the disastrous Japanese launch, the Dreamcast's arrival in America, where Sega hoped to regain much of the ground it had lost over the years, was a raging success. Orchestrated by Peter Moore, a marketing executive who had come to Sega from Reebok specifically to launch the Dreamcast, the event, which was planned around the palindromic date 9.9.99, set the template for videogame systems launches.

There were the lines of consumers trailing around blocks of streets. There were the panoramic advertisements plastered over hoardings in major cities. There were the hired celebrities. There was the high-profile sponsoring of an awards show. There was the enigmatic 'It's Thinking' ad campaign, designed by top-flight advertising firm Foote, Cone & Belding (marketers for MTV and Levi's), designed to imply industry-changing technological power and imbue this little box of plastic, metal and wires with the quivering of machine intelligence.

32

It worked. Ten months after the stumbling Japanese launch, Dreamcast sold 100,000 units in just a few hours to become, as employees of Sega of America would remind everyone at every opportunity, the highest earning entertainment launch yet, beating the previous record holder, the opening weekend gross of *Star Wars: The Phantom Menace*. By 1 p.m., all 705 branches of Toys 'R' Us had sold out of systems. Within 24 hours, benefiting from its alluring catalogue of launch games, the console had sold close to a quarter of a million units and, along with sales of games and peripherals, had netted Sega close to US$100 million dollars (almost enough to clear the cost of the marketing spend...). Within two and a half months, more than a million Dreamcasts had been sold in North America, almost as many as were sold in Japan in the entire first year following the console's release.

In Britain, however, the launch was delayed for an entire month due to issues with the online service. Sega Europe projected onto the Houses of Parliament confusing, potentially controversial images of the Union Jack alongside the slogan 'Show the continentals who's the daddy', with scant mention of the product or even the fact that it was a videogame system.

The UK TV ad campaign was similarly obscure, showing barbers racing to shave kids' heads and children throwing stones at bobbing buoys. The campaign was further dogged by accusations of false advertising. The Advertising Standards Agency ruled that Sega's claim of 'up to six billion players' had to be removed from the ads, for the entirely reasonable logic that the console did not yet support online play. As in the US, no in-game images were shown. The first time that footage of a Dreamcast game was broadcast in the marketing campaigns was several months after the machine's launch, when Sega Europe changed agencies prior to the launch of *Sega Bass Fishing*.

Around the world, meanwhile, the shadow of PlayStation 2 continued to loom large. In the past, the first videogame console to market often enjoyed an advantage over its latecomer rivals. The memory of PlayStation's decisive victory over Sega's Saturn, and Sony's whispering campaign in anticipation of the supposedly paradigm-shifting PlayStation 2, proved viciously effective. Hundreds of thousands of potential Dreamcast buyers decided to wait a year for Sony's console to arrive, to see for themselves how the two machines compared.

Light Speed Dash!

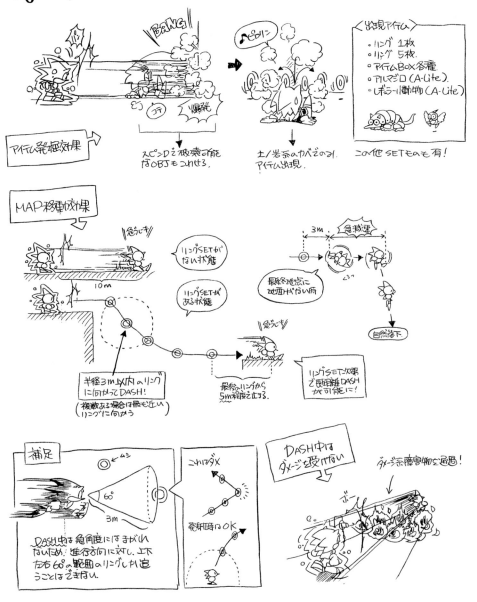

Sonic Adventure, design document (restored), 1998

Borders Down

Peter Moore, president, Sega of America

I was at Reebok in Boston. After 18 years, I was 45 years old and it was time to do something different. I got a call from an executive recruiter who said, 'What do you know about videogames?' Very little, I answered. 'What do you know about Sega?' Well, the only thing I knew was that I had bought my son a Sega Saturn for $500 and, pretty soon after that, heard they weren't making games for it any more. I went to San Francisco and sat down with Bernie Stolar. We ended up going to Japan together for a cursory interview. I was offered a job as senior VP of marketing. My skillset was perfectly matched to what was required – I was a marketer of sneakers to young men and that, at the time, fitted the profile of the gamer: a 15-year-old or so male. I felt confident that my skills in sports marketing transferred well. No matter where Sega was, they had an innovative product and I loved the idea of it being the 'challenger' brand to Sony's PlayStation.

Bernie Stolar, president and COO, Sega of America

I felt Sega needed a new marketing and sales approach, so I brought in Peter Moore. He had a great feel for and insight into branding. I also brought in a guy named Chris Gilbert, from Cerwin Vega Speakers. He knew retail sales like Peter knew branding. Peter Moore went on to work with Microsoft with Xbox and Xbox 360, and was the chief competitive officer and head of eSports at Electronic Arts, and is now CEO of Liverpool Football Club. I'd say I picked the right guy there. I firmly believe we had an incredible team for the Dreamcast launch. A great product needs a great team. We had both. I went out and hunted for these individuals. Honestly, the people that were at Sega, when I first got there, well, I don't believe they had the ability to step up and be winners. I only work with winners.

Peter Moore, president, Sega of America

I was told the launch was going to be 9.9.99. I sat down with the marketing agency to discuss the product specs and positioning. My job was to build out the marketing platform: TV commercials, print ads, figure out how we were going to launch and work with retailers to build programmes around their needs. In April, I gave a detailed presentation on our launch message: the Dreamcast was always on, intelligent, aware. We had a tagline: 'It's thinking'. We convinced Japan that we had the right strategy. They didn't understand our campaign, or the launch spot with a lady in a leather suit stealing a Dreamcast. They shrugged their shoulders but let us get on with it. It was the classic: we'll give you enough room to hang yourself.

Simon Cox, launch editor, *Official Dreamcast Magazine* (US)

A high-level exec confessed to me that the 9.9.99 and 'It's thinking' campaigns produced amazing awareness from the public in their New York test market. As many as 45% of those they spoke to in the target demographic had seen the 9.9.99 ad and knew that the Dreamcast was coming. But guess what? Hardly any of them knew what the fuck the Dreamcast actually was.

Bernie Stolar, president and COO, Sega of America

You have to work with people who are both intelligent and hard-working. They have to believe they are winners too, in order to become winners. It's no different than if you're building a sports team. You want the best and the brightest available. That's exactly what we had at Sega. At the same time, I had a number of very loyal people who then left Sony to come work for me at Sega. Both Steve Ackeroyd and Shuji Utsumi were in business development at Sony. They came to work for me at Sega. We all had a mutual respect and vision. Gretchen Eichenger was in Third Party at Sony. She left as well to join me at Sega. We had an amazing team.

Peter Moore, president, Sega of America
The night of the launch I was in New York city, in Times Square. We had about 510,000 units available for the launch, and we had to spread them around. Toys 'R' Us and Electronics Boutique were the main retail outlets, which shows how different things were back then. It was the night of the VMAs. I attended that as part of the launch then we had the console at midnight. We did $99 million in those 24 hours. Perhaps it's not that large today, but back then it was a record breaker.

Scot Bayless, senior producer, Sega of America
Sega had, for several years, been launching new hardware at great cost, and failing to reap anything close to a sufficient return on that investment. The Dreamcast did $132 million in sales right out of the gate in North America, but so what? The company spent more than that just getting it to market. Unless the Dreamcast had been able to achieve a massive attach rate, there was almost no way it could have saved Sega's hardware business. The damage had already been done.

Peter Moore, president, Sega of America
Did Sega go too early? No. What would have been different going head-to-head with PlayStation 2? We had an opportunity we grasped. The lesson we saw with Xbox 360 was to get out, get installed and get publishers behind you. You build momentum. You build a lead. The first to 10 million wins. We had an incredible launch portfolio. We couldn't just delay it. Any delay would have had a massively negative effect on the publishers who had been working on games for 18 months. You can't do that. You go. You believe in it. You go and you go hard.

Bernie Stolar, president and COO, Sega of America
I wanted the Dreamcast to have the best launch line-up of titles possible. This is paramount. I was working a minimum of 10 hours a day in the office, non-stop. It was very difficult work and there was little work/life balance. I felt some people didn't want me there, and that was not helpful. I didn't care: I wanted Dreamcast to succeed. I was proud of the team I had built and that the launch was successful. Yes, I felt proud.

Mark Higham, editor, *Official Dreamcast Magazine* (UK)
In those early days, it was all very strange, because Sega wanted to proofread every page of the magazine. They knew they weren't going to get the online thing working in time for the launch, but they couldn't tell us. So we wrote long features about everything that the Dreamcast could do, and then they came along on press day and pulled out all the references to the online capabilities. They wouldn't tell us why, just that there were some concerns that they wouldn't be up and running from day one, so they didn't want to risk building consumers' expectations.

Sonic Adventure, production artworks, 1999

To Make Friends and Influence People

Even in 1998, a year prior to Dreamcast's launch, Sega was busily courting third-party publishers, aware that the fortunes of every videogame system largely rest on the success of its software library, which must be rich, diverse, and, above all, expansive.

 Internally, Sega had reorganised its development staff into nine autonomous, second-party developers, led by many of the titans of the industry, including Yu Suzuki (AM2), Yuji Naka (Sonic Team), Toshihiro Nagoshi (AM4/ Amusement Vision) and Tetsuya Mizuguchi (United Game Artists). With unprecedented freedom kicked up by Sega's do-or-die position, these teams would together build Dreamcast's enviable, glittering, sometimes offbeat software library. But the company's executives knew these nine teams couldn't do it alone. They would need outside assistance.

In an interview published in the July 1998 edition of *Sega Saturn Magazine*, Sega's president, Shoichiro Irimajiri, was bullish about the strength of Sega's relationships with third-party gamemakers like EA, Capcom and Ubisoft, on whose work he knew the Dreamcast would keenly rely. 'Most of the third parties are saying that

40

they want to devote their big titles to Dreamcast because of the superiority of the hardware,' he boasted.

This was certainly true for game publishers whose businesses were centred on finding success in the arcades, then porting those games to the home. Sega's NAOMI system represented the cutting edge of arcade hardware, and the buttery ease of porting a NAOMI game to the Dreamcast made Sega seem a safe and easy bet for companies such as Capcom, which brought dozens of its titles, from *Power Stone* to *Cannon Spike* to *Marvel vs. Capcom 2*, from the arcade into the living room.

For those Western game publishers who were fully focused on the console market, it was a different story. The memory of PlayStation's trouncing of the Sega Saturn was still fresh, and Sony had developed a talent for seeding doubt about Sega's product, while simultaneously hyping up its own incoming machine to a preposterous degree. Carefully cut trailers showcased pre-rendered animations in such a way that implied to consumers that they were seeing in-game footage. One executive claimed that the PlayStation 2 was so powerful it would be like

41

playing Pixar's animated film *Toy Story*. Such was the level of hype surrounding Sony's machine that Japan's Ministry of Trade placed export controls on it, claiming the machine was so technologically advanced it could be used to power missile guidance systems.

In the shadow of this looming threat, Sega was only too aware of the need to secure the backing of third parties as quickly as possible. With unusual frankness and just a hint of desperation, Irimajiri said, 'The most important thing is that we get the most considerable share of the market before the PlayStation 2 comes out, and then carry on the momentum. That's our basic strategy.' Then, he added, 'My biggest concern is PlayStation 2.'

Irimajiri's hunch proved correct. In reality, Sony's machine was comparable in specs to the Dreamcast, and significantly harder to develop games for, with notoriously irksome architecture. The damage, however, was done years before the truth was out. The third-party publishers who had voiced their interest quickly disappeared, leaving Sega with scant support.

Howard Lincoln, chairman, Nintendo of America (speaking in 2000)

Sega has a very difficult uphill fight to battle against Nintendo and Sony. They have difficult relationships with gamers, retailers and third-party publishers. They certainly have the history of being able to make great games – that's not an issue. Whether they're going to have the financial resources to pull [Dreamcast] off is anyone's guess.

Peter Moore, president, Sega of America

Sony's job was to sow fear, uncertainty and doubt about Dreamcast. They did a brilliant job, not only of placing doubt in the minds of the consumer, but also in the minds of third parties. We were still shedding the negative hangover of the Saturn. Now, there was a deep-seated love of Sega, similar to that which Nintendo enjoys today. The juggernaut that was the PlayStation 2 was on the horizon. But Sony 'fudded' us. All that talk of the Emotion Engine, and the games being like playing *Toy Story*. They managed to convince everyone that theirs would be a superior machine that would leapfrog anything that the Dreamcast could be.

Bing Gordon, vice-president, Electronic Arts

We would get together and say, 'OK, are we going to put 10 games together and be there at [the Dreamcast's launch], and put our corporate will behind this, or not?' I remember our CTO talking about the processor and going, 'Oh my God, I don't know anybody who has even heard of this chip. It's non-standard and there are no libraries for it.'

Mark Higham, editor, *Official Dreamcast Magazine* (UK)

In those early days, everyone dearly wanted the Dreamcast to work – especially the third parties. They were pissed off with Sony – many publishers felt like Sony had them over a barrel – and Sega were the great white hope. [But then] Sega started squeezing third parties over margins while doing everything they could to push their own games.

Bernie Stolar, president and COO, Sega of America

We were in talks about *Grand Theft Auto III*, *Warcraft: Online* (as it was known at the time), *Max Payne* and other titles coming to Dreamcast, and this would have helped tremendously. *Black & White* and *Fable* both began as Dreamcast titles as well. I remember ports were being made for PC games such as *Alien vs. Predator*, *Commandos 2: Men of Courage*, *Half-Life*, *Outcast*, *System Shock 2* and others.

Kenji Kanno, director, *Crazy Taxi*

Ultimately, I think customers judge the strength of a games machine on the strength of its line-up of games. That was the big question: how many major publishers would join the battle and add their major games to sit alongside the quality of what we, at Sega, were making?

44

Peter Moore, president, Sega of America

A lot of publishers signed a one-game deal with Sega. The idea was to release one game, see how it sold and wait and see whether they wanted to then ramp up production and continue to make games for the platform. When you see a juggernaut like PlayStation 2 arriving and simultaneously you're not seeing announcements about new Dreamcast games, that gives you, as a consumer, pause for thought. This is where the 'fudding' came in – placing doubt in the consumer's mind. Frankly, Sony did it brilliantly.

Jet Set Radio/Jet Grind Radio, production artwork, 1999

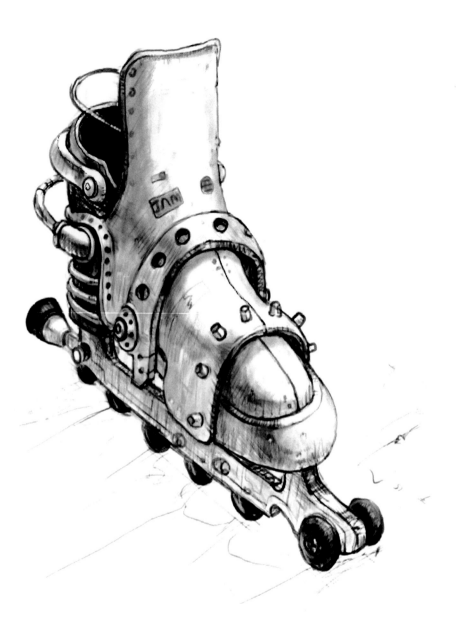

Jet Set Radio/Jet Grind Radio, production artwork, 1999

Hardware Production Drawings

Naoto Ohshima, designer, *Sonic Adventure*

Right from the start, I had concerns. We just didn't get much cooperation from third parties, while the marketing of the console failed to capture the fun of the games.

Greg Zeschuk, CEO, Bioware

Publishers were wary of Sega's ability to support the system with marketing and promotion – that's where the Dreamcast lost the battle, not on the quality of the system.

Bing Gordon, vice-president, Electronic Arts

There was a pushback from Sega, which was having cash-flow problems, and they couldn't afford to give us the same kind of licence that EA had over the last five years. So EA basically said, 'You can't succeed without us.' And Sega said, 'Sure we can. We're Sega.' And, at that point during negotiations, when someone is trying to call your bluff, you have to question whether you want to knuckle under or not. And because of the way they had flip-flopped on the configuration, and because the Dreamcast had become the system that EA developers least wanted to work on in the history of systems at EA, that was pretty much it. I got quoted in the press saying, 'Dreamcast can't succeed without EA.' They hated me for that.

Takayuki Kawagoe, producer, *Jet Set Radio*

I was thrilled imagining what kind of stuff we could achieve with the specifications of the machine. However, I was concerned if third parties, especially major companies, would be interested so early in the day.

Philip Oliver, managing director, Blitz Games

The big publishers were happy making loads of money from PlayStation and didn't want to dilute the market with another console when they were creaming in money from the most stable platform the industry had ever seen.

Keiji Okayasu, game director, *Shenmue*

At first, other software manufacturers seemed like they were trying to see how it was going as they didn't want to take a risk. People would often say that Sega was ahead of its time and I feel like the Dreamcast was no exception. Players were not prepared for the new, unfamiliar features such as the modem and portable memory card. As one of the developers, I still believe it was a really good system. Since *Dragon Quest* and *Final Fantasy* were very popular at that time, it might have been different if those two titles were published for the Dreamcast...

Charles Bellfield, vice-president of communications, Sega of America

I would say that companies like Ubisoft, in my perception at the time, were created on Dreamcast. Companies like Acclaim survived a lot longer because of Dreamcast; Activision as well. Capcom was hugely successful on the platform. The first year, we were widely and successfully supported.

Tetsuya Mizuguchi, director, head of United Game Artists

The truth is that we needed more games. We needed games that would appeal to a broad audience, and this became a struggle with Sony. Sony ran a very effective PlayStation 2 campaign. They chose their words carefully. I was frustrated with our efforts by comparison. Sony was constantly appealing to this broad audience.

A Phantasy Online

From the very start, Isao Okawa, the co-founder of Sega and a kingmaker at the executive level, the only person at the company with the power to hire and fire CEOs and presidents, had believed that the future of videogames was in the online realm.

Since the early 1980s, computer scientists had been experimenting with online games on university networks. But it was only at the advent of the mainstream internet that the full potential of interconnected, online games was revealed. Despite numerous experiments with add-ons for the Super Nintendo and Sega Saturn, no console manufacturer had yet managed to seamlessly integrate online play into its hardware and, in doing so, to foster a connected community of players. The Dreamcast, Okawa pledged, was going to change all of that. The system launched not only with a built-in 56k modem, ready to plug into the stuttering dial-up internet services of the time, but Okawa also offered a year's worth of free internet access with every Dreamcast sold, paid for, extraordinarily, out of his own pocket. The internet was going to define videogames, even if it cost Okawa his personal wealth.

In September 2000, Sega launched its online network, dubbed SegaNet, in America. While only a few games had, to date, taken advantage of the inbuilt modem (the only online-enabled Dreamcast game in the US by this point was Sonic Team's delightful but slender competitive puzzle game, *ChuChu Rocket!*), SegaNet was intended to show off the company's renewed commitment to online play. Paying $21.95 a month, any subscriber who signed up for a two-year contract was given a free Dreamcast console and keyboard. It was a brave experiment, and one that inevitably came with the types of problems associated with emergent technology at this scale. Sega's servers sagged under the weight of the tens of thousands of newcomers to the digital realm, and, in terms of the ecosystem needed to support the venture, the lack of broadband infrastructure made connections patchy and unreliable, while the lack of affordable, long-term surfing packages caused many customers to run up stratospheric phone bills.

While Sega claimed that a third of European Dreamcast owners subscribed to Dream Arena (Sega's European online service), in the US that number was, according to one estimate, as low as 15%. Only a fistful of games fully exploited the Dreamcast's online potential.

But one of these, *Phantasy Star Online*, resurrected the company's dormant science-fiction RPG series and recast it as a massive online multiplayer game modelled on the giants of the PC world such as *Everquest*. It presented a new and alluring vision of  interconnected play in the living room. Through an ingenious chat system, which translated words and phrases back and forth between players using different languages, *Phantasy Star Online* encouraged teamwork between strangers to take down hulking beasts while searching for loot.

For players who managed to connect, the Dreamcast expanded the horizons of an entire medium and, for those intrepid early explorers, it seeded everlasting memories.

158

Phantasy Star Online, Secretary, Nurse and Trunk Girl character production artworks, 2000

A Phantasy Online

Yuji Naka, head of Sonic Team

The president of Sega at the time, Isao Okawa, was very vocal about the future of games being online.

Yu Suzuki, head of Sega AM2

Okawa had a huge interest in the internet at that time and repeatedly said that, in the future, the internet would spread to everyone, like water cascading from the top of Mount Fuji to its foot. The idea of an internet-enabled Dreamcast was like a bridge for his dreams. But, unfortunately, data speeds were just not fast enough at that time.

Hideki Sato, head of Sega's console R&D (speaking in 1998)

We knew we needed something special to distinguish our console from others. It was here that we first considered the option of adding a modem as a standard feature. With graphics and sounds, if you don't increase the power of a new console by a magnitude of ×100, the average user won't really notice the change. That's why you have to find some new direction, some new angle, when you create a new console. The modem represents that new direction we are presenting to players with the Dreamcast.

Bernie Stolar, president and COO, Sega of America

I believed that the future of games was not DVD: that was merely a stop-gap. It was going to be massive multiplayer online gaming, with digital downloads being the main delivery system. I was a big believer in that and still am. I saw network play and the internet evolving and I knew cloud gaming was coming. Look at what Dreamcast could do with its modem. We were way ahead of our time. That's why we built Dreamcast as the first online multiplayer gaming system in the console space. A lot of people wonder though why Sega did not include a DVD player anyway. Fact is, Sega could not afford it. Online was our future and what would define Dreamcast in the marketplace. We were even in talks with Blizzard about *World of WarCraft*, which was at the time known as *WarCraft: Online*.

Hideki Sato, head of Sega's console R&D (speaking in 1998)

Now, on the Saturn, we had the Saturn modem and the XBAND online service, with about 15,000 users. When we looked at how they were using the XBAND service, we discovered that the usage was split about 50/50 between fighting match-ups, on the one hand, and email on the other. To be honest, there weren't really a lot of networked games available to begin with, so I'm not sure how meaningful the data about the fighting games was, but the part about the email showed us that this was a significant user need. From there we asked, could we capitalise on this and perhaps simplify email, and find new kinds of play based around that need? Could we develop a virtual space for networked communications, but give it a game-like feel? We want to create a community for Sega users to communicate with each other: we think a new kind of gameplay could emerge from such a space. So it may be the modem that is the key to all this, to broadening the horizons of games.

Charles Bellfield, vice-president of communications, Sega of America

In September 2000, we had *NFL 2K* up and running and playing between players in San Francisco and New York. That, on a console, through a telephone connection, was unheard of at the time.

Christophe Kagotani, journalist

The online stuff was just coming too early. The market wasn't ready. People wanted something new and simple. DVD was one answer, and Sony used it perfectly. At the same time, Sega wasn't able to explain to people that Dreamcast could offer great quality 3D. People still thought Sony had the edge.

Yuji Naka, head of Sonic Team

We chose to make an online *Phantasy Star* game because we thought the series was most suited to the online environment. Since it was my first attempt at such a big online game, it was a matter of trial and error. We tested and retested and discarded a lot of things before eventually coming up with the final product. It was a very different experience of game design and development.

Takao Miyoshi, director, *Phantasy Star Online*[1]

At first, we had to think of how the people using the internet would communicate among themselves. Once we started to think about it, we realised that everyone will be strangers at first, so we had to think of a method to go around that. We decided that everyone would come together around a common goal. In *Phantasy Star Online*, this would be people playing the game in order to adventure together. Then it was time to figure out how to get a first-time player talking to the other people and how to get them started on their adventure.

Yuji Naka, head of Sonic Team

For me, my main goal was not to make an RPG that had cool movies and pretty graphics but rather a game that you'll have fun playing with other people. I wanted to be able to make my own story, to adventure with my friends.

Koji Aizawa, editor, *Famitsu*

More than 250,000 people were playing *Phantasy Star Online* in Japan. That's one of the most successful online videogames in the country. But it was too late for Dreamcast and Sega. And the calling cost in Japan is expensive. That was really a big problem.

Naoto Ohshima, designer, *Sonic Adventure*

I truly believe the Dreamcast contributed to the development of the internet infrastructure in Japan.

60

Phantasy Star Online, Anna, Kroe and Shino character production artworks, 2000

Sega Dreamcast: Collected Works

Loss of a Dream Maker

Born in Osaka in 1926, and educated at Waseda University, Isao Okawa founded CSK Corporation, a computer services company, in 1968. Two decades later, in 1984, CSK became Sega's largest shareholder, a move that promoted Okawa to the position of company chairman. A bright, attractive man, ever-ready with an anecdote, Okawa came to see Sony Corporation and its PlayStation console as, in the words of one *New York Times* journalist, his 'arch-enemy'. Saturn's loss of market share at the hands of the PlayStation only redoubled Okawa's resolve. He invested a reported $900 million of his personal fortune into its successor, the Dreamcast. This money had been made when he was an early backer and major stockholder in a number of other Japanese technology firms, including the ASCII Corporation, Bell System 24 and Japan Card System.

Okawa was fully taken with the idea that, firstly, internet connectivity was the future of home videogaming, and also the notion that, if the Dreamcast was to be Sega's final piece of hardware before it turned into a software company, the project would burn fierce and burn bright.

144

62

In 1999, Nakayama left Sega, reportedly at Okawa's bidding, after the Dreamcast failed to meet its projected targets, and Okawa took his place as assistant president of the company. Then, the following year, Shoichiro Irimajiri left, and Okawa was promoted to president. By the time Okawa came to occupy the top spot, the Dreamcast had been abandoned by most third-party game publishers. Despite a strong debut in the US, it was now struggling there, just as it was struggling in Japan and Europe. The idea that Sega might have to cease production of the Dreamcast, and become only a software company, may have been unthinkable in the mid-1990s, but by this point it was not unexpected. In fact, Okawa had confided to senior colleagues that it had always been his long-term plan. 'I have worked in software all my life, and I feel uncomfortable being in the hardware business,' he told the *New York Times* in a 2000 interview. 'In fact, when I became chairman of Sega in 1997, I said we should stop producing hardware.'

144

Still, Dreamcast, he pledged, would not go down without a fight. Okawa donated 85 billion yen (US$692 million), including 32.7 billion yen worth of Sega stock, back

63

to the company. He began brokering talks with Microsoft to attempt to convince them to enable the Xbox to run Dreamcast games. Okawa, however, was fighting on two fronts: both for Sega's future, and also his own. On 16 March 2001, he died of blood cancer. Shortly before his death, he forgave Sega's debts to him, a final act of generosity that smoothed the difficult transition of the next few years, and gave Dreamcast a final surge of life.

More than 6,000 people attended a memorial service to celebrate Okawa's life. Upon learning of the death of his friend, Sega's co-founder, David Rosen, sent a telegram to Okawa's family in which he described Okawa as 'a man of great vision', someone who 'dedicated his energy and his many abilities to whatever task he undertook', and who provided inspiration both to younger staff and Sega management alike.

Tetsuya Mizuguchi, head of United Game Artists

Okawa was so aggressive in his aims. He had such ambition, to bring internet technology into videogames. After his death, that curiosity sort of fell away. Without his energy, something went out of the company. He was an extremely charismatic man; a godfather to Sega really. It was a big loss, and played a part in the death of the Dreamcast.

Peter Moore, president, Sega of America

Okawa was something of a divisive visionary but I loved him.

Bernie Stolar, president and COO, Sega of America

I did not like Okawa. I'm the one who actually wanted the modem. I very much liked Hayao Nakayama; he understood games and how important content was. Nakayama-San and I shared the same vision. We are friends to this day. Yes, for him I have the utmost respect.

Peter Moore, president, Sega of America

We lost Okawa while I was there. He was passionate about Sega. Even though he was an incredibly wealthy man who owned very large call centres in Okinawa, his love for Sega knew no bounds. He knew what he wanted and he pledged to put everything behind it in order to make it successful. He was energetic and a visionary from a technology perspective, but also wanted to drive forward Japanese industry. I enjoyed my time with him. It was such a shame when he died. He was a benefactor of the company. One great gesture is that, when he knew he had limited time left, he gave the equity he owned in Sega back to Sega to allow them to continue without the restraint of financial issues, to be as successful as they could. It was an extraordinarily generous gesture, and typical of the man I knew. He was an energetic visionary leader, able to be agile and responsive even within the formal structure of a Japanese company.

Yu Suzuki, head of Sega AM2

He used to ask everyone about their dreams, and tell them his. He always had interesting stories. He was very attractive as a person, in that he would attract people toward him, like a magnet. We were not friends, per se – we were in the totally different positions within the company – but he was always supportive of what I did, I suspect because he liked innovation.

Masayoshi Kikuchi, director, *Jet Set Radio*

I remember Okawa surprised us all by sending everyone involved in the development of *Sonic Adventure* high-grade Wagyu beef to thank us for our efforts. I didn't receive it as I was not involved in that project, but I went to my colleague's house to eat his! We enjoyed Sukiyaki together. It is such a good memory.

Toshihiro Nagoshi, head of Amusement Vision   66

Okawa never directly helped me with ideas for games, but I learnt an awful lot from him about how to manage a group of people.

Tetsu Katano, programmer, *Sonic Adventure*

My favourite memory is that I received a grateful handshake from Okawa, the chairman of Sega at that time. He said 'thank you', while offering his hand to me, when *Sonic Adventure* was released. I remember realising at the time how that handshake and those appreciative words could go right to my heart.

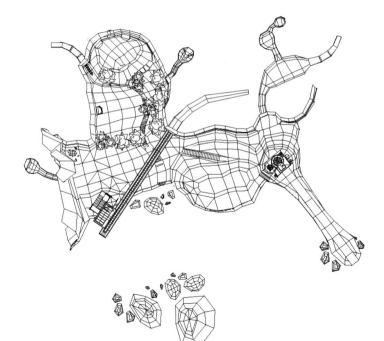

67

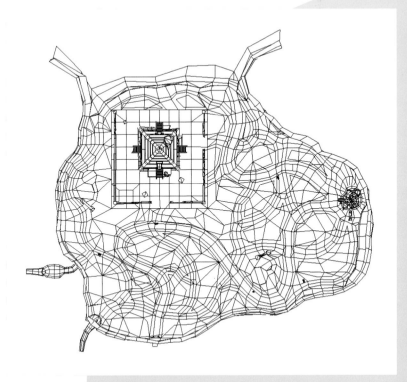

Sonic Adventure, environment wireframes, 1998

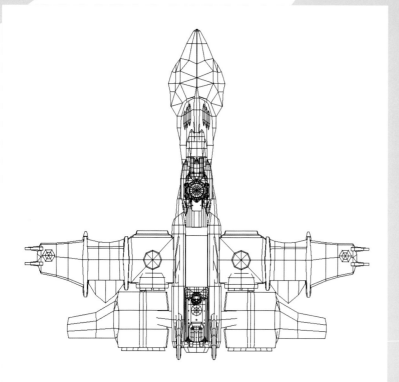

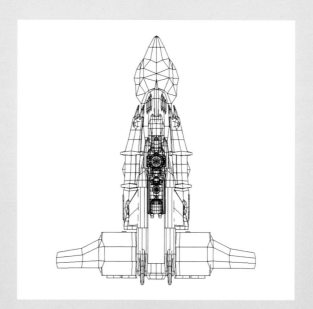

Sonic Adventure, environment wireframes, 1998

Loss of a Dream Maker

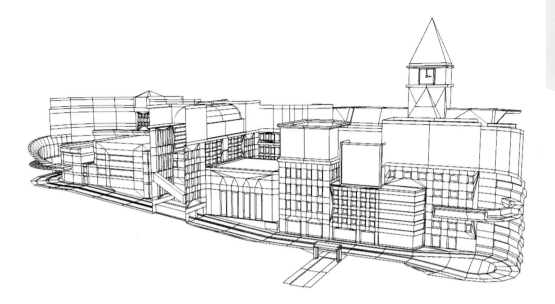

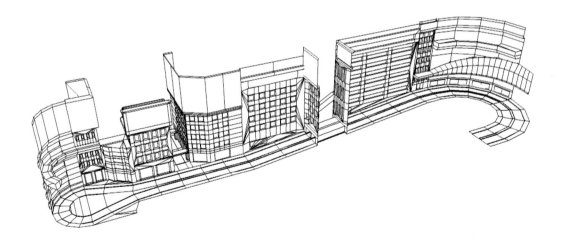

Sonic Adventure, environment wireframes, 1998

Insert Credit to Continue

That the Dreamcast entered the world an underdog was never in question. When Sega first announced the console, Howard Lincoln, the former chairman of Nintendo of America, commented that, in the light of Sega's financial situation, the Dreamcast project was nothing short of 'completely irresponsible.' Despite the success of the American launch, within

just a few months it had become clear how desperately the Dreamcast was struggling. It struggled against the retailers still smarting from Sega's recent failures. It struggled against the third-party publishers wanting to wait and see how things played out before lending the console their full support. Most of all, it struggled against the shimmering promise of its rival, the PlayStation 2.

Six months after the Dreamcast came to America, the longed-for PlayStation 2 launched in Japan. Shortly afterwards, Kmart, one of the largest American retailers, announced it would no longer stock the Dreamcast console or its games. Rumours were also circulating that Microsoft, which had partnered with Sega to make its Windows CE platform run on Dreamcast, was planning to enter the console business.

So the month before the PlayStation 2's American launch, Peter Moore and the rest of Sega's US team travelled to Tokyo for a crisis meeting. Moore arrived in Japan with a report called 'Manifesto of the Future.' It contained a presentation, which they delivered to Sega's Japanese executives and internal studio heads, including Yu Suzuki (AM2), Yuji Naka (Sonic Team), Rikiya Nakagawa (AM1/Wow Entertainment) and Toshihiro Nagoshi (AM4/Amusement Vision). Moore argued that Sega should shift its focus away from hardware fully onto making games. Sega simply could not compete at the levels now required for a videogame hardware manufacturer to make a success of a console.

'I remember it like it was yesterday,' Charles Bellfield later recalled. 'We presented a strategy in September 2000 that said we were not viable as a hardware player in the US beyond Christmas 2000 and that we needed to get out of the hardware business. That meeting was the first time Japan had ever heard that we could not be successful against the power of Microsoft, who had not yet announced their intention to come into the space, but we knew they were.' Unmoved by the arguments, and dismayed at Moore and his team's apparent capitulation in the face of challenge, Sega's studio heads reportedly got to their feet and walked out of the meeting room.

Despite Moore and his team's prediction meeting such indignation in Tokyo, they were proved correct. Sega tripped into 2001 more than two million units short of its hardware targets, despite having given Dreamcasts away for free in the United States to subscribers to its SegaNet web service. That month, the *New York Times* claimed that Nintendo was considering buying Sega, a story dismissed as false by one of Sega's Japanese executives. Then, at the end of January, a Japanese news service wrote that Sega had discontinued the Dreamcast.

In desperation, Sega countered the news, saying that the manufacturing plant had only temporarily ceased production due to a surplus of inventory. It was, of course, a lie. Finally, on 24 January, the company came clean. Sega put out a press release stating that it would now become a gamemaker, not a console manufacturer, publishing its creations on any and all platforms.

Less than three years into its lifespan, the Dreamcast was finished.

72

Jake Kazdal, artist, *Rez*

We were all called into our biggest meeting room for a mystery meeting. It was unlike anything that had happened before and people seemed apprehensive. Mizuguchi didn't have his usual smile, which, if you know the guy, you'll know is strange. He just dropped the bomb on us. Sega was ceasing production of the Dreamcast and we would be supporting the PlayStation 2. Utter silence. It was like a tomb. I remember looking around at these veterans who had been with the company for much longer than me, literally with their mouths agape, and the absolute shock and unease at what had just taken place. I'll never forget it. I loved the Dreamcast and the phenomenal suite of new games we had been banging out. It was crushing.

Tetsuya Mizuguchi, head of United Game Artists

I was having a major dilemma at the time. As a gamemaker, I want many people to play my games. Now, I love Sega. I love the Dreamcast. I wanted both to succeed. But, as a game developer, I want to provide a game to players on other platforms, because my priority is to reach as large an audience as possible. So I was in a difficult position: wanting the Dreamcast to succeed, but also wanting Sega to become a software company, with all the freedoms that brought. A TV documentary crew was following our team while we were making *Rez*. Midway through filming, we heard that Sega was going to cease production of the Dreamcast, and leave the hardware business. On camera, we had to continue as though everything was fine. I didn't even know if we had to finish the game.

Charles Bellfield, vice-president of communications, Sega of America

When you consider the strength of the PlayStation 2 hype, the cost of marketing a new platform in the North American market... When you consider that Microsoft had announced a $500 million marketing program for the launch of Xbox and that Nintendo has a $5 billion war chest... Sega did not have the ability to compete against those companies.

Tetsu Katano, programmer, *Sonic Adventure*

I don't want to admit this, but it was a failure because the overall power of Sega was not as strong as the other companies.

Peter Moore, president, Sega of America

We didn't get a large enough install base to sustain manufacturing. In any console launch, you have a period of time – between one and three years – and, if you don't hit your target of install base to attach ratio, whereby people buy software for the hardware, then you are finished, because typically you are losing money for every piece of hardware you sell. We just could not convince customers this was the platform to buy, or that a ton of software was coming out for it.

Yu Suzuki, head of Sega AM2

Since I was one of the board members, I knew that the production of the Dreamcast was going to end. Of course, I felt disappointed as we all put our heart and soul into the console.

Peter Moore, president, Sega of America

We gave it a tremendous shot. The Japanese Dreamcast was starting to fail when the US and European ones launched. Even so, we created an amazing team, and had a launch line-up that, today, would still be one of

74

Shenmue, dragon mirror production artwork, 1999

Shenmue, phoenix mirror production artwork, 1999

the best of all time: *Soul Calibur*, *Trickstyle*, *Sonic Adventure* and so on. All innovative. New IP. What would I have done differently? I can't think of anything. People still stop me today to talk about the Dreamcast. I still have my Dreamcast and still play it. The PS2 overwhelmed us. They showcased games like *The Bouncer*, visually impressive, but with little substance. But they managed to convince the consumer to wait.

Keiji Okayasu, game director, *Shenmue*

I had already left Sega when the end of Dreamcast production was announced so I wondered: does that mean they will only be developing software from now on? By that point I was like a player: an outsider.

Bernie Stolar, president and COO, Sega of America

I knew that Sega was going to cease being a hardware company before we even released Dreamcast. Okawa wanted Sega to only be a software company. I figured that out the day I got there.

Mike Brogan, development director, Sega Europe

There is no future in selling hardware in any market. Through competition, hardware eventually becomes a commodity. The future is in software. Sega's fault was to think that its core business was selling consoles, but consoles tend to be a one-time buy for most consumers, until the next version comes along. Software is a repeat purchase, so there's far more profit in it. If a company has to sell hardware then it should only be to leverage software, even if that means taking a hit on the hardware. I think some of the senior people in Sega never really understood that.

Yuji Naka, head of Sonic Team

Until the very final moments, I was really against Sega leaving the hardware business. In a way, I feel that, had that decision not been made, Sega would have gone bankrupt – so maybe it was a good business decision. But, at the same time, I also feel like, what the hell, we should have given it a go, and we should have taken that risk. But that's just my personal opinion, because I loved the hardware side of things at Sega.

Jake Kazdal, artist, *Rez*

There is no good reason why the Dreamcast failed. I think Sony's marketing was effective in making everyone believe the PS2 was more powerful than God. But really, there is no good reason.

Bernie Stolar, president and COO, Sega of America

It wasn't a commercial failure. Sega did very well with the product. I think, corporately, they just wanted to be a software company. Bigger players with bigger bank accounts entering the arena also played a role...

Hideki Naganuma, composer, *Jet Set Radio*

I don't remember exactly where I was when I learned that Dreamcast production was going to end, but I do clearly remember feeling very disappointed. I think Sega was too far ahead of its time, maybe 10 or 15 years ahead. Sega was making a game system that was understood by hardcore players with particular tastes, but, unfortunately, there were not enough people like that. Understandably, companies can't run a business if their products don't sell... But, on the other hand, genuine Sega fans who like edgy stuff might leave us if we made mainstream stuff which would have been well received by a mass audience. So it's not simple.

Shenmue, dragon mirror and phoenix mirror production artworks, 1999

Insert Credit to Continue

Kenji Kanno, director, *Crazy Taxi*

I was disappointed as an employee of Sega. I also had a great deal of anxiety because we would no longer be able to create stuff as a first party. Being able to deliver our original software was the one of privileges of being a first-party studio. So I felt uneasy when I heard that production of the Dreamcast was going to end. I think we were ahead of our time. It's normal to play online now but at that time people thought, 'What? Connecting to the internet?', 'Playing with strangers?'. We probably should have made an effort to understand the market and provide content in simpler and easier ways so the audience would be more familiar with the new system.

Masayoshi Kikuchi, director, *Jet Set Radio*

As a creator, when I heard the news I was excited that we would be able to create games for another company's console. There was more than one reason all of this happened the way that it did, but it all comes down to the fact that there was no blockbuster title for the Dreamcast.

Takayuki Kawagoe, producer, *Jet Set Radio*

It was at the end of 2000 when I heard production of the Dreamcast was going to end. I just felt so gutted. It was because of a lack of huge RPG titles. I then had to make the painful decision to start developing a number of games for PlayStation 2 before we announced that production of the Dreamcast was going to end. I loved those days when I was staying locked up and working hard in the second building of the headquarters with my peers to achieve the same ambitions; 'Rule the world with the Dreamcast' and 'Wow the world with innovative creation for the Dreamcast'. I'm still thankful to all the team members even now. I have good memories, especially about talking passionately with peers in the cafeteria.

Peter Moore, president, Sega of America

I felt I wasn't being heard any more. I had a view on where the industry was going and what we needed to do. *Grand Theft Auto III* had shipped and I saw the future of more mature Western content from developers like Rockstar. Console hardware was starting to power experiences that looked less like kids' games and more like movies. The opportunity to develop more mature experiences did not suit Sega. They still wanted to make Japanese-based games. We were too reliant on internal studios, who rarely travelled outside Tokyo, and who certainly did not take creative briefs. They made what they wanted to make, which in a sense was a strength, but which ultimately ceded ground to the blockbusters that dominate the landscape today. Everything was turning towards the West.

Tetsuya Mizuguchi, head of United Game Artists

85

There was no simple reason why the Dreamcast ended. Sega people love to carry the new technology. It's a very ambitious company.

Charles Bellfield, vice-president of communications, Sega of America

We had the content right. We had the marketing right. The product was designed right. The philosophy of networked capabilities was right. The team was right. The partners we had were right. But we didn't have the budget to build the confidence of the brand for our competitors. The first Xbox console was a far bigger failure than the Dreamcast. But Microsoft had much more money than Sega. And the Xbox was an ugly motherfucker.

Dream On

No videogame console that enjoyed as brief a lifespan as that of the Sega Dreamcast has left such a tall, long and vibrant legacy. Sega failed to convince many of those consumers, retailers and third parties that had abandoned the company in the Saturn years to return to the fold. But, for the men and women who worked for one of the company's nine autonomous, internal game-making teams, the Dreamcast represented a golden opportunity. They could make the games they had always dreamed of, for a system that, despite the bad-mouthing of Sony, was beautifully constructed, powerful and elegant and, in its embrace of internet connectivity, nothing short of a midwife to gaming's online future. The Sega of 1998, with little to lose and everything to gain, gave its teams unprecedented freedom, and only the lightest supervision, conditions that produced dazzling curios, novelties and classics, the likes of which we may never again see in the mainstream videogame industry.

The Dreamcast's games have a unique creative vibrancy and frisson. There's *Space Channel 5*, a camp, music video-themed

170

86

space opera, and *Jet Set Radio*, a game that combines the skater-graffiti culture of ice-cool Shibuya teens with the rhythmic joys of navigating an urban playground. There's *Samba De Amigo*, which turns the dry mathematical timekeeping of the rhythm action genre into a showboating carnival of Latin maraca-shaking (complete with arguably the greatest videogame peripheral yet made). In *Crazy Taxi*, we hurl a cab around San Francisco, delivering ungrateful customers from A to B with cop-baiting pizzazz. *Phantasy Star Online* scattered us to the far reaches of the galaxy while simultaneously bringing players without a shared language together, in moments of tender and unforgettable intimacy. *Seaman* gave us the chance to raise a fish voiced by Leonard Nimoy. *Shenmue*, that bold, astonishing adventure (and, at $20 million, the most expensive videogame ever made at the time) laid the blueprint followed by most of the open-world titans of the contemporary videogame landscape. And, of course, there was *Rez*, which blended sound, art and interactivity with such elegance that the president of Sony Music was moved to claim it was nothing less than the future of music.

There are less well-known treasures, as well: *Bangai-O*, a bewitching puzzle shooter from one of Tokyo's best-respected small studios, Treasure, which also released *Ikaruga*

for the system, a colour-matching shoot-'em-up whose sharp style is yet to be bettered. For the arcade aficionados, there's *Border Down*; for the RPG nut, there's *Skies of Arcadia* and *Napple Tale*; while, for those players who prefer a more mundane kind of thrill, *Tokyo Bus Driver* gave players a glimpse of life on the sleepy bus routes of the city's suburbs.

Alas, in the final reckoning, the world passed the Dreamcast by. The system represented the future of nothing much at all, save perhaps its devotees' unquenchable pining for a time when videogames were drawn in bright, delicious colours and with a creativity, freedom and abandon that has never been matched since. Dreamcast's legacy lives on, not only in the imaginations of its players, but also via a still-steady stream of independent releases by game developers who have eschewed the allure of the current consoles to instead release their new creations for that little white box, so carefully and robustly constructed, so beautiful and so doomed.

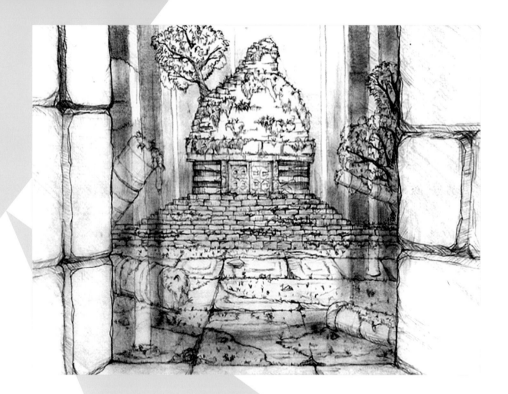

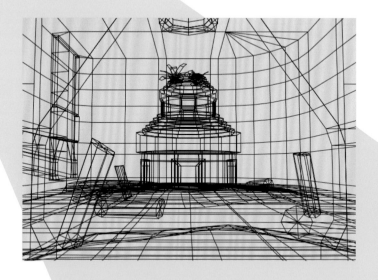

Sonic Adventure, environment production artwork/wireframe, 1998

Dream On

Bernie Stolar, president and COO, Sega of America

Honestly, I'm not surprised at all at how well-loved the Dreamcast is today; it was an incredible system with unique gameplay experiences. Great systems like that do not just fade away. It was a superior hardware system, ahead of its time.

Peter Moore, president, Sega of America

It had great software, wonderful new IP. And it was such a robust little machine: look at how many of the things are still working fine to this day. They go and go. Then the online element was so unique, so innovative. I'm not frustrated or bitter. If there are winners and losers, Sony won. It taught me a lot of lessons that I still use today: 'Why should you buy? Why now? How will it be different?'

Naoto Ohshima, designer, *Sonic Adventure*

The secret to the Dreamcast's longevity is simple: every one of us at Sega worked so very hard together to make the Sega's last system and I believe customers sensed our passion.

Hideki Naganuma, composer, *Jet Set Radio*

Even to this day, I receive lots of messages from fans from all over the world via social networks like Twitter. When I receive a message like '*Jet Set Radio* and your music were a huge part of my childhood. Its graphics and music still feel fresh to today', I am moved that what I created was genuinely appreciated and was not a waste of time. I think it proves that the original, unique stuff [we designed for the Dreamcast] will never die out with age.

Hideki Naganuma, composer, *Jet Set Radio*

I think it remains one of the best-loved game systems because we had lots of titles which were aggressive and edgy that had not been made by any other companies at that time. Our stance was 'let's create something we love and then people who like the game will become a fan and people who don't understand our game just won't buy it.' We had to see how many people liked our game. It's that simple. On the other hand, if we were making a mainstream game which will be well received by a mass audience, that kind of game would pay your bills temporarily but it would not be a game which will go down in history. Based on my experience, the cult-type game loved by fewer people will be loved for a long time and receive recognition throughout the ages compared to temporary blockbuster games. I think that's exactly what the Dreamcast and Sega's games, specifically *Jet Set Radio*, does.

Jake Kazdal, artist, *Rez*

91

I think it was such a breath of fresh air, so full of originality, it had that same warm fuzzy feeling the Super Famicom did, and was just full of love. Weird original concepts executed fantastically, it was a brief but bright star in the skies of gaming.

Keiji Okayasu, director, *Shenmue*

I can sum up the enduring love the people have for the Dreamcast in a single word: originality. I don't actually know how many but there are many Dreamcast games which haven't been ported to the other systems as they are only available on the Dreamcast.

92

Sonic Adventure, environment production render/in-game screenshot, 1998

Dream On

Tetsuya Mizuguchi, director, *Rez* and *Space Channel 5*

I did my best. You know, we all did. We made history, in some ways. And that is OK. Times change. They always do. Sega stopped making hardware, but the spirit of the challenger, that spirit that led to the creation of the Dreamcast? That has never left those of us who were involved.

Kenji Kanno, director, *Crazy Taxi*

I still think Dreamcast is a masterpiece. It's a dream machine created with nothing but love.

Takayuki Kawagoe, producer, *Jet Set Radio*

I think the reason the Dreamcast is still viewed so fondly is that there were lots of vibrant games, including arcade games, which showed a spirit to challenge users and other manufacturers. I have such fond memories of all the titles I produced. Other than that, I like *Roommania #203* because it has a completely new system, where the player doesn't control characters and also the story and the world-view was superb. I also enjoyed *Marvel vs. Capcom 2* because I like American comics. As a system, it was too early and edgy though.

Yu Suzuki, head of AM2

People love the Dreamcast because it typifies Sega's approach to hardware, produced with an engineering spirit and developer passions. The games for the machine were very Sega, too. Lovable games of high quality; that's the reason it continues to fascinate people today. I hope Sega will come back with a rambunctious spirit and start creating consumer hardware again.

93

Controller concept, GK Dynamics, 1998

Hardware Development

95

Controller concept, GK Dynamics, 1998

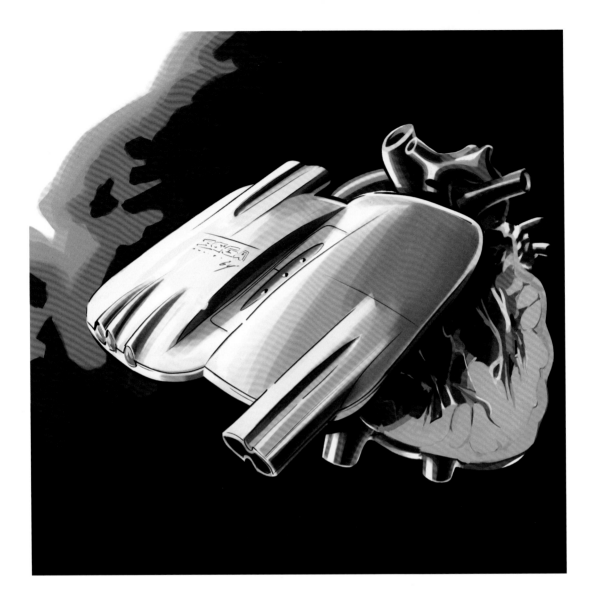

'Energy Form' console concept, GK Dynamics, 1998

Hardware Development

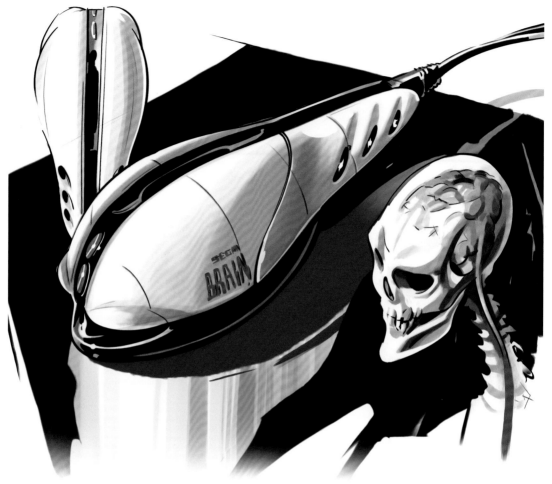

'Energy Form' console concept, GK Dynamics, 1998

'Toy Feeling' console concept, GK Dynamics, 1998

Hardware Development

'Toy Feeling' console concept, GK Dynamics, 1998

'Toy Feeling' console concept, GK Dynamics, 1998

Hardware Development

101

'Toy Feeling' console concept, GK Dynamics, 1998

'Toy Feeling' console concept, GK Dynamics, 1998

Hardware Development

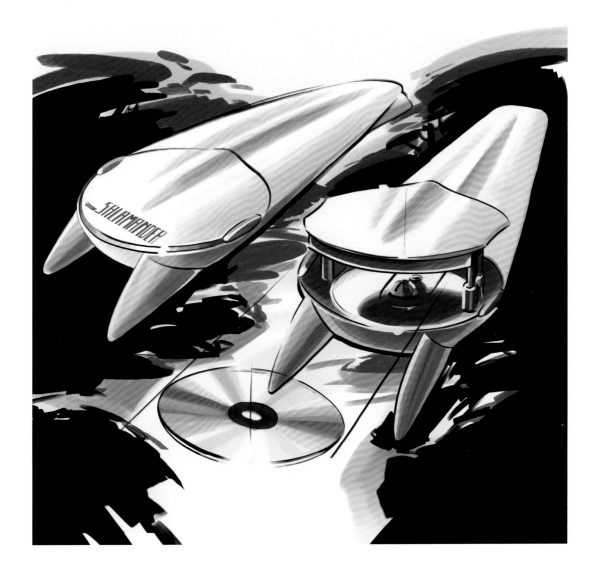

103

'Energy Form' console concept, GK Dynamics, 1998

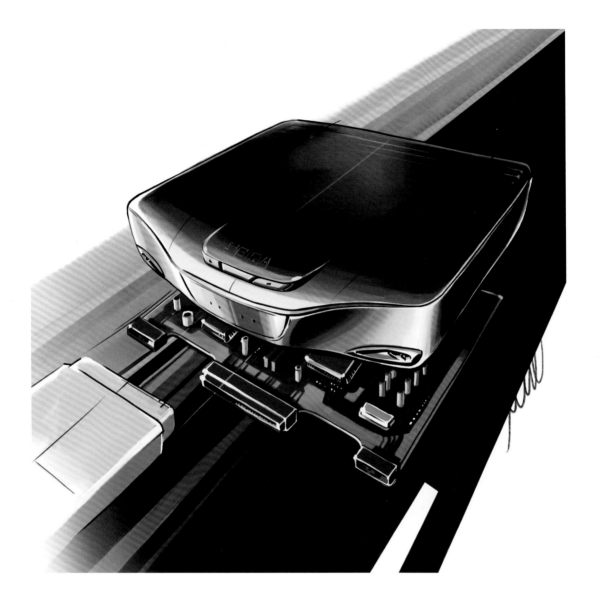

'Energy Form' console concept, GK Dynamics, 1998

Hardware Development

105

'Energy Form' console concept, GK Dynamics, 1998

Dreamcast, 1998
Combining innovative hardware, design and motion-sensing capability years before it was considered the norm, the Sega Dreamcast was a true pioneer of its age and the very first 128-bit console to market. The Dreamcast shares much with Sega's NAOMI arcade hardware, making the console particularly suited to 3D gaming and the flurry of Sega arcade ports that released during its official lifespan of a little over two years.

Dreamcast Controller, 1998
The Dreamcast Controller is widely recognised for its onboard visual memory unit (VMU) slot, which allows for the docking of the innovative storage device. Featuring an analogue control stick, D-pad, four front-facing buttons and dual analogue triggers, the Dreamcast Controller is also notable for its bottom-connected cable and rear slot, primarily for the connection of the Sega Vibration Pack.

Hardware Showcase

Visual Memory Unit, 1998
Functioning not only as a memory card, when plugged into the Dreamcast controller and compatible Dreamcast peripherals, the VMU doubles up as a second screen to complement in-game action. Among the VMU's features is its ability to serve as an independent handheld gaming device – as exemplified in *Sonic Adventure*'s 'Chao Adventure' minigame, which allows players to power-up their Chao creatures while on the move.

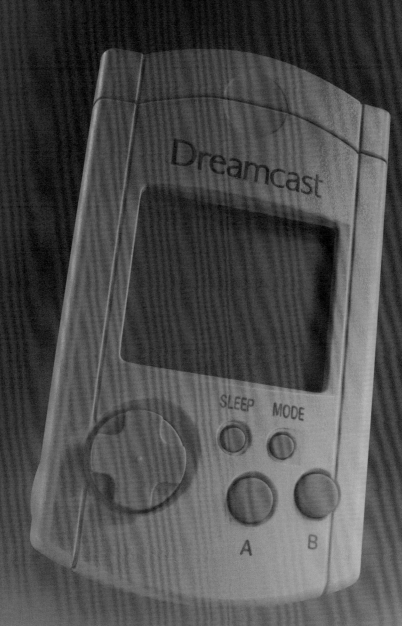

Fishing Controller, 1999
Available in stores shortly after the release of *Sega Bass Fishing*, this unique controller is designed to simulate an authentic fishing rod – albeit without an actual 'rod' attachment. Featuring a reel, analogue stick, A, B, X, Y buttons and rumble, the controller also includes motion-sensing capabilities. Manufactured under licence from Sega, to this day, the Fishing Controller remains videogaming's only official fishing peripheral.

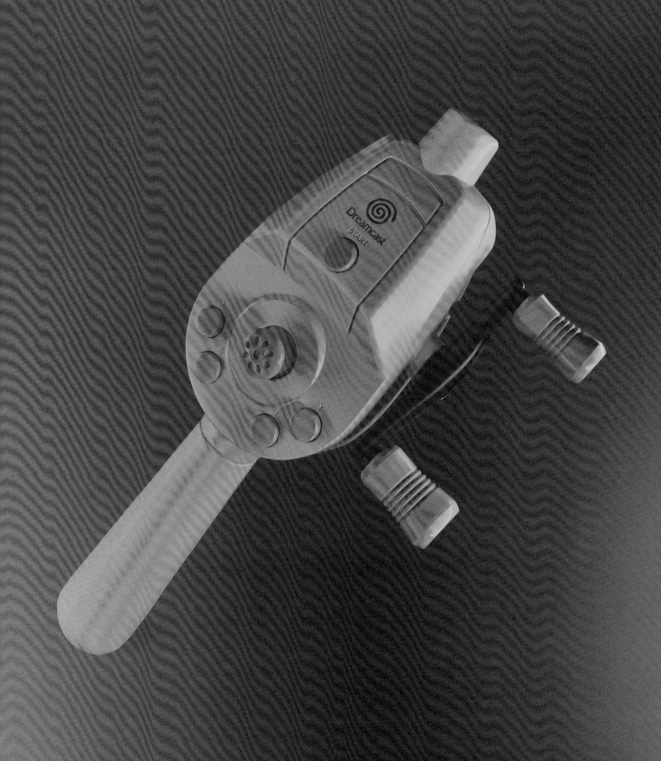

Dreamcast Arcade Stick, 1998
Continuing Sega's long tradition of console stick releases, the Dreamcast Arcade Stick is the perfect companion for gamers wishing to replicate the arcade experience at home. Best suited with 2D titles of the shoot 'em up and fighting genres, the peripheral houses six neon-green buttons, a start button, an eight-axis non-analogue stick and a VMU slot.

Hardware Showcase

Dreamcast Gun (Asia and Europe only), 1999
With an onboard expansion port, the Dreamcast Gun is compatible with the VMU and Vibration Pack. Arriving on the market shortly after the Columbine High School massacre, Sega opted not to release their pistol-shaped accessory in North America – making it available only in Europe and Asia instead. A licensed accessory by Mad Catz was to be the only official Dreamcast light gun available in the US.

Dreamcast Twin Stick (Japan only), 1999
Released only in Japan, the Twin Stick is intended for use with *Cyber Troopers Virtual-On: Oratorio Tangram*. As its name suggests, the controller features two joysticks. Having fewer buttons than most Dreamcast controllers – two buttons at the head of each stick, and both a 'start' and 'pause' button – the Twin Stick also reserves space for a VMU.

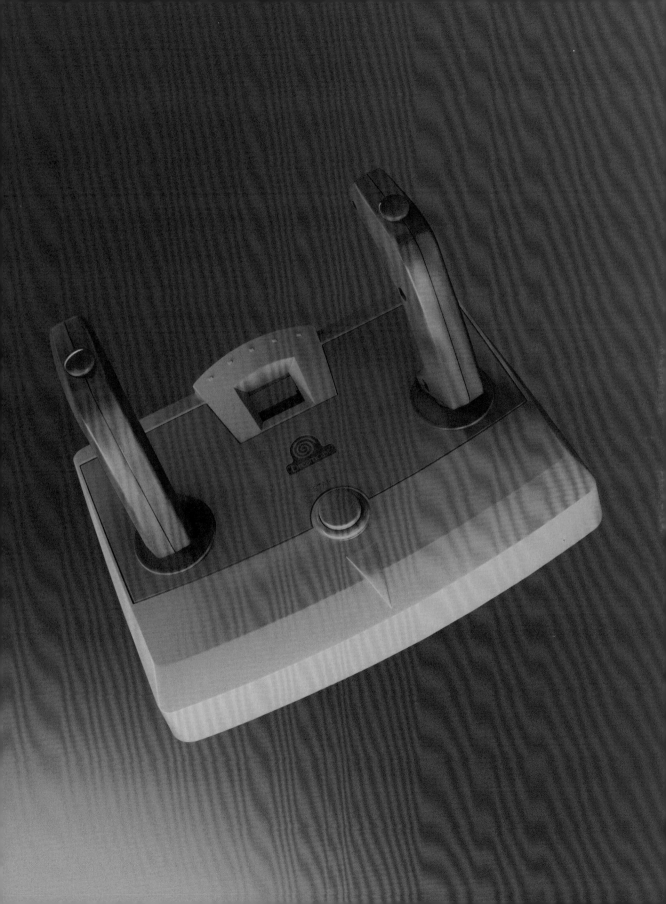

Dreameye (Japan), 2000
Pairing with the Dreamcast via its controller port, the Dreameye is a webcam peripheral capable
of imagery and video to a maximum of 640×640 pixels. Amongst the accessories included in the box
are a microphone headset and microphone card that can be docked in the Dreamcast Controller.
Although no games were compatible with the Dreameye, the camera shipped with photo-editing
software *Visual Park*.

Dreamcast Karaoke (Japan only), 2001
Complete with a microphone and Sega Kara software, the Dreamcast Karaoke functions as an online-only add-on, which allowed users to sing along to music via Sega's servers. These servers were switched off in 2006, taking the entire Sega Kara music library with it. With no available music today, the user is now limited to applying effects and adjusting the volume of their own voice through the hardware.

Hardware Showcase

Divers 2000 Series (Japan only), 2000
Manufactured in association with Sega, CSK and the Fuji Television Network, the Divers 2000 is
a 14-inch CRT television with a functional Dreamcast built in. Bundled with a Controller, Dreameye,
keyboard and remote control, the TV unit features MIDI in/out connectivity, and rows of lights on
its side that flash in sequence with on-screen action. Limited to a run of 200.

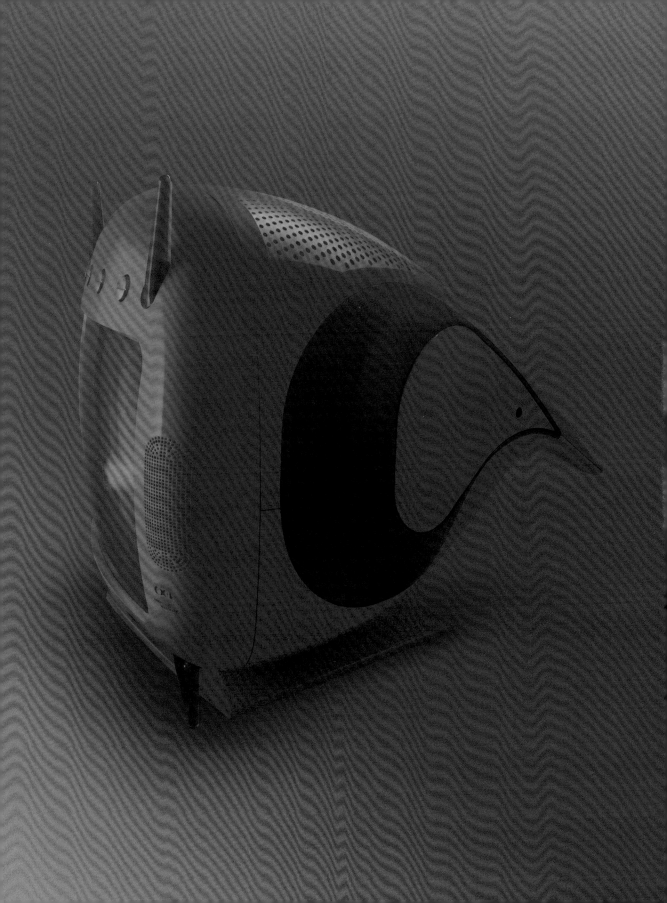

01

02

COSMIC SMASH

03

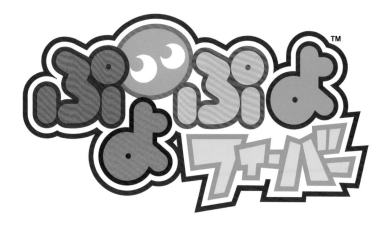

04

05

127

06

01

02

03

Game Production Artwork

04

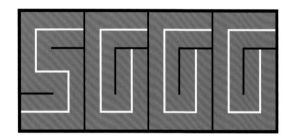

05

129

06

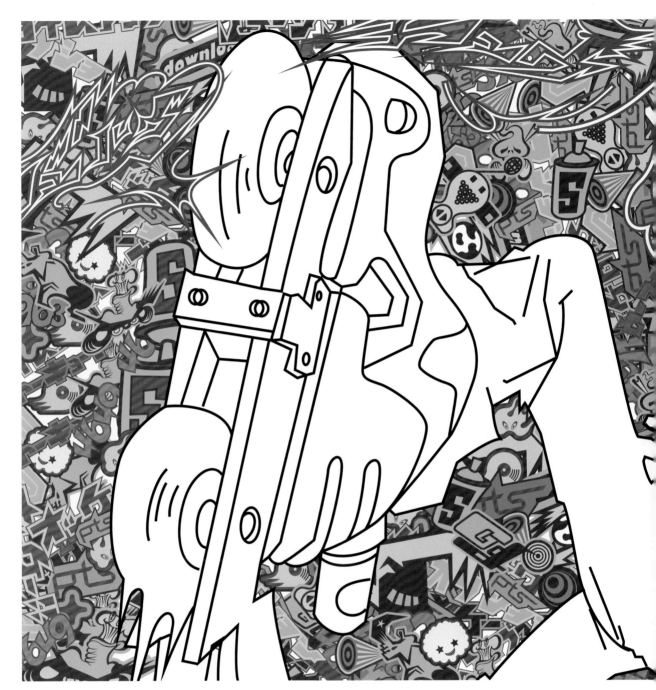

01

Game Production Artwork

01

Game Production Artwork

02

01

02

03

04

136

Game Production Artwork

02

01

Game Production Artwork

139

02

Game Production Artwork

02

01

02

Game Production Artwork

03

04

05

143

01

02

03

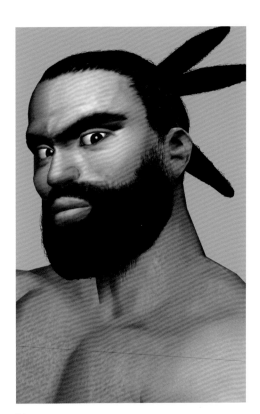

04

144

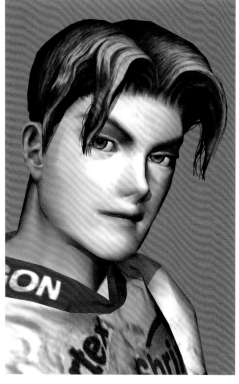

05

06

145

07

08

01

Game Production Artwork

147

01

149

02

151

02

01

02

03

04

05

153

06

154

Game Production Artwork

155

157

158

159

02

01

162

01

165

01

02

169

02

01

02

04

170

03

05

06

07

08

02

173

03

01

02

174

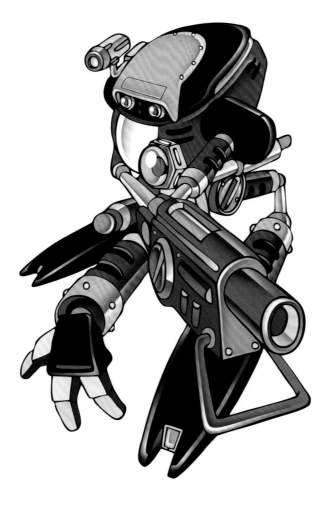

03

175

04

01

02

03

05

04

06

01

02

03

178

04

179

05

06

180

181

02

182

183

01

185

02

Sega Dreamcast: Collected Works

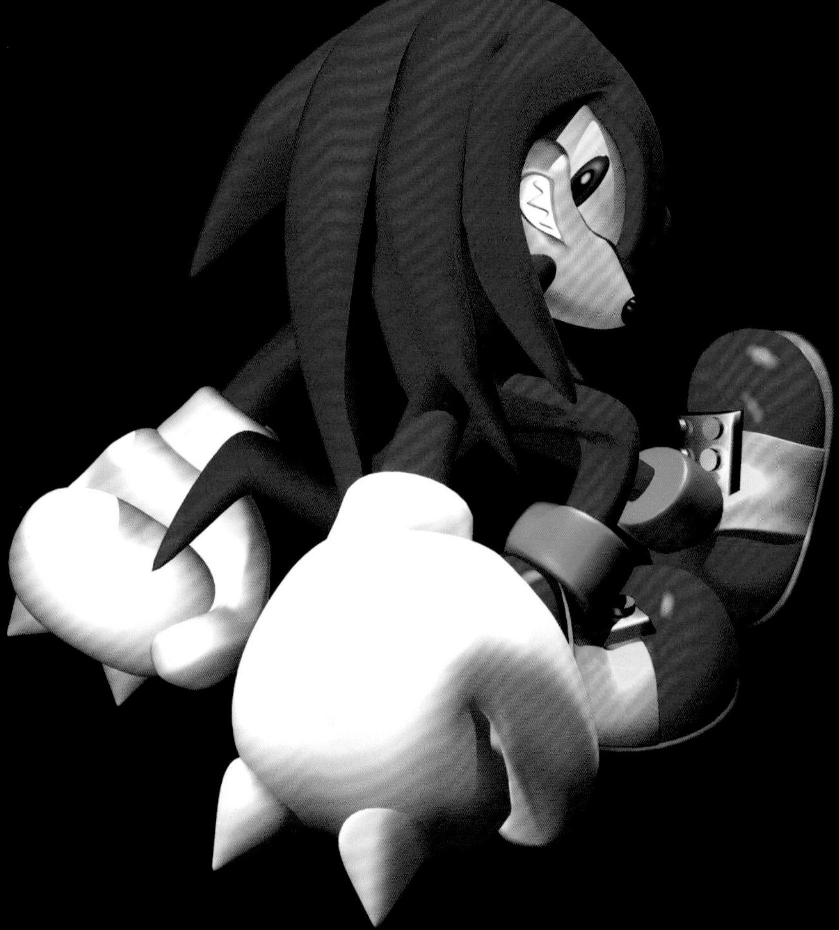

01

02

02

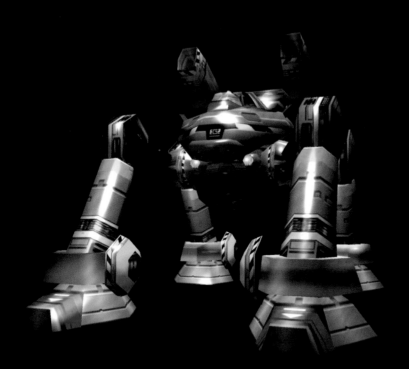

01

03

188

04

189

05

06

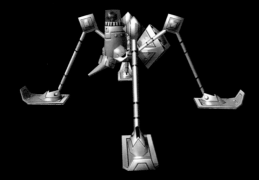

01

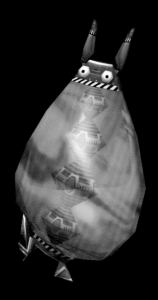

02

03

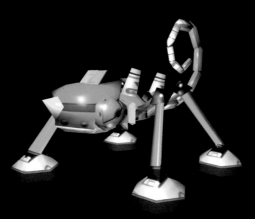

190

04

191

05

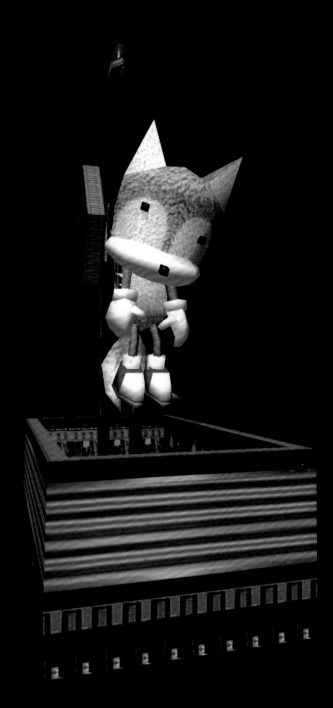

01

Game Production Artwork

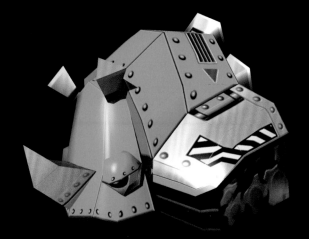

02

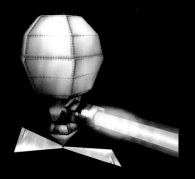

03

04

193

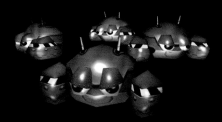

05

01

02

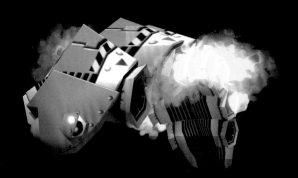

03

194

04

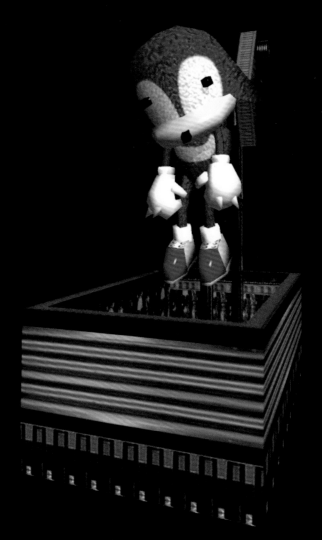

195

05

01

02

Game Production Artwork

02

03

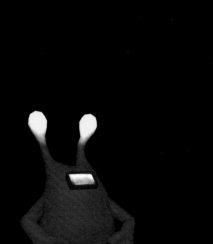

04

199

05

200

201

Sega Dreamcast: Collected Works

202

203

01

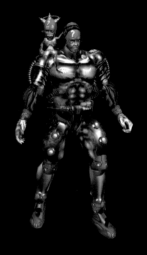

02

03

204

04

06

05

205

Sega Dreamcast: Collected Works

01

02

03

04

06

05

01

02

03

05

04

209

06

Production Artwork Key

126.01
Jet Set Radio, logotype, 2000

126.02
Jet Set Radio, logotype, 2000

126.03
Cosmic Smash, logotype, 2001

127.04
Puyo Puyo Fever, logotype, 2004

127.05
Crazy Taxi, logotype, 1999

127.06
Space Channel 5, logotype, 1999

128.01
Phantasy Star Online, logotype, logotype, 2000

128.02
Crazy Taxi 2, logotype, 2001

128.03
Samba de Amigo, logotype, 1999

129.04
The House of the Dead 2, logotype, 1998

129.05
Segagaga logotype, logotype, 2001

129.06
Virtua Fighter 3, logotype, 1996

130–131.01
Jet Set Radio, box artwork, 2000

132.01
Jet Set Radio, production artwork, 2000

133.02
Phantasy Star Online, box artwork, 2000

134.01, 134.02
Get Bass/Sega Bass Fishing, box artwork, production rendering, 1999

135.03, 135.04
Sega Rally 2, production renderings, 1999

136.01
18 Wheeler: American Pro Trucker, box artwork, 2000

137.02
Outtrigger, production artwork, 2001

138.01
Shenmue, Ryo Hazuki production rendering, 1999

139.02
Shenmue, Shenhua Ling production rendering, 1999

140.01
Shenmue, Ryo Hazuki production rendering, 1999

141.02
Shenmue, Chai production rendering, 1999

142.01
Shenmue, Nozomi Harasaki production rendering, 1999

142.02
Shenmue, Ryo Hazuki production rendering, 1999

143.03
Shenmue II, Wuying Ren production rendering, 2001

143.04
Shenmue II, Joy production rendering, 2001

143.05
Shenmue II, Xiuying Hong production rendering, 2001

144.01
Virtua Fighter 3tb, Aoi Umenokoji production rendering, 1998

144.02
Virtua Fighter 3tb, Lau Chan production rendering, 1998

144.03
Virtua Fighter 3tb, Akira Yuki production rendering, 1998

144.04
Virtua Fighter 3tb, Jeffry McWild production rendering, 1998

145.05
Virtua Fighter 3tb, Lion Rafale production rendering, 1998

145.06
Virtua Fighter 3tb, Jacky Bryant production rendering, 1998

145.07
Virtua Fighter 3tb, Pai Chan production rendering, 1998

145.08
Virtua Fighter 3tb, Dural production rendering, 1998

146.01
Jet Set Radio, Beat production artwork, 2000

147.02
Jet Set Radio, Gum production artwork, 2000

148.01
Jet Set Radio, Garam production artwork, 2000

149.02
Jet Set Radio, Cube production artwork, 2000

150.01
Jet Set Radio, Love Shockers production artwork, 2000

151.02
Jet Set Radio, Noise Tanks production artwork, 2000

152.01
Jet Set Radio, Corn/Tab production artwork, 2000

152.02
Jet Set Radio, Yoyo production artwork, 2000

152.03
Jet Set Radio, Soda/Slate production artwork, 2000

153.04
Jet Set Radio, Sugar/Piranha production artwork, 2000

153.05
Jet Set Radio, Bis/Mew production artwork, 2000

153.06
Jet Set Radio, Combo production artwork, 2000

154.01
Phantasy Star Online, HUcast production artwork, 2000

155.02
Phantasy Star Online, HUmar production artwork, 2000

156.01
Phantasy Star Online, HUnewearl production artwork, 2000

157.02
Phantasy Star Online, RAmar production artwork, 2000

158.01
Phantasy Star Online, RAcast production artwork, 2000

159.02
Phantasy Star Online, RAcaseal production artwork, 2000

160.01
Phantasy Star Online, FOnewearl production artwork, 2000

161.02
Phantasy Star Online, FOmarl production artwork, 2000

162.01
Phantasy Star Online, FOnewm production artwork, 2000

163.02
Phantasy Star Online, Rico Tyrell AKA 'Red Ring Rico' production artwork, 2000

164.01
Shenmue, Ryo Hazuki production artwork, 1999

165.02
Shenmue, Shenhua Ling production artwork, 1999

166.01
Shenmue, Longsun Zhao production artwork, 1999

167.02, 168.01
Shenmue, Chai production artwork, 1999

169.02
Shenmue, Iwao Hazuki production artwork, 1999

170.01
Crazy Taxi 2, Slash production artwork, 2001

170.02
Crazy Taxi 2, Iceman production artwork, 2001

170.03
Crazy Taxi 2, Hot-D production artwork, 2001

170.04
Crazy Taxi 2, Cinnamon production artwork, 2001

171.05
Crazy Taxi, Axel production artwork, 2000

171.06
Crazy Taxi, Joe production artwork, 2000

171.07
Crazy Taxi, Gena production artwork, 2000

171.08
Crazy Taxi, Gus production artwork, 2000

172.01
Sonic Adventure, Sonic the Hedgehog production artwork, 1998

173.02
Sonic Adventure, Knuckles the Echidna production artwork, 1998

173.03
Sonic Adventure, Miles 'Tails' Prower production artwork, 1998

174.01
Sonic Adventure, Big the Cat production artwork, 1998

174.02
Sonic Adventure, Amy Rose production artwork, 1998

175.03
Sonic Adventure, E-102 Gamma production artwork, 1998

175.04
Sonic Adventure, Chao production artwork, 1998

176.01
Puyo Puyo Fever, Rider production artwork, 2004

176.02
Puyo Puyo Fever, Ms. Accord production artwork, 2004

176.03
Puyo Puyo Fever, Carbuncle production artwork, 2004

177.04
Puyo Puyo Fever, Amitie production artwork, 2004

177.05
Puyo Puyo Fever, Onion Pixy production artwork, 2004

177.06
Puyo Puyo Fever, Tarutaru production artwork, 2004

178.01
Puyo Puyo Fever, Donguri Gaeru production artwork, 2004

178.01
Puyo Puyo Fever, Yu production artwork, 2004

178.02
Puyo Puyo Fever, Raffine production artwork, 2004

179.04
Puyo Puyo Fever, Frankensteins production artwork, 2004

179.05
Puyo Puyo Fever, Ocean Prince production artwork, 2004

179.06
Puyo Puyo Fever, Arle Nadja production artwork, 2004

180.01
Outtrigger, Lina production rendering, 1999

181.02
Outtrigger, Jay production rendering, 2001

182.01
Outtrigger, Alain production rendering, 2001

183.02
Outtrigger, Talon production rendering, 2001

184.01
Sonic Adventure, Sonic the Hedgehog production rendering, 1998

185.02
Sonic Adventure, Eggman production rendering, 1998

186.01
Sonic Adventure, Knuckles the Echidna production rendering, 1998

187.02
Sonic Adventure, Amy Rose production rendering, 1998

188.01
Sonic Adventure, Egg Viper production rendering, 1998

188.02
Sonic Adventure, Egg Hornet production rendering, 1998

188.03
Sonic Adventure, Egg Walker production rendering, 1998

189.04
Sonic Adventure, E-101 Mark II production rendering, 1998

189.05
Sonic Adventure, E-103 Delta production rendering, 1998

189.06
Sonic Adventure, E-104 Epsilon production rendering, 1998

190.01
Sonic Adventure, Sweeper production rendering, 1998

190.02
Sonic Adventure, Buyoon production rendering, 1998

190.03
Sonic Adventure, Egg Keeper production rendering, 1998

190.04
Sonic Adventure, Leon production rendering, 1998

191.05
Sonic Adventure, Sonic Doll production rendering, 1998

192.01
Sonic Adventure, Tails Doll production rendering, 1998

193.02
Sonic Adventure, Rhinotank production rendering, 1998

193.03
Sonic Adventure, Egg Beam production rendering, 1998

193.04
Sonic Adventure, Bladed Spinner production rendering, 1998

193.05
Sonic Adventure, Beat production rendering, 1998

194.01
Sonic Adventure, Cart Kiki production rendering, 1998

194.02
Sonic Adventure, Ice Ball production rendering, 1998

194.03
Sonic Adventure, Boa-Boa production rendering, 1998

194.04
Sonic Adventure, Spiky Spinner production rendering, 1998

195.05
Sonic Adventure, Knuckles Doll production rendering, 1998

196.01, 197.02, 198.03
Space Channel 5, Ulala production renderings, 1999

199.02–199.05
Space Channel 5, Morolian production renderings, 1999

200.01
The House of the Dead 2, David production rendering, 1999

201.02
The House of the Dead 2, Steve/Andrew production rendering, 1999

202.01
The House of the Dead 2, Gary Stewart production rendering, 1999

203.02
The House of the Dead 2, James Taylor production rendering, 1999

204.01
Zombie Revenge, Black Magician production rendering, 1999

204.02
Zombie Revenge, UDS-TP II production rendering, 1999

204.03
Zombie Revenge, UDS-04C production rendering, 1999

205.04
Zombie Revenge, UDS-06B production rendering, 1999

205.05
Zombie Revenge, Warm Hedlin production rendering, 1999

205.06
Zombie Revenge, UDS-05 production rendering, 1999

206.01–206.03
Crazy Taxi, Axel's taxi production renderings, 2000

207.04–207.06
Crazy Taxi, BD-Joe's taxi production renderings, 2000

208.01–208.03
Crazy Taxi, Gus' taxi production renderings, 2000

209.04–209.06
Crazy Taxi, Gena's taxi production renderings, 2000

Making
Shenmue

Developer
Sega AM2

Release
29 December 1999

Interviewees
Yu Suzuki, creator
Keiji Okayasu, game director
Kenji Eno, director, *D2*

Shenmue, title screen tests, 1999

For a videogame that, at the time of its release was the most expensive yet made, and which laid the blueprint followed by most so-called 'open-world' games, *Shenmue* is a surprisingly ponderous adventure. Set in 1986, in the sleepy port city of Yokosuka, the game follows the humdrum life of 18-year-old Ryo Hazuki as he glumly hunts for his father's killer. It is a game that, in its opening chapters, at least, follows the monotonous routines of the suburb in which it's set. You spend your time rifling through drawers, wandering the streets, taking on deadbeat part-time jobs and, in the gaps between your daily chores, asking local pensioners what, if anything, they might know about Lan Di, the man Hazuki suspects of killing his father.

Today, it can all seem a little dry and routine. At the time, however, the chance to experience domestic tedium in the context of a videogame, where we were used to seeing only the rip-roaring extremities of human existence, was weirdly breathtaking. By forcing us to move at walking speed, or to always be home by bedtime, *Shenmue* slowed us down to the point where, finally, we had a chance to be truly present in the simulated world, to notice the flourishes and details (and what details: the slot machines in the game were tested to meet the standards of Las Vegas machines). It detached us from notions of power fantasy and allowed us to adjust properly to the rhythms and strictures of the character Ryo Hazuki's life, with all its teenage boundaries and impositions.

The resulting bond between player, character and world remains one of the strongest yet seen, as evidenced, years later, by the fans' insistence that Yu Suzuki finish that which he began.

Yu Suzuki

As a director, I used to publish one game per year on average at that time, sometimes two games per year, but that was the period when we challenged ourselves to create games in the shortest time. I liked new challenges and there were lots of things I wanted to do, so I remember feeling that producing one game per year would not be challenging enough. Since I was mostly working on arcade games, I wanted a game without any time constraints on the player. I created a prototype on Saturn and planned a full RPG based on *Virtua Fighter*'s setting and technology. At the time it was known as *Virtua Fighter RPG*. That evolved into *Shenmue*.

Keiji Okayasu

Shenmue was being developed for the Sega Saturn. Pretty soon they realised that the Saturn's specifications might not meet the expectations we had set for the software. So development moved to the Dreamcast instead. Two things went through my mind when I heard this: firstly, relief that there would be better hardware with higher specs, and, secondly, a sense of annoyance that we would have to start all over again in order to make the game compatible with this new hardware.

YS

I was initially quite particular about the structure of the game. I wanted there to be five hours of movie scenes, four hours of fighting, four hours of searching rooms for

215

Shenmue, Ryo Hazuki character model, 1999

Making Shenmue

clues, eight hours of conversation, four hours to study and train martial arts in-game, four hours in 'dungeons', four hours of story and 12 hours of 'other' activities. In total, that came to about 45 hours. I wanted to make a game you could play for a long time without getting tired of the gameplay.

KO

Suzuki told us that the old RPGs such as *Ultima* and *Wizardry* had once evolved into *Dragon Quest* and *Final Fantasy* and that the time had come to evolve those games into something different and new. I was a big fan of *Dragon Quest* and *Final Fantasy* as a player so, when I heard his thoughts, I was curious to hear what the difference was going to be from those two games. I thought, 'What is it he is trying to create?'

YS

When the title changed to *Shenmue*, I rethought the game design. I wanted the game to follow three principles: leisure, fullness and gentleness. I wanted the game to be open-world, with cinematic quick-time events and free-flowing battles. My goal was to make a game that fused gameplay and film.

KO

The hardest challenge was trying to understand what Suzuki wanted to create. All the team members automatically used *Dragon Quest* and *Final Fantasy* as reference points, because those were the most familiar RPGs. But Suzuki disapproved. When he tried to explain what he wanted, the rest of us struggled to understand him. We were at a loss about what to do, time and again. For example, normally in

RPGs, if a player talks to non-player characters [NPCs] to get important clues, they always repeat the same thing, no matter how many times they talk to them. But Yu was like, 'It's not right that they can only say the same thing over and over again like a tape recorder.' Then I told him that players might miss hearing important clues if they changed what they said. We decided to add a notepad to the system where players could jot down important information they'd collected.

YS

Every NPC in the game operated on their own 'schedule'. One day, during testing, we noticed that one area was empty. There were no people going about their lives there. It took us a while to figure out what had happened. One morning, all of the NPCs in the warehouse district had gone to get breakfast at the convenience store at the same specific time. Because there were so many bodies in the store, they became stuck in the shop. We had to install an automatic door and limit the occupancy to solve that one.

KO

I remember Suzuki saying that there should be a variety of vegetables in the vegetable shop. Someone asked him, 'Will players actually be able to buy and use those vegetables as an item?' Then Yu said, 'It would be ideal but too difficult so having them in the background is enough.' The first guy countered: 'Then what's the point of putting in all this effort just to make a mere background image?' And Suzuki replied, 'Because it's not a vegetable shop if it doesn't have lots of different vegetables.'

217

Shenmue, Wuying Ren production artwork, 1999

Making Shenmue

Shenmue, Shenhua Ling production artwork, 1999

YS

It's true: we managed to make the world's first open-world game.

KO

Shenmue was created by delving deeply into two questions, or tensions, really. Firstly, there was the question of realism. We soon realised that, if we pursued realism too stringently, *Shenmue* wouldn't work as a game. So how far should we go? Secondly, there was the question of scope: just how much effort should we put into areas which were not directly related to gameplay? Answering these questions was a real trial-and-error process.

KO

I remember more about the team management than technical stuff and development, because I was a facilitator for the big project with lots of developers from AM2, Sega employees from other departments, helpers from a subcontracting company and people from temporary-employment agencies. Prior to *Shenmue* I had experience leading a small team with around 10 people, so it was very much a first for me to be running a team which ran into triple digits.

YS

By the end of the project there were more than 300 people on the team. At the time, there was no project management software. We just used an action item list in Excel. At one point, that document had more than 10,000 to-dos.

KO

Of course we encountered some technical challenges while we were trying to create something new... But I was working hard every day to resolve relationship issues. Some personal conflicts were like something out of a TV drama. My responsibility was creating a good environment so that Suzuki and the rest of the team could focus on creating a game.

YS

Because of the type of the project, which was large-scale and agile, *Shenmue* gave us lots of things to discover, and valuable challenges. On the other hand, it was a very tough project to manage.

KO

To be honest, I had no idea how people would react to the game as it had lots of unprecedented elements. But it turned out that people loved those elements. To me, it was refreshing and surprising to hear that players found it fun to see each character's daily routine. As for sales, I wanted it to sell like crazy as it was such a tough project.

Kenji Eno

Shenmue is just an extraordinary game. It's a type of game I would also develop, but I don't think I could have done it at Yu Suzuki's level of quality. As an analogy, developing *Shenmue* is like setting up a perfect domino effect. It's beautiful when you watch all the dominos topple in succession, but the process of setting each one is not easy. One would ask, how can they make a game with all those details?

220

YS

Favourite is not quite the right word for this but *Shenmue* is the title to which I am more emotionally attached than any other.

221

Shenmue, Guizhang Chen, Yaowen Chen, Dou Niu and Nozomi Harasaki production artworks, 1999

Making
Space
Channel 5

Developer
United Game Artists

Release
29 December 1999

Interviewee
Tetsuya Mizuguchi, producer

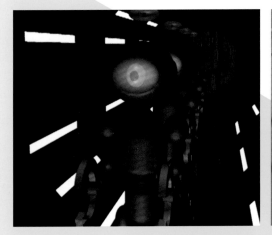

Space Channel 5, 'Project D.G.' proof of concept video, 1999

Tetsuya Mizuguchi's lunge from making racing games for Sega's arcade division to *Space Channel 5*, a soap-opera music game set in space, is almost as extreme as a *Sega Rally* hairpin bend. It was, however, a career move that Mizuguchi, a dedicated club-goer and music aficionado, had long been considering. Following a move of office from the corporate wasteland of Haneda to the thumping heart of Shibuya, ground zero for Tokyo's music and fashion scenes (and the setting for that other classic Dreamcast game, *Jet Set Radio*), Mizuguchi began work on a game that was quite unlike any other.

In *Space Channel 5*, you play as Ulala, a pink-haired news reporter ripped from cheesy American seventies sci-fi, who dances her way through an alien invasion while rescuing human hostages, while fighting for TV ratings. Camply idiosyncratic, the delightful weirdness of the project was only heightened in the sequel, which featured a cameo from Michael Jackson; the pair of games stand alone in the small pantheon of music games, and are a bright relic of a vanished era, never to be repeated.

Tetsuya Mizuguchi

I built a team called R&D 9, which was later rebranded United Game Artists. We started with about 10 people. I didn't like Haneda, where Sega was based at the time, as there was nothing around. Sega had been bought by CSK, a holding company that owned a building in the very centre of Shibuya, just two minutes from the station. At the time, the CEO changed to Shoichiro Irimajiri, who had come to the company from Honda. Everything was fresh and

new. I told Irimajiri I wanted to move to Shibuya, and to make *Rez*, and he told me, that's fine. I had managed to negotiate this complete freedom; I didn't have to convince anyone about my game ideas. I had the success of *Sega Rally* backing me up, I suppose. That's why they went for it.

TM

I wanted to do something new. I loved music and wanted to make new experiences. Arcade games were a huge market. But music games were, at most, a niche. Even *PaRappa the Rapper* was not out yet. I spent so much time thinking about what kind of project I wanted to make, and who I wanted to work with. The kernel of the idea for *Space Channel 5* was actually someone else's, initially: [Takashi] Yuda's. He had an idea to create a traditional music video that rolled as the player tapped the buttons correctly, in time with the music. It was a very serious fighting game that used a rhythm mechanic. I asked whether they would like me to produce their game idea, but, if they allowed me, I would change it dramatically. We started thinking about how we could make it fun and bright and quirky. That was the start of *Space Channel 5*.

TM

The executives asked me to come to one meeting in Haneda each week, a roundtable meeting to check the progress of the Dreamcast development and its games. They wanted me to report what was happening in Shibuya. I agreed to go but I hated it. I was completely concentrating on the game and the creative aspects of the work, then they wanted me to talk in the meetings about sales projections and competitors and whatnot. I just wanted to get back to Shibuya.

TM

For our research we watched all of Michael Jackson's music videos. We spent so many hours going to musicals, everything from *Stomp* to Broadway – every musical we could afford tickets to. Musicals were ideal reference material because they merge song and narrative. They create this kind of synergistic spiral that keeps the crowd going. We wanted to transport the same experience into something interactive, using a call-and-response dynamic. We did so much research, and that's how the elements that you see in my games were injected.

TM

We made a huge Morolian and placed it in Shibuya for the launch. We made a fake newspaper, with a headline about how an alien had invaded Shibuya, and we handed it out to passers-by. It was filled with articles. The entire interaction at Shibuya turned into this alien invasion scene. It was all staged, but it was almost like the news was hitting as the invasion was still occurring. It was this huge spectacle; very exciting.

TM

Now, Michael Jackson was a huge videogame fan. He came to visit Sega quite often. There was a thread of communication between him and us. During one of the visits we were about a month out of mastering *Space Channel 5*. We showed it to him. He said, 'How can I be a part of the game?' We were so close to launch and there was just no time

to make it happen. The ideal scenario for us was to save this for a sequel. So, in the end, we went back to him with a plan for a cameo appearance. I wasn't sure if he was going to be OK with what we proposed, or if he was going to ask for a larger scale involvement. But he was totally happy with our idea. He really just wanted to be a part of the project, I think. As soon as we had the 'yes', the team worked on it for about two weeks. It was such a short time.

TM

I told Michael that I needed vocal performances to put in the game: 'Hey!', 'Chu!' and all the rest of those exclamations. He recorded himself and sent me a tape. The problem was that he spoke incredibly softly. We put the effects in the game but they felt totally wrong because the main character has very high energy levels in her vocal recording. So I had to email him back to ask him if he'd re-record the vocals with higher energy. Finally he sent another tape. It was better, but still not quite as high energy as I'd hoped.

TM

It was difficult to catch people's reaction to the games, but when I saw people playing them, there was a good response. I think people who didn't take the time to play were probably more confused, but there was a strong word-of-mouth around *Space Channel 5*.

226

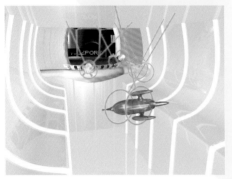

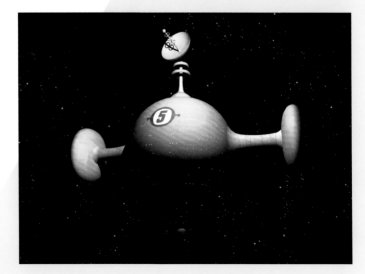

Space Channel 5, environment renders, 1999/2000

Making
Crazy Taxi

Developer
Hitmaker

Release
24 January 2000 (Dreamcast)

Interviewee
Kenji Kanno, director

Crazy Taxi, production artworks, 1999

Making Crazy Taxi

With a bit of effort, anything, a decent game designer will try to convince you, can be turned into a videogame. Taxi driving is no exception, although it took *Crazy Taxi*'s director, Kenji Kanno, several weeks to convince the rest of the development team of the soundness of his vision. Today, the idea seems dizzyingly obvious: race against the clock to collect passengers and deliver them to their chosen destinations, with your high-score measured in the dollars and cents of an aggregate fare. It is the inverse of the kind of fetch quest you might find in a role-playing game, where you must deliver the quest-giver themselves to their goal before desperately scanning the streets in search of another.

Kanno claims that the idea came to him when stuck in traffic. He longed to cross the central reservation and take off in the opposite direction. From this urge, Sega's AM3 division (before it was renamed, somewhat hopefully, as 'Hitmaker') assigned a team of 12 programmers and artists to work with Kanno. A year and a half later, *Crazy Taxi* debuted in arcades, injecting the coin-op industry with a burst of blue-sky thinking (and, like *Sonic Adventure*, *Super Monkey Ball* and all the rest, a burst of actual Sega blue sky overhead). The Dreamcast port, overseen by Kanno, showed just how smooth the transition from Sega's arcade hardware to home console could be.

231

Kenji Kanno

I always had a thing for amusement parks. I would become completely immersed and would be oblivious to the passing of time. During my university years, I was hoping to work for a company where I would get to design amusement parks, but there were only a few companies who do that kind of work. I asked my university professor for advice and he suggested that I apply to Sega or Namco as he'd heard they had launched a theme park division. That was the first springboard. During the interview with Sega, I remember telling the interviewers that I wanted to create spaces where people could have fun and forget the time.

KK

At that time, all the car games for arcade machines were racing games and they were very similar in terms of content. I felt that we needed to create a new style of racing game before the genre became completely stagnant; I wanted to make a car game which would provide players with a totally new experience. I started looking at ideas which would enable players to experience the dynamism of a car chase. A few months passed without coming up with good material, then one of my workmates from another team said 'You could just have a taxi driving at a furious speed' as a sort of joke. And the word 'taxi' stayed in my head. I thoroughly reworked the concept under the title '*Crazy Taxi*', then re-submitted it to my boss. What I wanted to achieve was a completely new type of car game.

KK

The most important thing was to stick to the concept throughout the project. The smallest misunderstanding could make the team go in different directions. It's hard to make sure that everyone working on the project is heading in the same direction and sticking to the original idea.

KK

Now, around half of my teammates were strongly against taxi driving as the subject matter and it took me about a month to convince them. They were worried that the concept wouldn't be cool enough to base an arcade game around. As for the stress, it was frustrating not being able to get what I had in my head into the game. I remember shouting for joy when I finally worked out the core game design. I'm sure people who saw me thought I was a nutcase.

KK

The first project I got involved in at Sega was a very tough one with lots of overtime. And I right away questioned myself: 'Why do I even want to work for Sega?' At that time, we started location testing our new game in real arcades. The first actual customers I watched play my game were two high-school girls. They started cheering as soon as they started playing. I could not stop crying seeing these total strangers having fun playing something I had created. I will never forget how moving it was. That gave me the answer I was looking for and that is why I'm still working at Sega. That said, I've also seen angry customers kicking the machines because they hate my game. That made me aware that most important thing is to picture a customer playing a game when you create something.

KK

I was developing *Crazy Taxi* for the arcade machine, when my boss and I concluded that we should not port it over to other machines in the future because if we did we would inevitably have to compromise our idea due to hardware limitations. But, after the arcade machine was released, my boss came up to me and said, 'A change of plan: we are porting it.' I remember being at my wit's end. The engineers and I were torn thinking, 'Can we really duplicate the original game on the new machine?'

KK

Memory was the main difference between the arcade machine and the Dreamcast, so the main question was whether or not we could display the entire levels. The engineers used all sorts of techniques and we came up with the system which displays streams in the course. It was the one and only challenge we came across.

232

233

Crazy Taxi, production renderings, 1999

Making
Jet Set Radio

Developer
Smilebit

Release
29 June 2000

Interviewees
Masayoshi Kikuchi, director
Takayuki Kawagoe, producer
Hideki Naganuma, composer
Tetsuya Mizuguchi, creator

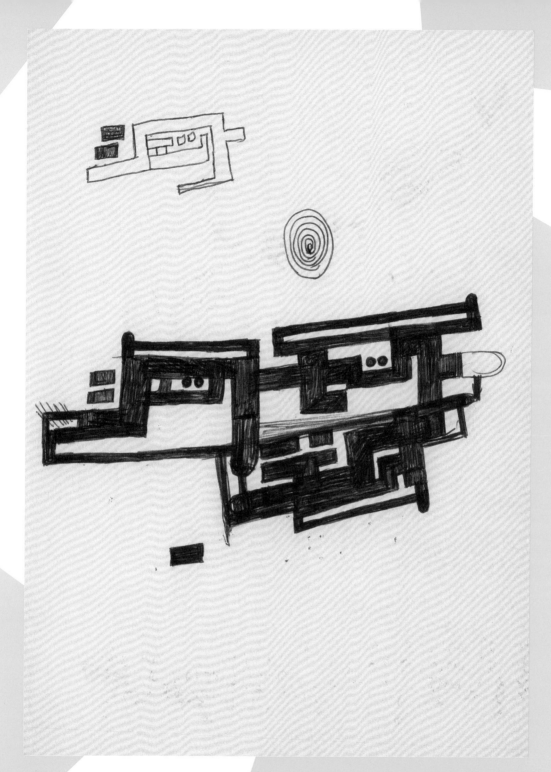

Jet Set Radio/Jet Grind Radio, logotype production artwork, grAphic tAkorA, 1999

Making Jet Set Radio

While an army of programmers and artists at AM2 doggedly pursued realism in Yu Suzuki's magnum opus *Shenmue*, their colleagues at Smilebit charged at full pelt in the opposite direction. No glum daily schedules played out beneath grey skies in *Jet Set Radio*'s world, which was painted in exuberant colours and swayed to a soundtrack that, two decades on, is as crisp as the day it was first burned to GD-ROM.

Set in Shibuya, that architectural shorthand for all that is young and vibrant and fashionable in Japan's capital, you skate on luminous rollerblades, spraying complicated murals on blank walls while pursued by furious policemen. *Jet Set Radio* has aged (the sequel, released shortly after the Dreamcast's demise, flattened out many of its interactive foibles) but the aesthetic is perennially fresh, a blaze of life and colour that quickly rubbed off to leave an indelible mark on Dreamcast's own legacy.

Masayoshi Kikuchi

I desperately wanted to create a game which young people in their teens and 20s and who didn't necessarily play videogames would find cool. That meant using different motifs. I wanted to create a new way to enjoy 3D space. It all kicked off when Ryuta Ueda, one of the art team on the *Panzer Dragoon* series, showed me some rough sketches of characters he had drawn. He said, 'Let's set up a project together.' We brainstormed ideas which we wanted to express in the form of a game. We grouped them together but it was just sort of a lump. Nothing was clear cut, and the game remained elusive for a while. But we were young and passionate.

Takayuki Kawagoe

Kikuchi and Ueda, the art director, wanted to make a new kind of action game. We came up with lots of ideas, one after another. There was particular character equipment, air tricks, grinding along rails and wall kicks. They also wanted to use a cel-shading technique, which we called 'manga dimension'.

MK

It took so long to make the game interesting. The turning point was when we made a prototype where characters could run through a 3D environment. It was as if we found a signpost in a foggy mess.

Tetsuya Mizuguchi

Our offices were in Shibuya, so often the creators of other games, who were working in Haneda, would visit us. I think they just wanted to escape Haneda. The *Jet Set Radio* team would come to look at our game, and show off theirs.

MK

Shibuya had an iconic place in Japanese pop culture. There was actually a Shinjuku motif as well, which took place at night for Benten-Cho, and a melancholy old streetscape, which made Japanese people feel nostalgic.

Hideki Naganuma

The first big title I worked on was *Sega Rally 2* for the Dreamcast. I composed some tracks which you could really dance to and created a sense of speed. The sound director knew I was good at making that music style so they made me main composer for *Jet Set Radio*. I was still a newbie so I didn't push for the job; they offered me the position.

237

HN

My main responsibility was composing tracks. The rest of my time was spent giving direction to outsourced artists, selecting tracks, creating looping tracks, and editing and processing music. I was also in charge of sound effects for bonus stages on other versions – *Jet Grind Radio* in North America and *De La Jet Set Radio* in Japan.

HN

I got the inspiration for the music from the game's charismatic style, and the cool characters created by Kota Ueda. At the start, I listened to a lot of music every day to research what would fit. Big Beat and Digital Rock were hot in UK clubs; I thought it would fit the game's world. Then I mixed in elements of funk and hip-hop. I had creative block at times but, as I was enjoying making music, I didn't feel any stress.

HN

One of my fondest memories of that time was when I was sleeping in the office when I was composing. I was making 'Rock It On', alone late at night at my desk, cutting shouty vocals by female singers into small bits, and I was changing the order of the words and repeating the same phrases to make meaningless words. I remember finding that very funny, thinking, 'How the hell is this middle-aged lady singing like this? She is so loud and crazy sounding!' and laughing hard by myself.

HN

Almost everything was done on my Mac. At first, I would narrow down ideas for the main theme and picture the final track, using the theme in my head. I'd then start composing the first and second bars in different ways, using guitar riffs, funky basslines, drum patterns and vocals. Then I'd start creating low-pass areas like the drums and the bass track. Then I overlapped middle-pass areas, such as guitar cutting, and synthesiser and piano chords and sometimes I put horn sections and then strings on the top.

HN

I did everything at my desk in the office: composing, recording and mixing. We also had meetings with programmers to discuss how to add drama, checking sound effects and fixing them until it was all perfect. I think the entire process lasted around ten months. In *Jet Set Radio*, the soundtrack can be heard non-stop, even in the loading screens, until you turn it off. I remember discussing a lot with the programmers how we could do that.

HN

Since we didn't have social media at the time, and I was in the office every day, we didn't get to hear player feedback directly. However, when the game was announced at E3 in 2000, I remember feeling very happy when I heard from the rest of the team that the game was well received, especially overseas.

TK

We were eager to release our game before the PlayStation 2 came out to prove that the Dreamcast was the superior machine.

HN

I felt proud that we had made a world-class game but I also heard via word-of-mouth that it wasn't selling as well as expected in Japan.

239

Jet Set Radio/Jet Grind Radio, logotype production artwork, grAphic tAkorA, 1999

Making
Segagaga

Developer
Sega AM3

Release
29 March 2001

Interviewee
Tez Okano, creator

SGGG (pronounced 'Segagaga') is a videogame about a console-maker on the verge of collapse, made by a console-maker on the verge of collapse. Released in March 2001, just as Sega began its withdrawal from the console manufacturing business, *SGGG* exemplifies why the company of the era is so painfully missed. Touching upon many genres, from business management sim to shoot 'em up, it is at heart a role-playing game. Except, instead of being asked to rescue the princess or divert world destruction, your challenge is to save Sega from the real-life forces against which every videogame company battles. *SGGG* invites us into the boardroom to ask, implausibly, 'Why don't you see if you can do any better?'

A glorious act of corporate postmodernism envisioned and executed by one of Sega's little-known, yet most vivacious designers, Tez Okano, *SGGG* subjects us to the challenges and frustrations with which Sega was intimately familiar at the time. The issues the game examines are evergreen, from the overworked, underpaid development staff ('High stress levels often drive our staff members to become... subhuman,' remarks one NPC. 'They're violent and need to be caged. But we need them to make good games. This is the unfortunate truth of the games industry.') to the hard-nosed executive wanting only safe, money-making sequels. The result is an extraordinary piece of self-reflection that was unprecedented, and unrepeated.

Tez Okano
The development started at a time when the Dreamcast was doing relatively well. I love the genre of 'metafiction': using yourself as the base content of a game was an appealing idea. There are tons of interesting and fun things in the games industry. I also believed that, if Sega was going to be the base content for a game, a favourable portrayal would seem a bit cheap. So bringing some of our weaknesses or not-so-favourable elements to a positive conclusion would be fun.

TO
The first time I made a presentation of the game [to Sega management], it was a huge success. We had such a laugh! But they didn't think that I was serious about making the game. So I had to go back for a second try: 'Actually, guys – that was not a joke.' Eventually, [Sega president Hisao] Oguchi gave me some money and then I entered the 'underground' phase of the project, spending two years in secrecy to develop it, unnoticed. When I finally brought the finalised version of the game to a meeting, it triggered tons of issues. Even so, Sega's situation had changed dramatically, and it was thought that such a game would not hurt the company.

TO
The hardest thing was to keep the project secret. I thought there would be little anyone could do about it once the game was completed, but, up to that moment, anything could have happened if someone found about its development. I'm basically a mangaka [comic artist], so in a way I know about direction. I was able to put many of my personal skills into this title, knowing the limited scale of its development, which went well

242

243

Segagaga, Tarou Sega, Yayoi Haneda, Secret Director Cool and Alisa character production artworks, 2000

Sega Dreamcast: Collected Works

Segagaga, Tarou Sega and Yayoi Haneda character production artworks, 2000

Making Segagaga

because I wasn't able to ask for anyone else's help inside Sega.

TO

SGGG was a name that I just wrote on my early game design document. There is no special meaning. There is absolutely no relation with the song 'Radio Ga Ga'. In my memo note, the two names that remained to call the game design document were 'Sega Sega' and 'Segagaga'. I was advised to put 'Sega' in the game name but I didn't think it was cool to do so. I chose the one which included the reference to Sega but with a touch that made the 'Sega factor' less intrusive.

TO

I was involved in every aspect of the game. I designed it but also supervised the programming, the sound, the graphics – everything. I was director, producer – everything from just one being: me. I was also in charge of promoting the game. You have to understand that we – no, I – had just about ¥30,000 (US$270) to promote this title! I used ¥20,000 (US$180) to get a mask made by a professional pro-wrestler that I could use to promote the game everywhere. In many ways, the game established some industry firsts in terms of budgets alone.

TO

[After I first showed the game to Sega management] I had a ton of changes on my hands: almost 300 issues to fix. I tried to narrow down those fixes to about 100. So you could think of the version that went to consumers as a light version of the original one. For example, one big fix was the opening, where I wanted to feature [Saturn-era Sega marketing

character] Segata Sanshiro but, because of copyright issues we could not secure him. The ending had to be changed as well because we used a character that was the property of a magazine here in Japan. I had to change that character to the *Get Bass* fish! Oh yes, I had also to change the red Ferrari which symbolised AM2 to... well, the only red thing that I could come up with was a shrimp. In Japanese, 'car' is 'kuruma', and there is a very popular shrimp, or 'ebi', that we eat here in Japan which is named 'kuruma ebi'! It was too bad – I wanted so much to see that Ferrari flying!

TO

There is one key phrase in the original game design document that introduces the project: 'To create a game with one hundredth of *Shenmue*'s budget and sell one hundred times more!' You have to remember that, at that time, the entire company was focused on *Shenmue*; the entire building #3 was used for the army developing the game. Now, I'm a man of ideas. Sega is not a company of ideas, it is a company of technologies, centred on amusement machines and quests, like simulating the human body, for instance. We were hardware-driven since the beginning. When a guy like me steps in, it is uncomfortable. Imagine that I come to a meeting and say: 'Guys! I have a new idea that...' The reply would be: 'Please, we are busy with *Shenmue*.'

TO

Using my colleagues in the game was difficult, of course! That is where I had to use my ingenuity to mask my true intention – pretending it was for a project based on Sega's history and so on. I remember going to see [Yuji] Naka. He is passionate about gaming, and he is very open-minded, so he gave me positive feedback about the game. But I remember he asked me not to use Sonic in weird ways. So Sonic appears at the end of the game in quite a positive way.

TO
There is one key sequence in the game when our beloved CEO, Mr [Shoichiro] Irimajiri, appears. I wanted him to appear in a very realistic way; I asked the animation company to really make him look as close to real as possible. At first, he looked too much like an animated character – I had to insist that we focus on realism. And then he stepped down. So we ended up using a mosaic effect on his appearance in the game...

TO
Of course [Sega's decision to stop Dreamcast production] was a shock but, having said that, it was not entirely a surprise. Really, Sega is a company that made money from arcades, not the consumer market. The money we made from arcades went to finance the consumer activity and develop another aspect of Sega. So the fact that the Dreamcast didn't have the rocket start we all hoped for was an early indication, maybe, of things to come. It is true that, being from the AM divisions, my view of the consumer division was a bit 'cold'. While gaming as a whole was going well, at that point we also started to see early signs of the boom fading away. I'm talking here about the entire industry, not just Sega. The Japanese bubble burst in 1993 – that was the start of the recession and

the economic downturn. At the same time, the gaming industry was continuing like it was still boom time. Coincidentally, we were making *SGGG* at this turning point.

TO
Near the end of the game, the hero is fired because his company closes, and he finds refuge in a game store near Sega that actually existed. The store manager is Alex Kidd – he was also fired from Sega, when Sonic arrived. The message to the hero is that no matter how bad things look, there is no point in crying over the industry. You have to carry on – just like Alex Kidd, who is working hard.

TO
The game ends in a very special, though perhaps strange way. The main character decides to keep making games even after realising how it is sometimes very challenging. After you make a game such as this, it is hard to leave the industry, and I'm pleased to see that everybody from the team found their place.

TO
Later we released a mobile phone version of the *R720* shooting game from *SGGG*. That is really one part of the game I love, and it's very popular. It's from the very end of the game – the hero experiences the greatest shooting game of all time. *R720* goes beyond the [pioneering cockpit-based Sega coin-op] R360 by sending the player into space for just ¥500. There, the shooting starts. We made a tribute to our hardware history and to shoot-'em-up culture. I'm a fan of the *Thunder Force* series that was created by Technosoft – after the demise of

246

Segagaga, President Hitomajiri character production artworks, 2000

Sega Dreamcast: Collected Works

Segagaga, Alex Kidd production artwork, 2000

Making Segagaga

that company, I managed to get permission to include the *Thunder Force V* soundtrack in *SGGG*, and even a video of *Thunder Force VI* that the original Technosoft team was making at that time. Anyway, at the end of *SGGG,* you experience parts of *Thunder Force IV* and *V.*

TO

As the game goes on, you are asked if you are really good enough to defeat Sega's history. It goes crazy from that point – the SG-1000 system arrives, with all its popular characters from that time flying around. Defeated, the SG-1000 turns into a Mark III and gets reinforced with the FM Pack. Then comes the Mega Drive with Super 32X and Mega CD! Of course, next is Saturn. That was how excited we were about our company, our achievements, our industry's history and culture.

TO

As I said, I didn't have much money to promote the game. But, again, some great people stepped in. Our star PR, [Tadashi] Takezaki, and [Taku] Sasahara of AM3, really invested their energy and creativity into promoting the game in any ways they could. This really influenced the popularity of the title and ultimately its sales. For example, they even managed to get the game a full-page story in the newspapers! It was uneasy for me trying to keep secrets on this game while also asking for help in promoting it. But Takezaki and Sasahara both found the idea of the game fun and wanted to help make it a success. Their efforts, combined with the official end of the Dreamcast, made the game some kind of a symbol, and that made it sell quite well.

TO

My greatest memory from the release was our tour in Akihabara. Normally, you would invite a celebrity to sign copies on a tour that would go to Tokyo, Osaka and Nagoya, for instance, and the players would get their copy signed at launch events. But, hey, we didn't have any money for that, so we thought up the Akihabara tour! With my mask, I was of course the guy who signed the copies of the game.

TO

We had a four-location tour throughout this one district of Tokyo. I was amazed that fans went to the four locations, buying a copy at each one and getting me to sign them. We had the Sega Shinja, the 'Sega believers', and they loved the company so much they would buy every single title we released. For fun, we made the four locations sacred Sega places, and gave the Shinja ranks – from Master System Shinja to Dream Shinja. This created a unique relationship between us and our fans.

TO

Many people thought this game was a pure parody. Well, that's true, in part. Many think *SGGG* is a game which makes a fool of gaming and the industry. But the fact that we did not have a single angry criticism from Sega Shinjas is certainly because there is no bigger fan of Sega than me.

Making
Rez

Developer
United Game Artists

Release
22 November 2001

Interviewees
Tetsuya Mizuguchi, creator
Jake Kazdal, artist

Rez, production artwork, Jake Kazdal, 2001

Making Rez

Rez takes the relatively restrictive and tired old format of the on-rails shooter – the kind Sega perfected years earlier with *Space Harrier*, *Panzer Dragoon* and all the rest – and, via a unique fusion of sound and pyrotechnics, elevates the form to something close to a religious experience. In this way, it represents the quintessential Dreamcast game: it's familiar, yet freshly alluring in ways that are difficult to quantify and articulate.

The game's story – something about a rogue AI trapped in the system – does nothing to snag on the memory, but the setting, a world of vector forests and waveform mountains, and the pounding electronic soundtrack, are unforgettable. By transposing the arcade shooter to a club, and by pairing every sci-fi bullet with the crystalline tssh'ing of a hi-hat and every explosion with the toppy bark of a snare drum, Tetsuya Mizuguchi and his team broke new experiential territory that remains uncharted in digital art today.

Rez may have once divided the critics but time has silenced detractors: it is the videogame at its most imaginative, its most original, its most artistically consistent and, with the curtains shut, its most world-narrowingly exhilarating.

Tetsuya Mizuguchi

I travelled a lot while working on *Sega Rally*. I was taken to a street parade in Zurich, Switzerland, where 300,000 people had gathered in the city centre for a concert. It blew me away. I think it appealed to the art student in me: the merging of sound and light, and the meaning behind it all perfectly synched in my head. I'd had a number of thoughts brewing for years. Something to do with the marriage of gaming and music, creating music as you shoot down enemies. When home console technology arrived at a point where I felt able to bring the idea to life, I knew it was time. I wanted to make a game that could put the player into a trance-like state.

Jake Kazdal

I was introduced to Mizuguchi over email by our mutual friend Kenneth Ibrahim, who had worked previously with Mizuguchi-san at Sega's AM3 studio. If you played *Sega Rally* you'll know his voice, because he is the guy who says: 'Long medium left!' It was just a few weeks before E3 1998 and I hustled together a demo tape of my animation and artwork. Mizuguchi was kind enough to make time to meet me during the show, where we secured a meeting room at the Sega booth and I showed him my demo reel. We had dinner and a few drinks later in the week. Then we started talking a bit about his vision for what would become *Rez*, and I started shamelessly begging for a job.

TM

I would recall the music from the game *Xevious*, which I had played as a child. I figured if that music kept coming into my head all these years later, it must have a special power. Jun Kobayashi was a VJ friend of mine. He was an artist, really. We discussed my idea for *Rez*. We talked about Kandinsky, the artist who would paint while inspired by music. That is what we wanted to do with *Rez*. We experimented, using all kinds of art styles. We went to clubs, where we would watch people's reactions to the music.

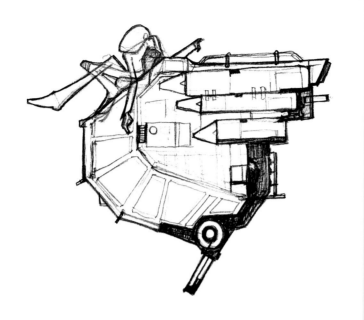

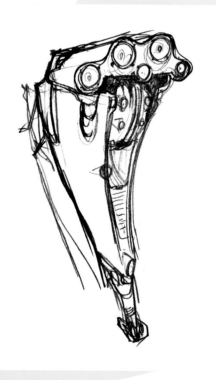

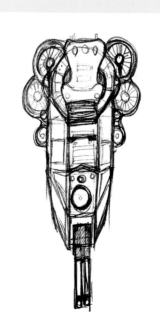

Rez, production artworks, Jake Kazdal, 2001

Making Rez

JK

Miz invited me out to Tokyo to tour the new game studio he was building, which became UGA, right in the heart of Shibuya. He took me to a trance party for the weekend in the forest, many hours' drive from Tokyo. He ended up offering me the job, which changed my life forever.

TM

At Shibuya, I expanded the team to 70-odd people. It was a tough process. We were making *Space Channel 5* and *Rez* simultaneously. But that also helped me to not go mad; I could switch between games: one was pure entertainment, and the other was quite deep and elemental. I worked so hard. I slept at my desk. I never went home. It was gruelling but fun. I was so caught up in my games that I didn't have time or space to think about the larger Dreamcast project. I just knew that, if I could make something special, then it would help the Dreamcast.

JK

I was the only non-Japanese person on the *Rez* team. The first few months were tough, no doubt. People were so sweet and patient with me, but they were busy and I spent a lot of time just writing down words that kept popping up at meetings and finding people later to break them down for me. Within a year or so, though, I was pretty chatty, and only really screwed up by not learning to read [Japanese] and missing out on the inter-team text chat. I used my eyes and hands to communicate more than my words.

TM

We had to do a lot of research because there weren't really any games like this or, at least, not enough to consider it a genre. I took my team to Taiko drumming festivals and we watched hours of recordings of street musicians. It wasn't just a case of listening to the music. We also took notice of the shapes and colours, and how we felt as the performance progressed. These were all things we wanted to translate into our game. The basic idea was that shooting would produce sounds, which could synch with the music. Quantisation was key to ensure that the sounds players made fell in step with the music. This would mean that any player could play the game 'in time', as it were; the rhythms of play would always be synched, and play would feel good. When we first made this work it felt like magic.

JK

I designed, modelled and animated a bunch of enemies for World 1 and 2 in *Rez*, and translated most of the text into English. One of my biggest influences was almost accidental. I had been out clubbing in Tokyo one weekend and got entranced with the WinAmp sound visualisations a VJ was using. I videotaped a bunch and showed it to Mizuguchi the next week while we were deep in visual development early on in *Rez*, and that drove the style for the rest of the project.

TM

Nobuhiko 'Ebizo' Tanuma, my creative partner who was sound director on the game, travelled to Kenya and shot a video there, on the street. People were eating dinner outside, then suddenly one guy starts up a rhythm. Then everyone around him starts to join in; the women begin to sing. I watched the

255

video many times, especially the way the sound built up. It was a big step in the creative development of the game. How can we groove, with any action becoming music? How do these actions become part of the soundscape? How do we make sure they are in time? We played around but it still didn't feel good. Then, finally, we added new elements, like the DJ playing, changing the backing track, which gave it movement and mood. When shooting the cubes changed the backtrack, it all started to fall into place. It felt like we finally had the mechanics working.

JK
The reaction generally to both *Space Channel 5* and *Rez* was very positive, but sales were not. I remember the stress taking its toll on Mizuguchi, and we were disappointed neither game became a runaway hit. In hindsight, I don't think anyone could have foreseen just how popular these games would continue to be, even now, a decade and a half later.

TM
In 2001, before the game's release, I had the chance to show *Rez* at the PlayStation Party in Shibuya, Tokyo. I remember it clearly. I decided to show the game without words. I just wanted to play it in front of people, through a huge sound system, without any comments, then leave the stage. The day before, I dyed my hair silver. I didn't know the Sony people – it was like playing an away game. I was so nervous. I took to the stage in this huge club. After I played, I went backstage, and I didn't know how people had reacted because it was so dark.

Suddenly, I heard my name from the stage. It was the chairman of Sony Music, Shigeo Maruyama, calling me back. Everyone respected him. And he said, on stage, 'I think this game could change the history of music.' After the party I thanked him, and he told me, 'That wasn't marketing talk. That's how I really feel.' Until that party, the Sega marketing people didn't seem very excited about *Rez*. But that night, there were Sega people in the audience and they saw me play. And then they saw Maru-san come on stage and compliment me. The next time I went to the Haneda office, it was very different. Sega was like: 'We'd better start supporting this game.'

JK
I loved that we were this crazy, experimental team in the heart of youth scene in Shibuya. I didn't know how lucky I was when it first happened. Mizuguchi was the perfect guy to lead the team, and we went deep, trying to break new ground and establish new genres and I think we wildly succeeded. As a CEO now, years later, I realise how much sales have to drive design decisions, but at the time we had a long leash and big dreams. Silky smooth anti-aliased *Rez* on Dreamcast still gives me goosebumps. When I think of the long hours of development with the kit booting up, the boot-up sounds, I still just get this warm fuzzy feeling. Working with people so talented and driven, on a bold, daring adventure into uncharted territory deep in the heart of Tokyo, it shaped me as a human and I'll never forget any of that. People to this day tear up when I tell them I worked on *Rez*. I couldn't be prouder of what we achieved.

256

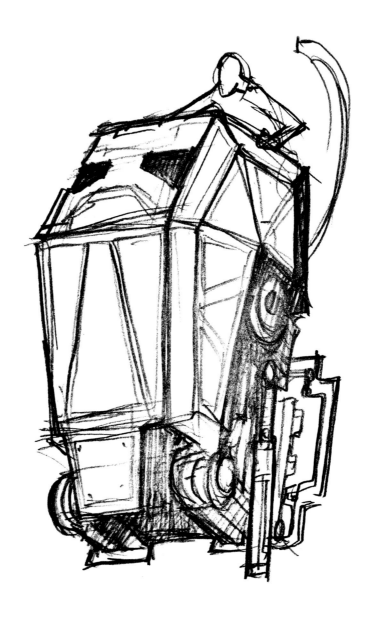

Rez, production artwork, Jake Kazdal, 2001

Sega Dreamcast: Collected Works

In-Game Artwork

260

In-Game Artwork

261

02

03
04

263

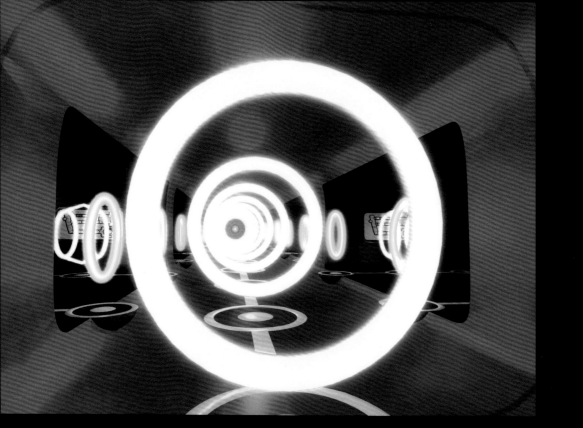

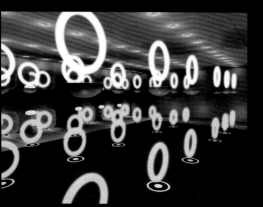

264

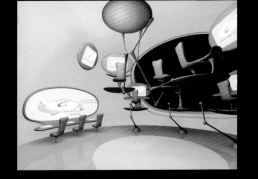

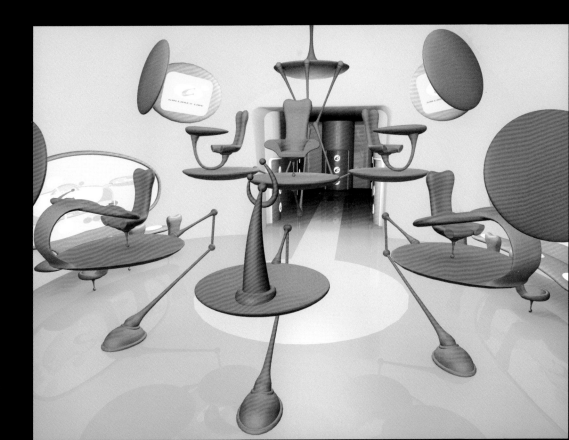

01

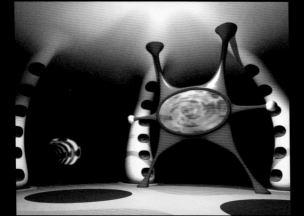

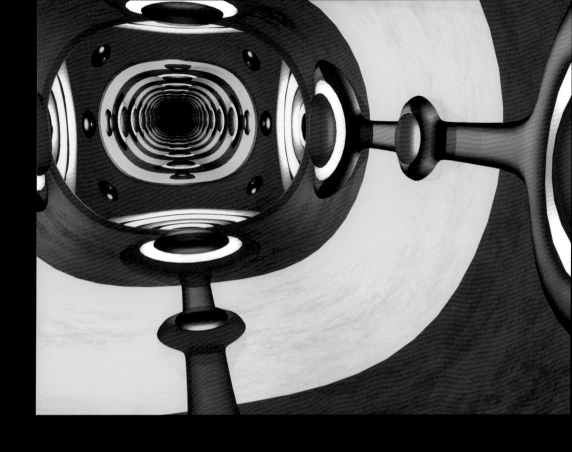

269

270

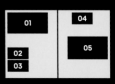

In-Game Artwork

01		03
	02	04
		05

In-Game Artwork

274

In-Game Artwork

275

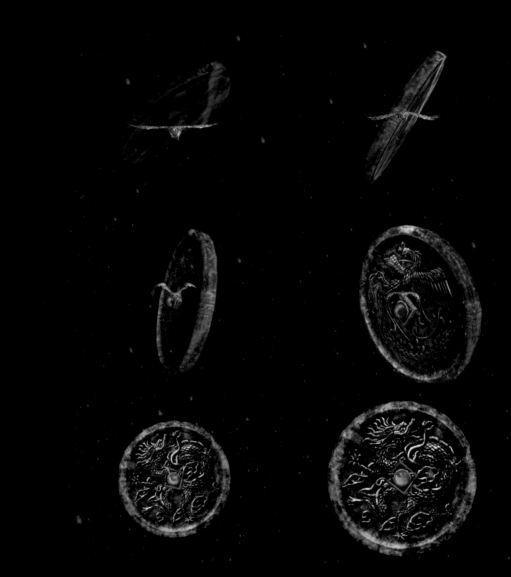

276

In-Game Artwork

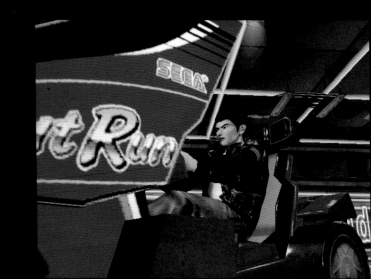

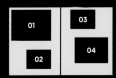

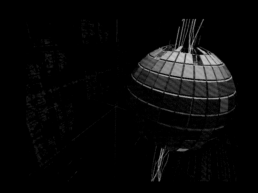

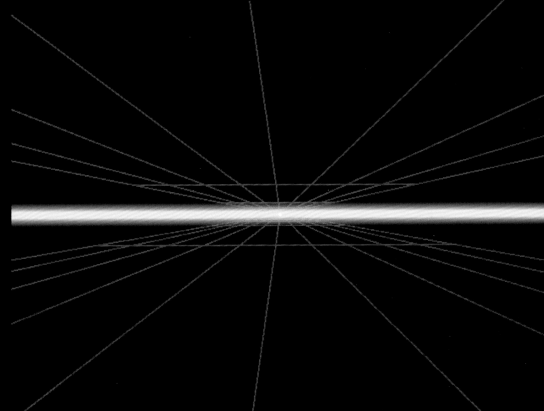

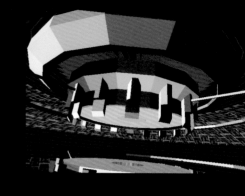

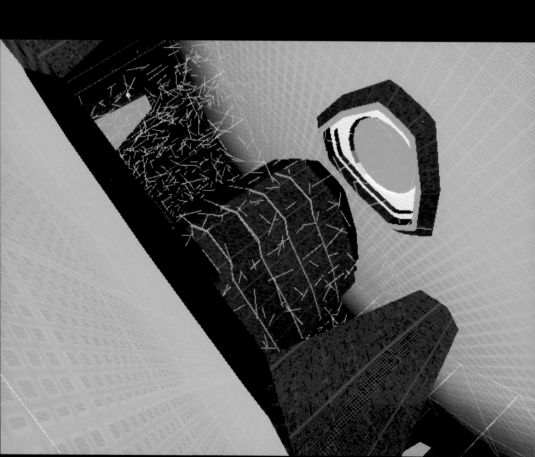

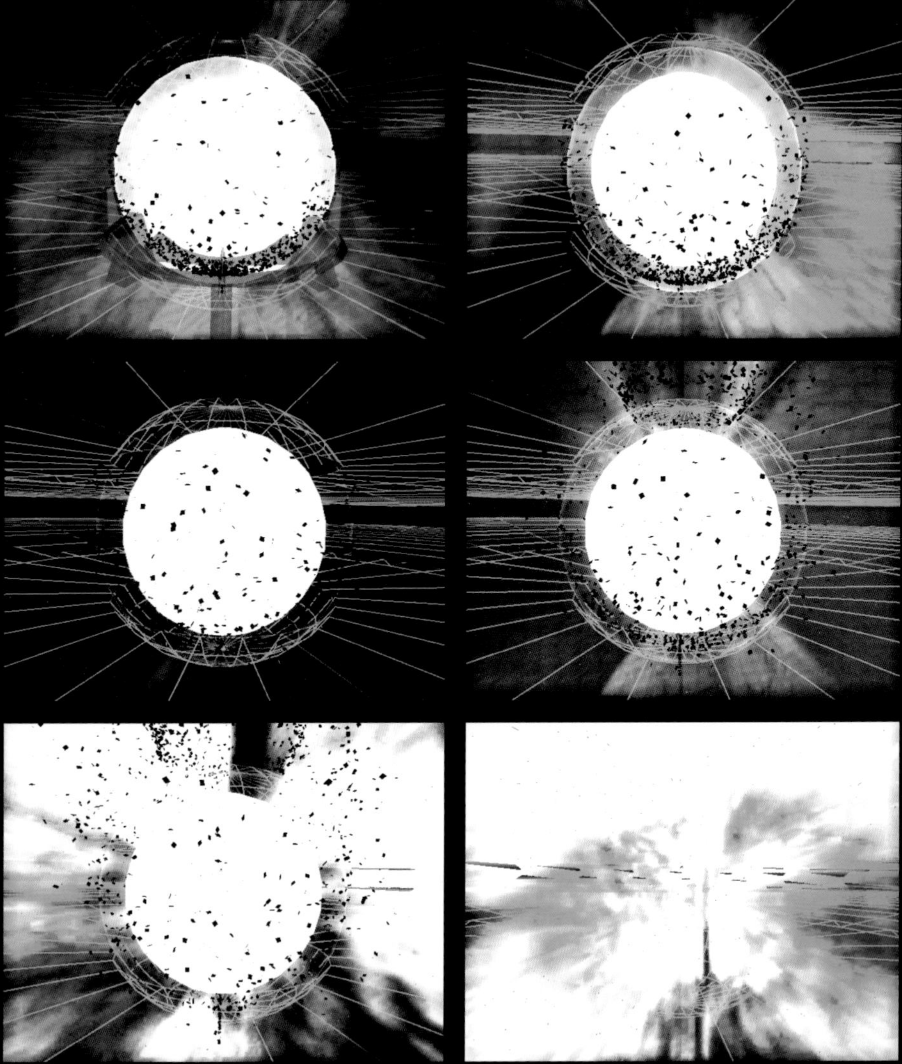

287

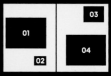

In-Game Artwork